Intermediate
Conversational
French

HOLT, RINEHART AND WINSTON
New York   Toronto   London

Julian Harris
André Lévêque

University of Wisconsin

Intermediate Conversational French

Third Edition

Credits

(Numbers refer to pages. Credits are listed in order of appearance on a page, from left to right, from top to bottom.)

xvii–HR & W Library   xx–Helena Kolda   12–Peter Buckley   16–Helena Kolda   27–Fritz Henle, from Monkmeyer Press   28–François Vikar   33–New York Public Library   45–New York Public Library   46–Photo Giraudon   51–Helena Kolda   61–Jean Roubier, from Rapho-Guillumette   62–Helena Kolda   67–New York Public Library   75–Silberstein, from Monkmeyer Press   81–New York Public Library   88–New York Public Library   89–French Cultural Services   90–Peter Buckley   95–The Metropolitan Museum of Art, Rogers Fund, 1920   105–The Metropolitan Museum of Art, Bequest of Mrs. H. O. Havemeyer, 1929   106–New York Public Library   123–Bettmann Archive   124–Peter Buckley   136–Bettmann Archive   138–Photo Giraudon   143–Photo Yvon   152–Robert Doisneau, from Rapho-Guillumette   164–Photo Feher, French Government Tourist Office   180–Helena Kolda   185–French Embassy Press and Information   193–Photo Giraudon   206–New York Public Library   207–French Government Tourist Office   210–French Cultural Services   211–French Cultural Services   214–Standard Oil   222–New York Public Library

Printed in the United States of America

Library of Congress Catalog Card Number: 79–172937

ISBN 0–03–088063–7

45678   038   98765432

INTRODUCTION

The basic philosophy of the book. Like the other Harris and Lévêque books, *Intermediate Conversational French* is based upon four assumptions: (1) that language is something you *do*, (2) that learning a language means learning to *use* it, (3) that the most natural and efficient way to learn a foreign language is to practice using it—first by hearing and speaking and then by reading and writing in the language, and (4) that, at least for literate adults, a systematic study of the grammar of the language is an invaluable aid and a great time-saver.

From practice to principle. Conversation Units precede grammar units so that students practice understanding and using phrases before they learn the grammatical principles the phrases exemplify. Throughout the book we put greater emphasis on practice than on grammar, for no one has ever learned a foreign language without a lot of practice. Although we do not slight grammar, we try even in the grammar units, to help students learn to use French instead of just learning *about* the language.

We have found, moreover, that when correct examples are "planted" in a conversation, most students understand quickly and sharply the relevant grammatical explanations when they see them in the following grammar unit. In this way, they accept the explanations for what they are, namely, a series of generalizations that are relevant to and useful for the business of learning to use the language. And as the examples used in the grammar units are taken from the conversations that have a modicum of human interest, the context of the dialog carries over into the grammar unit and supplies flesh and blood for the otherwise dry bones of the structure of the language. Thus the students develop the habit of learning to use authentic patterns of the language instead of trying to figure out how you *would* say something, and, equally important, they realize early in the game the fundamentally important fact that grammar merely describes usage instead of determining it.

The English version of the conversation units. We hold that insofar as possible French should be the language of the classroom and that every possible means should be used to bring the students quickly to the point where they can practice using the phrases of a dialog correctly, intelligently and with confidence. In order to get *them* to use French, *we* provide an easy, idiomatic English version of the dialogs, because (1) it gives the students a clear understanding of the precise meaning of the text more quickly than they could possibly get it any other way; (2) as the meaning of the text is already clear, it prevents the students from thumbing through the vocabulary and making a word-for-word *mistranslation* of it; (3) it shows them that their task is not to translate the phrases but to practice understanding and using them; and (4) it makes it possible for the instructor to devote substantially all the time of class meetings to the business of teaching them to use French. It goes without saying that we do not recommend that the English version be used in the classroom.

Should the dialogs be memorized? Some experts still seem to think students should memorize dialogs and devote an enormous amount of time to purely mechanical exercises so that they learn phrases "to the point of automaticity." We disagree. Memorization and purely mechanical exercises seem to us a throwback to the ancient practice of rote memorization and endlessly repeating or copying material to be learned. We think students should always try to associate the meaning with the sound and the intonation of every phrase they hear or repeat. We are convinced that students learn sounds, words, syntax, verb forms, or patterns of speech quicker and better when they learn them in meaningful contexts.

For four hundred years, some of the world's best minds have advocated the abandonment of rote memorization and the adoption of the practice of giving students the ability to use what they learn, to "inwardly digest" what they are taught. Montaigne said "Savoir par cœur n'est pas savoir," and he deplored the fact that students were taught to swallow lessons whole and bring them out later "with their feathers still on." Following their lead, we do not recommend, and never have recommended the memorization of dialogs. If anyone wanted students to be able to recite dialogs, he should of course have them commit them to memory; but since we want them to be able to understand and use the phrases, we have them practice understanding and using them. It is as simple as that. Neither of the authors of this book could repeat a single one of the dialogs from memory, but we can use the phrases handily. Moreover, when students *do* memorize a dialog, they still have to practice using the phrases before they can actually use them correctly and with confidence. Why give them the preliminary chore of memorizing—which is certainly unnecessary and uninspiring, and, we think, pedagogically useless?

The exercises of the conversation units. The exercises that accompany the dialogs are constructed so that they will give the students practice in hearing, understanding, repeating, using, and varying the phrases of the dialogs.

The substitution exercises can be extremely helpful for learning to use new expressions if they are done intelligently; but it is absolutely essential that students make the effort to understand what they are saying at all times. In doing this type of exercise, the student must keep in mind both the expression that is being practiced and the words that are to be substituted. As he must think consciously of the words that are to be substituted, and as the expression that is being repeated has to be retained at a deeper level of consciousness, this exercise seems to us to drive home an expression far more effectively than any amount of repetition. Nevertheless, as this type of exercise can be done very easily by the student at home, we recommend that only two or three examples be used in class—and very rapidly—as a warm-up exercise to prepare the students for the more sophisticated exercises that follow.

Even after doing substitution exercises and the "exercices d'application" students sometimes find it difficult to do the "Répondez en français" and the "Demandez à quelqu'un" exercises. Some students even at this level still try to translate the question into English, figure out the answer in English, and then translate the answer back into French—a roundabout procedure that practically always results in answers that are full of mistakes. Such students should be told (or reminded) that it is much more instructive and *much easier* just to answer the question in French without translating at all. If a student persists in the translating routine, the instructor can sometimes break him of the habit by asking him to repeat the question in French before answering it. It sometimes happens that a student cannot answer a question because he does not remember a detail of the dialog; in such cases, we think he should be encouraged to say, in French, of course, that he does not know the answer. For example, in answer to the question: "Comment Jean décide-t-il d'aller à Saint-Cloud?" we think it would be all right for a student to say: "Je ne sais pas comment Jean décide d'aller à Saint-Cloud." It is far less important to know the details of the story than to know how to use French phrases correctly.

The grammar units. The grammar units are frankly intended to give students a clear grasp of the morphology and syntax of the language. We have made it a point to present grammar in large blocks rather than in small parcels; for while small parcels are easier to master from day to day, they are also easier to forget. Besides, we feel that students at this level should see not only the details but the larger picture. And it is important that they distinguish between known material and new material so that they will not devote a lot of time to poring over what is (or should be) perfectly obvious. It is true that the grammar units would be frighteningly long if they contained only new material; but as practically all of them contain some known material, and as we proceed always from the known to the unknown, the exercises can be done very rapidly. Students should answer simple questions without a moment's hesitation, and they will do so if the instructor expects it; but if the instructor asks a question as if he were calling on a student to explain the second law of thermodynamics, the exercises will be slow, boring, and useless. Students should be reminded that the exercises are not intended to test their ability to remember details of the dialog but to give them practice in using actively the material in hand—and to do so at an easy conversational tempo. Whenever an exercise seems to drag, we suggest that the instructor answer a question or two himself so as to get the class back to the optimum tempo. If students are kept "on their toes" the work will be more agreeable both to instructor and students.

Paraphrase, clichés and redundancy. Many an American has found that when he sets foot upon French soil (to use a fairly outworn cliché), he can speak French well enough to express his needs; but when French people begin to talk, he hasn't the vaguest idea of what they are saying! They seem to be talking at break-neck speed and to be using words he cannot identify. If the American says he doesn't understand, the Frenchman promptly repeats what he has to say but he is likely to try to make himself clear by using a paraphrase and lots of words that seem even less comprehensible! As a matter of fact, we all use many words and phrases that convey very little if any meaning. Our conversation is full of clichés and redundancies. Instead of simply saying "Yes," people often say things like: Okay, Okedoke, You bet, Sure thing, That's for sure, Right, You are right, You said it, and so on.

In formal writing, the French normally express themselves with admirable clarity, precision, and simplicity; but in everyday conversation, they use clichés as everyone else does. It is therefore necessary to be aware of this fact in order to know how to listen for meaning and not try to identify every word of every utterance you hear. We have included in this book and in the Teacher's Manual a few exercises that will show students how simple phrases are often laced with a lot of unnecessary verbiage. We find that if students run through such exercises rapidly until they can rattle them off, realizing, meanwhile, that they contain a certain amount of superfluous verbiage, they will be a little more aware of the way ordinary French people talk in everyday conversation. Here are some samples:

1. Répétez les phrases suivantes en ajoutant **Et puis alors** . . . et **tout simplement.**

Ex.: Il est parti. —**Et puis alors, il est parti tout simplement.**

1. Il est rentré. 2. Elle s'est fâchée. 3. J'ai été opéré. 4. Nous sommes allés au Louvre. 5. Il s'est couché. 6. Ils se sont mis à table.

2. Répétez les phrases suivantes en ajoutant **Je n'en sais rien, moi, mais il est sans doute possible que** . . . et en employant le subjonctif.

Ex.: Elle est allée en Suisse. —**Je n'en sais rien, moi, mais il est sans doute possible qu'elle soit allée en Suisse.**

1. Elle est arrivée. 2. Elle n'est plus à Paris. 3. C'est un bon film. 4. Il a du talent. 5. Il fera beau demain. 6. C'est un voleur.

3. Changez chacune des phrases suivantes en employant les mots **pas mauvais(e,es) du tout.**

Ex.: Il est bon, ce poisson. —**Il n'est pas mauvais du tout, ce poisson.**

1. Il est très bon, ce vin rouge. 2. Elle est bonne, cette pêche. 3. Il est bon, ce petit restaurant. 4. Il est intéressant, ce film. 5. Ils sont délicieux, ces fruits. 6. Elles sont exquises, ces poires.

The grammarians have always disapproved of redundancy, tautology, pleonasm, clichés, and various other kinds of illogical and/or meaningless or near meaningless usage. Indeed, there was a time when the negative was expressed in French by the word "ne" alone and when the word "pas" simply meant "a step." But people tended to say "Je n'irai pas" (I won't go a step) so often that they eventually came to say "Je ne dirai pas," "Je ne veux pas" and so on. Redundancy is a linguistic factor that should not be ignored.

Pronunciation. Although pronunciation has been studied in first year French, we find that many intermediate students need systematic help in improving their pronunciation. Consequently, we have included a considerable section entitled "How to improve your accent" that is intended to provide such help (pp. 225–238). An important part of this section is a transcription of the dialogs in the International Phonetic Alphabet. Some teachers will want to use the transcription in classes and others may leave it to individual students. We have tried to make the entire section simple enough for students to use it by themselves.

The present edition. The present edition differs from the previous one in a number of ways.

(1) We have revised some of the dialogs to introduce useful expressions, to enliven responses, and to clarify phrases that seemed a little involved.

(2) We have shortened some of the dialogs and we have added brief introductions to set the stage for those in units 7, 9, 11, 17, 19, 21, 23, and 25, introducing additional items of vocabulary and idiom and enriching somewhat the content of the exercises. (The other dialogs already had such introductions.)

(3) We have expanded some of the footnotes to the dialogs and put them all into French.

(4) We have constructed exercises entirely in French to replace most of those in which English was used. We have retained the *Thèmes*, however, for the use of instructors who find them valuable (as we do) and who can find the time to use them. And we have retained a few "Dites en français" exercises to give students practice in *not translating*(!) word for word from English. For whatever anyone may say about the evils of translation (and be it said that no one opposes phony translation more strongly than we do), most experienced teachers know that students, even advanced ones, will try in vain to *figure out* how to say things like "When he got there" or "After he left" unless and until they are taught to use the expressions "A son arrivée" and "Après son départ." Students *can* be taught to think in French; but teaching them to do so is quite different from merely telling them to see no English, hear no English, speak no English.

(5) We have examined with care every item of every grammar unit, rewriting sentences or paragraphs, and recasting some of the units, reworking many of the exercises and introducing illustrative examples that are more concrete, more timely, and, we hope, more arresting. To teach the expression "de plus en plus," for example, we ask students to use it in phrases like: "Les villes sont surpeuplées," "Les rues sont encombrées," "Les impôts sont élevés," and so on.

The Teacher's Manual, Laboratory Manual, Tapes, and **Records.** We have revised the materials that accompany the present edition of the book in the light of experience and have introduced new features that, we hope, will be interesting and useful. We have included in the Teacher's Manual some discussion of certain features of our method that may be of use to inexperienced teachers and to those who have not used our *Basic Conversational French*. We have also inserted an idiomatic version of the *Thèmes;* for while all the expressions that are used in the *Thèmes* have been repeatedly used in the exercises, it is sometimes difficult to think, on the spur of the moment, of the most natural French equivalent of idiomatic English.

The laboratory program is designed to help students prepare their assignments. The textbook may, of course, be used without a laboratory, but we find that students working with the tapes learn faster and better than when they are merely assigned a lesson as homework. Although first-year students of a foreign language should not be sent to the laboratory to work on material before the instructor gives them preliminary instruction on it, we have found that at the intermediate level students can prepare their assignments so efficiently that the classwork can be conducted at a much more rapid and stimulating pace.

There are thirty taped lessons, corresponding to the thirty units in the textbook. The conversation lessons include repetition of the conversation itself, a "questionnaire," substitution exercises, and a dictée. The grammar lessons contain substitution exercises, "exercices d'application," and practice in reading and aural comprehension. The exercises in the laboratory manual and on the tapes are different from those in the textbook.

Acknowledgements. We are endebted to so many colleagues, both at Wisconsin and in other institutions, for suggestions and help in revising this book that it would be impossible to say here precisely what we owe them. It would be ungracious, however, not to say we have made use of many ideas, hints, queries, and criticisms that have been sent us by numbers of correspondents during the last few years. We are grateful to them and we hope their letters have all been duly acknowledged. In any case, it is certain that but for their suggestions, the book would be a very different one.

J. H.
A. L.

CONTENTS

---

* Idioms and expressions practiced in the exercises are listed under each chapter.

REFERENCE MATERIALS

CONTENTS   XV

Vue aérienne de Chambord

YOUR FRENCH ACCENT

Although most intermediate students of French have learned to speak simple French with some skill, there are few who would not profit by a fresh look at the basic differences between the way we speak English and the way French is spoken, as well as a renewed effort to get the habit of producing the individual sounds of the language as French people do. If you want to develop a good French accent, it is necessary (1) to learn to utter French words in groups without stressing some syllables and slighting others as we do in English and (2) to cultivate French intonation patterns. Specific suggestions and exercises for improving your French accent will be found on pp. 225–238.

ARRIVEES
L'AVION EST ARRIVE
VOL
PROVENANCE
LUFTHANSA 264 HAMBOURG
ALITALIA 326 MILAN
AIR INTER 640 MARSEILLE
AIR INTER 424 PAU
AIR INTER 538 CLERMONT FD
AIR FRANCE 765 DUSSELDORF
AIR FRANCE 426 NICE
LONDRES
MULHOUSE
ZURICH
LONDRES
CASABLANCA
STRASBOURG
ROME
ARRIVEES
L'AVION EST ARRIVE
VOL
PROVENANCE
AIR FRANCE 795 STOCKHOLM
AIR INTER 336 LORIENT
LUFTHANSA 267 STUTTGART
AIR INTER 356 BREST
AIR FRANCE 1520 BASTIA
SWISSAIR 708 ZURICH
AIR INTER 618 MARSEILLE
AIR FRANCE ALGER
AIR FRANCE MOSCOU
AIR FRANCE
AIR INTER
AIR FRANCE
AIR FRANCE
AIR INTER
VOL
PROVENANCE
SWISSAIR GENEVE
LUFTHANSA FRANCFORT
AIR FRANCE VENISE
AIR FRANCE MILAN
AIR FRANCE
AIR INTER BIARRITZ
BORDEAUX
GENEVE
TOULOUSE
NICE
ROME
TEL AVIV
LONDRES

RETOUR À PARIS

De passage à Paris après une longue absence, Jean Hughes décide d'aller revoir ses amis parisiens, Roger et Marie Duplessis, maintenant mariés et qui demeurent depuis quelque temps à Saint-Cloud.* Il vient de faire signe à un chauffeur de taxi. Le taxi s'arrête.

Passing through Paris after a long absence, John Hughes decides to go to see his Parisian friends again— Roger and Marie Duplessis (who are) married now and who have been living for some time in Saint-Cloud. He has just signaled to a taxi driver. The taxi stops.

[1](Au chauffeur)

JEAN. —[2]13, avenue du Palais, à Saint-Cloud. [3]C'est près du pont de Saint-Cloud, à l'entrée de l'autoroute de l'Ouest.

LE CHAUFFEUR. —[4]Entendu, monsieur. Montez, s'il vous plaît.

JEAN. —[5]Volontiers. Il y a dix minutes que j'attends un taxi. (Jean monte dans le taxi.)

LE CHAUFFEUR. —[6]Si ça ne vous fait rien, je vais prendre les quais.†
[7]C'est peut-être un peu plus long, mais on perd moins de temps.

[1](To the driver)

JOHN. —[2]13 Avenue du Palais in Saint-Cloud. [3]It's near the Saint-Cloud bridge at the entrance to the Freeway to the West.

THE DRIVER. —[4]Okay. Get in, please.

JOHN. —[5]Glad to. I have been waiting for a cab for ten minutes. (John gets into the taxi.)

THE DRIVER. —[6]If it is all right with you, I am going to follow the river. [7]It is perhaps a little longer, but you lose less time.

---

* **Saint-Cloud,** un faubourg agréable à l'ouest de Paris. Il possède un beau parc et a autrefois servi de résidence royale.
† **Les quais** sont les rues qui bordent la Seine.

JEAN. —⁸Comment ça?

LE CHAUFFEUR. —⁹Ils sont "sens unique". ¹⁰Le long des quais, toutes les voitures vont dans le même sens. ¹¹Ça va beaucoup plus vite.

JEAN. —¹²Combien de temps faut-il pour aller à Saint-Cloud?

LE CHAUFFEUR. —¹³Il faut environ vingt ou vingt-cinq minutes, tout au plus. ¹⁴Le temps c'est de l'argent, vous savez, ¹⁵surtout pour un chauffeur de taxi.

(*Un peu plus tard*)

JEAN. —¹⁶Sommes-nous déjà à Saint-Cloud?

LE CHAUFFEUR. —¹⁷Non, Monsieur. Nous sommes toujours à Paris. ¹⁸On ne sait jamais où Paris commence et où il finit.

JOHN. —⁸How's that?

THE DRIVER. —⁹They are one-way streets. ¹⁰Along the river, all the cars go in the same direction. ¹¹It goes much faster.

JOHN. —¹²How long does it take to go to Saint-Cloud?

THE DRIVER. —¹³It takes about 20 or 25 minutes, at the very most. ¹⁴Time is money, you know, ¹⁵especially for a taxi driver.

(*A little later*)

JOHN. —¹⁶Are we already in Saint-Cloud?

THE DRIVER. —¹⁷No, sir. We are still in Paris. ¹⁸You never know where Paris begins and where it ends.

I. SUBSTITUTIONS. Répétez les phrases suivantes, en substituant les mots indiqués:

1. (a) Jean est [de passage] à Paris.

de nouveau/ de retour/ toujours (*still*)/ souvent/ rarement

(b) Nous sommes [de passage] à Paris.

de nouveau/ de retour/ toujours/ souvent/ rarement

2. Il décide [d'aller revoir ses amis].

de prendre l'autobus/ d'appeler un taxi/ d'aller à pied/ d'aller à Saint-Cloud/ de rester quinze jours à Paris

3. Les Duplessis habitent [à Saint-Cloud].

près du pont de Saint-Cloud/ près de l'entrée de l'autoroute de l'Ouest/ près de la Seine/ près des quais/ à une demi-heure de Paris

4. Il vient de faire signe [à un chauffeur de taxi].

à un taxi/ à un vendeur de journaux/ à un ami/ à un camarade

5. Le taxi va le long [des quais].

des boulevards/ de la Seine/ des vieilles rues/ des Champs-Elysées

6. Si ça ne vous fait rien, je vais [prendre les quais].

acheter un journal/ dîner en ville/ prendre les grands boule-
vards/ prendre l'autoroute de l'Ouest/ rester à la maison

7. Il faut environ 20 ou 25 minutes tout au plus [pour aller de Paris à Saint-
Cloud].

pour aller à l'aéroport/ pour lire le journal/ pour
déjeuner/ pour monter en haut de la tour Eiffel

II. Répondez aux questions suivantes, en employant l'expression indiquée:

A. depuis

1. Jean est-il à Paris depuis quelques jours? (Oui.) **2.** Les Duplessis sont-ils à Saint-
Cloud depuis longtemps? **3.** Êtes-vous ici depuis longtemps? **4.** Jean attend-il un taxi
depuis longtemps? **5.** Les Duplessis sont-ils mariés depuis longtemps?

B. il y a . . . que

1. Y a-t-il quelques jours que Jean est à Paris? **2.** Y a-t-il longtemps que les Duplessis
sont à Saint-Cloud? **3.** Y a-t-il longtemps que vous êtes ici? **4.** Y a-t-il longtemps que
Jean attend un taxi? **5.** Y a-t-il longtemps que les Duplessis sont mariés?

C. il faut (*it takes*)

1. Faut-il longtemps pour aller de Paris à Saint-Cloud? **2.** Combien de temps faut-il?
3. Faut-il plus d'une demi-heure? **4.** Faut-il plus longtemps quand on prend les quais?
5. Faut-il plus longtemps quand on prend les rues "sens unique"?

D. aller, aller voir

1. Où Jean va-t-il? **2.** Pourquoi va-t-il à Saint-Cloud? **3.** Pourquoi les voitures
vont-elles plus vite le long des quais? **4.** Allez-vous souvent en voyage? **5.** Allez-vous
voir des amis quand vous êtes de passage dans une ville? **6.** Qui Jean va-t-il voir à
Saint-Cloud?

III. Répétez les phrases suivantes, en remplaçant le passé composé par le présent de **venir de** et l'infinitif:

EX.: —Jean est parti.
     —Jean vient de partir.

1. Jean est arrivé à Paris. **2.** Il a déjeuné. **3.** Il a fait signe à un taxi. **4.** J'ai déjeuné.
5. J'ai joué au tennis. **6.** J'ai acheté une voiture. **7.** Êtes-vous arrivé? **8.** Avez-vous
pris des photos? **9.** Avez-vous vu ce film?

RETOUR À PARIS

IV. Répondez en français par une phrase complète à chacune des questions suivantes:

1. Où est Jean? **2.** A-t-il des amis à Paris? **3.** Qui sont ses amis parisiens? **4.** Qu'est-ce qu'il décide de faire? **5.** Où demeurent Roger et Marie? **6.** Demeurent-ils à Saint-Cloud depuis longtemps? **7.** Qu'est-ce que c'est que Saint-Cloud? **8.** Où se trouve Saint-Cloud? **9.** Comment Jean décide-t-il d'aller à Saint-Cloud? **10.** Qu'est-ce qu'il fait pour avoir un taxi? **11.** Que fait le taxi quand Jean fait signe au chauffeur? **12.** Quelle adresse Jean donne-t-il au chauffeur? **13.** Est-ce près du pont de Saint-Cloud? **14.** Quelle est l'autoroute qui commence près de là? **15.** Combien de temps y a-t-il que Jean attend un taxi? **16.** Comment appelle-t-on les rues qui bordent la Seine? **17.** Est-ce que c'est la route la plus courte? **18.** Alors, pourquoi le chauffeur va-t-il prendre cette route? **19.** Pourquoi les voitures vont-elles plus vite le long des quais? **20.** Pourquoi le chauffeur veut-il aller vite? **21.** Combien de temps faut-il pour aller à Saint-Cloud? **22.** Quelle question Jean pose-t-il au chauffeur un peu plus tard? **23.** Que répond le chauffeur? **24.** Est-ce que Jean est toujours à Paris quand il pose cette question au chauffeur? **25.** Est-ce qu'on sait toujours où une ville commence et où elle finit?

V. Demandez à quelqu'un:

1. combien de temps il faut pour aller à Saint-Cloud. **2.** combien de temps il faut pour aller de New York à Paris. **3.** combien de temps il faut pour aller de Paris à Versailles. **4.** combien de temps Jean va rester à Paris. **5.** combien de temps il va passer chez les Duplessis. **6.** combien de temps il y a que Jean est à Paris. **7.** depuis quand il est de retour à Paris. **8.** combien de temps il y a que Jean attend un taxi. **9.** combien de temps il y a que les Duplessis sont mariés. **10.** depuis quand les Duplessis habitent à Saint-Cloud.

VI. THÈME.

John is passing through Paris. He has been there for three days. He decides to go and see Roger and Marie who now live in Saint-Cloud. He takes a taxi. It takes a half-hour to go to Saint-Cloud. The taxi stops near the Saint-Cloud bridge. John gets out (**descend**) and walks along the Avenue du Palais. He arrives at number 13 (**au numéro 13**) where his friends live. He is very happy to see his Parisian friends again.

Présent de l'indicatif

1   The tenses of French verbs.

The tenses of French verbs correspond in part with those of English verbs, *but only in part*. Even the use of the present indicative should be studied with care. For example, in English the present tense takes three different forms (*I talk* fast usually, *I am talking* fast now, *I do talk* fast when I am in a hurry); but in French the single form **Je parle** is used with all three meanings:

Elle parle vite d'ordinaire.	*She talks* fast usually.
Elle parle vite maintenant.	*She is talking* fast now.
Je ne parle pas vite d'ordinaire,	*I do not talk* fast usually,
mais **je parle** vite quelquefois.	but *I do talk* fast sometimes.

2   Uses of the present indicative common to French and English.

A. The present indicative is used to express an action that takes place or to describe a situation that exists at the present time.

Jean est à Paris.	*John is* in Paris.
Il décide d'aller voir ses amis.	*He decides* to go to see his friends.
Il fait signe à un taxi.	*He signals* a taxi.
Le taxi s'arrête.	*The taxi stops.*

B. The present indicative is used to express an action in progress at the present time.

— Où **allez-vous?**	*Where are you going?*
— **Je vais** à Saint-Cloud.	*I am going* to Saint-Cloud.
— Que **faites-vous?**	*What are you doing?*
— **J'attends** un taxi.	*I am waiting* for a taxi.

C. The present indicative is used to express habitual actions in the present.

Que **faites-vous** le samedi?　　　What *do you do* on Saturdays?
Le samedi, **je vais** au cinéma.　　On Saturdays, *I go* to the movies.

D. The present indicative is used to express action in the near future.

Que **faites-vous** ce soir?　　　　What *are you doing* tonight?
Je reste à la maison.　　　　　　*I'm staying* at home.

3　　Special uses of the present indicative in French.

A. With an expression of time preceded by **depuis** or **il y a . . . que,** the present tense expresses an action (or describes a situation) that began in the past and is still going on at present.

J'attends **depuis** dix minutes.　　⎫
Il y a dix minutes **que** j'attends.　⎬　I *have been waiting* for ten minutes.
　　　　　　　　　　　　　　　　⎭

In interrogative sentences asking *How long?* either **Depuis combien de temps** or **Combien de temps y a-t-il** may be used:

Depuis combien de temps attendez-　⎫
vous?　　　　　　　　　　　　　⎬　How long *have you been waiting?*
Combien de temps y a-t-il que vous　⎪
attendez?　　　　　　　　　　　⎭

B. **Voilà . . . que** is frequently used like **Depuis** and **Il y a . . . que** in declarative sentences, but it is little used in asking questions.

Voilà dix minutes **que** j'attends un　　I *have been waiting* for a taxi for ten
taxi.　　　　　　　　　　　　　　　minutes.

C. If you are asking for a specific date or time of day, you say **Depuis quand** instead of **Depuis combien de temps.**

Depuis quand êtes-vous ici? . . . Je suis ici depuis le 15 septembre (hier soir,
sept heures du matin).
Cf. **Depuis, Il y a . . . que,** and **Voilà . . . que** with the passé composé, par. 6 D.

D. The present tense of **venir** followed by **de** and an infinitive expresses an action of the immediate past.

Jean **vient de faire signe** à un　　John *has just signaled* to a taxi driver.
chauffeur de taxi.
Le taxi **vient de s'arrêter.**　　　　　The taxi *has just stopped.*

4   Forms of the present indicative.

A. Affirmative forms.

These forms of the present indicative of regular verbs and of **avoir** and **être** will be found on p. 271 and p. 275.

B. Negative forms.

Saint-Cloud **n'est pas** loin de Paris.	Saint-Cloud *is not* far from Paris.
On **ne sait pas** où Paris commence.	You *don't know* where Paris begins.
Ça **ne fait rien.**	That *makes no* difference.
On **ne sait jamais.**	You *never know.*

Note that **ne** precedes the verb and that **pas** (or **rien** or **jamais**) follows it. In compound tenses **ne** precedes the auxiliary, **pas (rien, jamais)** follows it.

Je **n'ai pas trouvé** de taxi.	I *didn't find* a taxi.
Je **ne suis jamais allé** à Saint-Cloud.	I *have never been* to Saint-Cloud.

C. Interrogative forms.

1. Interrogation with **est-ce que?**

Any declarative statement becomes a question if it is preceded by the expression **est-ce que?**

Jean est à Paris.	**Est-ce que** Jean est à Paris?
Il est Américain.	**Est-ce qu'**il est Américain?

Americans tend to use the **est-ce que?** form of questions to the exclusion of the rather commoner pattern of inversion. Both forms should be mastered.

2.   Interrogation by inversion.

If the subject of the verb is a personal pronoun, you can ask a question by inverting the order of pronoun and verb.

Il est à Paris.	**Est-il** à Paris?
Elle a des amis à Paris.	**A-t-elle** des amis à Paris?

When the verb ends in a vowel, **-t-** is inserted between the verb and **il, elle,** or **on: Va-t-il? A-t-il? Parle-t-on** français en Suisse?

Note that for the first person singular, the inverted form is rarely used. For the first person singular, you normally say: **Est-ce que je parle? Est-ce que je suis ...? Est-ce que j'ai ...?**

If the subject of the verb is a noun, you can ask a question by inserting the appropriate pronoun after the verb.

Jean est à Paris.   Jean **est-il** à Paris?
Jean a des amis.   Jean **a-t-il** des amis?

When questions consist only of a noun, a verb, and an interrogative expression (**Où? Combien? Quel?** etc.), the noun itself usually follows the verb.

Comment **va Jean?**
A quelle distance **est Saint-Cloud?**
Combien **coûte cette voiture?**
Où demeurent **les Duplessis?**

3. (a) With n'est-ce pas?

You often ask a question by simply adding **n'est-ce pas?** to a declarative statement — especially when you expect an answer that agrees with what you are saying. This expression corresponds to a number of English expressions such as: "Don't you?" "Wouldn't he?" "Shall I not?" "Didn't they?"

Ses amis demeurent à Saint-Cloud, **n'est-ce pas?**
Ça ne vous fait rien, **n'est-ce pas?**
Vous venez de déjeuner, **n'est-ce pas?**

(b) By intonation.

You can ask a question simply by uttering a declarative sentence with a questioning tone.

Ça ne vous fait rien?
Nous sommes à Saint-Cloud?
Vous venez de déjeuner?

This pattern is much more common in French than in English.

I. SUBSTITUTIONS. Répétez les phrases suivantes, en substituant les mots indiqués:

1. [Jean est] de passage à Paris.
   Nous sommes/ Elle est/ Jean et Roger sont/ Êtes-vous
   . . .?/ Elle n'est pas/ N'êtes-vous pas . . .?/ Je ne suis pas

2. Il y a trois jours [qu'il est] ici.

que nous sommes/ que je suis/ qu'elle est/ qu'ils sont/ qu'elles sont

3. [Il a] de bons amis à Paris.

J'ai/ Nous avons/ Avez-vous . . .?/ A-t-il . . .?/
Ont-ils . . .?/ Je n'ai pas/ N'avez-vous pas . . .?

II. Mettez chacune des phrases suivantes au pluriel. Cet exercice doit
être fait rapidement.

EX.: Je suis. **Nous sommes.**
    Je finis de bonne heure. **Nous finissons** de bonne heure.

A. être et avoir

1. Je suis. **2.** J'ai. **3.** Il est. **4.** Il a. **5.** Est-il? **6.** A-t-il? **7.** Es-tu? **8.** As-tu?
9. Il n'a pas d'amis à Paris. **10.** N'a-t-il pas d'amis à Paris? **11.** N'as-tu pas d'amis
à Paris? **12.** Elle n'est pas à Paris.

B. aimer, rester, chercher, décider (de), monter, fumer, étudier

1. Il aime voyager. **2.** J'aime voyager. **3.** Elle n'aime pas rester à la maison. **4.** Je
cherche un taxi. **5.** Cherches-tu un taxi? **6.** Je décide de prendre l'autobus. **7.** Tu
montes dans l'autobus. **8.** Je ne fume pas. **9.** Tu ne fumes pas? **10.** J'étudie tous
les soirs. **11.** Il n'étudie pas tous les soirs. **12.** Tu n'étudies pas ce soir?

C. finir, réussir à (et l'infinitif), choisir, obéir (à)

1. Je finis de bonne heure. **2.** Il ne finit pas de bonne heure. **3.** A quelle heure
finit-il? **4.** Je réussis d'habitude. **5.** Il ne réussit pas toujours. **6.** Je réussis à finir
de bonne heure. **7.** Il réussit à trouver un taxi. **8.** Elle choisit une robe. **9.** Je ne
choisis pas toujours très bien. **10.** Il obéit toujours à la loi. **11.** Obéis-tu toujours à
la loi? **12.** Je n'obéis pas toujours.

D. perdre, attendre, entendre, vendre, descendre

1. Je perds beaucoup de temps. **2.** Il ne perd pas trop de temps. **3.** Qu'est-ce que tu
attends? **4.** Qu'est-ce que tu entends? **5.** J'entends venir un autobus. **6.** Il vend des
journaux. **7.** Je descends à l'Opéra. **8.** Où descends-tu? **9.** Tu ne descends pas ici?
10. Tu ne vends pas cette auto? **11.** Elle vend des fleurs. **12.** Qu'est-ce que tu vends?

E. acheter, préférer, peser, commencer, espérer, lever, s'appeler*

1. J'espère. **2.** J'achète. **3.** Je m'appelle Dupont. **4.** Comment t'appelles-tu? **5.** Je
n'espère pas. **6.** Combien pèses-tu? **7.** Je commence tout de suite. **8.** Tu espères.
9. Il préfère aller. **10.** Je me lève. **11.** Il pèse 70 kilos. **12.** Comment s'appelle-t-il?

---

* For verbs that have two stems, see pp. 273–274.

PRÉSENT DE L'INDICATIF

F. aller, partir, sortir, ouvrir, connaître, croire, prendre, faire, voir, venir

1. Je vais à Saint-Cloud. 2. Il va à Saint-Cloud. 3. Je pars à midi. 4. A quelle heure pars-tu? 5. A quelle heure sors-tu? 6. Il ouvre les yeux. 7. Je ne connais pas les Duplessis. 8. Crois-tu cette histoire? 9. Je prends l'autobus. 10. Il prend l'avion. 11. Qu'est-ce que tu fais cet après-midi? 12. Il fait des courses. 13. Je ne vois pas de taxi. 14. Qu'est-ce que tu vois? 15. Il vient d'arriver. 16. Je viens de déjeuner.

III. Répondez en français par une phrase complète à chacune des questions suivantes:

1. Êtes-vous Américain? 2. Avez-vous des amis à Paris? 3. Où demeurent vos parents? 4. A quelle heure arrivez-vous en classe? 5. A quelle heure finissent vos cours aujourd'hui? 6. Attendez-vous souvent un autobus? 7. Perdez-vous beaucoup de temps le soir? 8. A quelle heure commencez-vous à travailler le soir? 9. A quelle heure finissez-vous d'habitude? 10. Allez-vous souvent au cinéma? 11. Aimez-vous aller au cinéma? 12. Combien de temps faut-il pour aller en ville?

IV. Mettez chacune des phrases suivantes à la forme interrogative par l'inversion du pronom sujet et du verbe:

1. Vous êtes de retour. 2. Il est marié. 3. Ils demeurent ici. 4. C'est près d'ici. 5. Il y a une pharmacie près d'ici. 6. Jean est de retour. 7. Les Duplessis habitent à Saint-Cloud. 8. Jean va voir ses amis. 9. Jean décide de prendre un taxi. 10. Les Duplessis sont contents de revoir Jean.

V. Demandez à quelqu'un:

1. s'il (si elle) est Américain(e). 2. si Roger et Marie sont Français. 3. si Roger et Marie sont mariés. 4. si Roger et Marie ont des amis américains. 5. si Roger et Marie demeurent à Paris. 6. où Roger et Marie demeurent. 7. depuis quand Roger et Marie demeurent à Saint-Cloud. 8. s'il (si elle) demeure à Saint-Cloud. 9. où il (elle) demeure. 10. à quelle heure sa classe finit. 11. à quelle heure il (elle) finit son travail. 12. à quelle heure il (elle) commence à travailler le soir. 13. s'il (si elle) va au cinéma ce soir. 14. s'il (si elle) attend souvent un autobus. 15. combien de temps il faut pour aller de Paris à Saint-Cloud.

VI. A. Répétez chacune des phrases suivantes en employant **depuis cinq minutes:**

1. Il pleut. **2.** J'attends un taxi. **3.** Il est ici. **4.** Le téléphone sonne. **5.** Elle parle au téléphone.

B. Même exercice en employant **Il y a cinq minutes que . . .**

C. Même exercice en employant **Voilà cinq minutes que . . .**

VII. A. Posez la question à laquelle répond chacune des phrases suivantes en employant **Depuis combien de temps . . .?**

1. Je suis ici depuis 10 minutes. **2.** J'attends un taxi depuis un quart d'heure. **3.** Voilà quinze jours que nous sommes ici. **4.** Il pleut. **5.** Il est à table.

B. Même exercice en employant **Combien de temps y a-t-il que . . .?**

C. Posez la question à laquelle répond chacune des phrases suivantes en employant **Depuis quand . . .?**

1. Il est ici depuis le premier septembre. **2.** Il est à Paris depuis le 15 août. **3.** Nous sommes en ville depuis 10 heures du matin. **4.** Il fait froid depuis le premier novembre.

VIII. DICTÉE.

1. Où achetez-vous votre journal? **2.** Je l'achète au bureau de tabac. **3.** Quelle saison préférez-vous? **4.** Je préfère l'été. **5.** Il gèle aujourd'hui. **6.** Cette route mène à Saint-Cloud. **7.** Combien pesez-vous? **8.** Je pèse soixante-dix kilos. **9.** Nous commençons à huit heures. **10.** J'espère qu'il est à la maison. **11.** Je me lève à sept heures. **12.** Nous nous levons à sept heures. **13.** Comment vous appelez-vous? **14.** Je m'appelle Henri (Henriette).

Deux amis à table

CHEZ LES DUPLESSIS

Roger a reçu Jean à bras ouverts, et Jean a été très heureux de retrouver son ami, qu'il n'avait pas vu depuis longtemps. Malheureusement, Marie était en train de faire des courses au moment de l'arrivée de Jean. En attendant son retour, nos deux amis parlent de ce qu'ils ont fait au cours des deux dernières années.

ROGER. —[1]Tu as beaucoup voyagé depuis ton départ il y a deux ans, n'est-ce pas?

JEAN. —[2]Oui, pas mal! [3]Comme tu le sais, en quittant Paris, je suis retourné à Philadelphie. [4]De là, je suis allé à Pittsburgh, où j'ai passé quelques mois dans les laboratoires d'une compagnie de pétrole. [5]Puis on m'a envoyé au Vénézuéla.

ROGER. —[6]Tu es allé aussi au Moyen-Orient, n'est-ce pas?

JEAN. —[7]Attends! Je n'ai pas encore fini de parler de mes voyages... [8]Du Vénézuéla, je suis parti pour la Tunisie. [9]J'ai quitté la Tunisie pour l'Égypte, l'Égypte pour l'Iraq. [10]Puis j'ai passé quelque temps à Tel-Aviv. [11]On m'envoie maintenant aux États-Unis, passer un congé de trois mois que je n'ai pas volé.

Roger welcomed John with open arms, and John was very happy to be with his friend, whom he had not seen in a long time. Unfortunately Marie was doing errands when John got there. While waiting for her to get back, our two friends talk about what they have done in the course of the last two years.

ROGER. —[1]You have traveled a lot since you left two years ago, haven't you?

JOHN. —[2]Yes, quite a bit! [3]As you know, when I left Paris, I went back to Philadelphia. [4]From there I went to Pittsburgh, where I spent several months in the laboratories of an oil company. [5]Then they sent me to Venezuela.

ROGER. —[6]You also went to the Middle East, didn't you?

JOHN. —[7]Wait! I haven't finished telling about my travels... [8]From Venezuela, I set out for Tunisia. [9]I left Tunisia for Egypt, Egypt for Iraq. [10]Then I spent a little time in Tel-Aviv. [11]Now they are sending me to the United States for a three months leave— which I have really earned (which I have not stolen).

ROGER. —¹²Comparée à la tienne, ma vie a été bien tranquille. ¹³Depuis notre mariage, Marie et moi nous sommes restés bien sagement à la maison, ¹⁴sauf bien entendu quelques petits voyages d'agrément.

JEAN. —¹⁵J'ai reçu l'invitation à ton mariage quand j'étais dans la jungle vénézuélienne. ¹⁶Je n'ai pas pu venir assister* à la cérémonie. C'était trop loin.

ROGER. —¹⁷En tout cas, reste dîner avec nous ce soir. ¹⁸Marie sera enchantée de te revoir, et nous reparlerons du bon vieux temps.

ROGER. —¹²My life has been very calm in comparison to yours. ¹³Since our marriage, Marie and I have remained very quietly at home, ¹⁴except, of course, for a few little pleasure trips.

JOHN. —¹⁵I got the invitation to your wedding when I was in the jungle of Venezuela. ¹⁶I couldn't come to (be present at) the ceremony. It was too far.

ROGER. —¹⁷In any case, stay to dinner with us this evening. ¹⁸Marie will be delighted to see you again, and we will talk over the good old days again.

I. SUBSTITUTIONS. Répétez les phrases suivantes, en substituant les mots indiqués:

1. Jean a été [très heureux] de retrouver son ami.
   bien content/ fort content/ bien aise/ enchanté/ ravi (*extremely happy*)

2. Tu as beaucoup [voyagé] depuis ton départ.
   appris/ grandi/ maigri (*lost weight*/ engraissé (*put on weight*)

3. Marie était sortie au moment [de son arrivée].
   de son départ/ de son retour/ de l'arrivée du taxi/ de l'arrivée de l'agent de police/ de l'arrivée des pompiers (*firemen*)

4. En attendant son retour, nos amis parlent [de ce qu'ils ont fait].
   de ce qu'ils vont faire/ de leurs familles/ de leurs voyages/ de leur travail/ du bon vieux temps

5. Comparée à la tienne, ma vie a été [bien tranquille].
   bien sage/ bien occupée/ bien agitée/ peu brillante/ bien monotone

---

* **Assister à** is used to refer to specific events — performances, lectures, church services — but not to places such as schools, theaters, movie houses, stadiums. Ex.: **Elle a assisté à la cérémonie, à la représentation, à un match. Elle est allée au cinéma, à l'école, au stade, au théâtre, à l'église.**

6. Elle n'a rien acheté sauf [le journal].

un pain/ des timbres/ du lait/ une robe et
un manteau/ quelques bouteilles de vin

7. Reste [dîner] avec nous.

déjeuner/ prendre le thé/ prendre le café/ passer la soirée

II. Répondez aux questions suivantes, en employant l'expression indiquée:

A. assister à *(to attend, to go to a specific event)*

1. Jean a-t-il assisté au mariage de Roger? **2.** Avez-vous assisté au match de football samedi dernier? **3.** Avez-vous assisté à la conférence du professeur hier soir? **4.** Avez-vous jamais assisté à la messe de minuit à Notre-Dame de Paris? **5.** Avez-vous jamais assisté à une représentation de *Carmen?*

B. aller à *(to attend, to go to a place)*

1. Êtes-vous allé au stade samedi dernier? **2.** Êtes-vous allé au théâtre la semaine dernière? **3.** Êtes-vous jamais allé au musée du Louvre? **4.** Êtes-vous allé à l'école à Chicago?

C. retrouver *(to meet again, to meet, to join)*

1. Jean est-il content de retrouver ses amis? **2.** Êtes-vous content(e) de retrouver vos amis après un long voyage? **3.** A quelle heure est-ce que je vous retrouverai? **4.** Où est-ce que je vous retrouverai? **5.** Où allez-vous retrouver vos amis?

III. Répondez en français:

1. Comment Roger a-t-il reçu Jean? **2.** Qu'est-ce que Marie était en train de faire? **3.** Où était Marie au moment de l'arrivée de Jean? **4.** De quoi les deux amis parlent-ils en attendant son retour? **5.** Quand Jean a-t-il quitté la France? **6.** A-t-il beaucoup voyagé? **7.** Où est-il allé en quittant Paris? **8.** Combien de temps a-t-il passé à Pittsburgh? **9.** Où a-t-il travaillé à Pittsburgh? **10.** Où l'a-t-on envoyé ensuite? **11.** Dans quels pays d'Afrique est-il allé? **12.** Combien de temps a-t-il passé à Tel-Aviv? **13.** Où va-t-il maintenant? **14.** Pourquoi l'envoie-t-on aux États-Unis? **15.** Qu'est-ce que Jean pense de son congé? **16.** Est-ce que Roger et Marie ont beaucoup voyagé depuis leur mariage? **17.** Quelle sorte de voyages ont-ils faits? **18.** Où était Jean quand il a reçu l'invitation à leur mariage? **19.** Est-ce qu'il a assisté à la cérémonie? **20.** Pourquoi n'a-t-il pas pu venir? **21.** Est-ce que Jean va rester dîner? **22.** De quoi parleront-ils ensemble?

CHEZ LES DUPLESSIS

IV. Demandez à quelqu'un:

1. où habitent les Duplessis depuis qu'ils ont quitté Paris. **2.** où ils habitent depuis leur départ de Paris. **3.** ce que Marie était en train de faire quand Jean est arrivé chez les Duplessis. **4.** où elle était à l'arrivée de Jean. **5.** où elle était au moment de son arrivée. **6.** si Jean est content d'être de retour à Paris. **7.** si Jean a assisté au mariage des Duplessis. **8.** pourquoi il n'a pas assisté au mariage.

V. Répétez les phrases suivantes en remplaçant **partir de** par **quitter:**

EX.: Je suis parti de l'Égypte. — **J'ai quitté l'Égypte.**

1. Je suis parti de la Tunisie. **2.** Il est parti de l'Iraq. **3.** Nous sommes partis de Tel Aviv. **4.** Nous sommes partis des États-Unis. **5.** Nous sommes partis de la maison. **6.** Elle est partie de Paris. **7.** Il est parti du Vénézuéla. **8.** Ils sont partis du Japon.

VI. THÈME.

When John arrives at the Duplessis', Marie is not at home. She is in town. Roger hopes that she is going to be back soon. She is buying a loaf of bread. But sometimes it takes a long time to buy a loaf of bread. Sometimes you (**on**) meet your (**ses**) friends. You never know. Sometimes you waste a great deal of time.

While waiting for Marie to come back (Marie's return), John and Roger talk together. John talks about what he has done since he left Paris two years ago.

Passé composé/ Article défini/ Prépositions "de" et "à"

5   The **passé composé** and the **imparfait**.

The *passé composé* and the *imparfait* are both used to express an action or state of being in the past: the *passé composé* is used to tell WHAT HAPPENED, whereas the *imparfait* is used primarily to tell what was going on at the time when the action took place. The *passé composé* is the normal past tense in spoken French; the *imparfait* is a special tense that is used only in special cases. Its use will be described in Unit 6.

Note that in formal written French the *passé simple* is normally used instead of the *passé composé*. Students learning to read French would do well to familiarize themselves with the *passé simple* of regular verbs and of frequently used irregular verbs. (See pp. 215–217.)

6   Examples of the use of the **passé composé**.

(A)

—Qu'est-ce que **vous avez fait** pendant les vacances?	What *did you do* during the vacation?
—**J'ai voyagé.**	I *took* a trip.
Je suis allé en Californie.	I *went* to California.
En route, **nous avons visité** le parc de Yellowstone.	On the way, *we visited* Yellowstone Park.
Et vous, qu'**avez-vous fait?**	And what *did you do?*
—Moi, **j'ai été** malade.	I *was* sick.
J'ai eu une crise d'appendicite.	I *had* appendicitis.
On m'a **opéré. Il y a eu** des complications. **J'ai passé** trois semaines à l'hôpital. **Je n'ai pas pu** quitter mon lit. **J'ai** même **cru** un jour que j'allais (*imparfait*) mourir.	I *was operated on. There were* complications. I *spent* three weeks in the hospital. I *couldn't* leave my bed. One day, I even *thought* I was going to die.

(B)

— **Avez-vous vu** ce nouveau film?	*Have you seen* this new film?
— Oui. **Je l'ai trouvé** excellent.	Yes. *I thought* it was excellent.
Est-ce qu'**il** vous **a plu?**	*Did you like* it?
— Oh, **je l'ai trouvé** comme ci comme ça.	Oh, *I thought* it was so-so.

(C)

— Cet hiver a **été** très rigoureux, n'est-ce pas?	This winter *was* very severe, wasn't it?
— Oui, **il a fait** froid tout l'hiver et **il a neigé** tout le temps.	Yes. *It was* cold all winter and *it snowed* all the time.

Note with care that in the above examples the *passé composé* is used regardless of what you would say in English. Students often suppose that if you say: "I was" "I had" "I could" "I thought" in English, the French *imparfait* would automatically be called for; but this is frequently not the case.

(D)

{**Je ne suis pas allé** au cinéma {depuis longtemps.	*I haven't been* to the movies in a long time.
{Il y a longtemps que **je ne suis pas** {**allé** au cinéma.	
Il y a longtemps que **je ne vous ai pas** vu.	*I haven't seen you* in a long time.

Compare **Depuis** with present indicative, par. 3 A.

7   Forms of the **passé composé.**

The forms of the *passé composé* will be found on p. 267.

For the negative and interrogative forms of the *passé composé*, you use the negative and interrogative forms of the auxiliary verb.

Vous avez voyagé. Avez-vous voyagé? Je n'ai pas voyagé.

8   Forms of the past participle.

Past participles have four forms: masculine and feminine singular and masculine and feminine plural, aim**é**, aim**ée**, aim**és**, aim**ées**; fini, fin**ie**, fin**is**, fin**ies**; perd**u**, perd**ue**, perd**us**, perd**ues**. All four forms of these (and of most other participles) are pronounced alike. In the case of irregular verbs whose participle ends in **t**, the **t** is pronounced only in the feminine forms: ouvert, ouverte, ouverts, ouvertes; fait, faite, faits, faites. Likewise, the **s** of participles ending in **s** is silent in masculine forms and is pronounced **z** in feminine forms: pris, prise, pris, prises; mis, mise, mis, mises.

9   Agreement of the past participle of verbs conjugated with **avoir**.

The masculine singular form of the past participle of these verbs is used except when the verb is preceded by a direct object; but when the verb *is* preceded by a direct object, the past participle agrees with it in gender and number.

Marie a été malade. (*No agreement.*)
Elle a e**u** une crise d'appendicite. (*No agreement, dir. obj. follows.*)
On l'a opér**ée**. (*Agreement with preceding direct object* **l'** — *which refers to Marie.*)
J'ai acheté des fleurs. (*No agreement, dir. obj. follows.*)
Voilà les fleurs que j'ai achet**ées**. (*Agreement with preceding direct object* **que** — *which refers to* **les fleurs.**)
Je les ai achet**ées** dans la rue. (*Agreement with preceding direct object* **les** — *which refers to* **les fleurs.**)

Note, however, that the past participles does not agree with **en**:

Marie en a acheté aussi. (*No agreement, even though* **en** *replaces* **des fleurs.**)

10   Verbs conjugated with **être**.

A few verbs, which denote generally motion or change of condition, are conjugated with the auxiliary verb **être**:

INFINITIVE	PAST PARTICIPLE
aller *to go*	allé
venir *to come*	venu
sortir *to go out*	sorti
entrer *to go in*	entré
partir *to go away, to leave*	parti
arriver *to arrive*	arrivé
retourner *to return*	retourné

Infinitive	Past Participle
monter *to go up*	monté
descendre *to go down*	descendu
tomber *to fall, to fall down*	tombé
rester *to stay, to remain*	resté
naître *to be born*	né
mourir *to die*	mort
devenir *to become*	devenu

Compounds of these verbs (**revenir, ressortir, rentrer, repartir, remonter, redescendre,** etc.) are also normally conjugated with **être.**

Note that many verbs that seem to imply motion are conjugated with **avoir.**

EX.: J'ai quitté la maison. J'ai voyagé tout l'été. J'ai marché un peu. J'ai couru à la porte. J'ai avancé un peu. J'ai reculé.

A. Rentrer, revenir, retourner.

Rentrer means to go back home. **Revenir** means *to come back to where you are* (including home). When you leave the house in the morning you could say: **Je reviendrai vers cinq heures, Je rentrerai vers cinq heures,** or **Je serai de retour vers cinq heures.** You could NOT use **retourner** here. **Retourner** means to return someplace else — to which you have been before. An American who is in the U.S. but who has been to France could say: **Je retournerai en France l'année prochaine. Ensuite je reviendrai en Amérique.** If he is in France, he could say: **Je reviendrai en France l'année prochaine. Je retournerai en Amérique au mois de septembre.**

B. Partir, sortir, quitter.

Partir means to leave, to set out. It is the opposite of **arriver.**

Le train est parti à l'heure. Jean est parti hier matin.

Sortir is used more specifically to express the idea of going out of an enclosed place: a house, room, office, building, garden, park, etc. It is the opposite of **entrer** or **rentrer.**

Nous sommes entrés au théâtre à huit heures. Nous en sommes sortis à onze heures.

Quitter also means to leave, but it is conjugated with **avoir** and must always have an expressed object: **J'ai quitté la maison, Paris, l'Europe, l'aéroport, etc.**

C. Entrée, sortie, arrivée, retour, départ.

These nouns are normally used after prepositions to express ideas that we usually express in English with some form of a verb.

The French words for *exit* and *entrance* are **sortie** (*f*) and **entrée** (*f*).

A mon **arrivée** à Paris . . .	When I *got to* Paris . . . (lit. upon my arrival in Paris . . .)
Après son **départ** . . .	After he *left* . . .
Avant son **retour** . . .	Before he *got back* . . .
A la **sortie** du village . . .	As (we) *left* the village . . .

11 Agreement of the past participle of verbs conjugated with **être** (except reflexive verbs).

The past participle of these verbs agrees with the subject.

Le petit **Michel** est n**é** à Saint-Cloud.
Marie est n**ée** en Bretagne.

Jean et Roger sont all**és** en ville.
Marie et sa mère sont all**ées** en ville.

Nous (*m* or *m* and *f*) sommes par**tis.**
Nous (*f*) sommes par**ties.**
Vous (*m sg*) êtes par**ti.**
Vous (*f sg*) êtes par**tie.**
Vous (*m pl* or *m* and *f*) êtes par**tis.**
Vous (*f pl*) êtes par**ties.**

When **monter, descendre, sortir,** and **rentrer** are used as transitive verbs (that is, when they take a direct object), they are conjugated with **avoir.**

J'ai monté (descendu) les bagages.

The agreement of the past participle of reflexive verbs will be explained in par. 45.

12   Definite articles **le, la, les** and prepositions **de** (of, from) and **à** (to, at).

A. Forms used with masculine singular nouns beginning with a consonant — other than a mute "h".

  le: **le** taxi, **le** chauffeur
  du: **du** taxi, **du** chauffeur
  au: **au** taxi, **au** chauffeur

B. Forms used with feminine singular nouns beginning with a consonant — other than a mute "h".

   la: **la** voiture, **la** maison
  de la: **de la** voiture, **de la** maison
   à la: **à la** voiture, **à la** maison

C. Forms used with all singular nouns beginning with a vowel or mute
"h".

   l':   **l'**ami, **l'**homme (*m*)
            l'entrée, **l'**annonce (*f*)
  de l':   **de l'**ami, **de l'**homme
            de l'entrée, **de l'**annonce
  à l':   **à l'**ami, **à l'**homme
            à l'entrée, **à l'**annonce

D. Forms used with plural nouns of both genders.

   les: **les** taxis, **les** voitures
  des: **des** taxis, **des** voitures
  aux: **aux** taxis, **aux** voitures

Note (1) that consonant **s** (or **x**) of **les, des,** and **aux,** is linked when
immediately followed by a noun beginning with a vowel or mute "h":
les amis, des hommes, aux enfants.

(2) A few French nouns may be either masculine or feminine:
artiste, camarade, collègue, élève, pianiste, touriste, secrétaire, etc.

13   Use of the definite article.

The definite article is normally expressed in French either when the
noun is used in a specific sense (The books are on the table) or in a

general sense (Books are useful). Note the difference between English and French usage in the following phrases.

Le jus d'orange est bon pour la santé.	*Orange juice* is good for the health.
Le déjeuner est à midi.	*Lunch* is at noon.
L'homme aime **la liberté.**	*Man* loves *liberty.*
Le départ de Jean.	John's *departure.*
Le retour de Marie.	Marie's *return.*
La vie est chère.	*Living* is expensive.
La réclame est nécessaire au commerce.	*Advertising* is necessary for trade.

The definite article is not used with nouns that are in apposition **(M. Adam, professeur à la Sorbonne);** in references **(voir page 2);** in lists **(Hommes, femmes, enfants, tout le monde s'amusait. Il n'a ni père, ni mère, ni proches parents);** or with nouns denoting nationality or profession when they follow the verb **être (Il est avocat. Nous sommes Américains).** It is usually omitted in titles: **Retour à Paris, Huis clos.**

14 Prepositions and definite articles with geographical names.

A. Prepositions and definite articles with names of countries that are masculine.

au (aux) (*to* or *in*)	Mon père est **au Canada.** Je vais **aux États-Unis.** On a envoyé Jean **au Vénézuéla.**
du (des) (*from*)	Je suis parti **du Mexique.** Jean vient **des États-Unis.**

Most countries in the Western Hemisphere are masculine. Ex.: **les États-Unis, le Mexique, le Canada, le Brésil, le Pérou, le Chili, le Nicaragua,** etc.

B. Prepositions are used alone with names of continents and with countries that are feminine.

en (*to* or *in*)	Jean est allé **en France.** On l'a envoyé **en Égypte** et **en Arabie.** Roger et Marie habitent **en Europe.**

de (*from*)   Jean vient **d'Égypte.**
                                                  Il vient **d'Afrique.**

All the continents and most European countries are feminine. Ex.: **la Suisse, la Russie, la Suède, la Belgique, l'Allemagne.**

C. Prepositions are used alone with names of cities.

à (*to* or *in*)   Il est **à Paris.**
                                          Il va **à Genève.**
                                          Son père est **à Londres.**

de (*from*)   Il vient **de Philadelphie.**

In the case of cities whose names have a definite article (Le Havre, La Nouvelle-Orléans) you use the forms **au** and **du** and **à la** and **de la** as you would expect: **au Havre, à la Nouvelle-Orléans.**

I. EXERCICES D'APPLICATION.

A. Mettez chacune des phrases suivantes au passé composé:

1. Je vais en ville. 2. Il vient lundi. 3. Il revient bientôt. 4. Il sort tout de suite.
5. Il ressort tout de suite. 6. Il entre. 7. Il rentre. 8. Nous partons mardi. 9. Nous repartons samedi. 10. Ils montent dans le taxi. 11. Elle remonte dans sa chambre.
12. A quelle heure allez-vous en ville? 13. A quelle heure retournez-vous en ville?
14. Qu'est-ce qu'il devient? (*What's becoming of him? What has become of him?*)

B. Répondez affirmativement par une phrase complète:

1. Êtes-vous sorti hier soir? 2. A quelle heure avez-vous quitté la maison? 3. Avez-vous dîné au restaurant? 4. Combien de temps êtes-vous resté au restaurant? 5. Où avez-vous passé la soirée? (au théâtre.) 6. A quelle heure avez-vous quitté le théâtre?
7. En quittant le théâtre êtes-vous retourné au restaurant? 8. A quelle heure êtes-vous rentré chez vous?

C. Demandez à quelqu'un:

1. s'il est allé au Canada l'été dernier. 2. quel jour il a quitté la maison. 3. quand il est parti des États-Unis. 4. s'il est allé à Montréal. 5. s'il est allé à Québec en quittant Montréal. 6. s'il est allé voir l'Île d'Orléans. 7. s'il est retourné à Montréal. 8. quand il est revenu aux États-Unis. 9. quand il est rentré à la maison.

II. Répondez en français:

1. Qu'est-ce que vous avez fait l'été dernier? **2.** Comment avez-vous passé les vacances? **3.** Avez-vous voyagé? **4.** Voyagez-vous tous les étés? **5.** Avez-vous été malade? **6.** Avez-vous eu une crise d'appendicite? **7.** Quel temps a-t-il fait l'été dernier? **8.** L'été a-t-il été très chaud? **9.** Est-ce qu'il a beaucoup plu? **10.** Avez-vous jamais visité Yellowstone? **11.** Avez-vous trouvé Yellowstone intéressant? **12.** Combien de temps avez-vous passé à Yellowstone? **13.** Quand avez-vous quitté la maison? **14.** Vos parents voyagent-ils souvent? **15.** Ont-ils voyagé l'été dernier? **16.** Ont-ils jamais vu les chutes du Niagara? **17.** Comment ont-ils trouvé les chutes du Niagara?

III. EXERCICES D'APPLICATION.

A. Employez **près de** avec chacun des noms suivants:

le pont, l'hôtel, la Seine, l'entrée, les quais, la voiture.

B. Employez **le long de** avec chacun des noms suivants:

la rue, le boulevard, la Seine, les quais, le parc.

C. Employez **Il fait signe à** avec chacun des noms suivants:

le chauffeur, le garçon, l'homme, le professeur, la jeune fille.

D. Employez **au cours de** avec chacun des noms suivants:

le voyage, la conversation, l'année, les vacances.

E. Employez **Nous allons à** avec les noms suivants:

la maison, le parc, les Champs-Elysées, le théâtre, le cours (*course*) de français, le stade.

F. Employez la préposition indiquée avec chacune des expressions suivantes: **l'arrivée de mon père, le départ de Jean Hughes, le retour de mon ami.**

1. Employez la préposition **à** (*at, on, upon*).
2. Employez la préposition **avant.**
3. Employez la préposition **après.**

G. Employez les phrases indiquées avec les noms suivants: **l'entrée, la sortie, le parc, le kiosque, le bureau de tabac.**

1. Employez **Il s'arrête à.**
2. Employez **C'est près de.**

PASSÉ COMPOSÉ/ ARTICLE DÉFINI/ "DE" ET "À"

H. Employez les phrases indiquées avec les noms suivants: **l'Afrique, la Hollande, l'Angleterre, la Chine, l'Allemagne, la Russie, la Suisse l'Amérique.**

1. Employez **Je vais en.**
2. Employez **Je viens de.**

IV. EXERCICE SUR L'EMPLOI DE L'ARTICLE DÉFINI. Dites en français:

1. Dinner is at seven. **2.** Milk is good for the health. **3.** French people like wine. **4.** Americans like automobiles. **5.** Boys like girls. **6.** Children go to school. **7.** Men love liberty. **8.** Women prefer luxury (**le luxe**). **9.** School begins at 8:30. **10.** At the entrance of the West Freeway. **11.** Near the Saint-Cloud bridge. **12.** Near the entrance. **13.** John has just signaled to a taxi driver. **14.** He has just signaled to the driver. **15.** He finds Roger at the door of the house.

V. Exercice sur l'emploi des expressions **arrivée, retour, départ:** Dites en français:

1. When he got here (there) . . . **2.** When he got back . . . **3.** After he left . . . **4.** Before we left . . . **5.** Before we got back . . . **6.** When you get back . . . (When you return) **7.** When you got back . . . (When you returned) **8.** After my father got back . . . **9.** Before my father left . . .

VI. THÈME.

We decided to have dinner downtown. We looked for a restaurant. We went in. We ordered (**commander**) a good dinner. The waiter brought the dinner. We finished early. We left the restaurant. We got into a taxi. The driver lost his way. He wasted a lot of time. We got home very late.

(Note how dry, how elementary, these statements about "what happened" are. You will see in Unit 6 how the *imparfait* can be used to put flesh and blood on the dry bones of the narration.)

Cuisine de restaurant

UN ACCIDENT

Marie et Roger ont invité Jean à dîner chez eux. A la fin du repas, Jean parle d'un accident qui a eu lieu sur le Nil pendant son séjour en Égypte.

JEAN. —¹Marie, ton dîner était délicieux. ²Je ne savais pas du tout, il y a deux ans, que tu étais si bonne cuisinière.

MARIE. —³J'apprécie vivement ton compliment. ⁴Mais dis-nous un peu* ce que tu as fait au cours de ces deux dernières années.

JEAN. —⁵L'année dernière, à cette date, j'étais en Égypte. ⁶Vous souvenez-vous du terrible accident qui a eu lieu sur le Nil?

ROGER. —⁷Je me souviens de quelque chose—⁸un bateau qui transportait des passagers sur le Nil, n'est-ce pas?

JEAN. —⁹J'étais dans le voisinage au moment de l'accident.

Marie and Roger invited John to have dinner with them. At the end of the meal, John is telling about an accident that happened on the Nile when he was in Egypt.

JOHN. —¹Marie, your dinner was delicious. ²I didn't have any idea two years ago that you were such a good cook.

MARIE. —³I appreciate your compliment very much (keenly). ⁴But how about telling us what you have done in the course of these last two years?

JOHN. —⁵Last year, on this date, I was in Egypt. ⁶Do you remember the terrible accident that took place on the Nile?

ROGER. —⁷I remember something— ⁸a boat that was carrying passengers on the Nile, wasn't it?

JOHN. —⁹I was in the neighborhood at the time of the accident.

---

* Notez que **un peu** est ici une simple formule d'atténuation. Cf. **Voyons un peu** Let's take a look *or* Let's just take a look; **un peu partout** practically everywhere.

ROGER. —[10]Qu'est-ce qui est arrivé, au juste?

JEAN. —[11]Voilà. C'était un très vieux bateau. [12]Depuis soixante-dix ans il transportait des passagers sur le Nil. [13]Il y avait de la place pour une soixantaine de passagers. [14]Le jour de l'accident, on en a embarqué plus de cent cinquante. [15]Le bateau venait à peine de quitter la rive lorsque l'eau a commencé à entrer à l'intérieur.

MARIE. —[16]Pourquoi le capitaine n'est-il pas retourné au bord?

JEAN. —[17]Il a essayé. [18]Le bateau était à quelques mètres du bord quand l'accident a eu lieu. [19]Il était même si près du bord [20]qu'on a lancé des cordes à des gens sur la rive du fleuve. [21]Naturellement, plus ils tiraient sur les cordes, plus le bateau s'inclinait. [22]Il a fini par chavirer. [23]Une centaine de personnes se sont noyées. [24]La plupart des passagers ne savaient pas nager.

MARIE. —[25]C'est en vérité une bien triste histoire.

ROGER. —[26]C'est affreux! Mais c'est la vie . . . [27]Si nous allions prendre le café au salon?

ROGER. —[10]Just what happened?

JOHN. —[11]Here's what happened. It was a very old boat. [12]For seventy years, it had been carrying passengers on the Nile. [13]There was room for about sixty passengers. [14]The day of the accident, they took on more than a hundred and fifty. [15]The boat had scarcely left the shore when water began to come in.

MARIE. —[16]Why didn't the captain go back to shore?

JOHN. —[17]He tried to. [18]The boat was just a few yards from the shore when the accident took place. [19]It was so near the shore, even, [20]that they threw ropes to people on the bank of the river. [21]Naturally, the more they pulled on the ropes, the more the boat listed. [22]It finally turned over on its side. [23]About a hundred persons were drowned. [24]Most of the passengers didn't know how to swim.

MARIE. —[25]That is really a very sad story.

ROGER. —[26]It's awful! But such is life . . . [27]How about going into the living room to have coffee?

I. SUBSTITUTIONS. Répétez les phrases suivantes, en substituant les mots indiqués:

1. Je ne savais pas que tu étais [si bonne cuisinière].

si bon musicien/ si bon étudiant/ si bon nageur/ si bon violoniste/ si bon mathématicien

2. Dis-nous un peu [ce que tu as fait] au cours de tes voyages.

ce que tu as vu/ où tu es allé/ ce qui t'est arrivé/ ce qui s'est passé

3. L'année dernière, à cette date, j'étais [en Égypte].

en Israël/ à Tel-Aviv/ sur la Mer Méditerranée/ au Caire (*at Cairo*)

4. Je me souviens [de quelque chose].

de l'accident/ de l'histoire/ du capitaine/ de ce vieux bateau

5. Le bateau venait à peine de [quitter la rive] quand l'accident a eu lieu.

partir/ se mettre en route/ se mettre en marche/ quitter le bord

6. Il a fini par [chavirer].

retourner au bord/ remonter le Nil/ regagner le port/ rentrer sain et sauf au port

7. [Une centaine] de personnes se sont noyées.

Une dizaine/ Une vingtaine/ Une soixantaine/ Des centaines

8. C'est [affreux]! Mais c'est la vie.

effroyable/ épouvantable/ horrible/ terrible

II. Mettez chacune des phrases suivantes à l'imparfait:

A. venir de

1. Le bateau vient de quitter le bord. **2.** Jean vient d'arriver en Égypte. **3.** On vient d'embarquer plus de cent cinquante personnes. **4.** On vient de lancer des cordes à des gens sur la rive. **5.** Je viens de revenir d'Égypte.

B. plus . . . plus (moins)

1. Plus ils tirent sur les cordes, plus le bateau s'incline. **2.** Plus le bateau s'incline, plus l'eau entre. **3.** Plus l'eau entre, plus le bateau s'incline. **4.** Plus ils essayent, moins ils réussissent.

C. il y a

1. Il y a de la place pour soixante passagers. **2.** Il y a de la place pour une soixantaine de passagers. **3.** Il n'y a pas de place pour plus de soixante personnes. **4.** Il n'y a pas de place pour plus d'une soixantaine de personnes. **5.** Il n'y a pas de place pour nous.

III. Dites, en employant le passé composé de **finir par** et l'infinitif:

1. Le bateau a chaviré. **2.** On a embarqué plus de cent cinquante personnes. **3.** Il est retourné au bord. **4.** Tous les passagers sont montés dans le bateau.

IV. Répétez les phrases suivantes, en commençant par **La plupart (de)**...:

1. Les passagers ne savaient pas nager. **2.** Les gens ont tiré sur les cordes. **3.** Les chauffeurs de taxi sont bavards (*chatty*). **4.** Les jeunes gens aiment les sports. **5.** Les Françaises sont bonnes cuisinières. **6.** Les voyageurs aiment prendre des photos.

V. Posez en français la question à laquelle répondrait chacune des phrases suivantes, en commençant par **A quelle distance** ...? (*How far* ...?):

1. Le bateau était à quelques mètres du bord. **2.** Versailles est à dix-huit kilomètres de Paris. **3.** New York est à 5000 kilomètres de Paris. **4.** Le Caire est à une centaine de kilomètres de Suez. **5.** Marseille est à plus de deux mille cinq cents kilomètres du Caire.

VI. Répondez en français par une phrase complète à chacune des questions suivantes:

1. Comment Jean a-t-il trouvé le dîner de Marie? **2.** Savait-il qu'elle était si bonne cuisinière? **3.** Qu'est-ce qu'elle demande à Jean de leur dire? **4.** Où était Jean l'année dernière à cette date? **5.** Où l'accident a-t-il eu lieu? **6.** Est-ce que Roger se souvient de l'accident? **7.** Qu'est-ce que le bateau transportait? **8.** Où était Jean au moment de l'accident? **9.** Le bateau était-il vieux? **10.** Depuis combien de temps transportait-il des passagers? **11.** Pour combien de passagers y avait-il de la place? **12.** Combien de passagers a-t-on embarqué le jour de l'accident? **13.** Qu'est-ce qui est arrivé quand le bateau a quitté la rive? **14.** Qu'est-ce que le capitaine a essayé de faire? **15.** A quelle distance le bateau était-il du bord quand l'accident a eu lieu? **16.** A qui a-t-on lancé des cordes? **17.** Qu'est-ce qui est arrivé quand les gens qui étaient sur la rive ont tiré sur les cordes? **18.** Est-ce que le bateau a réussi à retourner au bord? **19.** Combien de personnes se sont noyées? **20.** Est-ce que tous les passagers savaient nager?

VII. Demandez à quelqu'un:

1. ce que Jean pense du dîner de Marie. **2.** quand Jean était à Paris. **3.** s'il savait que Marie était bonne cuisinière. **4.** ce que Jean a fait au cours des deux dernières années. **5.** où a eu lieu l'accident dont parle Jean. **6.** où il était au moment de l'accident. **7.** ce qui est arrivé. **8.** depuis quand le bateau transportait des passagers. **9.** combien de passagers il y avait le jour de l'accident. **10.** pourquoi le bateau a chaviré. **11.** si le bateau était loin du bord quand il a chaviré. **12.** où Roger propose d'aller prendre le café.

VIII. THÈME.

Two years ago I was on a boat on the Mississippi near St. Louis. It was an old boat that had been carrying passengers on the river for more than fifty years. It had hardly left the shore when they (**on**) told the captain that water was coming in. Immediately, the captain stopped the boat and gave orders (**l'ordre**) to go back to the shore. He told the passengers that there would be no danger if they remained calm. Most of them knew how to swim and were not at all afraid.

The captain finally succeeded in returning to shore. All's well that ends well.

Vieux bateau sur le Mississippi

UN ACCIDENT

Imparfait/ Partitif

15 The passé composé and the imparfait.

As we have seen in the story of the accident on the Nile (pp. 29–30), John uses both the *passe composé* and the *imparfait* as he tells the story. Now if a very young child had been telling the story, he might have reported every detail in the *passé composé* and joined each detail to the preceding one by saying "et puis" somewhat as follows: *Le jour de l'accident on a embarqué plus de cent cinquante passagers. Le bateau a quitté la rive et puis l'eau a commencé à entrer, et puis le capitaine a essayé de retourner au bord, et puis le bateau est retourné à quelques mètres du bord, et puis on a lancé des cordes à des gens sur la rive, et puis les gens ont tiré sur les cordes et le bateau s'est incliné et il a fini par chavirer.* But John, who speaks French like a mature Frenchman, merely puts the principal happenings in the *passé composé* and makes use of the *imparfait* for all sorts of circumstantial details — which makes the story much more artistic and dramatic. He starts out by giving background information, in the *imparfait*, of course: *J'étais en Égypte . . . J'étais dans le voisinage . . . C'était un très vieux bateau . . . Il transportait . . . Il y avait de la place pour une soixantaine de passagers . . .* (Drama is imminent.)

Roger, impatiently, says: *Qu'est-ce qui est arrivé au juste?* (*passé composé*). Now that the background is clear, the actual narrative begins: *Le jour de l'accident on a embarqué plus de cent cinquante personnes.* But even then, instead of saying "bientôt" or "quelques minutes plus tard", he injects still another dramatically descriptive clause in the *imparfait: Le bateau venait à peine de quitter la rive lorsque l'eau a commencé à entrer à l'intérieur.*

Marie interrupts to ask: *Pourquoi le capitaine n'est-il pas retourné au bord?* But John goes on with his story after answering: *Il a essayé.* He keeps the circumstances in the imperfect and puts the main facts in the *passé composé* as before: *Le bateau était à quelques mètres du bord quand l'accident a eu lieu. Il était si près du bord qu'on a lancé des cordes à des gens sur la rive du fleuve.* Then, instead of saying: the people pulled on the ropes so hard that they turned the boat over, thereby spoiling the dramatic effect, he introduces two clauses in the *imparfait: Naturellement, plus ils tiraient sur les cordes, plus le bateau s'inclinait.*

Then, suddenly, the climax: *Il a fini par chavirer. Une centaine de personnes se sont noyées.* Then, as if in answer to the question "Pourquoi?" he adds: *La plupart des passagers ne savaient pas nager.*

In a word, the *passé composé* is used to report what happened and the *imparfait* to report the circumstances in which the occurrences took place — where, when, how, why, etc.

16 Forms and use of the **imparfait**.

(1) Formation of the *imparfait* is explained in par. 120, p. 266.
(2) Use.

A. The *imparfait* with the *passé composé.*

1. The *imparfait* is used with the *passé composé* to describe the circumstances in which an event took place:

C'était un très vieux bateau. Le bateau était à quelques mètres du bord quand l'accident a eu lieu.

2. The *imparfait* is used with the *passé composé* to explain why an occurrence took place:

Ils se sont noyés parce qu'ils ne savaient pas nager.

B. The *imparfait* with another *imparfait.*

The *imparfait* is used with another *imparfait* to describe (1) habitual or (2) progressive actions that were going on simultaneously:

(1) Je partais tous les matins à sept heures et je rentrais à cinq heures du soir.
(2) Plus ils tiraient sur les cordes, plus le bateau s'inclinait.

C. The *imparfait* is used to describe the situation at the time of, or prior to, a past action. (The past action may be implied rather than expressed.)

Je pensais que vous étiez en Amérique (before I met you on the street).
Je ne savais pas que tu étais si bonne cuisinière (before eating dinner).

D. The *imparfait* is used to describe the way a person felt, looked, or seemed in the past — especially with the verbs **savoir, croire, penser, espérer, être, avoir, porter, être content, avoir peur,** etc.

Je ne savais pas que vous étiez ici. Je vous croyais à Paris.
J'espérais arriver à l'heure. J'avais peur d'être en retard.
L'hôtel était confortable. L'hôtelier était aimable. Les femmes de chambre portaient des coiffes bretonnes.

17   Special uses of the **imparfait**.

A. The *imparfait* is used with **depuis** or **il y avait . . . que** and an expression of time to report an action that had been going on for a specified time before another occurrence took place.

Il y avait dix minutes que j'attendais quand le taxi est arrivé.	I had been waiting for ten minutes when the taxi arrived.
Depuis soixante-dix ans il transportait des passagers sur le Nil.	It had been carrying passengers on the Nile for seventy years (when the accident occurred).

B. The *imparfait* of **venir de** with an infinitive is used to express an action that had immediately preceded another past occurrence.

Le bateau venait de quitter la rive quand l'eau a commencé à entrer.	The boat had just left the shore when water began to come in.

C. The *imparfait* is used with the conjunction **si** to express a mild request or a suggestion.

Si nous allions prendre le café au salon?	Suppose we go and have coffee in the living room? *or* How about going to have coffee in the living room?

D. The *imparfait* is used in if-clauses of conditional sentences. (See p. 130.)

E. The *imparfait* is used to express present action in indirect discourse that depends upon a verb in the *passé composé*.

Il a dit: "Je vais en Égypte". (*Direct discourse.*)
Il a dit qu'il allait en Égypte. (*Indirect discourse.*)

18 Comparison of the meaning of the **passé composé** and of the **imparfait.**

Je ne vous croyais pas si bonne cuisinière (*before eating dinner*).

Je n'ai pas cru ce qu'il m'a dit (*after he told me*).

L'avion survolait la ville pendant la cérémonie. (*The plane was incidental.*)

L'avion a survolé la ville plusieurs fois. (*The plane's flights are the principal action.*)

J'avais peur d'être en retard, car mon auto ne marchait pas bien. (*The way he felt before he arrived where he was going.*)

Quand j'ai vu l'agent de police près de mon auto, j'ai eu peur. (*My reaction when I saw the policeman.*)

19 Nouns.

A. Gender.

You know that French nouns fall into two classes or "genders," that nouns used with **le** or **un** are masculine, that those used with **la** or **une** are feminine, and that articles, adjectives, and pronouns agree in gender and number with the noun they modify or refer to. Simple as that all is, English speaking persons often find it difficult to master the role of gender in French. But if you do the exercises in this book systematically, you will have little trouble with the gender of nouns, because the dialogs as well as the grammar units are designed to give you practice in using authentic French phrases instead of isolated words. Instead of learning the gender of words (Ex.: **l'eau** is feminine), you should always use nouns in phrases that make the gender clear (Ex.: **de l'eau chaude**). If you practice using nouns in such phrases, they will enter your subconscious mind correctly and be available for use whenever you need them. And the phrases will probably serve also as patterns for generating other authentic French phrases.

As you read in French, however, you will learn the meaning of many nouns without paying attention to their gender. This is natural, because in reading you concentrate on the meaning of phrases rather than on the gender of words. But whenever you want to use such words in speaking or writing, you should make it a point to use them correctly from the first. For example, let us assume that you want to say something about a telegram, that you have met the words **télégramme** and **dépêche** in your reading, and that you do not know the gender of either. (1) You look up their gender. (2) You construct phrases such as "un long télégramme" and "une dépêche urgente". (3) Then you repeat each of them several times, sounding clearly the article, the noun and the adjective. The sound, the rhythm, and the meaning of the phrases will help you learn once and for all to use the words correctly. Do not imagine that it would be more efficient to learn "Télégramme is masculine" and "Dépêche is feminine"; for after memorizing these statements you would still have to learn to use the nouns with the right article and the right form of the adjective.

B. Forms.

1. In written French.

(a) To form the plural of most French nouns, you add **s** to the singular: **le fauteuil — les fauteuils, la chaise — les chaises, le détail — les détails, le bal — les bals, le pneu — les pneus, une auto — des autos, le vice — les vices, la vertu — les vertus,** etc.

(b) Instead of an **s**, you add an **x** to the singular of a few French nouns: **le vœu — les vœux** (*wishes*), **le cheveu — les cheveux, le château — les châteaux, le lieu — les lieux** (*places*), **le chameau — les chameaux, le bijou — les bijoux** (*jewels*), **le chou — les choux** (*cabbages*), **le genou — les genoux** (*knees*), etc.

A few frequently used nouns have a slightly irregular plural in **x: le travail — les travaux, le cheval — les chevaux, le journal — les journaux, le mal — les maux** (*evils*), etc.

(c) The plural of nouns whose singular form ends in **s**, **x**, or **z**, remains unchanged: **le fils — les fils, le sens — les sens, un vers** (*a line of poetry*) **— des vers, la voix — les voix, le choix — les choix, le gaz — les gaz, le nez — les nez,** etc.

2. In spoken French.

As the singular and plural of most nouns are pronounced alike, the distinction between the singular and plural is usually indicated by the form of the article or an adjective — or both: **le taxi — les taxis, mon ami — mes amis, le petit garçon — les petits garçons,** etc.

C. Nouns used in a partitive sense.

French usage in regard to expressing the partitive idea is very strict: a noun used in a partitive sense must be preceded by the word

de — either in combination with the definite article or alone. It is not always easy for English-speaking people to know when a noun is used in a partitive sense, because we sometimes express the partitive idea by the word *some* or *any* but, more often, we merely imply it. Most people would say "Do you want coffee?" rather than "Do you want some coffee?" or "Do you want any coffee?" But if you refer to *a part of* whatever you are talking about, you are using the noun in a partitive sense, and in French you *must* express the partitive idea. Compare the following:

Le beurre est un aliment.	Butter is food (all butter).
J'ai acheté **du** beurre ce matin.	I bought butter this morning (a part of the butter that they had for sale at the store).
Le beurre est dans le réfrigérateur.	The butter is in the refrigerator (all the butter I bought).
Voulez-vous **du** beurre?	Do you want butter? (a part of the butter I bought).

As a general rule, verbs such as **avoir, acheter, manger, vouloir** are usually followed by nouns used in a partitive sense, since you usually have, buy, eat, or want only a part of whatever you are talking about: **J'ai des amis, J'achète du tabac, Je mange de la viande, Je voudrais du rosbif;** but verbs like **aimer, préférer, détester, admirer** are usually followed by nouns in a general or specific sense since you like, prefer, dislike, or admire whatever you are talking about in *general:* **J'aime (Je n'aime pas) le café noir, Je préfère le café au lait, Je déteste les bananes, J'admire les peintures de Renoir.** ("I like *some* coffee" means "I like *some kinds* of coffee" — an idea that is not expressed by the partitive in French. One might say: **J'aime certaines espèces de café.**)

20 Use of partitive forms **du, de la, de l', des,** and **de.**

A. When a noun used in a partitive sense is the direct object of an affirmative or interrogative form of a verb, it is preceded by **du, de la,** or **des** — depending upon the gender and number of the noun: Voulez-vous **du café? de la crème? des fruits?** If the noun begins with a vowel, the form **de l'** is used for both masculine and feminine singular nouns: Donnez-moi **de l'argent, de l'eau.**

B. When a noun used in a partitive sense is the direct object of a negative form of a verb, it is preceded by **de** (or **d'**) alone, regardless of gender or number.

Je ne bois **pas de café (pas de crème, pas d'eau minérale, pas de vin).**	I don't drink coffee (cream, mineral water, wine).
Je ne prends **plus de café.**	I no longer drink coffee.
Je ne prends **guère de café.**	I hardly ever drink any coffee.
Je ne prends **jamais de café.**	I never drink coffee.

1. Note, however, that **ne . . . que** (*only*) is not negative and must be followed by **du, de la,** etc.:

Je **ne** prends **que du café (que de la crème, que de l'eau).**

2. Note also that when nouns are *not* used in a partitive sense, the form of the article is the same after a negative as after other forms of the verb.

J'aime **le café** (la crème, l'eau minérale, le vin).
Je n'aime **pas le café** (la crème, l'eau minérale, le vin).

3. Note also that the definite article alone is used in the following expressions:

Je n'ai pas **le temps . . . , l'occasion . . . , l'argent pour . . . , l'habitude de . . .**

21 Special uses of **de** alone.

A. After expressions of quantity.

De is used alone after expressions of quantity: **beaucoup de** sucre, **un peu de** crème, **un kilo de** beurre, **des quantités de** fruits, **un tas de** choses, **une bouteille de** lait.

B. When the plural form of a noun is preceded by an adjective.

Ordinarily **de** is used instead of **des** when a plural noun is preceded by an adjective: **de bons restaurants, d'autres restaurants, d'autres idées.** (Note exceptions in par. 29, C, D, E.)

22   The indefinite article **un, une, (des)**.

J'ai **un frère**.
J'ai **une sœur**.
J'ai fait **un voyage**.

J'ai **des frères**.
J'ai **des sœurs**.
J'ai fait **des voyages**.

The partitive form **des** can be thought of as the plural of **un, une.**

When the verb is negative, both **un, une,** and **des** are replaced by **de** alone.

Je n'ai pas de frère (de frères).
Je n'ai pas de sœur (de sœurs).
Je n'ai pas fait de voyage.

I. EXERCICES D'APPLICATION.

A. Mettez chacune des phrases suivantes à l'imparfait, en commençant par **A ce moment-là** . . . :

EX.: — Il a dix ans.
    — A ce moment-là il avait dix ans.

1. Il est à Paris. 2. Il est étudiant. 3. Je suis en Amérique. 4. Je travaille tous les soirs. 5. Je finis mon travail à midi. 6. J'obéis toujours à la loi. 7. Je réussis toujours. 8. Je vends des journaux.

B. Répétez les phrases suivantes, en commençant par **Il y avait dix minutes que** . . . :

EX.: — J'attendais un taxi.
    — Il y avait dix minutes que j'attendais un taxi.

1. J'étais à la maison. 2. J'écoutais des disques. 3. Je jouais aux cartes. 4. Je préparais le dîner. 5. Je parlais avec mes amis.

C. Répétez les phrases précédentes, en ajoutant . . . **depuis dix minutes.**

D. Répétez les phrases suivantes, en commençant par **Je ne suis pas allé au cinéma hier soir parce que** . . . :

1. Je n'avais pas le temps. 2. Je n'avais pas d'argent. 3. J'avais autre chose à faire. 4. J'avais du travail à faire. 5. Je ne me sentais pas très bien. 6. Je devais téléphoner à ma mère. 7. Je voulais me coucher de bonne heure. 8. J'étais en train de lire un roman passionnant (*very interesting*). 9. J'étais fatigué. 10. J'attendais un coup de téléphone.

IMPARFAIT/ PARTITIF

41

E. Répétez les phrases suivantes, en commençant par **J'ai dit que . . .** et en remplaçant le présent par l'imparfait:

EX.: — Je ne peux pas.
   — **J'ai dit que je ne pouvais pas.**

1. Je vais à la bibliothèque. **2.** Je suis occupé. **3.** Je pars pour le week-end. **4.** Je travaille à un rapport (*term paper*).

F. Mettez chacune des phrases suivantes à l'imparfait:

EX.: — Plus il tire sur les cordes, plus le bateau s'incline.
   — **Plus ils tiraient sur les cordes, plus le bateau s'inclinait.**

1. Plus il essaie, moins il réussit. **2.** Plus il étudie, moins il sait. **3.** Plus il voyage, plus il aime son pays. **4.** Plus il réfléchit, plus il comprend. **5.** Plus il connaît de gens, moins il les aime.

G. Répétez les phrases suivantes, en remplaçant l'impératif par **si** et l'imparfait:

EX.: — Allons prendre le café au salon.
   — **Si nous allions prendre le café au salon?**

1. Restez dîner avec nous. **2.** Parlons du bon vieux temps. **3.** Restons à la maison ce soir. **4.** Allons au cinéma. **5.** Racontez-nous votre voyage. **6.** Faisons une partie de bridge. **7.** Partons tout de suite. **8.** Prenons l'autobus.

II. Remplacez le présent de **venir de** par l'imparfait:

EX.: — Je viens de finir.
   — **Je venais de finir** (*I had just finished*).

1. Je viens d'arriver ici. **2.** Nous venons de déjeuner. **3.** Est-ce que Jean vient d'arriver à Paris? **4.** Est-ce que vous venez de jouer au tennis?

III. Combinez deux phrases en une seule, en employant l'imparfait de **venir de** avec l'infinitif suivi de **quand**:

EX.: — Je suis rentré. Vous avez téléphoné.
   — **Je venais de rentrer quand vous avez téléphoné.**

1. Je suis sorti. Il a commencé à neiger. **2.** Le bateau a quitté le bord. L'eau a commencé à entrer. **3.** Jean est arrivé à Paris. Il est allé revoir ses amis. **4.** Nous sommes entrés dans la maison. Nous avons entendu le téléphone.

IV. Substitutions. Répétez les phrases suivantes en substituant les mots indiqués:

1. Je ne vous croyais pas [si bonne cuisinière].

   si bonne musicienne/ si bonne ménagère
   (*housekeeper*)/ si bon artiste/ si bon peintre

2. C'était [un très vieux bateau].

   une très vieille chaise/ un très vieux fauteuil/
   une très vieille auto/ un très vieux pneu

3. Il y avait de la place pour une centaine de [passagers].

   personnes/ voyageurs/ gens/ hommes

V. (a) Répétez les noms suivants au pluriel:

EX.: un journal — **des journaux**
     la vertu — **les vertus**

1. une chaise. 2. le détail. 3. un bal. 4. un pneu. 5. un travail. 6. le fils. 7. un cheveu. 8. un cheval. 9. un exercice. 10. un vers.

(b) Répétez les noms suivants au singulier:

1. les chaises. 2. les fils. 3. des pneus. 4. des bals. 5. des exercices. 6. les vertus. 7. les vices. 8. des vers. 9. des cheveux. 10. des chevaux.

VI. Répondez en français:

1. Le dîner de Marie était-il bon? 2. Est-ce que Marie était bonne cuisinière il y a deux ans? 3. Savait-elle faire la cuisine il y a deux ans? 4. Où Jean était-il l'année dernière? 5. Était-il sur le bateau qui a chaviré? 6. Que faisait Jean quand il était à Paris il y a deux ans? (Il était ingénieur-chimiste.) 7. Que faisait-il quand il était à Pittsburgh? 8. Est-ce que les Duplessis savaient que Jean était en France? 9. Est-ce que Jean savait qu'ils avaient un fils? 10. La plupart des passagers savaient-ils nager? 11. Roger croyait-il que Jean était dans la jungle vénézuélienne?

VII. Répondez affirmativement et négativement par une phrase complète:

1. Avez-vous fait des courses hier? 2. Avez-vous acheté un journal? 3. Avez-vous acheté des journaux? 4. Avez-vous acheté du beurre? 5. Y a-t-il du beurre sur la table? 6. Prenez-vous du café le matin? 7. Est-ce que vous

IMPARFAIT/ PARTITIF

preniez du café quand vous aviez dix ans? **8.** Avez-vous reçu des lettres aujourd'hui? **9.** Avez-vous reçu une lettre hier? **10.** Avez-vous apporté des fruits?

VIII. Employez les noms **lait** (*m*) et **limonade** (*f*) dans chacune des phrases suivantes:

1. Aimez vous . . . ? **2.** J'aime . . . . **3.** Je n'aime pas . . . . **4.** Voulez-vous . . . ? **5.** Donnez-moi . . . . **6.** Je bois . . . . **7.** Je ne bois pas . . . . **8.** Je bois beaucoup . . . . **9.** Je ne bois pas beaucoup . . . . **10.** Je ne bois plus . . . . **11.** Je ne bois guère . . . . **12.** Je ne bois que . . . .

IX. EXERCICE SUR L'EMPLOI DE L'ARTICLE DÉFINI ET LE PARTITIF. Dites en français:

(A)

1. Cats and dogs are animals. **2.** Butchers are merchants. **3.** Horses are quadrupeds. **4.** Apples and pears are fruit (*plural*).

(B)

1. A lot of things. **2.** Many people (**gens**). **3.** A kilo of bread. **4.** A little bread. **5.** A glass of milk. **6.** A dozen eggs.

(C)

1. John has friends in Paris. **2.** He has good friends. **3.** He has other friends in America. **4.** I bought some flowers this morning. **5.** I bought some beautiful flowers. **6.** I am going to buy some more (**d'autres**) flowers tomorrow.

Grotte de Lascaux, dessins préhistoriques

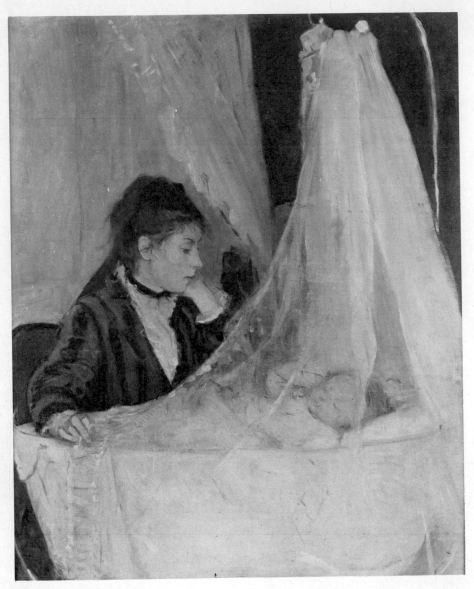

Le berceau, Berthe Morisot

LE PETIT MICHEL

Fièrement, Roger et Marie montrent à Jean leur fils, le petit Michel. Jean, qui a d'autres soucis, traite toute la scène avec une indulgence légèrement moqueuse.

ROGER. —¹Est-ce que Michel est réveillé, Marie? ²Voilà bien deux heures qu'il dort.

MARIE. —³Je crois l'avoir entendu remuer dans son lit tout à l'heure. ⁴Veux-tu le voir, Jean?

JEAN. —⁵Certainement. ⁶J'ai si souvent entendu parler de lui que je tiens absolument à faire sa connaissance.

(Dans la chambre de Michel.)

MARIE. —⁷Je te présente notre jeune fils Michel.

JEAN. —⁸Quel gentil petit garçon! ⁹Regardez ces grands yeux bleus et ce joli sourire!

MARIE. —¹⁰Il est maintenant de bonne humeur, sans doute parce qu'il a dormi tout l'après-midi. ¹¹Quand il vient de se réveiller, il est quelquefois de très mauvaise humeur.

Roger and Marie proudly show John their little son Michel. John, who is not particularly interested in babies, treats the scene with a slightly bantering though friendly tone.

ROGER. —¹Is Michel awake, Marie? ²He has been asleep for two solid hours.

MARIE. —³I think I heard him stir in his bed a while ago. ⁴Do you want to see him, John?

JOHN. —⁵Certainly. ⁶I have heard of him so often that I am very eager to meet him.

(In Michel's room)

MARIE. —⁷Let me introduce our young son Michel.

JOHN. —⁸What a nice little boy! ⁹Look at those big blue eyes and that cute smile!

MARIE. —¹⁰He is in a good mood (humor) now, because he has slept all afternoon, no doubt. ¹¹When he has just wakened, he is sometimes in a very bad mood.

JEAN. —¹²J'ai peine à le croire. ¹³Quel âge a-t-il?

JOHN. —¹²I can scarcely believe it. ¹³How old is he?

MARIE. —¹⁴Il aura treize mois le premier septembre et il pèse onze kilos.

MARIE. —¹⁴He will be thirteen months old on September 1st and he weighs eleven kilos (24.2 pounds, approximately).

JEAN. —¹⁵Est-ce qu'il sait marcher?

JOHN. —¹⁵Can he walk?

ROGER. —¹⁶Voyons, Jean, savais-tu marcher quand tu avais un an?

ROGER. —¹⁶Come, John, could you walk when you were one year old?

JEAN. —¹⁷Franchement, je ne me rappelle pas ... ¹⁸D'ailleurs, avec une telle mère, ou plutôt avec de tels parents, rien n'est impossible.

JOHN. —¹⁷Frankly, I don't remember . . . ¹⁸Anyway, with such a mother, or rather with such parents, nothing is impossible.

MARIE. —¹⁹Oh! voilà bien notre Jean, qui adore se moquer des gens, ²⁰tout en leur faisant des compliments.

MARIE. —¹⁹Oh! Isn't that just like John — who *loves* to kid people ²⁰while paying them compliments.

JEAN. —²¹Marie, tu me prêtes toute sorte de mauvaises intentions. ²²Malgré tout, nous sommes les meilleurs amis du monde, n'est-ce pas?

JOHN. —²¹Marie, you are attributing all sorts of bad meanings to me. ²²In spite of everything, we are the best friends in the world, aren't we?

I. SUBSTITUTIONS. Répétez les phrases suivantes, en substituant les mots indiqués:

1. Jean traite la scène avec une indulgence [légèrement] moqueuse.
   un peu/ tant soit peu (*ever so slightly*)/ un tout petit peu/ assez

2. Voilà bien deux heures [qu'il dort].
   qu'il est ici/ que je suis arrivé/ que nous sommes partis/ que j'attends

3. (a) Je crois l'avoir entendu [remuer] dans son lit.
   crier/ appeler/ pleurer/ faire du bruit

   (b) Je crois entendre venir [un avion].
   le train/ l'autobus/ un taxi/ les pompiers (*the firemen*)

4. J'ai si souvent entendu parler [de lui] que je tiens absolument à faire sa connaissance.
   d'elle/ de votre cousine/ de sa fiancée/ de son frère

5. Il aura [treize] mois au mois de [septembre].

onze . . . août/ quatorze' . . . octobre/ seize . . . janvier/ dix-huit . . . mars

6. Quand il vient de se réveiller, il est quelquefois de [mauvaise] humeur.

très mauvaise/ bonne/ très bonne/ excellente

7. Voilà le meilleur restaurant [de la ville].

de New York/ des États-Unis/ du quartier/ du monde

II. Répondez aux questions suivantes, en employant l'expression indiquée:

A. savoir (et l'infinitif)

1. Savez-vous jouer au bridge? **2.** Savez-vous jouer du piano? **3.** Saviez-vous marcher quand vous aviez un an? **4.** Saviez-vous parler quand vous aviez deux ans? **5.** Est-ce que le petit Michel sait marcher?

B. entendre (et l'infinitif)

1. Est-ce que Marie a entendu remuer le petit Michel? **2.** Jean a-t-il entendu parler du petit Michel? **3.** Avez-vous entendu parler des Duplessis? **4.** Avez-vous entendu venir une auto? **5.** Avez-vous entendu passer un avion? **6.** Avez-vous entendu sonner le réveil (*alarm-clock*)?

III. Combinez deux phrases en une seule, en employant **tout en** et le participe présent:

EX.: — Il adore se moquer des gens. Il leur fait des compliments.
   — Il adore se moquer des gens tout en leur faisant des compliments.

1. Il regardait le journal. Il déjeunait. **2.** Il regardait la télévision. Il lisait le journal. **3.** Il lisait le journal. Il écoutait des disques. **4.** Jean et Roger se parlaient. Ils se promenaient. **5.** Nous nous parlions. Nous nous promenions.

IV. Répétez les phrases suivantes, en remplaçant **comme ça** par **un tel (une telle, de tels, de telles)**:

EX.: — Je n'ai jamais vu une auto comme ça.
   — Je n'ai jamais vu une telle auto.

1. Avec un père comme ça, rien n'est impossible. **2.** Avec des parents comme ça, tout est possible. **3.** Des amis comme ça sont rares. **4.** On ne voit pas souvent des femmes comme ça. **5.** Je n'ai jamais vu un château comme ça.

LE PETIT MICHEL

V. Répondez en français:

1. Comment s'appelle le fils de Roger et de Marie? **2.** Qu'est-ce qu'il fait à ce moment-là? **3.** Depuis combien de temps dort-il? **4.** Pourquoi Marie croit-elle qu'il est réveillé? **5.** Est-ce que Jean a déjà fait sa connaissance? **6.** Pourquoi tient-il à faire sa connaissance? **7.** Où Roger, Jean et Marie vont-ils ensemble? **8.** Que dit Marie en présentant son fils à Jean? **9.** Comment Jean trouve-t-il le petit garçon? **10.** Qu'est-ce qu'il admire particulièrement? **11.** Pourquoi Michel est-il de bonne humeur? **12.** Est-il toujours de bonne humeur? **13.** Quand est-il de mauvaise humeur? **14.** Quel âge a-t-il? **15.** Combien pèse-t-il? **16.** Est-ce qu'il sait marcher? **17.** Saviez-vous marcher quand vous aviez treize mois? **18.** Vous rappelez-vous quand vous avez commencé à marcher? **19.** Quel compliment Jean fait-il à Marie et à Roger? **20.** Est-ce que Jean aime se moquer des gens tout en leur faisant des compliments? **21.** Est-ce que vous aimez vous moquer des gens? **22.** Quelle sorte d'intentions Marie prête-t-elle à Jean? **23.** Est-ce que ce sont de bons amis?

VI. Demandez à quelqu'un:

1. si l'enfant des Duplessis est un garçon ou une fille. **2.** comment s'appelle l'enfant. **3.** s'il est réveillé. **4.** depuis combien de temps il dort. **5.** si Jean a entendu parler de lui. **6.** si Jean a fait sa connaissance. **7.** pourquoi il est de bonne humeur. **8.** s'il est toujours de bonne humeur. **9.** si le petit Michel sait marcher. **10.** à quel âge un enfant commence à marcher. **11.** quel âge a le petit Michel. **12.** combien il pèse. **13.** de quelle couleur sont les yeux du petit Michel. **14.** si Jean savait marcher quand il avait un an. **15.** si Jean aime se moquer des gens.

VII. THÈME.

Parents are always proud of their children, and of course the Duplessis love their young son. When Michel was born a year ago, John was still in Egypt. He is very eager to see him, but little Michel has been asleep for two hours.

Marie thinks she hears him move in his bed. She goes to his room. Michel has just awakened, and because he has slept two hours he is in a good humor. He is (**C'est**) a nice little boy with (**aux**) big blue eyes and the prettiest smile in the world. Roger says he weighs eleven kilos, and that he can almost walk. John answers that with such parents he must (**doit**) be the best baby in the city.

VIII. Mettez les phrases suivantes au passé, en remplaçant le présent de l'indicatif par le **passé composé** ou l'**imparfait**, selon le cas:

C'est un très vieux bateau, qui depuis fort longtemps transporte des passagers sur le Nil. Il vient de quitter la rive, lorsque quelqu'un se met à crier que l'eau entre à l'intérieur. Personne ne soupçonne alors ce qui va arriver. Mais aussitôt les passagers se précipitent d'un côté du navire. Plus il y a de gens, plus le bateau s'incline, si bien qu'il finit par chavirer. Ceux qui savent nager regagnent le bord. Les autres font tout ce qu'ils peuvent, mais que peuvent-ils faire?

De la rive, les gens regardent ce triste spectacle. Une centaine de personnes périssent dans ce déplorable accident.

Petits campagnards

Adjectifs

23 Agreement of Adjectives.

Adjectives agree in gender and number with the noun they modify.

24 Interrogative adjective **quel** (what).

	SINGULAR	PLURAL
MASCULINE	quel?	quels?
FEMININE	quelle?	quelles?

Ex.: **Quel temps** fait-il? **Quelle heure** est-il? A **quelle heure** dînez-vous? **Quels** sont les mois de l'année?

25 Demonstrative adjective **ce** (this, that, these, those).

	SINGULAR	PLURAL
MASCULINE	ce (cet)	ces
FEMININE	cette	ces

Ce is used before masculine singular nouns or adjectives that begin with a consonant (other than a mute "h"), **cet** before those that begin with a vowel or mute "h". Ex.: **ce matin, ce soir, cet après-midi, cet hôtel.**

The suffixes **-ci** and **-là,** which formerly meant *here* and *there*, are sometimes attached to nouns to sharpen the meaning of a preceding demonstrative adjective. Nouns (and demonstrative pronouns) with these suffixes are sometimes used in oppositions: J'aime mieux cette **auto-ci** que **celle-là (cette auto-là).** I like *this car* better than *that one* (*that car*).

Note, however, that these suffixes are not used indiscriminately. The suffix **-là** is used with many expressions of time — referring either to the past or the future. Ex.: **Ce jour-là** *that day*, **cette année-là** *that year*, **ce matin-là** *that morning*, **cette semaine-là** *that week*, **à ce moment-là** *at that time*, **à cette heure-là** *at that hour*. But on the other hand, the suffix **-ci** is used much less frequently. Ex.: **ce mois-ci** *this month*, **à cette heure-ci** *at this hour*, **ces jours-ci** *these days*. You would not normally use the suffix **-ci** with **cette année, cette semaine, ce matin, en ce moment.** And, for *this day* you would of course say **aujourd'hui.**

26 Possessive adjectives mon, ton, son, etc.

SINGULAR		PLURAL	
MASCULINE	FEMININE	MASCULINE, FEMININE	
mon	ma (mon)	mes	*my*
ton	ta (ton)	tes	*your*
son	sa (son)	ses	*his, her, its*
notre	notre	nos	*our*
votre	votre	vos	*your*
leur	leur	leurs	*their*

A. Note particularly that possessive adjectives agree in gender and number *with the noun they modify* — not with the noun to which they refer.

Roger parle de **son père** et de **sa mère** (*his*, singular).
Marie parle de **son père** et de **sa mère** (*her*, singular).
Jean parle de **ses voyages** (*his*, plural).
Roger et Marie parlent de **leur fils** (*their*, singular).
Ils parlent de **leurs amis** (*their*, plural).

B. The feminine forms **ma, ta, sa,** are used before feminine singular nouns or adjectives that begin with a consonant (other than a mute "h"); **mon, ton, son,** before those that begin with a vowel or a mute "h".

ma sœur, **ma** petite sœur, **mon** autre sœur
ma nouvelle adresse, **mon** adresse

ADJECTIFS

27   Indefinite adjectives.

	SINGULAR		PLURAL		
	MASCULINE	FEMININE	MASCULINE	FEMININE	
	un autre	une autre	d'autres	d'autres	*another, other*
	l'autre	l'autre	les autres	les autres	*the other*
	le même	la même	les mêmes	les mêmes	*the same*
	quelque	quelque	quelques	quelques	*some, a few*
	un tel	une telle	de tels	de telles	*such (a)*
	tout le	toute la	tous les	toutes les	*all, all the*
	aucun	aucune			*no, not one*
	chaque	chaque			*each*
			plusieurs	plusieurs	*several*
			certains	certaines	*some*

Note particularly the following: **quelque temps** *some time*, **tout le temps** *all the time*, **tout l'été** *the whole summer*, **toute la journée** *all day*, **toute l'année** *all year*, **tous les jours** *every day*, **tous les soirs** *every evening*, **tous les ans** *every year*, **tous les trois ans** *every three years*, **chaque jour (mois, année)** *each day (month, year)*, **certaines personnes** (*some people*).

28   Descriptive adjectives.

A. Contrary to English usage, most descriptive adjectives follow the noun they modify.

Un homme intelligent (habile, riche, estimé, détestable, etc.)
Une famille aisée (*well to do*) (bourgeoise, protestante, catholique, juive, allemande, etc.)
Une rue large (étroite, pavée, sombre, tranquille, commerçante, etc.)
Un ciel gris (bleu, couvert, nuageux, pluvieux, etc.)
De l'eau minérale gazeuse naturelle (*natural sparkling mineral water*)

A few of the adjectives that follow have slightly irregular forms: **actif — active, doux — douce, heureux — heureuse, sérieux — sérieuse, neuf — neuve, blanc — blanche, gras — grasse,** etc.

B. The following descriptive adjectives normally precede the noun they modify:

	SINGULAR		PLURAL	
	MASCULINE	FEMININE	MASCULINE	FEMININE
	beau (bel)	belle	beaux	belles
	bon	bonne	bons	bonnes
	mauvais	mauvaise	mauvais	mauvaises
	joli	jolie	jolis	jolies
	gentil	gentille	gentils	gentilles
	grand	grande	grands	grandes
	gros	grosse	gros	grosses
	long	longue	longs	longues
	petit	petite	petits	petites
	jeune	jeune	jeunes	jeunes
	vieux (vieil)	vieille	vieux	vieilles
	nouveau (nouvel)	nouvelle	nouveaux	nouvelles

The forms **bel, vieil,** and **nouvel** are used before masculine singular nouns that begin with a vowel or mute "h".

C. Descriptive adjectives are frequently used after the verb **être:**

Il est intelligent. Elle est belle. Ils sont actifs. Nous sommes contents.

The same is true of nouns used as adjectives:

Il est musicien. Elle est violoniste. Il est Américain. Elle est Italienne. Ils sont Russes.

29 Remarks about descriptive adjectives that normally precede the noun modified.

The uses and meanings of these adjectives are rather subtle. Here are a few remarks that will help to clarify this very complicated question:

A. Grand, grande frequently means *large* in the sense of *tall:* **un grand arbre.** But it often has other meanings: **une grande maison** *a big house,* **de grands yeux** *big eyes,* **de grands pieds** *big feet,* **les grandes personnes** *grown-ups,* **un grand garçon** *a big boy,* **une grand-mère** *a grandmother.*

Un grand homme means "a great man" — *not* a tall man. If you want to say "He's a tall man" in French, you could say "C'est un homme grand"; but French people would be more likely to say **Il est grand** or **C'est un homme de haute taille.**

B. **Gros, grosse** ordinarily means *big, large* — in the sense of *voluminous.* You would say: **un gros livre, un gros chien, un gros poisson, une grosse voiture, une grosse fortune, une grosse orange, un gros dahlia.** You would *not* use the word **grand** with such nouns as **orange** or **poisson. Un grand dahlia** would refer to the height of the plant rather than to the size of the flower.

C. **Jeune** usually means *young.* But note the following: **une jeune fille** *a girl,* **des jeunes filles** *girls,* **un jeune homme** *a young man.* The plural of **un jeune homme** is **des jeunes gens;** but **des jeunes gens** also means *young people* in general. Ex.: **Marie était avec deux jeunes gens** (boys). **Marie, Roger et Jean sont des jeunes gens** (mixed).

D. **Petit, petite** usually means *small.* But note the following: **une petite fille** *a little girl,* **des petites filles** *little girls,* **une petite-fille** *a granddaughter,* **un petit pain** *a roll,* **des petits pains** *rolls,* **des petits pois** *green peas.*

E. **Bon, bonne** *good;* **mauvais, mauvaise** *bad.* These words also mean *right* and *wrong:* **la bonne route, la mauvaise route, la bonne réponse, la mauvaise adresse.**

Bon is also used in the following expressions: **faire bon voyage** *to have a good trip,* **acheter à bon marché** *to buy at a favorable (low) price,* **du bon vin** *wine of good quality,* **du bon beurre** *butter of good quality,* **si j'ai bonne mémoire** *if I remember correctly.*

F. **Vieux, vieille** *old (aged);* **ancien, ancienne** *old (former).* **Ancien, ancienne** usually follows the noun modified and means *old* or *ancient;* but when it precedes, it means *former.* Ex.: Un **vieux** sénateur, *an elderly senator;* Un **ancien** sénateur, *a former senator.*

But when **ancien** follows the noun modified (as it usually does), it has about the same meaning as **vieux.** Ex.: **un livre ancien** *an old book,* **un vieux livre** *an old book.*

G. Nouveau, nouvelle *new (recent, additional).* EX.: **Il a écrit un nouveau livre. Neuf, neuve** *new (brand new, unused).*

Un nouveau livre is merely *a new book.* But **un livre nouveau** is *a book that has just been published.*

H. Pauvre usually follows the noun and means *poor* — the opposite of rich: C'est **un homme pauvre.** But when **pauvre** precedes the noun it means *unfortunate:* **Le pauvre homme!** *The unfortunate fellow! The poor fellow!*

30 Comparative of adjectives: Regular.

A. *Superiority* is expressed by **plus . . . que.**

Roger est **plus** grand **que** Marie.	Roger is taller than Marie.
Il fait **plus** chaud en Égypte **qu'en** France.	It is warmer in Egypt than in France.

B. *Equality* is expressed by **aussi . . . que.**

Marie est **aussi** intelligente **que** Roger.	Marie is as intelligent as Roger.
Il fait **aussi** chaud aujourd'hui **qu'**hier.	It is as warm today as (it was) yesterday.

Note that after a negative, **aussi** is often replaced by **si.** Il ne fait pas **si** chaud aujourd'hui qu'hier.

C. *Inferiority* is expressed by **moins . . . que.**

Marie est **moins** grande **que** Roger.	Marie is less tall than Roger.
Le Havre est **moins** beau **que** Paris.	Le Havre is less beautiful than Paris.

31 Superlative of adjectives: Regular.

A. Le plus (la plus, les plus).

Paris est **la plus grande** ville de France.	Paris is the largest city in France.

B. Le moins (la moins, les moins).

L'hiver est la saison **la moins agréable.**	Winter is the least pleasant season.

Note that the superlative forms of adjectives normally stand in the same position in relation to the noun modified as their positive forms.

Le petit garçon. Le plus petit garçon.
Le garçon intelligent. Le garçon le plus intelligent.

32 Irregular comparison of adjectives.

POSITIVE	COMPARATIVE	SUPERLATIVE
bon—bonne	meilleur—meilleure	le meilleur—la meilleure
bons—bonnes	meilleurs—meilleures	les meilleurs—les meilleures
mauvais—mauvaise	pire	le pire—la pire
mauvais—mauvaises	pires	les pires

The old irregular comparative of **petit (moindre)** is still used in set expressions. Ex.: Je n'en ai pas **la moindre idée.** C'est **le moindre de mes soucis.** Il n'a pas **la moindre chance** de réussir.

I. EXERCICES D'APPLICATION.

A. Répétez les noms suivants, en remplaçant l'article défini par un adjectif démonstratif :

EX. : — le matin
    — **ce matin**

    — l'hôtel
    — **cet hôtel**

le soir, la semaine, l'année, la soirée, l'arbre, l'hôpital, la rue, la jeune fille, les garçons, les jeunes gens.

B. Répétez les noms suivants, en remplaçant **ce, cet, cette, ces** (*this, these*) par **ce, cet, cette, ces . . . -là** (*that, those*) :

EX. : — ce matin
    — **ce matin-là**

ce soir, cet été, cette année, cet après-midi, cette nuit, cet hiver, cette semaine.

C. Répétez les noms suivants, en ajoutant la forme convenable de **tout:**

EX.: — la journée
    —**toute la journée**

l'hiver, la soirée, les jours, l'année, les ans, les jeudis, le temps, l'après-midi, les matins, la matinée, les samedis soirs.

D. Répétez les noms suivants, en remplaçant l'article défini par **chaque** (*each*):

EX.: — le matin
    — **chaque matin**

le soir, la semaine, le samedi, l'hiver, le jour, l'après-midi.

E. Répétez les phrases suivantes, en mettant chacun des adjectifs indiqués avant ou après le nom suivant le cas:

1. *C'est un garçon: beau/ grand/ petit/ intelligent/ gentil/ gros.
2. Voilà une jeune fille: belle/ blonde/ petite/ intelligente/ gentille.
3. C'est un arbre: jeune/ bel/ grand/ gros/ vieil/ petit/ vigoureux/ vert.

F. Répétez les noms suivants, en employant la forme convenable de l'adjectif:

1. **(long)**   un voyage, une promenade, une histoire, des histoires.
2. **(nouveau)**   un livre, une route, des livres, des idées (*f*).
3. **(gentil)**   un garçon, un petit garçon, une famille.

II. SUBSTITUTIONS. Répétez les phrases suivantes, en substituant les mots indiqués:

1. Voilà un homme qui est [plus intelligent] que sa femme.
   moins intelligent/ plus grand/ plus gentil/
   aussi agréable/ moins agréable/ moins gentil

2. Ces jeunes filles sont [plus belles] que leurs mères.
   aussi jolies/ moins intelligentes/ plus sages/ moins agréables

3. Marie est [meilleure] cuisinière que sa sœur.
   aussi bonne/ moins bonne/ bien meilleure

---

* *He is, she is, it is, they are* are expressed in French by **c'est** or **ce sont** when **est** is followed directly by **le, la, les, un, une, des,** or a possessive adjective (**mon, son,** etc.) Ex.: **C'est la voiture de mon père. C'est une bonne voiture. C'est sa voiture. Ce sont des photos excellentes. Ce sont mes photos. Ce sont de bonnes photos.**

For an explanation of the use of **ce** with the verb **être,** see par. 65 D.

4. Ce journal est [meilleur] que celui-là.

plus petit/ plus volumineux/ moins intéressant/ bien meilleur

5. La tour Eiffel est [aussi célèbre] que Notre-Dame de Paris.

moins belle/ plus haute/ moins vieille/
moins ornée (*less ornate*)/ aussi solide

6. J'ai passé [trois semaines] en France.

quelques semaines/ quelques mois/ quelque temps/ quelques jours

7. C'est un petit monsieur [agréable].

fort riche/ très habile/ riche et estimé/ détestable

8. C'est une jeune femme [charmante].

douce (*pleasant, gentle*)/ affectueuse/ exquise/ ravissante (*entrancing*)

III. Répondez en français, en employant la forme convenable de l'adjectif possessif:

1. Où demeurent vos parents? **2.** Où habite votre famille? **3.** Quel âge a votre père? **4.** Votre mère est-elle allée en France? **5.** Où habitent les parents du petit Michel? **6.** Que fait le père de Michel? **7.** Comment s'appelle la mère de Michel? **8.** Comment Jean a-t-il trouvé le dîner de Marie? **9.** Est-ce que Jean a parlé des voyages qu'il a faits? **10.** A-t-il assisté au mariage de Marie et de Roger? **11.** A-t-il reçu l'annonce du mariage de Marie et de Roger? **12.** Est-ce que les Duplessis sont les meilleurs amis de Jean?

IV. Demandez à quelqu'un:

1. l'heure qu'il est. **2.** son âge. **3.** la date de son anniversaire. **4.** le nom du fils de Marie et de Roger. **5.** la couleur de ses yeux. **6.** le temps qu'il fait aujourd'hui. **7.** à quelle heure il va dîner. **8.** à quel âge il a commencé à parler.

V. Répondez en français:

1. Quelle est la meilleure saison de l'année pour voyager? **2.** Quel est le meilleur moment de la journée pour travailler? **3.** Où habite votre meilleur ami? **4.** Où habite votre meilleure amie? **5.** D'où viennent les meilleures oranges? **6.** Quel est le meilleur moment de la journée pour faire des courses? **7.** Quel est le moment le moins favorable pour travailler? **8.** Quelle est la plus mauvaise saison de l'année? **9.** Quelle est la pire saison de l'année?

Cloître roman de Moissac

Facteur faisant sa tournée

LE FONCTIONNAIRE

Roger a des difficultés avec une administration financière. Il raconte à Jean comment les choses se sont passées.

ROGER. —[1]Je dois retourner cet après-midi aux bureaux d'une administration financière [2]m'occuper d'une affaire d'impôts pour mon usine. [3]Il s'agit d'une deuxième visite. [4]La première fois, j'ai été fort mal reçu.

JEAN. —[5]Que veux-tu dire? Qu'est-ce qui s'est passé?

ROGER. —[6]Quand je suis entré, un employé m'a fait comprendre que je le dérangeais beaucoup.

JEAN. —[7]C'était pourtant son métier, après tout.

ROGER. —[8]Tu ne sais pas ce que c'est qu'un fonctionnaire.

JEAN. —[9]C'est quelqu'un au service du gouvernement.

Roger is having trouble with his taxation office. He tells John how it all came about.

ROGER. —[1]This afternoon I have to go back to the Income Tax Bureau [2]to take care of an income tax item for my factory. [3]It is [a question of] a second visit. [4]The first time, they gave me a very cool welcome.

JOHN. —[5]What do you mean? What happened?

ROGER. —[6]When I went in, an employee gave me to understand that I was bothering him a great deal.

JOHN. —[7]But it was his business, after all.

ROGER. —[8]You don't know what a civil servant is.

JOHN. —[9]It's someone who works for the government.

ROGER. —[10]Précisément. Travailler pour le gouvernement lui donne de l'autorité. [11]Or, le gouvernement le paie d'ordinaire assez mal, et sa vie n'est pas exactement passionnante. [12]Il est donc mécontent. [13]Il a l'impression qu'il n'est pas récompensé de ses services [14]comme il devrait l'être. [15]Quelquefois il se venge sur le public. [16]Cet employé s'est vengé en m'obligeant à revenir le voir aujourd'hui.

JEAN. —[17]Qu'est-ce qu'il t'a dit?

ROGER. —[18]Il m'a dit que, d'après la lettre qu'il m'avait envoyée, [19]j'aurais dû venir le voir la veille. [20]Je lui ai répondu que je n'avais pas pu, [21]à cause d'un rendez-vous d'affaires important. [22]«Important ou non, il fallait venir» m'a-t-il répondu. [23]Il ne m'a fallu qu'un instant pour me rendre compte [24]qu'il valait mieux ne pas insister. [25]Je suis sorti en lui disant que je serais heureux de revenir le voir.

JEAN. —[26]Les fonctionnaires sont partout les mêmes, tu sais.

ROGER. —[10]Exactly. Working for the government gives him authority. [11]But the government usually pays him rather poorly and his life is not very exciting. [12]So he is not happy. [13]He has the impression that he is not rewarded for his services [14]as he should be. [15]Sometimes he takes it out on the public. [16]This public servant took vengeance by requiring me to come back to see him today.

JOHN. —[17]What did he say to you?

ROGER. —[18]He said that according to the letter he had sent me, [19]I should have come to see him the day before. [20]I told him I couldn't, [21]because of an important business engagement. [22]"Important or not, you should have come" he answered. [23]It took me only a moment to realize [24]that it was better not to insist. [25]I left saying that I would be glad to come back to see him (at his convenience).

JOHN. —[26]Public servants are the same everywhere, you know.

―――――

I. SUBSTITUTIONS. Répétez les phrases suivantes en substituant les mots indiqués:

1. Je dois retourner [cet après-midi] aux bureaux d'une administration financière.

ce soir/ demain/ d'aujourd'hui en huit/ demain après-midi

2. Il doit revenir me voir [ce soir].

samedi prochain/ d'aujourd'hui en quinze/ la semaine prochaine/ lundi

3. Un employé m'a fait comprendre que [je le dérangeais beaucoup].

j'étais en retard/ il était fort mécontent/ j'avais
tort/ les fonctionnaires n'étaient pas à mon service

4. Tu ne sais pas ce que c'est qu' [un fonctionnaire].

un fonctionnaire français/ un employé du gouverne-
ment/ un petit employé/ une administration financière

5. Il s'agit [d'une deuxième visite].

d'une affaire d'impôts/ d'une déclaration d'impôts/ de payer
mes impôts/ d'un fonctionnaire de l'administration des finances

6. Travailler pour le gouvernement lui donne [de l'autorité].

de l'importance/ de la considération/ du pouvoir sur les gens/ un pouvoir considérable

7. [Or,] le gouvernement le paie d'ordinaire assez mal.

En même temps/ Comme vous le savez/ Cependant/ Et pourtant

8. Il m'a dit que j'aurais dû [venir la veille].

venir plus tôt/ venir le voir la veille/
venir lui parler la veille/ être à l'heure

9. Il ne m'a fallu [qu'un instant].

qu'un moment/ qu'un petit moment/ que
quelques minutes/ que quelques instants

II. Demandez à quelqu'un:

1. ce qui s'est passé*. **2.** ce qui se passe. **3.** ce qui se passera. **4.** ce qui
arrivera. **5.** ce qui arrive. **6.** ce qui est arrivé. **7.** ce qui lui est arrivé*.
8. ce qui leur est arrivé. **9.** ce qui est arrivé à Charles. **10.** ce qui s'est passé
sur le Nil. **11.** ce qui est arrivé au bateau. **12.** ce qui est arrivé aux passagers.

III. Répétez les phrases suivantes, en remplaçant le nom par **y**:

1. Je suis allé au Louvre hier. **2.** Je vais retourner au Louvre aujourd'hui.
3. Voulez-vous venir au Louvre avec moi? **4.** Voulez-vous retourner au
Louvre avec moi demain? **5.** Êtes-vous déjà allé à la Comédie-Française?
6. Je vais souvent au théâtre.

---

* Both **arriver** and **se passer** mean *to happen;* but if something happens *to someone* or *to something*, **arriver (à)** must be used — not **se passer**.

IV. Répondez en français:

1. Où Roger doit-il retourner cet après-midi? **2.** Pourquoi doit-il y retourner?
3. S'agit-il d'une première visite? **4.** Comment a-t-il été reçu la première fois?
5. Qu'est-ce que l'employé lui a fait comprendre? **6.** Qu'est-ce que c'est
qu'un fonctionnaire? **7.** Est-il d'ordinaire bien payé? **8.** Quelle impression
a-t-il souvent? **9.** Sur qui se venge-t-il quelquefois? **10.** Comment cet employé s'est-il vengé? **11.** Quand Roger aurait-il dû venir le voir? **12.** Pourquoi Roger n'est-il pas venu le voir? **13.** L'employé a-t-il accepté son excuse?
14. De quoi Roger s'est-il rendu compte? **15.** Lui a-t-il fallu longtemps pour
s'en rendre compte? **16.** Qu'est-ce que Roger lui a dit en sortant? **17.** Que
dit Jean à propos des fonctionnaires?

V. Demandez à quelqu'un:

1. où Roger doit retourner cet après-midi. **2.** de quoi il doit s'occuper. **3.** de
quoi il s'agit. **4.** ce qui s'est passé la première fois. **5.** ce que l'employé lui a
fait comprendre. **6.** s'il sait ce que c'est qu'un fonctionnaire. **7.** ce qui
donne de l'autorité aux fonctionnaires. **8.** s'ils sont d'ordinaire bien payés.
9. pourquoi ils sont mécontents. **10.** sur qui ils se vengent quelquefois.
11. quand Roger aurait dû venir le voir. **12.** pourquoi il n'est pas venu.
13. de quoi Roger s'est rendu compte. **14.** ce qu'il a dit en sortant.

VI. Révision de **rentrer, aller, retourner.** Dites en français:

1. He went to the office. **2.** He went back home. **3.** He went to the restaurant.
4. He went back to the office. **5.** He went to the laboratory. **6.** He went back
to the restaurant. **7.** He went back home.

VII. THÈME.

One afternoon, Roger asked John if he would like (wanted) to go out with him.
John gladly accepted his friend's invitation. He thought of course that they
were going to take a walk together. But when they arrived near the offices of
the Internal Revenue Service **(Ministère des Finances)**, Roger said that he
had a little errand to do. John waited for his friend a quarter of an hour,
half an hour, one hour, more than one hour. He knew that administration is
never simple. Yet when Roger returned, he said to his old friend: "Old man,
I know that it is not your fault. But I have not come from Egypt to Paris to
wait at the door of some official of the Internal Revenue Service."

VIII. Mettez les phrases suivantes au passé, en remplaçant le présent de l'indicatif par le **passé composé** ou l'**imparfait**, selon le cas:

J'entre. Le fonctionnaire me dit de m'asseoir, et comme je suis d'humeur accommodante, je m'assieds. Ce fonctionnaire est de très mauvaise humeur, et il commence à me faire comprendre que je suis un être fort déplaisant. J'ai beau lui expliquer que ce n'est pas ma faute: il me dit que, venant en ce moment, je le dérange beaucoup. Même, il n'y a pas de pire moment, me dit-il, car il doit envoyer demain son rapport mensuel. Pourquoi est-ce que je viens le voir en ce moment? Est-ce que je le fais exprès?

Je me rends compte que ce n'est pas la peine d'insister, et je m'en vais, en lui promettant de revenir.

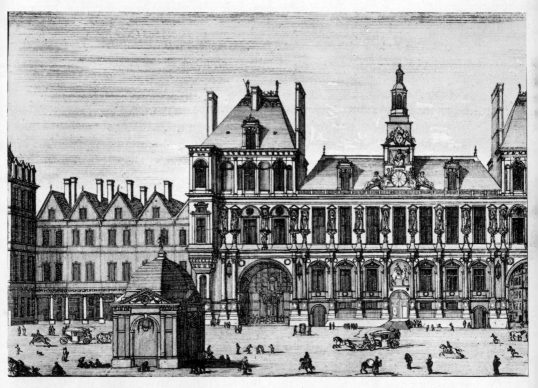

L'Hôtel de Ville de Paris, commencé sous François Ier en 1538

LE FONCTIONNAIRE

Devoir, Falloir, Pouvoir, Vouloir, Savoir

33 Remark about these verbs.

These verbs are irregular both in form and meaning. They are doubly difficult for English-speaking persons because their English equivalents are strangely irregular and because in both languages some of the forms have two or more different meanings. Therefore, the forms and meanings of these verbs must be studied carefully, understood sharply, and practiced systematically. This lesson should be reviewed frequently.

34 **Devoir** (must, have to, should, ought, to be supposed to) (expressing commitment, obligation, probability, and followed by an infinitive.) The forms of devoir will be found on p. 288.

A. **Devoir** expressing commitment.

PRESENT: Je dois aller en ville cet après-midi. (*I am supposed to* . . .)
IMPERFECT: Je devais y aller hier. (*I was supposed to* . . .)

B. **Devoir** expressing obligation.

PRESENT: Je dois payer mes impôts. (*I must* . . .)
CONDITIONAL: Je devrais payer mes impôts . . . (*I ought to* . . .)
　　　　　Les fonctionnaires ne sont pas payés comme ils
　　　　　devraient l'être. (. . . *ought to be* . . .)
CONDITIONAL PERFECT: J'aurais dû aller le voir la veille. (*I ought to have gone* . . .)

C. **Devoir** expressing probability.

PRESENT: Il doit être au moins trois heures. (*It must be . . .*)

Il doit y avoir un bon restaurant sur la place. (*There must be . . .*)

Je dois avoir laissé ma montre à la maison. (*I must have . . .*)

PASSÉ COMPOSÉ: J'ai dû laisser ma montre à la maison. (*I must have . . .*)

35 **Devoir** meaning "to owe".

Devoir is normally followed by an infinitive (as in the preceding examples); but it is also used as a transitive verb meaning "to owe" and is followed by a noun.

Il me doit cent francs.

36 **Falloir** (must, to have to, to be necessary, etc.) followed by an infinitive, a clause in the subjunctive, a noun, or an expression of time. The forms of falloir will be found on p. 291.

A. **Falloir** followed by an infinitive.

PRESENT: Il faut payer ses impôts. (*One must . . .*)

Il faut quelquefois attendre dans les bureaux. (*One has to . . .*)

FUTURE: Si vous allez en ville, il faudra attendre l'autobus. (*You'll have to . . .*)

PASSÉ COMPOSÉ: Hier il a fallu attendre une demi-heure. (*I, you, we, they — depending on the context — had to . . .*)

B. **Falloir** followed by a clause in the subjunctive.

PRESENT: Il faut que je fasse des courses. (*I must, I have to . . .*)

This pattern is very frequently used. (Cf. Grammar Unit 22.)

C. **Falloir** followed by a noun or an expression of time.

Il faudrait beaucoup d'argent. (*It would take . . .*)

Il faut du courage pour faire cela. (*It takes . . .*)

Il faut vingt minutes pour aller à Saint-Cloud. (*It takes . . .*)

Il faudra une heure. (*It will take . . .*)

Il faudrait des journées entières. (*It would take . . .*)

Il ne m'a fallu qu'un instant. (*It took me only . . .*)

Est-ce qu'il vous faudra longtemps? (*Will it take you . . .*)

DEVOIR, FALLOIR, POUVOIR, VOULOIR, SAVOIR

37 Pouvoir (can, may, to be able, etc.) The forms of **pouvoir** will be found on p. 296.

A. The present indicative of **pouvoir** means either *may* or *can*.

Est-ce que **je peux** vous **aider**? *May I or Can I help you?*

The future is frequently used instead of the present.

Vous pouvez (or **pourrez**) visiter le musée. (*You can . . .*)

B. The *imparfait*, the *passé composé*, and the conditional all mean *could*.

1. The *imparfait* means *could* in the sense of *was able to:*
Comme **je ne pouvais pas aller** voir ma mère, je lui ai donné un coup de fil. (*Since I couldn't . . .*)

2. The *passé composé* means *could* in the sense of *I succeeded in:*
J'ai pu trouver un taxi. (*I could get . . .*)
Je n'ai pas pu trouver de taxi. (*I couldn't get . . .*)

3. The conditional means *could* in the sense of *would be able:*
Vous pourriez aller en ville à pied. (*You could . . .*)

C. The conditional perfect means *could have* in the sense of *would have been able to:*

J'aurais pu attendre l'autobus. (I *could have* . . .)*

38 Vouloir (to want), **vouloir bien** (to be willing), **vouloir dire** (to mean). The forms of **vouloir** will be found on p. 304.

The meaning of the present indicative of **vouloir** in the affirmative is much stronger than *wish* or *want* in English. **Je veux** is so strong that it is practically always replaced by **je veux bien** (*I'm willing*) or **Je voudrais** (conditional) (*I would like . . .*)

The negative form is even stronger: **Je ne veux pas** (*I won't*). Instead of this, one is more likely to say: **Non merci, je regrette.**

Vouloir dire is *to mean*. EX.: Qu'est-ce que ça **veut dire**? (*What does that mean?*) Que **veut dire** ce mot? (What *does that word mean?*)

---

* Notez que **pouvoir** est toujours suivi du présent de l'infinitif. Bien qu'on dise en anglais: I could have gone there, en français, on dit: J'**aurais pu y aller** (lit.: *I would have been able to go there*).

39   Savoir (to know, to know how).

A. Present indicative of savoir.

Savez-vous la date? (*Do you know . . .*)
Sait-elle faire la cuisine? (*Does she know how to . . .*)
Savez-vous jouer du piano? (*Do you know how to . . .*)

B. *Imparfait* of **savoir.**

Je ne savais pas votre adresse à ce moment-là. (*I didn't know . . .*)

C. *Passé composé* of **savoir.**

Quand **j'ai su** votre adresse... (*When I learned, found out . . .*)

D. Future of savoir.

Quand **je saurai** son adresse... (*When I find out, learn . . .*)

The forms of **savoir** will be found on p. 299.

40   Distinction between savoir and connaître.

These verbs both mean "to know" but **savoir** has a much broader usage than **connaître.**

A. (1) **Savoir** may be followed by an infinitive. In this case it means "to know how to".

Elle sait faire la cuisine.
La plupart des passagers ne **savaient** pas nager.

(2) **Connaître** *cannot* be used in this way.

B. (1) **Savoir** may be used to govern clauses introduced by **que, quand, où, combien, si, ce qui, ce que,** and many other expressions.

Je sais que Jean est à Paris, quand il est arrivé, où il habite, pourquoi il est venu en France, combien de temps il va rester à Paris, ce qui lui est arrivé en Égypte.

Tu ne sais pas ce que c'est qu'un fonctionnaire.

(2) **Connaître** *cannot* be used in this way.

C. Both verbs may take a direct object:

(1) **Savoir** is normally used when the direct object is a specific bit of information such as a date, the time of day, an address, a rule, etc.

Je sais la date. **Je ne sais pas** son adresse. **Elle sait** la leçon par cœur.

(2) **Connaître** is normally used when the object of the verb is a person, a place, a work of art, a work of literature, a body of knowledge, etc. It means "to know" in the sense of "to be acquainted with", "to be familiar with", "to have knowledge of", "to know about".

Je connais les Duplessis. **Je ne connais pas** Saint-Cloud. **Je connais** les sculptures de Maillol. **Je ne connais pas** les romans de Sartre. **Je connais** les mathématiques. **Je ne connais pas** grand-chose à l'économie politique.

D. The two verbs may be used practically interchangeably (alas!) in a few cases:

Je sais le grec. **Je connais** le grec.
Savez-vous l'histoire de la prise de Troie? **Connaissez-vous** cette histoire?

I. SUBSTITUTIONS. Répétez les phrases suivantes, en substituant les mots indiqués:

1. Il devait [arriver hier] mais il a manqué son avion.
quitter Paris/ partir pour Marseille/
revenir à Paris/ retourner à Londres

2. Je ne trouve pas ma montre. J'ai dû la laisser [à la maison].
dans la salle de bain/ sur mon bureau/
dans mon bureau/ dans mon tiroir

3. Il devrait [travailler davantage].
jouer plus souvent au tennis/ prendre plus d'exercice/
se coucher plus tôt/ aller plus souvent à la bibliothèque

4. Roger aurait dû [rester à la maison].
se coucher de bonne heure/ rester au lit/
se reposer un peu/ boire beaucoup d'eau

5. [Voulez-vous bien] me donner son adresse?
Voudriez-vous . . . ?/ Pouvez-vous . . . ?/
Pourriez-vous . . . ?/ Ne voulez-vous pas . . . ?

GRAMMAR 10

II. Répétez les phrases suivantes, en remplaçant l'impératif par l'expression indiquée:

A. Employez **Il faut** (ou **Il ne faut pas**) et l'infinitif.

EX.: — N'allez pas trop vite.
— **Il ne faut pas aller trop vite.**

1. Restez calme. **2.** Soyez à l'heure. **3.** Ne soyez pas en retard. **4.** Ne perdez pas votre temps. **5.** Allez voir ce film. **6.** Partez à temps. **7.** Ne courez pas dans la rue. **8.** Soyez gentil pour tout le monde. **9.** Attendez un instant. **10.** Venez me voir. **11.** Visitez le musée. **12.** Appelez un taxi.

B. Employez **Vous devez** (*you must*) et l'infinitif.

C. Employez **Vous devriez** (*you should, you ought to*) et l'infinitif.

D. Employez **Vous auriez dû** (*you should have*) et l'infinitif.

III. Employez **Savez-vous** ou **Connaissez-vous** avec chacune des expressions suivantes:

1. ... l'hôtel George V? **2.** ... l'adresse de cet hôtel? **3.** ... où se trouve cet hôtel? **4.** ... quand il a été construit? **5.** ... la rue Montaigne? **6.** ... où se trouve cette rue? **7.** ... le Jardin des Tuileries? **8.** ... le latin? (deux réponses)

IV. Transposez chacune des phrases suivantes au conditionnel passé:

EX.: — Il ne faut pas avoir peur (*One mustn't be afraid*).
— **Il n'aurait pas fallu avoir peur** (*One shouldn't have been afraid*).

1. Jean doit aller revoir ses amis. **2.** Je peux travailler davantage. **3.** Je ne dois pas perdre mon temps. **4.** Il faut partir plus tôt. **5.** Nous devons être à l'heure. **6.** Je veux aller à la campagne pour le week-end. **7.** Jean veut assister au mariage. **8.** Peut-il venir au mariage?

V. Répondez en français:

1. Où Roger doit-il retourner cet après-midi? **2.** De quoi doit-il s'occuper? **3.** Doit-il attendre au bureau? **4.** Faut-il souvent attendre à la porte d'un bureau? **5.** Avez-vous des courses à faire? **6.** Est-ce que vous devez les faire aujourd'hui? **7.** Deviez-vous les faire hier? **8.** Auriez-vous dû les faire la

DEVOIR, FALLOIR, POUVOIR, VOULOIR, SAVOIR

semaine dernière? **9.** Voulez-vous les faire maintenant? **10.** Faut-il les faire tout de suite? **11.** Savez-vous le grec? **12.** Connaissez-vous l'*Iliade* d'Homère? **13.** Savez-vous la date de la mort d'Homère? **14.** Pourriez-vous me dire quand il a écrit l'*Iliade*? **15.** Savez-vous l'histoire de la prise de Troie? **16.** Connaissez-vous cette histoire? **17.** Voudriez-vous entendre cette histoire? **18.** Avez-vous pu lire l'*Iliade*?

VI. THÈME.

"You must see that film."

"I would like to see it. I couldn't go to the movies yesterday."

"Could you go (to it) tonight?"

"No, I can't go (to it) tonight. But I could go (to it) tomorrow."

"It is too late. You should have seen the film last week."

"I would have liked to see it. I was free Thursday; I could have seen it that night. You should have told me about it. One should not miss such films. When there are good films, will you please let me know **(me le faire savoir)?**"

"Yes, I am willing. I should have thought of it sooner."

LES MOYENS DE TRANSPORT

Les moyens de transport changent beaucoup d'une époque à l'autre. Autrefois les gens allaient à pied, quelquefois à cheval ou en voiture. Maintenant ils se déplacent en auto. Néanmoins les trains sont encore très employés en France.

ROGER. —¹On ne se doute pas ²qu'il a fallu des siècles ³pour donner aux Parisiens des moyens de transport commodes. ⁴Jusqu'au siècle dernier, ⁵personne, sauf Pascal, ⁶n'avait pensé à créer ce qu'on appelle les transports en commun.

JEAN. —⁷Pascal, le mathématicien, l'auteur des *Pensées?**

ROGER. —⁸En personne. ⁹Un jour il a eu l'idée ¹⁰d'établir des voitures payantes pour transporter les voyageurs à l'intérieur de la ville. ¹¹Malheureusement, ils ne se sont pas habitués tout de suite à son invention. ¹²Beaucoup d'entre eux n'avaient même pas de quoi s'offrir le nouveau moyen de transport. . . . ¹³As-tu entendu parler de M. Omnès?

The means of transportation change from one period to another. Formerly people traveled on foot, sometimes on horseback or in carriages. Now they travel by car. Nevertheless trains are still much used in France.

ROGER. —¹One does not realize (suspect) ²that it took centuries ³to provide Parisians with convenient means of transportation. ⁴Until the last century, ⁵no one but Pascal ⁶had thought of setting up what we call common carriers.

JOHN. —⁷Pascal, the mathematician, the author of the *Pensées?*

ROGER. —⁸The very same. ⁹One day he had the idea ¹⁰of establishing vehicles to transport passengers within a city — for pay. ¹¹Unfortunately, they didn't adopt (get used to) his invention right away. ¹²Many of them didn't even have enough money to pay for the new mode of transportation . . . ¹³Have you heard of Monsieur Omnès?

---

* Blaise Pascal vivait au dix-septième siècle. Il a écrit un *Traité des sections coniques*. Il a inventé une machine à calculer qu'on peut considérer comme l'ancêtre de l'ordinateur (*computer*).

JEAN. —[14]Non, je n'ai jamais entendu parler de lui.

ROGER. —[15]C'est lui qui, paraît-il, après avoir inventé ses voitures publiques, [16]leur a donné le nom d'omnibus, à cause de son nom: Omnès, omnibus* . . . Tu comprends? [17]M. Omnès a pensé à cela aux environs de 1830, [18]vers l'époque où l'on s'est mis à construire les chemins de fer. [19]A l'heure actuelle, beaucoup de voyageurs se servent des chemins de fer, [20]et aussi des autobus, qui ont succédé aux omnibus de M. Omnès.

JEAN. —[21]Chez nous, les trains servent surtout à transporter des marchandises.

ROGER. —[22]J'ai entendu dire que les trains américains transportent de moins en moins de voyageurs. [23]Pas en France. [24]Le chemin de fer reste le principal moyen de transport. [25]L'État a dépensé des sommes énormes pour moderniser le matériel. [26]Partout les lignes ont été électrifiées. [27]Les autorails, pour le transport des voyageurs, vont à une très grande vitesse. [28]Sans nous vanter, [29]nous autres Français avons réussi à créer un système [30]qui fait l'admiration des connaisseurs . . . de chemins de fer.

JOHN. —[14]No, I have never heard of him.

ROGER. —[15]It was he, it seems, who after inventing his public vehicles, [16]gave them the name omnibus, because of his name: Omnès, omnibus. You understand? [17]Monsieur Omnès thought of this one around 1830, [18]about the time (when) they began to build railroads. [19]Today many travelers use the railroads [20]as well as the buses that have taken the place of Monsieur Omnès' omnibuses.

JOHN. —[21]Back home, trains are used mostly for hauling freight.

ROGER. —[22]I have heard that American trains carry fewer and fewer passengers. [23]Not in France. [24]Railroads are still the chief means of transportation. [25]The government has spent enormous amounts to modernize the rolling stock. [26]The lines have been electrified everywhere. [27]The "autorails", for carrying passengers, run at very high speed. [28]Without boasting, [29]we (French) have succeeded in creating a system [30]that is greatly admired by the connoisseurs . . . of railroads.

---

* Jeu de mots sur son nom qui signifie en latin "tout".

I. SUBSTITUTIONS. Répétez les phrases suivantes, en substituant les mots indiqués:

1. On ne se doute pas qu'il a fallu [des siècles].
   très longtemps/ plusieurs siècles/ des
   centaines d'années/ trois cents ans

2. A ce moment-là, personne n'avait pensé à [créer ce qu'on appelle "les transports en commun"].
   donner des numéros aux maisons/ inventer une
   machine à calculer/ inventer un ordinateur/
   construire des autorails (*very fast passenger trains*)

3. Beaucoup d'entre eux n'avaient même pas de quoi s'offrir [ce moyen de transport].
   un bon repas/ de la viande tous les jours/ une maison/ des vêtements

4. Avez-vous jamais entendu parler [de M. Omnès]?
   de Pascal/ des *Pensées* de Pascal/ de ses inventions/ de
   sa machine à calculer/ de ses découvertes scientifiques

5. Je n'ai jamais entendu parler [de lui].
   de ses *Pensées*/ de ses inventions/ de sa machine
   à calculer/ de ses découvertes scientifiques

6. J'ai entendu dire [que les trains américains transportent de moins en moins de voyageurs].
   qu'ils transportent de plus en plus de marchandises/ que
   les autorails vont très vite/ qu'ils ne transportent que des
   voyageurs/ qu'ils remplacent de plus en plus les anciens
   trains/ qu'ils ne transportent pas de marchandises

7. A l'heure actuelle beaucoup de voyageurs se servent [des chemins de fer].
   du métro/ des autobus/ de leur auto/ de l'autorail/ des avions

8. Les trains servent [à transporter des marchandises].
   à transporter des voyageurs/ au transport des voyageurs/
   au transport des marchandises/ à transporter des marchandises lourdes/ au transport des marchandises lourdes

II. Répétez les phrases suivantes, en mettant après le verbe l'expression indiquée:

EX.: (de plus en plus) Les avions transportent des voyageurs.
Les avions transportent de plus en plus de voyageurs.

A. de plus en plus

1. Les camions (*trucks*) transportent des marchandises. 2. Les trains servent à transporter des marchandises. 3. Les autorails vont vite. 4. Les Américains voyagent en Europe. 5. Les impôts sont élevés. 6. Les villes sont surpeuplées (*overcrowded*). 7. Les rues sont encombrées (*congested*).

B. de moins en moins

1. Les trains américains transportent des voyageurs. 2. Les gens voyagent par le train. 3. La vie est tranquille. 4. Les villes sont propres. 5. Les gens sont patients. 6. Les fonctionnaires sont agréables.

III. Répétez les phrases suivantes, en remplaçant **maintenant** par **à l'heure actuelle:**

1. Maintenant les gens se déplacent en auto. 2. Maintenant il n'y a plus d'omnibus. 3. Maintenant beaucoup de gens se servent du chemin de fer. 4. Maintenant les trains en Amérique transportent surtout des marchandises. 5. Le chemin de fer n'est plus maintenant le principal moyen de transporter des voyageurs. 6. Maintenant beaucoup de lignes sont électrifiées. 7. Maintenant beaucoup de gens passent leurs vacances chez eux.

IV. Répondez en français:

1. Comment les gens se déplaçaient-ils autrefois? 2. Combien de temps a-t-il fallu pour donner aux Parisiens des moyens de transport commodes? 3. Qui a pensé à créer ce qu'on appelle "les transports en commun"? 4. Avez-vous jamais entendu parler de Pascal? 5. Quelle idée a-t-il eue un jour? 6. Ces voitures étaient-elles gratuites (*free*)? 7. Les gens se sont-ils habitués tout de suite à son invention? 8. Avaient-ils de quoi s'offrir ce moyen de transport? 9. Jean a-t-il jamais entendu parler de M. Omnès? 10. Quel nom M. Omnès a-t-il donné à ses voitures? 11. Comprenez-vous pourquoi il leur a donné ce nom? 12. Que veut dire le mot latin *omnibus?* 13. Quand M. Omnès a-t-il imaginé cela? 14. A quelle époque s'est-on mis à construire des chemins de fer? 15. A l'heure actuelle est-ce que beaucoup de voyageurs se servent des chemins de fer? 16. Comment s'appellent les voitures qui ont succédé aux omnibus? 17. En Amérique beaucoup de voyageurs se servent-ils encore des trains? 18. A quoi servent surtout les trains en Amérique? 19. Est-ce que les trains américains transportent de plus en plus de voyageurs? 20. Est-ce qu'en France les trains transportent de moins en moins de voyageurs? 21. Quels sont les autres moyens de transport? 22. Qu'est-ce que l'État a fait pour moderniser le matériel? 23. Est-ce que beaucoup de lignes ont été électrifiées? 24. A quoi servent les autorails? 25. Est-ce que les autorails vont très vite?

V. Demandez à quelqu'un:

1. s'il a fallu longtemps pour donner aux Parisiens des moyens de transport commodes. **2.** s'il a entendu parler de Pascal. **3.** s'il a entendu dire que Pascal a inventé une machine à calculer. **4.** quel nom M. Omnès a donné à ses voitures. **5.** à quelle époque on s'est mis à construire des chemins de fer. **6.** si beaucoup de voyageurs américains se servent encore des trains. **7.** ce que c'est qu'un autorail. **8.** si beaucoup de lignes ont été électrifiées. **9.** ce que le gouvernement français a fait pour moderniser le matériel des chemins de fer. **10.** ce que veut dire le mot latin *omnibus*. **11.** comment s'appellent aujourd'hui les anciens omnibus. **12.** s'il aime voyager par le train.

VI. THÈME.

Around 1835, when they began to build railroads in France, many people thought the railroad was an invention for children, suitable at best for **(bonne tout au plus à)** amusing the Parisians. When the line Paris–Saint-Germain was opened in 1837, the king, Louis-Philippe, wanted to make the first trip. His ministers explained to him that this trip was dangerous and, especially, hardly worthy **(peu digne)** of royal majesty. The king stayed at home.

On May 8th, 1842, hundreds of Parisians went by train to go through **(visiter)** the château of Versailles. On the way back, a terrible accident took place. Around fifty travelers were killed. They said it was the end of railroads!

Versailles la nuit (XVIIIème siècle)

Verbes pronominaux

41   Form of reflexive verbs.

Reflexive verbs (*verbes pronominaux*) are those that have a personal pronoun object which refers to the subject of the verb. The forms of the reflexive pronoun object are: **me, te, se, nous, vous, se.** The reflexive pronoun object is expressed even with the infinitive (Nous allons **nous occuper** de cela) and with the present participle (**En se réveillant,** le bébé a pleuré). All reflexive verbs are conjugated with **être.**

PRÉSENT: Je me demande (*I wonder*)
IMPARFAIT: Je me demandais
PASSÉ COMPOSÉ: Je me suis demandé

A complete table of forms of **reflexive** verbs will be found on p. 282.

42   Position of reflexive pronouns.

A. In affirmative forms, both the subject and object pronouns precede the verb thus: subject, object, verb.

Je me lève. Vous vous trompez. Il se trompe.

If the subject is a noun, it of course precedes the pronoun object:

Le taxi s'arrête.

In compound tenses, both pronouns precede the auxiliary verb:

Je me suis levé. Vous vous êtes trompé. Il s'est trompé.
L'auto s'est arrêtée.

B. In the inverted interrogative forms, the pronoun object precedes the verb and the pronoun subject follows it.

Vous trompez-vous? A quelle heure vous levez-vous? L'auto s'arrête-t-elle?

In compound tenses, the inverted pronoun subject follows the auxiliary verb — not the participle:

Vous êtes-vous trompé? A quelle heure vous êtes-vous levé? L'auto s'est-elle arrêtée?

C. In negative forms, **ne** precedes the object pronoun and **pas** follows the verb.

Je ne me trompe pas. Vous ne vous trompez pas. L'auto ne s'arrête pas.

In compound tenses, **pas** follows the auxiliary verb:

Je ne me suis pas trompé. Vous ne vous êtes pas trompé. L'auto ne s'est pas arrêtée.

43 Meaning of reflexive verbs.

In English, the few reflexive verbs that are commonly used (*to hurt oneself, kill oneself, delude oneself, kid oneself*, etc.) are clearly reflexive in meaning. But in French, reflexive verbs are much more numerous and they have a reflexive meaning, an active meaning, or a passive meaning.

REFLEXIVE MEANING

Il **s'**est accusé.	He accused himself.
Il **s'**est tué.	He killed himself.

ACTIVE MEANING

Je **me** demande quelle heure il est.	I wonder . . . (I ask myself.)
On **se** l'imagine.	One imagines it. (One imagines it to himself.)
Il **s'**est tu (*p. part. of se taire*)	He became silent.

PASSIVE MEANING

Je **me** suis trompé.	I was mistaken. (I have deceived myself.)
Le français **se** parle dans plusieurs pays.	French is spoken in several countries.

A reflexive verb is often used in French when we would use the ubiquitous word "get" in English: **se fatiguer** (to get tired), **se reposer** (to get rested), **se coucher** (to get to bed), **se lever** (to get up), **s'habituer à** (to get used to).

Elle se fatigue vite. Je me couche de bonne heure. Nous nous levons tard. Il s'habitue à son travail.

VERBES PRONOMINAUX

44 Use of reflexive verbs.

A. Many ordinary verbs may be used reflexively.
The difference in meaning is often slight:

J'arrête l'auto.	I stop the car.
L'auto **s'arrête.**	The car stops.

But sometimes the difference in meaning is striking:

Je lève la main.	I raise my hand.
Je **me** lève.	I get up.
J'appelle mon frère.	I call my brother.
Je **m'**appelle Jacques.	My name is Jacques.
J'en doute.	I doubt it.
Je **m'en** doute.	I rather think so. I suspect so.

B. Only a few common verbs are always reflexive.

L'enfant **s'écrie.**	The child cries out.
Jean **se moque** de nous.	John is kidding us.
Je **me souviens** de ce pays.	I remember that country.
Je **m'efforce** de finir mon rapport.	I am trying hard to finish my paper.

C. The reflexive pronoun is also found in a number of common expressions.

Cela **se fait.** Cela ne **se fait** pas.	That is done. That is not done.
Cela **se dit.**	That is said.
Cela **se peut.**	That is possible.
Cela **se comprend.**	That is comprehensible.
Ce mot **s'écrit** avec deux "c".	That word has two "c's".
Il **s'agit de** s'y habituer.	It's a matter of getting used to it.

45 Agreement of the past participle of reflexive verbs.

This is one of the trickiest details of French grammar. Most French people have to stop and think before they are sure. It is particularly difficult for English-speaking persons, because they are likely to think French verbs function just as English verbs do. This is often not the case. In English we say: You ask someone (*direct object*) for something; but in French "On **demande** quelque chose **à** quelqu'un" (*indirect object*). In English: You tell someone something; but in French "On **dit** quelque chose **à** quelqu'un." Therefore it is necessary to consider the way the French verb is used — not its English equivalent.

A. If the reflexive pronoun is a direct object of the French verb, the past participle of course agrees with it.

Elle s'est lev**ée** (*f sing*).	She got up.
Nous nous sommes arrêt**és** (*m pl*).	We stopped.
Ils se sont tromp**és** (*m pl*).	They were mistaken.
Elles se sont mises à travailler (*f pl*).	They began to work.
Une centaine de **personnes se** sont noy**ées** (*f pl*).	A hundred persons drowned.

B. If the reflexive pronoun is the indirect object of the verb, the past participle does not agree with it.

Elle s'est lavé les mains.	She washed her hands.
Elle s'est demand**é** quelle heure il était.	She wondered what time it was.
Ils se sont parl**é**.	They talked to each other.

C. If the reflexive pronoun is neither direct nor indirect object, the past participle agrees with the subject of the verb.

Elle s'en est all**ée**.	She went away.
Ils se sont enfui**s**.	They fled.
Elles se sont écri**ées**.	They cried out.

I. SUBSTITUTIONS. Répétez les phrases suivantes, en substituant les mots indiqués:

1. Jean se moque [de Marie].
de vous/ de nous/ de tout/ de toi

2. Est-ce que vous vous souvenez [de cet accident]?
de ce pays/ de cette histoire/ de ces gens/ de ce poème

3. Je ne me rappelle pas [son nom].
où il habite/ ce qu'il fait/ quel âge il a/ où j'ai fait sa connaissance

4. Je ne m'occupe pas [de vos affaires].
de ses affaires/ de ce qu'il fait/ de ce qu'il pense/ de ce qu'il dit

VERBES PRONOMINAUX

5. Elles se sont mises [à travailler].

à voyager/ à déjeuner/ à table/ en route

6. Je me suis habitué [à me lever de bonne heure].

à me coucher tôt/ à m'occuper de ma voiture/ à me servir d'une machine à écrire (*typewriter*)/ à faire une promenade tous les soirs

II. EXERCICES D'APPLICATION.

A. Mettez chacune des phrases suivantes au passé composé:

1. Je me lève très tôt. **2.** Je m'occupe de votre affaire. **3.** Je me trompe. **4.** Le taxi s'arrête. **5.** Jean se moque de nous. **6.** Marie se rappelle l'histoire.

B. Mettez chacune des phrases suivantes à la forme négative:

1. Je me moque de vous. **2.** Vous vous trompez. **3.** Je me suis moqué de vous. **4.** Vous vous êtes trompé. **5.** L'auto s'est arrêtée. **6.** Jean s'y est habitué.

C. Mettez chacune des phrases suivantes au pluriel:

1. Je m'habitue à travailler. **2.** Il s'est habitué à voyager. **3.** Je m'occupe de son affaire. **4.** Il s'est occupé de cela. **5.** Je me suis réveillé à huit heures. **6.** Tu t'es trompé. **7.** Je m'en doute. **8.** Il s'en va ce soir. **9.** Je me suis assis. **10.** Il s'est noyé.

D. Employez l'infinitif dans chacune des phrases suivantes, en commençant par le présent du verbe **aller:**

EX.: — Nous nous habituerons à cela.
   — **Nous allons nous habituer à cela.**

1. Nous nous réveillerons à sept heures. **2.** Je me dépêcherai. **3.** Vous vous occuperez de tout. **4.** Ils se retrouveront demain. **5.** Tu te lèveras de bonne heure.

III. Répétez les phrases suivantes, en remplaçant le verbe **commencer** par se mettre à:

EX.: — Je commencerai à travailler à midi.
   — **Je me mettrai à travailler à midi.**

1. Je commence à voyager. **2.** Nous commençons à déjeuner à midi. **3.** Il a commencé à jouer au bridge. **4.** Nous avons commencé à lire des romans policiers. **5.** Il a commencé à raconter l'histoire. **6.** Il commençait à étudier vers neuf heures. **7.** Il a commencé à pleuvoir. **8.** Il commence à neiger.

IV. Répétez les phrases suivantes, en remplaçant le verbe **se rappeler** par **se souvenir de:**

1. Je me rappelle cette histoire. 2. Je ne me rappelle pas son nom. 3. Je ne me rappelle pas son adresse. 4. Il ne se rappelle pas la date. 5. Vous rappelez-vous ce voyage? 6. Je me suis rappelé la date de son anniversaire. 7. Je ne me suis pas rappelé cette date. 8. Je ne me rappelais pas son adresse.

V. Mettez chacune des phrases suivantes au pluriel:

A. douter (de) (*to doubt*)

1. Je doute de sa sincérité. 2. J'en doute. 3. Je ne doute pas de sa sincérité. 4. Je n'en doute pas. 5. Il doute de ma sincérité. 6. Il en doute. 7. Il ne doute pas de ma sincérité. 8. Il n'en doute pas.

B. se douter de (*to suspect*)

1. Je me doute de ce qui va arriver. 2. Je m'en doute. 3. Je ne m'en doute pas. 4. Il se doute de ce qui va arriver. 5. Il s'en doute. 6. Il ne se doute pas de ce qui va arriver. 7. Il ne s'en doute pas.

VI. Répondez en français:

1. A quelle heure vous réveillez-vous d'habitude? 2. A quelle heure vous êtes-vous réveillé ce matin? 3. Vous trompez-vous quelquefois? 4. Vous occupez-vous quelquefois de votre auto? 5. Savez-vous vous occuper d'un cheval? 6. Vous êtes-vous jamais occupé d'un bébé? 7. Vous amusez-vous bien le* samedi soir? 8. Vous êtes-vous bien amusé l'été dernier? 9. Vous rappelez-vous l'histoire de l'accident? 10. Vous souvenez-vous de cette histoire? 11. Est-ce que beaucoup de passagers se sont noyés? 12. Pourquoi beaucoup de passagers se sont-ils noyés?

---

* Le samedi veut dire: Saturdays, on Saturdays, ou on Saturday. Sans l'article samedi veut dire *samedi dernier* ou *samedi prochain* selon le contexte.

VII. DICTÉE.

1. Un soir, Roger et Marie ont décidé d'aller au théâtre. **2.** Marie s'est habillée avant le dîner. **3.** Roger est arrivé en retard et s'est habillé vite. **4.** Ils se sont dépêchés. **5.** Ils ont été obligés de s'occuper du bébé avant de partir. **6.** Ils se sont trompés d'autobus. **7.** Ils sont arrivés au théâtre juste au moment où le rideau se levait. **8.** Ils se sont bien amusés.

Le théâtre de l'Odéon (vieille gravure)

Un dimanche d'été à la Grande-Jatte (détail), Seurat

VERBES PRONOMINAUX

CHEZ L'ANTIQUAIRE

Jean profite de son séjour à Paris pour acheter des cadeaux destinés à des personnes qui lui sont chères aux États-Unis. Un jour, dans une petite rue voisine de Saint-Germain-des-Prés, il remarque à la devanture d'un antiquaire un service de table qui lui plaît. Il entre, avec l'intention de l'acheter pour sa sœur, si le prix en est raisonnable.

L'ANTIQUAIRE. —¹Vous désirez quelque chose, monsieur?

JEAN. —²Je m'intéresse à ce service qui est à la devanture de votre magasin. ³Pourriez-vous me le montrer?

L'ANTIQUAIRE. —⁴Certainement, monsieur. ⁵Je n'en ai mis que quelques échantillons à la vitrine. ⁶Les autres pièces sont ici, dans ce placard. ⁷Je vais vous les faire voir.

John is taking advantage of his stay in Paris to buy some presents for his loved ones in the United States. One day, on a little street near Saint-Germain-des-Prés, he notices in the shopwindow of an antique dealer a set of dishes that he likes. He goes in with the idea of buying it for his sister, if the price of it is reasonable.

THE DEALER. —¹Something for you, sir?

JOHN. —²I am interested in the set of dishes that is in the window of your store. ³Could you please show it to me?

THE DEALER. —⁴Certainly, sir. ⁵I have put only a few samples in the window. ⁶The other pieces are here in this cupboard. ⁷I will show them to you (make you see them).

CHEZ L'ANTIQUAIRE

JEAN. —⁸Combien y en a-t-il en tout?

L'ANTIQUAIRE. —⁹Soixante-quinze, monsieur. ¹⁰Le service est complet. ¹¹Il n'y manque pas une seule pièce. ¹²A vrai dire, lorsque je l'ai acheté, une assiette manquait. ¹³Mais j'ai pu me la procurer chez un antiquaire de Concarneau.

JEAN. —¹⁴Savez-vous d'où provient ce service?

L'ANTIQUAIRE. —¹⁵Je l'ai acheté moi-même dans une vente aux enchères à Rennes. ¹⁶Il vient d'un vieux château en Bretagne dont on vendait le mobilier après décès. ¹⁷C'est de la très belle faïence de Quimper, monsieur. ¹⁸Au prix indiqué de 650 francs, c'est une occasion magnifique.

JEAN. —¹⁹Pouvez-vous vous charger de l'expédier en Amérique? ²⁰C'est un cadeau pour ma sœur.

L'ANTIQUAIRE. —²¹Laissez-moi seulement son adresse. ²²Nous nous chargerons de tout le reste, emballage et frais d'envoi.

JEAN. —²³Elle le recevra en bon état, n'est-ce pas?

L'ANTIQUAIRE. —²⁴Ne craignez rien, monsieur. ²⁵Nous le lui enverrons dans un bon emballage et nous garantissons tous nos envois.

JEAN. —²⁶Entendu. ²⁷Envoyez-le-lui vers le 15 septembre. ²⁸Il ne me reste plus qu'à vous payer, n'est-ce pas?

JOHN. —⁸How many are there in all?

THE DEALER. —⁹Seventy-five, sir. ¹⁰The set is complete. ¹¹Not a single piece is missing. ¹²To tell the truth, when I bought it, one plate was missing. ¹³But I succeeded in getting it from an antique dealer in Concarneau.

JOHN. —¹⁴Do you know where the set comes from?

THE DEALER. —¹⁵I bought it myself, at an auction in Rennes. ¹⁶It comes from an old château in Brittany whose furnishings were being sold after (the) death (of the owner). ¹⁷It is of the finest Quimper earthenware, sir. ¹⁸At the price of 650 francs, it is a magnificent bargain.

JOHN. —¹⁹Can you take care of shipping it to America? ²⁰It is a present for my sister.

THE DEALER. —²¹Just leave me her address. ²²We will take charge of the rest, packing and shipping charges (costs).

JOHN. —²³She will get it in good condition, won't she?

THE DEALER. —²⁴Fear nothing, sir. ²⁵We will send it to her well packed (in a good packing) and we guarantee all our shipments.

JOHN. —²⁶All right. ²⁷Send it to her about September 15th. ²⁸All I have left to do now is to pay you, isn't it?

I. SUBSTITUTIONS. Répétez les phrases suivantes, en substituant les mots indiqués:

1. Jean profite de son séjour à Paris pour [acheter des cadeaux].
   faire des emplettes/ visiter les musées/ acheter un service de table/
   revoir ses amis parisiens/ revoir les personnes qui lui sont chères

2. Il remarque à la devanture d'un antiquaire [un service de table] qui lui plaît.
   un objet d'art/ un tableau/ un beau vase/ un plateau
   d'argent (*a silver tray*)/ de l'argenterie (*silverware*)

3. Il choisit [des assiettes] qui lui plaisent.
   des cuillers d'argent (*spoons*)/ des fourchettes
   (*forks*)/ des couteaux (*knives*)/ des verres

4. Je vais vous les [faire voir].
   faire envoyer/ montrer/ expédier/ envoyer

5. Le service est complet; il ne manque pas [une seule pièce].
   une seule assiette/ un seul plat (*serving dish*)/
   une seule tasse (*cup*)/ une seule soucoupe

6. [Une assiette] manquait.
   une seule assiette/ un plat/
   un seul plat/ une tasse

7. J'ai pu me la procurer [chez un antiquaire de Concarneau].
   chez un antiquaire de Rennes/ dans une petite boutique à Rouen/
   dans une vente aux enchères/ au marché aux Puces (*flea market*)

8. Pouvez-vous vous charger de [l'expédier en Amérique]?
   l'emballage/ l'envoi/ l'assurance (*insurance*)/ tout le reste

9. Il ne me reste plus qu'à [vous payer].
   l'emballer/ le faire emballer/ l'expédier/ le faire assurer

II. EXERCICE: manquer et rester.

A. Répondez en français par une phrase complète à chacune des questions suivantes:

1. Combien d'assiettes manque-t-il? 2. Combien d'assiettes vous manque-t-il? 3. Combien d'assiettes reste-t-il? 4. Combien d'assiettes vous reste-t-il?

B. Posez en français la question à laquelle chacune des phrases suivantes répondrait, en commençant par **Combien** . . . :

1. Il manque une assiette. **2.** Il me manque une assiette. **3.** Il reste une douzaine d'assiettes. **4.** Il me reste une douzaine d'assiettes.

III. Répondez en français:

1. Pour qui Jean veut-il acheter des cadeaux? **2.** Que remarque-t-il un jour à la devanture d'un antiquaire? **3.** Que pense-t-il de ce service de table? **4.** Quelle question lui pose l'antiquaire quand il entre dans son magasin? **5.** Que demande Jean à l'antiquaire? **6.** Toutes les pièces du service sont-elles à la vitrine? **7.** Où l'antiquaire garde-t-il les autres pièces? **8.** Combien de pièces y a-t-il en tout? **9.** Le service était-il complet quand l'antiquaire l'a acheté? **10.** Est-ce qu'il manquait plusieurs assiettes? **11.** D'où vient le service en question? **12.** Où l'antiquaire l'a-t-il acheté? **13.** Quelle espèce de faïence est-ce? **14.** Quel est le prix du service? **15.** A qui ce service est-il destiné? **16.** Qui va se charger de l'envoi? **17.** Qu'est-ce que l'antiquaire dit à Jean de lui laisser? **18.** Quand Jean dit-il à l'antiquaire d'envoyer le service?

IV. Demandez à quelqu'un:

1. pour qui Jean décide d'acheter des cadeaux. **2.** où il remarque un service de table. **3.** si ce service lui plaît. **4.** combien de pièces il y a dans le service. **5.** s'il manque des pièces. **6.** s'il manquait des pièces quand l'antiquaire l'a acheté. **7.** où l'antiquaire l'a acheté. **8.** d'où vient ce service. **9.** où l'antiquaire s'est procuré l'assiette qu'il cherchait. **10.** le prix du service en question. **11.** où l'antiquaire va expédier le service. **12.** qui se chargera de l'emballage. **13.** qui va payer les frais d'envoi. **14.** si le service arrivera en bon état.

V. THÈME.

On a little street near Saint-Germain-des-Prés, John noticed one day some interesting prints (**estampes** *f*) on display at an antiquarian's shop. He stopped to look at them. They were in color, and showed views of fashionable Paris (**mondain**) around 1830: men wearing hats and clothes of the period (**de l'époque**), ladies in long dresses and carrying parasols (**ombrelles**). John walked into the store. The prints were quite expensive, but the owner was so nice and so convincing that John finally bought them. He had just left the store when he remembered that he could not take them along on his trips. "Well." he thought, "they will make nice presents for my relatives and friends in the U.S."

VI. Mettez les phrases suivantes au passé, en remplaçant le présent de l'indicatif par le **passé composé** ou l'**imparfait**, selon le cas:

C'est un petit magasin qui paraît assez insignifiant, rue Jacob. A la devanture, il y a quelques objets, pas grand-chose. J'entre. Un vieux monsieur, qui porte une calotte noire, vient à ma rencontre et me demande ce que je désire. Je lui dis que je veux acheter quelque chose pour ma sœur. Mais quoi? Je ne sais pas au juste. Il me montre toute sorte d'objets. Mon choix s'arrête enfin sur une pendule, qui me paraît tout à fait honorable. Je lui demande combien c'est. Deux mille cinq cent francs, me répond-il. C'est cher. Mais enfin, cela vient de Paris, ou des environs, et je ne m'attends pas à trouver une de ces magnifiques "occasions" du siècle dernier. Je le paie et je sors, avec ma pendule.

Les amateurs d'estampes, Daumier

CHEZ L'ANTIQUAIRE

Pronoms personnels

46   Forms of the personal pronouns.

Personal pronouns have two sets of forms: the unstressed forms, which are used with verbs, and the stressed forms, which are used primarily with prepositions. The unstressed forms are sometimes called "conjunctive" pronouns (because they are always used in conjunction with verbs) and the stressed forms, "disjunctive" pronouns.

47   Unstressed forms of the personal pronouns.

A. Subject: **je, tu, il (elle, on), nous, vous, ils (elles).**

Allez-**vous** au cinéma ce soir? — Oui, **je** vais au cinéma ce soir.
Où vend-**on** des cartes-postales?

Note that the indefinite personal pronoun **on** is always used with the third person singular form of the verb — even when it means *we, you, they,* or *people.* (Cf. par. 68 C, p. 148.)

B.   Object: **me, te, se, nous, vous; le, la, les; lui, leur; y; en.**

1. **Me, te, se, nous, vous** may be used either as direct or indirect object of a verb.

Il **me** voit (*direct object*).
Il **me** dit bonjour (*indirect object*).
Je **vous** crois (*direct object*).
Je **vous** demande pardon (*indirect object*).

2. **Le, la, les** are used as direct object only. They may refer to persons or things.

Connaissez-vous **Marie** Duplessis?	⎫
Connaissez-vous **la faïence** de Quimper?	⎬ Oui, je **la** connais.
Jean a-t-il acheté **le service** de table?	Oui, il **l'**a acheté.
Est-il allé voir **les Duplessis**?	Oui, il est allé **les** voir.

Note that in French, certain verbs take a direct object although the English equivalents require a preposition:

Attendre (*to wait for*) :   J'attends l'autobus. Je **l'**attends.
Chercher (*to look for*) :   Je cherche son adresse. Je **la** cherche.
Écouter (*to listen to*) :   J'écoute la musique. Je **l'**écoute.
Regarder (*to look at*) :   Jean regarde la devanture. Il **la** regarde.

Demander (*to ask for*)   Il demande le journal. Il **le** demande.

3. **Lui, leur** and **y** are indirect object forms.

Lui, leur are the indirect object forms that are used to refer to persons. They replace a noun preceded by the preposition **à**.

Avez-vous parlé **à Roger**?	Oui, je **lui** ai parlé.
Avez-vous parlé **à Marie**?	Oui, je **lui** ai parlé.
Écrivez-vous souvent **à vos amis**?	Non, je ne **leur** écris jamais.

Note that in French, certain verbs require the preposition **à** although their English equivalents do not require a preposition:

Plaire à (*to please*) :   Le service de table plaît-il **à Jean**?
Oui, il **lui** plaît.

Obéir à (*to obey*) :   Le chien obéit **à son** maître.
Il **lui** obéit.

Ressembler à (*to resemble*) :   L'enfant ressemble-t-il **à son père**?
Oui, il **lui** ressemble.

Dire à (*to tell*, *to say to*) :   J'ai dit au revoir **à Marie**.
Je **lui** ai dit au revoir.

Demander à (*to ask [someone]*) :   J'ai demandé l'heure **à Jean**. Je **lui** ai demandé l'heure.

Y is the indirect object form that is used to refer to places or things. It is the equivalent of a noun preceded by the preposition **à** and sometimes **dans** or **sur.**

Allez-vous souvent **au théâtre?** ⎞
Allez-vous souvent **à la banque?** ⎠ Non, je n'**y** vais pas souvent.

Répondez-vous toujours **aux lettres?** Non, je n'**y** réponds pas toujours.

Pensez-vous souvent **à vos vacances?** Oui, j'**y** pense souvent.

Serez-vous **sur la terrasse?** Oui, j'**y** serai.

Roger est-il **dans son laboratoire?** Oui, il **y** est.

4. **En** is used as the equivalent of a noun preceded by the preposition **de.**

If the noun is used in a partitive sense, **en** may be used to refer to persons or things.

Avez-vous **des assiettes** en faïence? Oui, j'**en** ai.

Avez-vous **des cousins?** Oui, j'**en** ai quatre.

If the noun is not used in a partitive sense, **en** is used primarily to refer to places and things. For persons, see par. 48 A.

Avez-vous besoin **d'assiettes?** Oui, j'**en** ai besoin.

Jean a-t-il parlé **de son voyage?** Oui, il **en** a parlé.

Avez-vous peur **des taxis?** Non, je n'**en** ai pas peur.

Vient-il **du Mexique?** ⎞
Vient-il **de Paris?** ⎠ Oui, il **en** vient.
Vient-il **des États-Unis?** ⎠

En is also used in a number of expressions such as:

Il **en** a assez. He is fed up with it.

Il veut **en** finir. He wants to be done with it.

Où **en** sommes-nous? Where are we (in it)?

Nous **en** sommes à la page 98. We are on page 98.

C. Position of pronoun objects.*

---

* Ces explications sont d'ordinaire résumées sous la forme suivante:

me	précède	le	précède	lui	précède	y	précède	en	précède le verbe.
te		la		leur					
se		les							
nous									
vous									

Néanmoins, puisque seulement deux pronoms compléments peuvent être employés avec un seul verbe, il nous paraît plus utile de s'habituer à employer les combinaisons de pronoms les plus usitées que d'apprendre par cœur la table précédente.

When a verb has both a direct and an indirect object, both of them precede the verb — except for affirmative imperatives. (See par. 49.)

1. The indirect object forms **me, te, se, nous, vous** precede the direct object forms **le, la, les, en.**

Voulez-vous bien **me le** montrer?
Je vais **vous les** faire voir.
J'ai pu **me la** procurer.
Ne **m'en** donnez pas.

It is useful to repeat all the possible combinations of pronoun objects: **me le, me la, me les, m'en; te le, te la, te les, t'en;** etc.

2. The direct object forms **le, la, les** precede the indirect object forms **lui, leur.**

Nous **le lui** enverrons dans un bon emballage.
L'antiquaire a-t-il montré les assiettes à Jean et à Marie? — Oui, il **les leur** a montrées.

Possible combinations: **le lui, la lui, les lui; le leur, la leur, les leur.**

3. The indirect object forms **lui, leur** precede **en.**

Avez-vous envoyé des fleurs à votre grand-mère? — Oui, je **lui en** ai envoyé.

L'antiquaire a-t-il montré des assiettes à Jean et à Marie? — Oui, il **leur en** a montré.

4. With reflexive verbs, the personal pronoun object precedes **y** or **en.**

Vous êtes-vous habitué à conduire en France? — Oui, je **m'y** suis habitué.

Roger s'est-il souvenu de l'accident? — Oui, il **s'en** est souvenu.

5. When **en** is used with the expression **il y a,** it follows **y.**

Il **y en** a. **Y en** a-t-il? Il **y en** a eu.

48 Stressed forms of the personal pronouns.

The stressed forms **moi, toi, lui, elle, nous, vous, eux, elles,** and the indefinite form **soi** may be used as the object of a preposition or with verbs.

A. Stressed forms of personal pronouns as the object of a preposition.

Il est arrivé **avant (après) moi.**
Elle est là, **devant (derrière) vous.**
Ils sont **parmi (près de, loin de, à côté de) nous.**
Il est actuellement **chez (auprès d') elle.**
Cela ne dépend pas **de moi (d'elle, d'eux).**
J'irai au cinéma **avec (sans) lui.**
Je compte **sur vous (sur lui, sur elle).**
On va **chez soi.** Chacun **pour soi.**
Pensez-vous à Charles? — Oui, je pense **à lui.**

Note that after prepositions the stressed forms are used only to refer to persons:

Nous parlons de Charles **(de lui)**, de Marie **(d'elle)**, des Duplessis **(d'eux).**
But: Nous parlons des vacances (de notre voyage, de ce journal). Nous **en**
parlons.

B. Stressed forms of personal pronouns with verbs.

1. Stressed forms are used in addition to, or instead of, an unstressed form — for emphasis.

Moi, je n'en sais rien.
Lui n'en sait rien non plus.
Je l'ai acheté **moi-même.**

Note that all these forms may be used in combination with the word
même: lui-même (*himself*), **vous-même** (*you, yourself*).

2. Stressed forms are used to specify the persons indicated by a plural form of a personal pronoun.

Elle et **moi** nous avons fait une promenade ensemble.
Lui et **elle** ont fait une promenade ensemble.

3. Stressed forms are used after **c'est, ce sont** (whether expressed or implied).

Qui a pris ma clé? — C'est **moi** (*or* **Moi**).
Est-ce votre frère? — Non, ce n'est pas **lui.**
Est-ce que ce sont vos camarades? — Oui, ce sont **eux.**

49　Use of personal pronoun objects with imperatives.

A.　Personal pronoun objects with affirmative imperatives.

Pronoun objects follow the verb and are joined to it by a hyphen.

Voilà des fruits. Regardez-**les**.
Voilà une pomme. Mangez-**la**.
Sers-**toi**. Servez-**vous**.

When an affirmative imperative has two pronoun objects:

1. The direct object forms **le, la, les** precede the indirect object forms **moi, toi, lui, nous, vous, leur.**

Voulez-vous voir le service de table? — Oui, montrez-**le-moi**.

Possible combinations: **le-moi, la-moi, les-moi; le-lui, la-lui, les-lui,** etc.

Note the use of **moi** and **toi** instead of **me** and **te** in these combinations. **Lui** means either *to him* or *to her* and **leur** means *to them* (either masculine or feminine).

2. When **en** is used, it follows the indirect object forms **m', t', lui, nous, vous, leur.**

Voulez-vous des hors-d'œuvre? — Oui, apportez-**m'en**.
Mes camarades voudraient du café noir. Apportez-**leur-en**.
Servez-**vous-en**.

B.　Personal pronoun objects with negative imperatives.

When used with negative imperatives, personal pronoun objects precede the verb and stand in the same order as before other verb forms. (See par. 47, C.)

Ne **m'en** parlez pas.
Ne **le lui** dites pas.
Ne **les lui** montrez pas.

———————

I. SUBSTITUTIONS. Répétez les phrases suivantes, en substituant les mots indiqués:

1. Elle [me] demande le nom de l'hôtel.
   lui / nous / vous / leur

2. Elle [me le] demande.

le lui/ nous le/ vous le/ le leur

3. L'antiquaire [m'] enverra les assiettes.

lui/ nous/ vous/ leur

4. L'antiquaire [me les] enverra.

les lui/ nous les/ vous les/ les leur

5. Montrez-[moi] les assiettes.

lui/ nous/ leur

6. Montrez-[les-moi].

les-lui/ les-nous/ les-leur

7. Ne [m'en] parlez pas.

lui en/ nous en/ leur en

II. Répondez aux questions suivantes, en employant le pronom approprié:

A. le, la, les

1. Jean connaît-il les Duplessis? **2.** Va-t-il retrouver ses amis? **3.** A-t-il vu le petit Michel? **4.** A-t-il acheté le service de table? **5.** Où Jean a-t-il remarqué le service de table? **6.** A-t-il entendu remuer le petit Michel? **7.** Connaît-il Marie?

B. lui, leur

1. Est-ce que le service de table plaît à Jean? **2.** Est-ce que les assiettes plaisent à Jean? **3.** Le petit Michel ressemble-t-il à sa mère? **4.** Ressemble-t-il à ses parents? **5.** Avez-vous parlé au chauffeur de taxi? **6.** Avez-vous parlé aux Duplessis? **7.** Est-ce que Roger pose des questions à Jean? **8.** Est-ce que Jean répond à Roger?

C. y, en

1. Est-ce que Jean est allé à Saint-Cloud? **2.** Doit-il aller à la boulangerie? **3.** Est-ce qu'il vient d'Égypte? **4.** A-t-il besoin de repos? **5.** A-t-il entendu parler d'une vente aux enchères? **6.** A-t-il parlé de son voyage en Égypte? **7.** Est-ce qu'il se souvient de l'accident? **8.** Avez-vous entendu parler de cet accident? **9.** Êtes-vous jamais allé en France? **10.** Jean voudrait-il retourner aux États-Unis?

III. Répétez les phrases suivantes en remplaçant les noms par des pronoms:

EX.: Il a montré l'assiette à Marie.

Il la lui a montrée.

1. Il a montré le service de table à Jean.   2. Il a montré le service de table à Marie.
3. Il n'a pas montré le service à Henri.   4. Il a vendu le service de table à Jean.   5. Il
a montré l'assiette à Jean.   6. Il a montré l'assiette à Marie.   7. Il a montré les assiettes
à Jean.   8. Il a expédié les cadeaux à ses amis.

IV. Répondez en français, en remplaçant les noms par les pronoms appropriés:

1. Où Jean a-t-il vu le service de table?   2. Où l'antiquaire a-t-il acheté ce
service?   3. Est-ce que l'antiquaire va montrer les assiettes à Jean?   4. Est-ce
que le service plaît à Jean?   5. Est-ce que Jean va donner le service à sa sœur?
6. Qui enverra le service à sa sœur?   7. Combien de pièces y a-t-il en tout?
8. Qui se chargera de l'emballage?   9. Qui paiera les frais d'envoi?   10. Est-ce
que le prix en est raisonnable?   11. Combien d'assiettes manquent?   12. Est-ce
que l'antiquaire garantit ses envois?   13. Jean a-t-il acheté beaucoup de
cadeaux?   14. Est-ce que Roger doit s'occuper d'une affaire d'impôts?

V. Répétez les phrases suivantes, en remplaçant les noms qui suivent les
prépositions par les pronoms appropriés:

1. Jean est allé chez les Duplessis.   2. Il pense souvent aux Duplessis.   3. Il
pense souvent à Marie.   4. Il parle du petit Michel.   5. Il va parler avec le
petit Michel.   6. On a dîné sans le petit Michel.   7. Jean est arrivé avant
Marie.   8. Lui et Roger ont parlé de Marie.   9. Marie s'est occupée du bébé.
10. Ensuite ils ont fait une promenade avec le bébé.

VI. Mettez chacune des phrases suivantes à la forme impérative, en remplaçant les noms par les pronoms appropriés:

EX.: — Voulez-vous bien me montrer le service?
— **Montrez-le-moi.**

1. Voulez-vous bien le montrer à Jean?   2. Voulez-vous bien le montrer à Marie?
3. Voulez-vous bien me passer le journal?   4. Voulez-vous bien le passer à Marie?
5. Voulez-vous bien le passer à Roger?   6. Voulez-vous bien venir me voir?   7. Voulez-
vous bien aller voir les Duplessis?   8. Voulez-vous bien aller en ville?   9. Voulez-vous
bien acheter des cadeaux?   10. Voulez-vous bien venir chez nous?

VII. Mettez chacune des phrases suivantes au négatif:

EX.: — Montrez-le-moi.
— **Ne me le montrez pas.**

1. Donnez-le-moi.   **2.** Envoyez-m'en.   **3.** Expédiez-les-lui.   **3.** Achetez-lui-en.
5. Parlez-lui-en.   **6.** Pensez-y.   **7.** Pensez à elle.   **8.** Allez-y.

Le Mont-Saint-Michel

Le canotage (*détail*), Manet

L'Opéra de Paris au début du siècle

UNE RENCONTRE

Un jour qu'il traverse la place de l'Opéra, Jean se trouve tout à coup face à face avec Hélène Frazer et sa mère. Ils échangent de cordiales poignées de main. Notez d'ailleurs que ces rencontres inattendues, à Paris ou ailleurs, entre personnes venant de pays éloignés sont moins rares qu'on ne le penserait, car la plupart des touristes fréquentent les mêmes endroits.

JEAN. —¹Mᵐᵉ Frazer! ²Hélène! ³Quelle surprise! ⁴J'ignorais que vous étiez ici!

Mᴹᴱ FRAZER. —⁵Moi non plus, je ne me doutais pas que vous étiez à Paris. ⁶Henri sera certainement heureux de vous revoir!

JEAN. —⁷Henri est aussi à Paris?

HÉLÈNE. —⁸Bien sûr. ⁹Mais tu connais mon frère: ¹⁰quand nous lui avons dit que nous irions faire des emplettes cet après-midi, ¹¹il a déclaré qu'il aimait mieux monter en haut de la tour Eiffel.

Mᴹᴱ FRAZER. —¹²Combien de temps comptez-vous rester à Paris, Jean?

One day when he is crossing the Opera Square, John is suddenly face to face with Helen Frazer and her mother. They shake hands cordially. But note that these unexpected meetings, in Paris or elsewhere, between people who have come from distant countries are not so unusual as you would think, because most tourists go to the same places.

JOHN. —¹Mrs. Frazer! ²Helen! ³What a surprise! ⁴I didn't know you were here!

MRS. FRAZER. —⁵Nor did I (even) suspect that you were in Paris. ⁶Henry will certainly be glad to see you again!

JOHN. —⁷Is Henry in Paris, too?

HELEN. —⁸Of course. ⁹But you know my brother: ¹⁰when we told him we were going shopping this afternoon, ¹¹he announced that he preferred to go to the top of the Eiffel Tower.

MRS. FRAZER. —¹²How long do you expect to stay in Paris, John?

JEAN. —[13]Je serai encore ici une vingtaine de jours. [14]J'ai retenu passage sur un avion qui partira pour New York de samedi en quinze.

MME FRAZER. —[15]Nous irons passer le week-end en Touraine. [16]Il y aura une place pour vous dans notre voiture, si vous n'avez rien de mieux à faire. [17]Mais je me rends compte que vous n'avez sans doute pas beaucoup de temps à votre disposition.

JEAN. —[18]Mais si. [19]En ce moment, je suis libre comme l'air, et je serai enchanté de vous accompagner. [20]Quand avez-vous l'intention de partir?

MME FRAZER. —[21]Nous nous mettrons en route vers huit heures du matin, vendredi prochain. [22]Dites-nous où vous êtes descendu et nous viendrons vous chercher.

JEAN. —[23]Ne vous dérangez pas pour moi.

HÉLÈNE. —[24]Ce n'est pas un dérangement. [25]Donne seulement ton adresse à maman.

JEAN. —[26]Je suis descendu à l'hôtel Meurice. [27]Nous nous retrouverons vers huit heures. [28]En attendant, dites bien des choses de de ma part à Henri, [29]que je reverrai d'ailleurs sous peu.

JOHN. —[13]I'll be here about three more weeks. [14]I have reserved space on a plane which will leave for New York two weeks from Saturday.

MRS. FRAZER. —[15]We are going to spend the weekend in Touraine. [16]There will be room for you in our car, if you have nothing better to do. [17]But I realize that you surely don't have much free time.

JOHN. —[18]Yes I do. [19]Right now I am as free as the air, and I shall be delighted to go with you. [20]When do you expect to leave?

MRS. FRAZER. —[21]We will start around eight o'clock (next) Friday morning. [22]Tell us where you are staying and we will come for you.

JOHN. —[23]Don't go out of your way on my account.

HELEN. —[24](It's) no bother. [25]Just give your address to mother.

JOHN. —[26]I am staying at the Meurice. [27]We will meet about eight o'clock. [28]Meanwhile, say hello to Henry for me. [29]I'll see him soon.

I. SUBSTITUTIONS. Répétez les phrases suivantes, en substituant les mots indiqués:

1. J'ignorais [que vous étiez ici].

   que vous aviez quitté l'Amérique/ que vous étiez
   de passage à Paris/ que vous deviez partir sous peu

2. Elle ne se doutait pas [que Jean était ici].

   qu'il était de passage à Paris/ qu'il devait
   partir bientôt/ qu'il devait partir sous peu

3. Elle ne se rendait pas compte [que Jean était ici].

   qu'il était de passage à Paris/ qu'il devait
   partir bientôt/ qu'il devait partir sous peu

4. Combien de temps [comptez-vous] rester à Paris?

   pensez-vous/ croyez-vous/ devez-vous/ avez vous l'intention de

5. Je serai ici encore [une vingtaine de jours].

   une dizaine de jours/ une quinzaine de
   jours/ environ un mois/ deux ou trois mois

6. J'ai retenu passage sur un avion qui partira pour New York [de samedi en quinze].

   d'aujourd'hui en huit/ dans huit jours/ d'aujourd'hui en quinze/
   dans quinze jours/ le premier août/ le vingt-et-un juillet

7. Nous nous retrouverons [à sept heures et demie].

   à midi/ à huit heures et quart/ à onze
   heures moins le quart/ à six heures dix

II. Répétez les phrases suivantes, en remplaçant les mots en italiques par l'expression indiquée:

A. en ce moment

1. Il est de passage à Paris *maintenant*. 2. Elle est *maintenant* étudiante à la Faculté des lettres. 3. *Maintenant* je suis libre comme l'air. 4. Je n'ai pas grand-chose à faire *maintenant*. 5. Il est *maintenant* à l'hôtel Meurice.

B. à ce moment-là

1. J'étais *alors* en Égypte. 2. Le bateau était *alors* près du bord. 3. Les Frazer étaient *alors* en Amérique. 4. Hélène était *alors* étudiante à la Faculté des Lettres. 5. Je n'avais *alors* pas grand-chose à faire.

UNE RENCONTRE

C. au moment où

1. *Quand* j'ai reçu votre invitation, j'étais au Vénézuéla.   2. *Quand* l'accident a eu lieu, le bateau était près du bord.   3. *Quand* l'eau a commencé à entrer, le capitaine a essayé de retourner au bord.   4. *Quand* Jean a rencontré Mme Frazer et sa fille, il ignorait qu'elles étaient en France.   5. *Quand* Roger est entré, l'employé était de mauvaise humeur.

III. Répétez les phrases suivantes, en employant **de ma part, de sa part,** etc.

EX.: — Elle est gentille de m'inviter.
    — **C'est gentil de sa part de m'inviter.**

1. Il est gentil de m'inviter.   2. Ils sont gentils de m'inviter.   3. Elles sont très aimables de m'inviter.   4. Vous êtes gentil de m'inviter.   5. Vous êtes très aimable de m'inviter.

IV. Répétez les phrases suivantes, en remplaçant les mots en italiques par **une dizaine de, une vingtaine de,** etc.:

1. John passera encore *environ vingt* jours à Paris.   2. Il est arrivé il y a *à peu près dix* jours.   3. *Environ cent* passagers se sont noyés.   4. Au moment de l'accident, le bateau était à *environ quinze* mètres de la rive.   5. Il y a *à peu près cinquante* kilomètres de Monaco à Nice.

V. Répondez en français:

1. Où Jean rencontre-t-il Hélène et sa mère?   2. Savait-il qu'elles étaient à Paris?   3. Mme Frazer se doutait-elle que Jean était à Paris?   4. Qui est Henri?   5. Qu'est-ce qu'il a décidé de faire cet après-midi-là?   6. Combien de temps Jean compte-t-il rester à Paris?   7. Quand doit-il quitter Paris? 8. Où ira-t-il quand il quittera Paris?   9. A-t-il retenu passage sur un bateau? 10. Combien de temps faut-il pour aller de Paris à New York en avion?   11. Où Hélène et sa mère iront-elles passer le week-end?   12. Comment iront-elles en Touraine?   13. Qu'est-ce que Mme Frazer offre à Jean?   14. Pourquoi Jean sera-t-il enchanté de les accompagner?   15. Quand se mettront-ils en route? 16. A quelle heure les Frazer viendront-ils chercher Jean?   17. A quel hôtel est-il descendu?   18. Quand Jean reverra-t-il Henri?   19. En attendant, qu'est-ce qu'il demande à Hélène de dire à son frère?

VI. Demandez à quelqu'un:

1. où était Jean quand il a rencontré Hélène et sa mère. **2.** s'il comptait les voir. **3.** s'il savait qu'elles étaient à Paris. **4.** si Henri avait envie de faire des emplettes cet après-midi-là. **5.** ce qu'il aimait mieux faire. **6.** combien de temps Jean compte passer encore à Paris. **7.** quand partira l'avion sur lequel il a retenu passage. **8.** si la Touraine est loin de Paris. **9.** s'il connaît bien la Touraine. **10.** si Mme Frazer se rend compte que Jean n'a pas beaucoup de temps à sa disposition. **11.** à quelle heure ils se mettront en route. **12.** l'adresse de Jean. **13.** le nom de l'hôtel où il est descendu. **14.** si Jean reverra Henri sous peu.

VII. THÈME.

One afternoon when he was walking across the Place de l'Opéra, John found himself face to face with Helen Frazer and her mother. He had not seen them for several months, and he was very much surprised to meet* them. Since they were planning to spend the weekend in Touraine, Mrs. Frazer asked John if he would like to come along.

"It is very nice of you to invite me," said John, "but are you sure that I won't inconvenience you?"

"You won't inconvenience us at all," Mrs. Frazer answered. "There is plenty of room in the car. We'll be leaving early Friday morning. What about our coming for you at your hotel at eight?"

"Fine **(Entendu),**" said John. "I'll be waiting for you when you come."

---

* Employez *rencontrer* qui signifie *rencontrer par accident* plutôt que *retrouver* ou *se retrouver* qui suggère un rendez-vous fixé d'avance.

Futur/ Impératif/ Adverbes/ Nombres cardinaux et ordinaux

50 Forms and use of the future tense.

A. Forms.

The future tense of regular verbs will be found on p. 270, that of **être** and **avoir** on p. 275. Note that the future of most irregular verbs is perfectly regular: **dire (je dirai), mettre (je mettrai), écrire (j'écrirai).**

The following are the commonest verbs whose future is irregular: **aller (j'irai), envoyer (j'enverrai), venir (je viendrai), faire (je ferai), voir (je verrai),** and **pouvoir (je pourrai).**

B. Use.

1. The future tense is used to express a future action or state of being.

Mon avion **partira** de samedi en quinze.
Nous **irons** passer le week-end en Touraine.
Je **serai** encore ici une vingtaine de jours.

2. The future tense is used in the result clause of "simple" conditional sentences (i.e., those that express what will happen if a given condition is fulfilled).

Si vous nous dites où vous êtes descendu, **nous viendrons** vous chercher.
Il y aura une place pour vous dans notre voiture, **si vous n'avez** rien de mieux à faire.

3. The future tense is used in temporal clauses introduced by **quand, lorsque, dès que, aussitôt . . . que, tant . . . que,** etc., when the verb of the other clause is in the future tense.

Nous viendrons vous chercher **quand** vous **serez** prêt.
Quand vous **viendrez,** je serai prêt.
Dès que j'arriverai, je vous le ferai savoir.

4. The future tense is used in a few set expressions that imply futurity.

Faites **comme vous voudrez.**	Do as you wish.
Je ferai **ce qui me plaira.**	I'll do as I please.

5. The future tense is used instead of the imperative in formal instructions.

Vous partirez tout de suite. **Vous irez** à Londres. **Vous vous présenterez** dès
ce soir à cette adresse.
Tu ne **tueras** pas. (*Thou shalt not kill.*)

51 Imperatives.

A. Regular verbs: **Donne, donnons, donnez; finis, finissons, finissez; vends, vendons, vendez.**

Donnez votre adresse à maman.
Finissez vite votre travail.

The **tu** form of the imperative of verbs of the first conjugation ends in "s" when followed by **y** or **en.** The same is true for the form **Va.**

Donne-moi du café.
Donnes-en à ton père.
Va dans ta chambre.
Vas-y.

B. Auxiliary verbs: **Être: sois, soyons, soyez; Avoir: aie(s), ayons, ayez.**

Soyez tranquille. **Ayez** la bonté d'attendre un instant.

C. Irregular verbs.

The imperative of most irregular verbs takes its forms from the present indicative. Exceptions: **Sachez que** . . . *I'll have you know* . . . ,
Veuillez followed by an infinitive . . . *Please* . . .

Disons que nous nous mettrons en route vers huit heures du matin.
Dites bien des choses de ma part à Henri.

D. Reflexive verbs.

1. Affirmative Imperative.

The imperative of reflexive verbs always expresses the personal pronoun object:

Se dépêcher: dépêche-**toi,** dépêchons-**nous,** dépêchez-**vous.**
S'en aller: va-**t'en,** allons-**nous-en,** allez-**vous-en.**

2. Negative Imperative.

In the negative forms, the object pronoun precedes the verb:

Ne **te dépêche** pas, ne **nous dépêchons** pas, ne **vous dépêchez** pas.
Ne **vous dérangez** pas.
Ne **vous en allez** pas.

For the order of other personal pronoun objects of imperative form see paragraph 49.

52 Adverbs.

A. Formation of adverbs.

1. Many adverbs are formed by adding the ending **-ment** to the feminine singular form of an adjective: **fière**-fière**ment; vive**-vive**ment; malheureuse**-malheureuse**ment; nouvelle**-nouvelle**ment;** and so on.

2. Adverbs corresponding to adjectives ending in **-ant** or **-ent** usually end in **-amment** or **-emment,** both being pronounced [amã]: **violent-violemment, prudent-prudemment, savant-savamment.**

3. If the masculine singular form of the adjective ends in a vowel, the adverb is usually formed by adding the ending **-ment** to the masculine singular: **hardi**-hardi**ment; joli**-joli**ment; aisé**-aisé**ment.** Cf. **gentil-**gentil**ment.**

4. Adjectives are used as adverbs in a few expressions: **sentir bon, sentir mauvais; chanter faux, chanter juste; parler haut, parler bas; coûter cher.**

Parlez plus **haut,** s'il vous plaît.
Ces roses ont coûté **cher.** Elles sentent **bon.**

Note that **vite,** which is scarcely ever used as an adjective, is very commonly used as an adverb:

C'est **vite fait.** Allez plus **vite.** Vous parlez trop **vite.**

B. Comparison of adverbs.

1. Regular comparison: vite, **plus** vite, **le plus** vite.

Marie parle **vite**. Sa sœur parle **plus vite**. Sa mère parle **le plus vite de** toute la famille.

SUPERIORITY: **plus** vite **que** . . .
EQUALITY: **aussi** vite **que** . . .
INFERIORITY: **moins** vite **que** . . .

2. Irregular comparison.

Bien *well*, **mieux** *better*, **le mieux** *best*.
Peu *little*, **moins** *less*, **le moins** *least*.

Il a déclaré qu'il aimait **mieux** monter en haut de la tour Eiffel.
Les choses vont de **moins en moins bien.**
Les choses vont de **plus en plus mal.**

NOTE: Don't confuse the adverb **bien** (*well*), **mieux, le mieux** with the adjective **bon** (*good*), **meilleur, le meilleur.** Don't confuse the adverb **mal** (*badly*) with the adjective **mauvais** (*bad*): **Il va mal** (*adverb*); **Il a un mauvais rhume** (*adjective*).

The irregular comparison **mal, pis, le pis** is used primarily in set expressions.

Les choses vont de **mal en pis.**

C. Position of adverbs.

1. Unstressed adverbs.

The normal (unstressed) position of the adverb is after the verb it modifies:

Donnez seulement votre adresse à maman. (*Just give* . . .)
Je me rends compte que **vous n'avez sans doute pas** beaucoup de temps à votre disposition.
Est-ce qu'Henri **est aussi** à Paris?
Je vous **croyais toujours** en Arabie.
Je **serai encore ici** une vingtaine de jours.
Je le **reverrai d'ailleurs** sous peu.

When verbs are in compound tenses, the adverb usually follows the auxiliary verb:

Jean **est déjà allé** chez les Duplessis.
Il **a bien fait** d'aller les revoir.
Il **a beaucoup mangé, beaucoup parlé.**
Il **n'est peut-être pas encore** revenu à Paris.
Henri **n'est malheureusement pas** venu avec Hélène.

2. Stressed adverbs.

A few adverbs or adverbial expressions of time such as **demain, hier, aujourd'hui, à huit heures précises** are normally somewhat stressed and usually come at the end of the phrase:

Nous viendrons vous chercher demain matin **à sept heures précises.**
Il est revenu **hier.**

53 Cardinal numbers (**un, deux, trois,** etc.).

(For table of numbers and phonetic transcription, see pp. 239–241.)

The cardinal numbers are used in general as in English to express quantity, time, dates, measures, etc.

Note that the French word for numbers is **les nombres** and that **les numéros** is used only to refer to numbers when something is numbered: **le numéro d'une chambre, d'une maison,** etc. (**La salle numéro dix. Il habite au numéro 23, rue Jacob.**)

54 Pronunciation of the final consonant of numbers.

A. The final consonant of numbers is ordinarily silent when the noun immediately following the number begins with a consonant. EX.: **deux minutes, trois fois, cinq jours, six francs, huit semaines, dix mois, vingt francs.** However, practically everyone pronounces the final consonant of **sept** and **neuf.**

B. The final consonant of numbers is pronounced (linked) when the noun immediately following the number begins with a vowel or a mute "h". EX.: **trois heures, cinq ans, huit heures, vingt et un ans,** etc. Note, however, that you *never* link the "t" in **cent un.**

C. The final consonant of **cinq, six, sept, huit, neuf,** and **dix** is pronounced when the numbers are used alone, in counting, or at the end
of a phrase. EX.: **Combien de cousins avez-vous? —J'en ai cinq.**

55 Use of cardinal numbers.

A. Although in English we use ordinal numbers for days of the month
(the third of September, the eighteenth of November) in French the
cardinal numbers are used except for the first of a month:

C'est aujourd'hui le premier octobre.
But: C'est aujourd'hui le deux octobre, le trois novembre, le quatre décembre,
le trente janvier, etc.

B. In English, for 1975 we say nineteen seventy-five, nineteen hundred
seventy-five, or nineteen hundred and seventy-five. In French, 1975
can be read only two ways: **mil neuf cent soixante-quinze** or **dix-
neuf cent soixante-quinze.** Note that in both cases the word **cent**
must be expressed.

56 Collective numbers ending in -aine.

The suffix **-aine** indicates an approximate quantity. **Une douzaine**
means twelve; but the other collective numbers are approximate: **une
centaine** *about a hundred.* Others are: **une dizaine, une quinzaine, une
vingtaine, une trentaine, une quarantaine, une cinquantaine, une
soixantaine.** Like other expressions of quantity, the collective numbers
are followed by the preposition **de.**

Je serai ici encore une vingtaine de jours.

57 Time of day.

A. Official time.

The twenty-four hour system is used in all official announcements:
railroads, planes, banks, theaters, offices, army, navy, etc. In this system, fractions of an hour are always expressed in terms of minutes after
the hour.

zéro heure vingt (0 h. 20)	12:20 A. M.
douze heures vingt (12 h. 20)	12:20 P. M.
une heure trente (1 h. 30)	1:30 A. M.
treize heures trente (13 h. 30)	1:30 P. M.
six heures cinquante (6 h. 50)	6:50 A. M.
dix-huit heures cinquante (18 h. 50)	6:50 P. M.
huit heures quarante-cinq (8 h. 45)	8:45 A. M.
vingt heures quarante-cinq (20 h. 45)	8:45 P. M.

B. Time in conversation.

To express the quarter-hours, you say **et quart, et demie, moins le quart.** EX.: **huit heures et quart** (8:15), **neuf heures et demie** (9:30), **onze heures moins le quart** (10:45).

To express minutes between the hour and the half hour following, you say **quatre heures cinq** (4:05), **quatre heures vingt-cinq** (4:25), etc.

But to express minutes between the half hour and the following hour, you measure back from the next hour: **cinq heures moins dix** (4:50), **cinq heures moins vingt** (4:40).

Many people use official time even in conversation.

58 Measurement.

A. Distance.

The standard unit of linear measure in the metric system, which is used in France — and most other countries, is **le mètre** (39.37 inches). A **kilomètre** is 1000 **mètres** (.62 mile).

A quelle distance le bateau était-il de la rive? (*How far . . . ?*)
Il était à quelques mètres de la rive.
Versailles est à 18 kilomètres de Paris.
Quelle est la longueur de la Seine? (*How long . . . ?*)
La Seine a 800 kilomètres de long.
Quelle est la largeur de la Seine à Paris? (*How wide . . . ?*)
A Paris la Seine a une centaine de mètres de large.

Note that in asking and answering questions in which distance, height, width, etc. are involved, you say: A quelle distance est Versailles de Paris? — Versailles est à 18 kilomètres de Paris.

Quelle est la longueur de la Loire?	— Elle **a** presque 1000 kilomètres **de long.**
Quelle est la hauteur de la tour Eiffel?	— Elle **a** 300 mètres **de haut.**
Quelle est la largeur de la Seine?	— Elle **a** 100 mètres **de large** à Paris.

B. Weight.

Le gramme is the standard unit of weight in the metric system. **Un kilogramme** = 1000 **grammes** (2.2 pounds). **Une livre** = (1/2 kilo) 500 **grammes.** 1/2 **livre** = 250 **grammes.**

Combien pesez-vous? — Je pèse 70 kilos.
Donnez-moi une livre de café.

C. Volume.

Le litre is the standard unit of volume in the metric system. **Un litre** = 1000 **centimètres cubes** (.9 quart).

Donnez-moi dix litres d'essence.
Il a bu un demi-litre de bière.

59 Ordinal numbers **(premier, deuxième, etc.).**

premier, première	huitième
second, seconde; deuxième	neuvième
troisième	dixième
quatrième	onzième
cinquième	douzième
sixième	vingtième
septième	vingt et unième, etc.

A. Only premier and second have feminine forms.

B. The word **an** (year) is used with cardinal numbers but **année** is used with ordinals: **cinq ans** five years; **la cinquième année** the fifth year.

Il a passé deux ans à Paris. Il est revenu au commencement de sa troisième année.

Note that the words **année, journée, matinée, soirée** often express a nuance of duration — as opposed to **an, jour, matin, soir:**

Il fait beau ce soir. Nous allons passer la soirée en ville.

C. **Premier** is used to refer to the first of a series of rulers, but the cardinal numbers are used to refer to others in the series: **François premier, Henri II (deux), Louis XIV, Napoléon III.**

D. To refer to a century you use ordinal numbers: **le vingtième siècle. Au dix-huitième siècle** *In the 18th century.*

60 Fractions.

Ordinal numbers are used in fractions except for **la moitié** (1/2), **le tiers** (1/3), **le quart** (1/4).

Thus, you say: **un cinquième** (1/5), **un vingtième** (1/20), etc. EX.: $2/3 + 1/12 = 9/12$ (3/4) is read: **deux tiers plus un douzième font neuf douzièmes (trois quarts).**

I. EXERCICES D'APPLICATION.

A. Mettez chacune des phrases suivantes au futur :

1. Je déjeune à midi. **2.** Je finis à cinq heures. **3.** Je vends ma voiture la semaine prochaine. **4.** Je vais en Europe cet été. **5.** Il est à l'heure. **6.** Il n'a pas le temps. **7.** Il y a de la place dans l'auto. **8.** Pouvez-vous m'envoyer votre adresse? **9.** Que faites-vous ce week-end? **10.** Il m'envoie son adresse. **11.** Je vois mes amis cet après-midi. **12.** Il vient à quatre heures. **13.** Il peut le faire. **14.** Je fais des courses demain.

B. Répétez les phrases suivantes, en remplaçant le futur par l'impératif :

1. Vous vous lèverez de bonne heure demain matin. **2.** Vous irez à la bibliothèque à huit heures. **3.** Vous passerez la matinée entière à travailler. **4.** Vous rentrerez à midi. **5.** Vous déjeunerez comme d'habitude. **6.** Vous vous reposerez un peu après le déjeuner. **7.** Vous travaillerez bien l'après-midi. **8.** Après le dîner vous vous mettrez au lit de bonne heure. **9.** Vous serez bien sage.

II. Répondez en français :

1. Où irez-vous pour le week-end? **2.** Quand partirez-vous? **3.** Combien de temps serez-vous encore ici? **4.** Si vous avez le temps, viendrez-vous me voir dimanche? **5.** Y aura-t-il une place dans la voiture des Frazer? **6.** Est-ce que Madame Frazer viendra chercher Jean? **7.** Sera-t-il prêt quand les Frazer viendront le chercher? **8.** Quand vous irez à Paris, monterez-vous en haut de la tour Eiffel? **9.** Ferez-vous beaucoup d'emplettes quand vous serez en France? **10.** Connaissez-vous la pièce de Shakespeare qui s'appelle en français *Comme il vous plaira?*

III. SUBSTITUTIONS.

A. Répétez les phrases suivantes, en substituant les mots indiqués:

1. Jean est [toujours] à Paris.
encore/ de retour/ aussi/ actuellement

2. Il est [sans doute] allé à Saint-Cloud.
probablement/ déjà/ peut-être/ sûrement

3. Il n'a [peut-être] pas encore acheté de cadeaux.
sans doute/ évidemment/ malheureusement/ sûrement

4. Les Frazer ne partiront sûrement pas [avant neuf heures].
avant demain matin/ avant lundi
prochain/ avant midi/ avant ce soir

5. Il a passé [plusieurs] jours à la campagne.
une dizaine de/ une douzaine de/ une quinzaine de/ une vingtaine de

B. Répétez les phrases suivantes, en remplaçant **bien** par **mieux que nous:**

EX.: — Il travaille bien.
— **Il travaille mieux que nous.**

1. Il étudie bien. **2.** Il nage bien. **3.** Il parle bien. **4.** Elle conduit (*drives*) bien.
5. Elle danse bien.

C. Répétez les phrases suivantes, en remplaçant **bon (bonne)** par **le meilleur (la meilleure) . . . du quartier:**

EX.: — C'est un bon restaurant.
— **C'est le meilleur restaurant du quartier.**

1. C'est un bon magasin. **2.** C'est une bonne épicerie. **3.** C'est un bon café. **4.** C'est une bonne cuisinière. **5.** C'est un bon cuisinier. **6.** C'est un bon médecin.

D. Répétez les phrases suivantes, en substituant les mots indiqués:

1. Elle va [mal].
très mal/ plus mal/ de plus en plus mal/ de
mal en pis/ bien/ mieux/ de mieux en mieux

FUTUR/ IMPÉRATIF/ ADVERBES/ NOMBRES

2. J'aime mieux [me reposer que travailler].

me coucher que me lever/ m'amuser que travailler/ aller
au cinéma que regarder la télévision/ me promener que
rester à la maison/ aller au restaurant que faire la cuisine

IV. Demandez à quelqu'un:

1. la distance de Paris à Versailles.   **2.** la distance de New York à Chicago.
3. à quelle distance était le bateau.   **4.** la longueur de la Seine.   **5.** la longueur
du Mississippi.   **6.** la largeur de la Seine à Paris.   **7.** la hauteur de la tour
Eiffel.   **8.** la hauteur des tours de Notre-Dame.

V. Répondez aux questions suivantes:

A. Employez . . . **est à** . . . avec la distance indiquée.

1. A quelle distance est Paris de Versailles? (18 kilomètres)   **2.** A quelle distance est
New York de Chicago? (environ 1500 kilomètres)   **3.** A quelle distance était le bateau
de la rive au moment de l'accident? (à quelques mètres)

B. Employez **a** . . . **de long, de large, de haut** avec la distance indiquée.

1. Quelle est la longueur de la Seine? (800 kilomètres)   **2.** Quelle est la longueur du
Mississippi? (4620 kilomètres)   **3.** Quelle est la largeur de la Seine à Paris? (100 mètres)
4. Quelle est la hauteur de la tour Eiffel? (300 mètres)   **5.** Quelle est la hauteur des
tours de Notre-Dame? (75 mètres)

VI. Lisez rapidement en français:

(A)

1, 11; 2, 12, 20, 22; 3, 13, 30, 33; 4, 14, 40, 44; 5, 15, 50, 55; 6, 16, 60, 66, 76; 7,
17, 70, 77, 67; 8, 18, 88, 84, 44, 24; 9, 19, 90, 99, 89, 49, 79; 100, 101, 105, 150,
155; 160, 165, 175, 180, 185, 195.

(B)

Le 1er mai, le 15 juin, le 5 janvier, le 29 juillet, le 17 avril, le 13 mars, le 1er août,
le 2 février.

(C)

Louis XII, Napoléon Ier, Henri IV, Louis XIV, François Ier, Napoléon III,
Charles X, Louis XVI.

1815, 1850, 1875, 1895; 1795, 1775, 1765; 1745, 1845, 1945; 1955, 1975, 1985.

10 h. 20; 12h. 52; 14 h. 30; 20 h. 45; 23 h. 59; 0 h. 10; 1 h. 27.

VII. Dites en français:

1. In May. **2.** In the month of May. **3.** In 1850. **4.** In the 19th century.
5. In 1970. **6.** In the 20th century. **7.** This year **(Cette année)**. **8.** Next
year. **9.** Last year (*two ways*). **10.** Two years. **11.** The first year. **12.** The
second year. **13.** Two years from now **(Dans deux ans)**. **14.** How far is it
from Rouen to Paris?

L'Agriculture au Moyen Age

À CHENONCEAUX

Jean et ses amis passent la journée à Chenonceaux. Ils viennent de visiter l'intérieur du château, construit au XVIᵉ siècle et qui est un des monuments les plus élégants de la Renaissance française. En sortant, ils échangent leurs impressions.

John and his friends are spending the day at Chenonceaux. They have just gone through the château, built in the sixteenth century, and one of the most elegant monuments of the French Renaissance. As they come out, they exchange their impressions.

HÉLÈNE. —¹J'adore ce château! ²Si j'avais à choisir entre tous ceux que nous avons vus, je choisirais celui-ci. ³Ce qui me plaît surtout, c'est qu'il est encore habitable.

HELEN. —¹I am crazy about this château! ²If I had to choose among all those we have seen, I would choose this one. ³What pleases me especially is that it is still livable.

HENRI. —⁴Voudrais-tu y habiter?

HENRY. —⁴Would you like to live in it?

HÉLÈNE. —⁵Cela dépend. ⁶Si j'avais tout ce qu'il faut, je serais très heureuse ici. ⁷Bien entendu, il faudrait avoir de nombreux serviteurs: cuisiniers, jardiniers, etc., recevoir des quantités d'invités . . .

HELEN. —⁵That depends. ⁶If I had everything that is needed, I should be very happy here. ⁷Of course you would have to have numerous servants: cooks, gardeners, and so on, have lots of guests . . .

JEAN. —⁸Comme les rois d'autrefois, par exemple . . . ⁹En un mot, Hélène, tu voudrais mener un genre de vie qui, je le crains, n'existe plus.

JOHN. —⁸Like the kings of olden times, for example . . . ⁹In a word, Helen, you would like to lead a life which, I fear, no longer exists.

HÉLÈNE. —[10]Pourtant, le château a été habité jusqu'à une date récente, n'est-ce pas?

JEAN. —[11]Mais oui, par les Menier, qui en sont toujours propriétaires. [12]C'est pour cela que le château de Chenonceaux est en meilleur état que celui de Chambord, [13]qui depuis des siècles reste plus ou moins vide.

HENRI. —[14]Personnellement, je n'échangerais pas Chambord pour Chenonceaux. [15]Vue à distance, la façade de Chambord est inoubliable.

MME FRAZER. —[16]Voyons, mes enfants, il ne s'agit pas d'échanger un château pour un autre. [17]Ni l'un ni l'autre ne vous appartient.

HÉLÈNE. —[18]Quelque chose m'intrigue: [19]pourquoi a-t-on construit une partie du château au milieu d'une rivière?

JEAN. —[20]Rien de plus simple: [21]Catherine de Médicis a décidé que si elle faisait construire cette galerie à deux étages au-dessus de la rivière, [22]elle pourrait passer de l'autre côté sans sortir de chez elle.

HÉLÈNE. —[23]Tiens, c'est une idée! [24]Je n'aurais jamais pensé à cela!

HELEN. —[10]However, the château was lived in until recently, wasn't it?

JOHN. —[11]Oh yes, by the Menier family (the Meniers), who still own it. [12]That is why the château of Chenonceaux is in better condition than (the one of) Chambord, [13]which has remained more or less empty for centuries.

HENRY. —[14]Personally, I would not exchange Chambord for Chenonceaux. [15]Seen from a distance, the façade of Chambord is unforgettable.

MRS. FRAZER. —[16]Come, children, it is not a question of exchanging one château for another. [17]Neither of them belongs to you.

HELEN. —[18]Something intrigues me: [19]why did they build a part of the château in the middle of a river?

JOHN. —[20]Nothing (is) easier: [21]Catherine de Medici decided that if she had that two-story wing built over the river, [22]she could cross the river without leaving the house.

HELEN. —[23]Well! That's an idea. [24]I would never have thought of that!

I. SUBSTITUTIONS. Répétez les phrases suivantes, en substituant les mots indiqués:

1. Ils passent [la journée] à Chenonceaux.
   la soirée/ la matinée/ deux jours/ le week-end

2. [En sortant,] ils échangent leurs impressions.

En sortant du château/ En quittant le château/ En
partant du château/ En se promenant dans les jardins

3. Il faudrait avoir [de nombreux serviteurs].

des cuisiniers/ des jardiniers/ des domestiques/
énormément d'argent/ une grosse fortune

4. Vue [à distance] la façade de Chambord est inoubliable.

de loin/ du parc/ de près/ du côté de
la forêt/ de l'autre côté de la rivière

5. Il ne s'agit pas d'échanger [un château] pour un autre.

un palais/ un tableau/ une propriété/ une maison de campagne

6. Ni l'un ni l'autre [ne vous appartient].

n'est à vous/ n'est à vendre/ ne vous
convient/ ne peut vous appartenir

7. Elle pourrait [passer de l'autre côté] sans sortir de chez elle.

passer l'été/ traverser la rivière/ regarder
la rivière/ voir passer les bateaux

8. Je n'aurais jamais pensé [à cela].

à construire cette galerie/ à faire construire cette galerie/
à choisir cet endroit/ à bâtir un château sur une rivière

II. Remplacez le passé composé du verbe par le passé composé de **faire**
et l'infinitif:

EX.: — Elle a construit le château.
— **Elle a fait construire le château.**

1. Catherine de Médicis a ajouté une galerie au château. **2.** Elle a dessiné les jardins.
3. Elle y a planté toute sorte de fleurs. **4.** Elle a bâti cette galerie. **5.** Elle a construit
ce pont. **6.** Elle a planté beaucoup d'arbres.

III. Répondez aux questions suivantes, en employant **ne . . . ni l'un ni
l'autre:**

1. Connaissez-vous le château de Chambord et celui de Chenonceaux? **2.** Ces
deux châteaux sont-ils habités à l'heure actuelle? **3.** Voudriez-vous être le
propriétaire de Chambord ou de Chenonceaux? **4.** S'il s'agissait de choisir
entre les deux, lequel choisiriez-vous?

IV. Combinez deux phrases en une seule, en employant **ne . . . ni . . . ni:**

EX.: — Je n'ai pas de frères. Je n'ai pas de sœurs.
— **Je n'ai ni frères ni sœurs.**

1. Je n'ai pas vu Chenonceaux. Je n'ai pas vu Chambord. **2.** Il n'a pas de père. Il n'a pas de mère. **3.** Nous ne connaissons pas son père. Nous ne connaissons pas sa mère. **4.** Je n'ai pas lu ce roman. Je n'ai pas lu cette pièce. **5.** Je n'ai pas mangé de pain. Je n'ai pas mangé de beurre.

V. Combinez deux phrases en une seule, en employant la préposition **à** et l'infinitif:

EX.: J'ai passé l'après-midi. J'ai visité le château.
J'ai passé l'après-midi à visiter le château.

1. J'ai passé la matinée. J'ai fait des courses. **2.** Nous avons passé la soirée. Nous avons joué aux cartes. **3.** J'ai passé deux heures. J'ai réparé ma voiture. **4.** J'ai passé toute la journée. J'ai travaillé chez moi. **5.** J'ai passé toute la nuit. J'ai écrit mon rapport (*term paper*). **6.** Nous avons passé toute l'année. Nous avons voyagé. **7.** Ils ont passé le week-end. Ils n'ont rien fait. **8.** Marie a passé l'après-midi. Elle a nettoyé sa maison.

VI. Répondez en français:

1. Quel château Jean et ses amis viennent-ils de visiter? **2.** Que font-ils en sortant? **3.** Quand ce château a-t-il été construit? **4.** Qu'est-ce qu'Hélène pense du château? **5.** Lequel des châteaux qu'elle a vus choisirait-elle? **6.** Pourquoi Chenonceaux lui plaît-il surtout? **7.** Voudrait-elle y habiter? **8.** Serait-elle heureuse si elle y habitait? **9.** De quoi aurait-elle besoin? **10.** Quand le château a-t-il été habité? **11.** Qui en sont actuellement les propriétaires? **12.** Connaissez-vous un autre château de la Renaissance? **13.** Pourquoi le château de Chambord n'est-il pas en aussi bon état que celui de Chenonceaux? **14.** Lequel des deux châteaux Henri préfère-t-il? **15.** Échangerait-il Chambord pour Chenonceaux? **16.** Combien d'étages a la galerie au-dessus de la rivière? **17.** Qui a fait construire cette galerie? **18.** Pourquoi Catherine de Médicis l'a-t-elle fait construire? **19.** Que dit Hélène à propos de l'idée qu'a eue Catherine de Médicis?

VII. Demandez à quelqu'un:

1. quand le château de Chenonceaux a été construit. **2.** qui l'a fait construire. **3.** où se trouve Chenonceaux. **4.** ce qu'Hélène pense du château. **5.** si elle

voudrait y habiter. **6.** à quelle condition elle voudrait y habiter. **7.** s'il y a longtemps que le château a été habité. **8.** à qui il appartient à l'heure actuelle. **9.** pourquoi le château de Chenonceaux est en meilleur état que celui de Chambord. **10.** où se trouve la galerie du château de Chenonceaux. **11.** combien d'étages a cette galerie. **12.** pourquoi elle a été construite.

VIII. THÈME.

The château of Chenonceaux was built in the first part of the 16th century by a rich financier. Later, it belonged to Diane de Poitiers, the beautiful lady who was so often praised **(célébrée si souvent)** by the artists and poets of the French Renaissance. She had a bridge built over the Cher to be able to cross it easily when she wanted to go hunting. After the death of King Henri II, his widow Catherine de Médicis, who liked neither the château of Chaumont where she lived nor Diane de Poitiers, forced the latter **(celle-ci)** to exchange Chenonceaux for Chaumont. The queen had beautiful gardens designed on the other side of the river and a double gallery built on the bridge. The splendid festivities **(fêtes)** she gave at Chenonceaux have remained famous to our day **(jusqu'à nos jours)**.

IX. Mettez les phrases suivantes au passé, en remplaçant le présent de l'indicatif par le **passé composé** ou l'**imparfait**, selon le cas :

A la fin du Moyen Age, à Chenonceaux, il y a là, au bord de la rivière, une forteresse féodale. Elle appartient à la famille de Marle, dont le nom reste à une tour, la tour de Marle. Cette famille est en train de se ruiner, et un riche bourgeois, Thomas Bohier, receveur des finances, surveille de près sa ruine (*its bankrupcy*). Il profite de ses difficultés financières pour acheter peu à peu ses terres. Puis il finit par mettre la main sur le château, qu'il fait démolir et qu'il remplace par l'admirable édifice actuel, construit sur la rivière à l'endroit où se trouvent les restes d'un vieux moulin.

Thomas Bohier n'a cependant guère l'occasion de profiter de son habileté, car il meurt peu après en Italie, où il accompagne son maître, le roi François Ier.

Conditionnel/ Infinitif/ Participe présent

61   Uses of the conditional.

A. The conditional tense is used in the result clause of conditional sentences that describe what *would* happen if a given condition *were* fulfilled. The if-clause in this type of conditional sentence is always in the *imparfait* and the result is in the *conditional*.

Si j'avais à choisir, **je choisirais** Chenonceaux.
Si j'avais tout ce qu'il faut, **je serais** très heureuse ici.

Sometimes an if-clause in the *imparfait* is implied rather than expressed as in English:

Bien entendu, **il faudrait** avoir de nombreux serviteurs.
En un mot, **vous voudriez** mener un genre de vie qui n'existe plus.
Je n'échangerais pas Chambord pour Chenonceaux.

B. In indirect discourse that depends upon a verb in a past tense, the conditional is used to express future action.

Nous lui avons dit que **nous irions** faire des emplettes cet après-midi.
Roger m'a dit qu'**il irait** au Louvre demain.

Note that this is parallel to English usage. What Roger said was: I shall go to the Louvre tomorrow. This could be reported in direct or in indirect discourse.

DIRECT: Roger m'a dit: «J'irai au Louvre demain.» (*I shall go . . .*)
INDIRECT: Roger m'a dit qu'il irait au Louvre demain. (*. . . that he would go . . .*)

C. The conditional is sometimes used to report a rumor or a conjecture.

D'après ce que j'ai entendu dire, les Duplessis **seraient** à la campagne.
Il y a longtemps que je n'ai pas vu Roger. **Serait-il** malade? (*Is he perhaps sick?*)

D. The conditional is sometimes used instead of the present tense simply for politeness.

Pourrais-je vous demander l'heure?
Pourriez-vous me prêter votre voiture?
Je voudrais vous demander un conseil.
Je ne **dirais** pas qu'il a tort.

62 Verbs followed by infinitives.

A. Verbs + **de** + infinitive.

The commonest verbs and verbal expressions which may be followed by the preposition **de** and an infinitive are:

> **achever de,** *to finish;* **cesser de,** *to cease, stop;* **se charger de,** *to take care of;* **conseiller de,** *to advise;* **décider de,** *to decide;* **défendre de,** *to forbid;* **demander de,** *to ask;* **dire de,** *to tell;* **s'efforcer de,** *to try hard;* **empêcher de,** *to prevent;* **essayer de,** *to try;* **s'excuser de,** *to apologize;* **faire bien de,** *to be right;* **finir de,** *to finish;* **forcer de,** *to force;* **se garder de,** *to avoid;* **juger bon de,** *to see fit to;* **manquer de,** *to fail to;* **oublier de,** *to forget;* **permettre de,** *to permit, make possible;* **prier de,** *to request, beg;* **promettre de,** *to promise;* **proposer de,** *to propose, suggest;* **refuser de,** *to refuse;* **regretter de,** *to regret, be sorry;* **remercier de,** *to thank;* **risquer de,** *to risk;* **suffire de,** *to suffice;* **tâcher de,** *to try;* **il suffit de,** *it is sufficient,* **venir de,** *to have just . . .*

Madame Frazer **a décidé d'**inviter Jean.
Il regretterait de les déranger.
Ils viennent de visiter le château.
Elle lui a demandé de les accompagner.
Elle l'a prié de les accompagner.
Il suffit de partir à huit heures. (*Leaving at eight o'clock is early enough.*)

B. Verbs + **à** + infinitive.

The commonest verbs and verbal expressions which may be followed by the preposition **à** and an infinitive are:

> **aider à,** *to help;* **apprendre à,** *to learn;* **s'attendre à,** *to expect;* **avoir à,** *to have to;* **avoir de la peine à,** *to have trouble in;* **chercher à,** *to try;* **commencer à,** *to begin;* **consentir à,** *to consent, agree;* **continuer à,** *to continue;* **enseigner à,** *to teach;* **s'habituer à,** *to get used to;* **hésiter à,** *to hesitate;* **inviter à,** *to invite;* **se mettre à,** *to begin;* **parvenir à,** *to succeed in;* **renoncer à,** *to give up;* **réussir à,** *to succeed in;* **tenir à,** *to insist upon, to feel urged to.*

Madame Frazer **a invité** Jean **à** aller en Touraine.
Il n'**hésite** pas **à** accepter.
Il tient à revoir les châteaux de la Loire.
Il ne **s'attendait** pas **à** les revoir.
Il n'**a** pas grand-chose **à** faire.
Il s'est habitué à voyager.

C. Verbs + infinitive alone.

The commonest verbs and verbal expressions which may take an infinitive without a preposition are:

aimer, *to like;* **aimer mieux,** *to prefer;* **aller,** *to go;* **avoir beau,** *to . . . in vain;* **compter,** *to count on;* **croire,** *to think;* **désirer,** *to want;* **devoir,** *to be supposed to, to have to;* **espérer,** *to hope;* **être censé,** *to be supposed to;* **falloir (il faut),** *be necessary;* **laisser,** *to allow, let;* **oser,** *to dare;* **penser,** *to expect;* **pouvoir,** *to be able;* **préférer,** *to prefer;* **savoir,** *to know how;* **sembler,** *to seem;* **il vaut autant,** *it is just as well;* **il vaut mieux,** *it is better;* **venir,** *to come;* **vouloir,** *to want to.*

Note also **J'ai failli** with infinitive (*I almost . . .*).

Il aimait mieux monter en haut de la tour Eiffel.
Combien de temps **comptez-vous** rester à Paris?
Nous viendrons vous chercher à votre hôtel.
Il vaut mieux partir de bonne heure.
Il a failli manquer son train. (*He almost missed his train.*)

The verbs **entendre,** *to hear;* **envoyer,** *to send;* **faire,** *to have something done;* **voir,** *to see,* which also take an infinitive without a preposition, should be studied carefully because their English equivalent is likely to mislead one.

J'ai entendu dire cela.	I have heard that *said.*
Il a fait construire ce château.	He had that château *built.*
Je vais vous **faire voir** le service.	I am going to *show* you the set.
Nous avons envoyé chercher les journaux.	We *sent for* the papers.
Nous avons vu passer l'auto des Frazer.	We *saw* the Frazer's car go by.

63 Use of prepositions (other than **de** and **à**) with infinitives.

A. The present infinitive is used after **par, pour, sans,** and such expressions as **avant de, afin de** (*in order to*), **loin de, à condition de, de peur de, au lieu de, de manière à.**

Madame Frazer et Hélène sont venues en ville **pour faire** des emplettes.
Elles ont commencé **par acheter** des parfums.
Avant de finir leurs courses, elles ont rencontré Jean.
Il a accepté **sans hésiter. Loin d'être** trop occupé, il est libre comme l'air.

Note that in English, the present participle (not the infinitive) is used after prepositions: *after leaving, without hesitating, before buying,* etc.

B. The perfect infinitive is used after **après.**

1. Forms of perfect infinitive.

REGULAR VERBS: **avoir donné,** *to have given,** *having given;* **avoir fini,** *having finished;* **avoir vendu,** *having sold.*
AUXILIARY VERBS: **avoir eu,** *having had;* **avoir été,** *having been.*
VERBS CONJUGATED WITH **être: être allé,** *having gone.*
REFLEXIVE VERBS: **s'être dépêché,** *having hurried;* **s'être couché,** *having gone to bed.*

2. Examples.

Après avoir passé quelques mois au Vénézuéla, Jean est parti pour l'Égypte.
Après être allé en Égypte, il est rentré à Paris.
Après s'être reposé, il retournera en Afrique.

64 Present participle with preposition **en.**

A. Forms.

The present participle of verbs may be found by adding the ending **-ant** to the stem of the first person plural of the present indicative (nous **all — ons: all — ant;** nous **finiss — ons: finiss — ant**), except for the verbs **avoir, être,** and **savoir** whose present participles are, respectively, **ayant, étant,** and **sachant.**

B. Use.

The present participle after **en** expresses:

(1) an action that immediately precedes another action.

En sortant, ils échangent leurs impressions. (*On going out . . .*)
En quittant Paris, elle est allée en Bretagne. (*On leaving* Paris . . .)

---

*Note that in English, the perfect participle (not the perfect infinitive) is used after the preposition AFTER: after having spent, gone, rested, etc.

(2) an action that takes place at the same time as another action:

En attendant Marie, ils parlent de leurs affaires. (*While waiting . . .*)

Tout en stresses the simultaneousness of the two actions:

Tout en attendant Marie, ils parlent de leurs affaires.
Tout en se promenant, ils parlent de leurs projets.

(3) an action upon which a second action depends.

En partant à huit heures, nous arriverons à Orléans à midi. (*By leaving . . .*)
C'est en parlant qu'on apprend à parler. (*By talking . . .*)

I. SUBSTITUTIONS. Répétez les phrases suivantes, en substituant les mots indiqués:

1. J'ai demandé [un chèque] à mon père.
   de l'argent/ des conseils/ une voiture/ une motocyclette

2. Je lui ai demandé [un chèque].
   de l'argent/ des conseils/ une voiture/ une motocyclette

3. [Je l'ai] demandé à mon père.
   Je les ai/ J'en ai/ J'en ai . . . deux/ J'en ai . . . plusieurs

4. J'ai prié mon père [de m'envoyer un chèque].
   de m'envoyer de l'argent/ de m'acheter une voiture/ de m'acheter une motocyclette/ de m'acheter un bateau à voile

5. J'ai failli [manquer mon train].
   être en retard/ tomber/ me faire mal/ mourir de faim

6. Il a renoncé à [aller en Touraine].
   voir d'autres châteaux/ visiter Chaumont/ faire ce voyage/ revoir Chambord

II. EXERCICES D'APPLICATION.

A. Complétez les phrases suivantes, en employant **monter en haut de la tour Eiffel** et en employant ou non une préposition:

EX.: — Henri décide . . .
— **Henri décide de monter en haut de la tour Eiffel.**

1. Henri tient . . . 2. Il voudrait . . . 3. Il n'hésite pas . . . 4. Il n'a pas hésité . . .

5. Il s'attend . . . **6.** Mme Frazer ne veut pas . . . **7.** Elle a refusé . . . **8.** Elle se garderait bien . . . **9.** Elle hésiterait . . . **10.** Elle n'a pas promis . . . **11.** Elle ne propose pas . . . **12.** Elle ne voudrait pas . . .

B. Complétez les phrases suivantes, en employant **partir de bonne heure:**

EX.: — Henri tient . . .
    — **Henri tient à partir de bonne heure.**

1. Il décide . . . **2.** Il s'efforce . . . **3.** Il essaye . . . **4.** Il s'attend . . . **5.** Il ne renonce pas . . . **6.** Il propose . . . **7.** Il a proposé . . . **8.** Il n'a pas renoncé . . .

C. Complétez les phrases suivantes, en employant **partir à six heures:**

EX.: — Il faut . . .
    — **Il faut partir à six heures.**

1. Il faudra . . . **2.** Il faudrait . . . **3.** Il suffit . . . **4.** Il suffirait . . . **5.** Il suffira . . .
6. Il vaudrait mieux . . . **7.** Il vaut autant . . .

III. Combinez deux phrases en une seule, en employant **en** et le participe présent:

EX.: — Ils sont sortis. Ils ont échangé leurs impressions.
    — **En sortant, ils ont échangé leurs impressions.**

1. Ils ont quitté la maison. Ils ont vu l'accident. **2.** Ils attendaient l'avion. Ils ont visité l'aéroport. **3.** Ils ont dîné. Ils ont échangé leurs impressions. **4.** Je me promenais dans la rue. J'ai rencontré mon cousin. **5.** Nous partirons à huit heures. Nous arriverons à Orléans à midi. **6.** Nous avons visité le Louvre. Nous avons vu la Vénus de Milo. **7.** Je lui écrirai aujourd'hui. J'aurai sa réponse après-demain. **8.** Il se lèvera de bonne heure. Il ne manquera pas son train.

IV. Combinez deux phrases en une seule, en employant **après** et l'infinitif passé:

EX.: — Ils ont visité Paris. Ils sont allés en Touraine.
    — **Après avoir visité Paris, ils sont allés en Touraine.**

1. Ils ont vu Notre-Dame. Ils sont allés au Louvre. **2.** Ils ont passé quelques jours à l'hôpital. Ils sont rentrés chez eux. **3.** Elles sont allées à la banque. Elles ont fait des emplettes. **4.** J'ai fini mon travail. Je suis allé prendre une tasse de café. **5.** J'ai lu *l'Avare.* J'irai voir la pièce à la Comédie-Française. **6.** Il s'est cassé le bras. Il n'a pas pu conduire son auto.

V. Répétez les phrases suivantes en employant les expressions indiquées:

1. Il a quitté la Touraine sans [aller à] Chambord.
   voir/ visiter/ essayer de visiter/ passer par

2. Ils sont allés en Touraine au lieu de [rester à Paris].
   visiter Londres/ aller en Bretagne/ retourner en Suisse/ rentrer aux États-Unis

3. [En quittant] Chambord, ils ont visité Blois.
   Après avoir quitté/ Après être allés à/ Avant d'aller à/ Après

VI. Répondez en français:

1. Seriez-vous content d'habiter dans un grand château? 2. Si vous aviez à choisir, choisiriez-vous Chambord ou Chenonceaux? 3. Si Chenonceaux était à vous, l'échangeriez-vous pour Chambord? 4. Si on habitait dans un château de la Renaissance, qu'est-ce qu'il faudrait avoir? 5. Si vous aviez une grosse fortune, achèteriez-vous une grande maison de campagne? 6. Si vous aviez une grande maison, voudriez-vous recevoir quantité d'invités? 7. Voudriez-vous mener le genre de vie des gens riches qui vivaient au seizième siècle? 8. Aimeriez-vous faire construire une maison au milieu d'une rivière? 9. Si vous alliez en France, iriez-vous visiter tous les châteaux de la Touraine? 10. Diriez-vous que ces châteaux sont trop grands pour la vie moderne?

Catherine de Médicis (1519–1589)

Le château de Chambord

AU CHÂTEAU DE BLOIS

*Continuant leur visite de la Tou-
raine, Jean et ses amis arrivent à Blois.
Le château a été construit à différentes
époques et dans trois styles différents:
la partie la plus ancienne par Louis
XII, une autre par François premier,
et la troisième par Gaston d'Orléans,
frère de Louis XIII.*

LE GUIDE (*d'une voix monotone*). —[1]Nous
sommes maintenant, messieurs
dames, dans le cabinet de Catherine de Médicis.* [2]Remarquez
la décoration en bois sculpté. [3]Ce
panneau-ci cache plusieurs armoires secrètes, où la reine conservait des papiers, des bijoux,
même des poisons, dit-on. [4]Il y
avait plus de deux cents panneaux, et quatre seulement d'entre eux étaient mobiles. [5]Ceux-ci
ressemblaient tellement à ceux-là
qu'il était impossible de les distinguer, [6]même en les examinant
de près . . .

(*Le guide et les visiteurs quittent le
cabinet de la reine.*)

*Continuing their trip to the Tou-
raine, John and his friends arrive in
Blois. The château was built in three
different periods and in three different
styles: the oldest part by Louis XII,
another by Francis the First, and the
third by Gaston d'Orléans, who was the
brother of Louis XIII.*

THE GUIDE (*in a monotone*). —[1]We are
now, ladies and gentlemen, in the
office of Catherine de Medici.
[2]Note the decoration in carved
wood. [3]This panel conceals several secret cupboards in which the
queen kept papers, jewels, even
poisons, they say. [4]There were
more than two hundred panels
and only four of them would open
(were movable). [5]The latter were
so much like the stationary ones
(the former) that it was impossible
to tell them apart, [6]even when
examining them closely . . .

(*The guide and the visitors leave the
office of the queen.*)

---

* Femme de Henri II, roi de France de 1547 à 1559.

HENRI. —[7]Qu'est-ce qu'elle faisait des poisons qu'elle conservait dans son armoire?

HÉLÈNE. —[8]C'était peut-être pour les gens qu'elle n'aimait pas!

MME FRAZER. —[9]Ne dites pas trop de mal de Catherine de Médicis. [10]J'ai entendu dire qu'elle valait mieux que sa réputation...

HÉLÈNE. —[11]La plupart des châteaux que nous avons visités sont vides. [12]Autrefois, ils devaient être meublés. [13]Que sont devenus les meubles?

JEAN. —[14]Même autrefois, les châteaux n'avaient pas beaucoup de meubles, [15]sauf ceux qui servaient de résidence habituelle à quelque grand personnage. [16]Les meubles qui restaient ont disparu pendant la Révolution.

HÉLÈNE. —[17]Je voudrais bien prendre une photo de ces fenêtres ornées de salamandres.* [18]Mais j'ai laissé mon appareil dans la voiture. [19]Veux-tu bien me prêter le tien?

JEAN. —[20]Mais oui. [21]Le mien ne vaut sans doute pas le tien. [22]Mais il fera l'affaire.

HÉNÈNE. —[23]Je ne sais pas m'en servir.

JEAN. —[24]Rien de plus simple. [25]Il suffit d'appuyer sur le bouton.

HENRY. —[7]What did she do with the poisons she kept in her cupboard?

HELEN. —[8]They were perhaps for the people she didn't like!

MRS. FRAZER. —[9]Don't criticize (Don't speak too much evil about) Catherine de Medici too much. [10]I have heard that she was better than her reputation...

HELEN. —[11]Most of the châteaux we have gone through (visited) are empty. [12]They must have been furnished formerly. [13]What has happened to (became of) the furniture?

JOHN. —[14]Even formerly, the châteaux didn't have much furniture, [15]except those that were used as the habitual residence of some important personage. [16]The furniture that was left disappeared during the French Revolution.

HELEN. —[17]I would certainly like to take a picture of those windows that are decorated (ornamented) with salamanders. [18]But I left my camera in the car. [19]Will you lend me yours?

JOHN. —[20]Why yes. [21]Mine is not as good as yours, no doubt. [22]But it will serve the purpose (do the job).

HELEN. —[23]I don't know how to use it.

JOHN. —[24]Nothing (is) simpler. [25]All you need do is to press the button.

---

* La salamandre était l'emblème (*m.*) de François Ier, roi de 1515 à 1547, et le porc-épic était celui de Louis XII (1498-1515).

CONVERSATION 19

I. SUBSTITUTIONS. Répétez les phrases suivantes, en substituant les mots indiqués:

1. Remarquez [la décoration en bois sculpté].
cette armoire/ ces fenêtres ornées de sala-
mandres/ cette cheminée/ ces panneaux

2. Remarquez [que ces panneaux sont mobiles].
que ceux-ci sont mobiles/ que la décoration est
en bois sculpté/ que ceux-ci ressemblent à ceux-
là/ que ces fenêtres sont ornées de salamandres

3. [Quatre] d'entre eux étaient mobiles.
Quelques-uns/ Plusieurs/ Peu/ Un certain nombre

4. J'ai entendu dire [qu'elle] valait mieux que sa réputation.
que Napoléon III/ que Marie-Antoinette/
que Louis XVI/ que Mme de Pompadour

5. Voulez-vous bien me prêter [le vôtre]?
votre appareil/ votre voiture/ la vôtre/ vos skis/ les vôtres

6. Rien de plus [simple].
facile/ commode/ utile/ confortable/ passionnant (*interesting*)

7. Il suffit [d'appuyer sur le bouton].
d'écouter le guide/ de partir avant midi/
de suivre les instructions/ de les lire de plus près

II. Répondez aux questions suivantes, en commençant par **Je ne sais pas ce qu(e)** . . .:

EX.: — Qu'est-ce qu'il est devenu?
— **Je ne sais pas ce qu'il est devenu.**

1. Qu'est-ce que les meubles sont devenus? 2. Qu'est-ce qu'ils sont devenus?
3. Qu'est-ce que Charles est devenu? 4. Qu'est-ce qu'il est devenu? 5. Que sont devenus les meubles? 6. Que sont-ils devenus? 7. Qu'est-ce que le château est devenu au moment de la Révolution française? 8. Qu'est-il devenu?

III. Répondez affirmativement en français en employant l'expression indiquée:

A. servir de (*to be used as*)

1. Le château de Blois servait-il de résidence? 2. Ce château servait-il de prison?
3. Le premier château de Versailles servait-il de château de chasse?

B. se servir de (*to use*)

1. Vous êtes-vous servi de son appareil? **2.** S'est-il servi de votre auto? **3.** Est-ce que je peux me servir de votre stylo? **4.** Savez-vous vous servir de mon appareil? **5.** Savez-vous vous en servir?

C. servir à et l'infinitif (*to be used to* or *for*)

1. Ce panneau servait-il à cacher des armoires secrètes? **2.** Ce panneau servait-il à cacher des bijoux? **3.** Ce panneau servait-il à cacher des papiers?

IV. RÉVISION: **entendre parler, entendre dire.** Répondez en français:

1. Avez-vous entendu parler des châteaux de la Loire? **2.** Avez-vous entendu dire que le château de Chenonceaux a été construit pour un financier? **3.** Avez-vous entendu parler de Diane de Poitiers? **4.** Avez-vous entendu dire que Chambord servait de château de chasse à François Ier?

V. Répondez en français:

1. Où sont le guide et les visiteurs du château? **2.** Qu'est-ce que le guide fait remarquer aux visiteurs? **3.** Que cache le panneau du cabinet? **4.** Qui était Catherine de Médicis? **5.** Que conservait-elle dans ses armoires secrètes? **6.** Combien de panneaux étaient mobiles? **7.** Combien d'autres ne l'étaient pas? **8.** Était-il possible de distinguer les uns des autres? **9.** Est-ce que Catherine de Médicis a une bonne réputation? **10.** Que dit Mme Frazer au sujet de cette réputation? **11.** La plupart des châteaux sont-ils meublés? **12.** Y avait-il autrefois des meubles dans tous les châteaux? **13.** Que sont devenus les meubles à l'époque de la Révolution? **14.** De quoi Hélène veut-elle prendre une photo? **15.** De quel roi la salamandre était-elle l'emblème? **16.** Quel était l'emblème de Louis XII? **17.** Pourquoi Hélène demande-t-elle à Jean de lui prêter son appareil? **18.** Est-ce qu'Hélène sait se servir de cet appareil? **19.** Est-il difficile de s'en servir? **20.** Que suffit-il de faire?

VI. Demandez à quelqu'un:

1. où le guide accompagne les visiteurs. **2.** ce qu'il leur fait remarquer. **3.** combien de panneaux il y avait dans le cabinet. **4.** combien d'entre eux étaient mobiles. **5.** s'il a entendu parler de Catherine de Médicis. **6.** s'il a entendu dire qu'elle a habité à Blois. **7.** si la plupart des châteaux sont meublés à l'heure actuelle. **8.** s'il reste beaucoup de meubles dans le château de Blois. **9.** ce que sont devenus les meubles. **10.** quel était l'emblème de

François premier. **11.** quel était celui de Louis XII. **12.** s'il est difficile de se servir d'un appareil photographique.

VII. THÈME.

Like several châteaux of the French Renaissance, Blois was used as a royal residence. The oldest part was built by King Louis XII. It is a charming construction of rose bricks and white stones, with a high roof and richly decorated windows. Above the doors, one may see the royal emblem, the porcupine. The part added by King Francis the First is famous for its beautiful circular staircase. It is in this part of the château that a well-known event took place in 1588, the assassination of the Duke of Guise by order of **(sur l'ordre)** King Henry III. The guide always shows the visitors the spot where the duke fell dead.

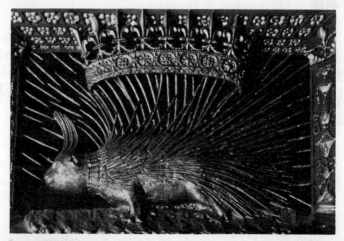

Le porc-épic, emblème de Louis XII

La salamandre, emblème de François Ier

Pronoms démonstratifs, possessifs et indéfinis

65 Demonstrative pronouns.

In English, the forms *this*, *that*, *these*, and *those* are used both as demonstrative adjectives and as demonstrative pronouns; but in French, there is one set of forms for the demonstrative adjective (see par. 25) and four sets of forms of demonstrative pronouns. Each of the four sets of forms has a clearly prescribed use.

A. The forms of **celui** with the suffix **-ci** or **-là.**

SINGULAR		PLURAL	
celui-ci m **celle-ci** f	} *this one*	**ceux-ci** m **celles-ci** f	} *these*
celui-là m **celle-là** f	} *that one*	**ceux-là** m **celles-là** f	} *those*

These forms are used to distinguish between persons or things *within a group*. They agree in gender and number with the noun to which they refer.

Remarquez ces panneaux en bois sculpté. **Celui-ci** cache plusieurs armoires secrètes.

Ceux-ci ressemblent tellement à **ceux-là** qu'il est impossible de les distinguer.

Note that while **ceux-ci** and **ceux-là** are translated *the latter and the former*, the opposition between the two is not so clear in French as it is in English. For oppositions, **les uns . . . les autres** is much more commonly used. (See par. 68, F.)

(For other uses of the suffixes **-ci** and **-là,** see par. 25.)

B. The forms of **celui** without the suffix **-ci** or **-là**.

These forms are always followed by a relative clause or a prepositional phrase.

(Les châteaux) **Ceux qui** servaient de résidence habituelle . . .
               Ceux que nous avons vus hier . . .
               Ceux dont le guide nous a parlé . . .
               Celui de la reine (*the queen's*) . . .

(Les chambres) **Celles que** nous avons visitées . . . .
               Celles de la reine . . . (*the queen's*)
               Celles où nous avons remarqué les salamandres . . .

(For **l'un** *the one*, see par. 68, F.)

C. **Cela,** *that, it;* **ceci,** *this.*

Cela (or **ça**) is used to refer (1) to something that has been said or done, or (2) to an unidentified object.

(1)

Cela dépend.	It (or that) depends.
Cela m'intéresse beaucoup.	That, (it), interests me a great deal.
Ça ne fait rien.	That (it) makes no difference.
Ça m'est égal.	It's all the same to me.
C'est **ça**.	That's it. That's right.
Comment **ça?**	How's that?

(Note that the pronoun **il** cannot be used in phrases of this type — even though we say "it" in English.)

(2)

Qu'est-ce que c'est que **ça?**	What's that?
Regardez-moi **ça**.	Just look at that.
Où avez-vous acheté **ça?**	Where did you buy that?

Ceci is used chiefly in oppositions: Donnez-moi **ceci** et gardez **cela**.

D. **Ce,** *this, that, it.*

1. **Ce** as subject of **être**.

Ce is used as subject of the verb **être** if the verb is followed by a personal pronoun, a person's name or a noun that is preceded by an article or possessive adjective.

C'est **mon père**. (*That's* my father. *He's* my father. *It's* my father.)

C'est **moi**. C'est **moi** qui ai parlé. C'est **une bonne idée**. C'est **un diplomate célèbre**. C'est **un beau château**. C'est **le château de Blois**. Ce sont **des artistes**.

C'est **vous** que je cherchais. (*You are the one* I was looking for.)

C'est **Hélène**. C'est **Madame Frazer**. Ce sont **les Frazer**.

2. **Ce** instead of **cela**.

Ce is often used instead of **cela** (see above):

C'est bien. C'est vrai. C'est impossible. C'est peu de chose, **Ce** n'est rien. **Ce** n'est pas la peine.

(For the use of **il est, elle est** with adjectives, see par. 28, C, p. 55.)

66 Possessive pronouns.

A possessive pronoun is the equivalent of a noun and the possessive adjective that modifies it. (For possessive adjectives, see par. 26.) EX.: J'ai laissé **mon appareil** dans la voiture. Voulez-vous bien me prêter **le vôtre? (Le vôtre** takes the place of **votre appareil.**) **Le mien** ne vaut sans doute pas **le vôtre** (i.e., Mon appareil ne vaut sans doute pas votre appareil.)

The forms of the possessive pronouns are:

SINGULAR		PLURAL		
MASCULINE	FEMININE	MASCULINE	FEMININE	
le mien	la mienne	les miens	les miennes	(*mine*)
le tien	la tienne	les tiens	les tiennes	(*yours*)
le sien	la sienne	les siens	les siennes	(*his, hers, its*)
le nôtre	la nôtre	les nôtres	les nôtres	(*ours*)
le vôtre	la vôtre	les vôtres	les vôtres	(*yours*)
le leur	la leur	les leurs	les leurs	(*theirs*)

Possessive pronouns agree in gender and number with the things possessed. Ex.: In answer to the question: — Avez-vous pris **des photos** (*f*)?, either Henri or Hélène could answer: — Oui, mais **les miennes** ne sont pas aussi bonnes que **les vôtres.**

The definite articles naturally have contracted forms when used with the prepositions **à** or **de:**

du mien, de la mienne, des miens, des miennes, etc.
au mien, à la mienne, aux miens, aux miennes, etc.

(un appareil) Je sais me servir **du mien,** mais je ne sais pas me servir **du vôtre.**

67 Use of preposition à to express possession.

If the subject of the verb **être** is a noun, personal pronoun, or a demonstrative pronoun, you normally express possession by using **à** with another noun or personal pronoun (stressed form) after the verb.

Cet appareil n'est pas **à moi.** *This camera is not mine.*
Est-il à vous? *Is it yours?*
Oui, **il est à moi** or Oui, **c'est à moi.** *Yes, it's mine.*
Celui-ci **est à Jean.** *This one belongs to John. This one is John's.*
Cette photo **est-elle à vous?** *Is this picture yours?*
Non, **elle est à Marie.** *No, it is Marie's. No, it belongs to Marie.*

In order to distinguish between two possible possessors, you can use the possessive pronouns **le mien, la mienne,** etc. after **C'est:**

C'est le mien. Ce n'est pas le vôtre.

But you cannot use the possessive pronouns after **Il est.**

68 Indefinite pronouns (Eng. *all, several, someone, some, others,* etc.)

For forms of indefinite *adjectives,* see par. 27, p. 54.

A. Tout, toute, tous, toutes *all; everything, everyone.*

Note that the **s** of the pronoun **tous** is always pronounced although it is silent in the adjective **tous.**

PRONOUN: Ils sont **tous** [tus] venus. *They all* came. *Everyone* came.
ADJECTIVE: **Tous** [tu] **les jours,** *every day;* **Tous** [tu] **les deux,** *both.*

B. Plusieurs *several.*

Avez-vous pris des photos? — Oui, j'en ai pris **plusieurs.**

PRONOMS DÉMONSTRATIFS, POSSESSIFS ET INDÉFINIS

C. **On** *one, someone, I, you, we, people, they.*

On y va. (*I'm* coming.)
On dîne à sept heures. (*We* dine . . .)
En France, **on** parle français. (*They* . . .)
On est venu vous voir. (*Someone* . . .)

Note that **on** is often replaced by **l'on** in written French after **où, si, et, lorsque,** and other words that end in a vowel sound.

D. **Quelqu'un, (quelqu'une), quelques-uns, quelques-unes** *someone; some, a few.*

The feminine singular is practically never used.

Quelqu'un est venu vous voir.
Quelques-uns de ceux que nous avons vus . . .

E. **Chacun, chacune** *each one.*

Chacune de ces assiettes est en bon état.

F. **L'un, l'une, les uns, les unes** *the one, the ones;* **l'autre, les autres** *the other, the others.*

Les uns sont en bois, **les autres** sont en fer forgé.
J'admire **l'un et l'autre.** (*both*)
Je n'admire **ni l'un ni l'autre.** (*neither*)
Ni l'un ni l'autre ne vous appartient. (*neither*)

G. **Le même, la même, les mêmes** *the same one, the same ones.*

Cet emblème est **le même** que celui que nous avons vu à Blois.

H. **Aucun, aucune** (used with **ne**) *none, not a one.*

— Avez-vous vu des châteaux de la Loire? — Non, je **n'**en ai vu **aucun.**

I. **Personne** (used with **ne**) *no one, nobody.*

Je **n'**ai trouvé **personne.**
Personne ne m'a dit que vous étiez ici.

J. **Rien** (used with **ne**) *nothing, not a thing.*

Il **n'**y a **rien** de plus simple. (**Rien** de plus simple.)
Rien n'est plus simple.

NOTE: **Ne** is omitted when **rien, personne,** or **aucun** is used without a verb.

Qu'est-ce que vous faites? — **Rien.**
Qui est venu? — **Personne.**

K. Certains, certaines, *some*

Certains disent . . . *Some people* say
Certaines de ces assiettes . . . *some of* these plates . . .

Note also the following "indefinite" expressions that are not regarded as pronouns: **Quelque chose,** *something;* **autre chose,** *something else;* **pas grand-chose,** *nothing much;* **peu de chose,** *practically nothing.*

— Avez-vous **quelque chose** à faire ce soir? — Je n'ai pas **grand-chose** à faire.

Note also that after **rien** and **quelque chose** an adjective is preceded by the preposition **de.**

Quelque chose d'intéressant. **Rien d'**extraordinaire.

I. SUBSTITUTIONS. Répétez les phrases suivantes, en substituant les mots indiqués:

1. Avez-vous vu [le château de Blois]?

   celui de Chambord/ ceux de la Loire/ celui de Diane de Poitiers/ celui que François premier a fait construire/ celui dont nous avons parlé

2. Avez-vous visité [la cathédrale de Chartres]?

   celle de Paris/ celles d'Angleterre/ celle dont j'ai pris des photos/ celle dont nous avons parlé

3. J'ai lu [des romans français].

   ceux de Camus/ celui où il s'agit de Meursault/ celui que je vous ai prêté/ celui dont je vous ai parlé l'autre jour

4. Cet appareil [est à moi].

   n'est pas à moi/ est à Henri/ est à lui/ est à nous/ n'est pas à nous

5. Cette auto est [aux Frazer].

   à eux/ à Mme Frazer/ à elle/ à Henri/ à lui

II. EXERCICES D'APPLICATION.

A. Répétez les phrases suivantes, en remplaçant le nom par le pronom démonstratif approprié:

EX.: — Les châteaux de François premier sont décorés de salamandres.
— **Ceux de François premier sont décorés de salamandres.**

1. Les châteaux de Louis XII sont décorés de porcs-épics. **2.** Les châteaux de Louis XIV sont décorés de soleils. **3.** Les cheminées de Chambord sont décorées de salamandres. **4.** Les cheminées de Chaumont ne sont pas décorées. **5.** Les cheminées de Blois sont décorées de salamandres. **6.** Hélène préfère l'emblème de François premier. **7.** Henri préfère l'emblème de Louis XII. **8.** J'aime beaucoup les décorations que nous avons vues à Blois. **9.** Henri préfère les décorations qu'il a vues à Chambord. **10.** Les emblèmes dont nous avons parlé sont célèbres. **11.** Je n'ai pas vu les emblèmes dont vous nous avez parlé. **12.** Les meubles anciens qui restent sont rares. **13.** Les meubles qui ont disparu ont sans doute été détruits. **14.** Les meubles dont nous avons parlé ont sans doute été volés (*stolen*). **15.** Que pensez-vous de ce panneau-ci? **16.** Remarquez ces panneaux-là.

B. Répétez les phrases suivantes, en remplaçant le nom par la forme appropriée du pronom possessif:

EX.: — Voilà mon appareil.
— **Voilà le mien.**

1. Où est votre appareil? **2.** Je trouve vos photos très bien. **3.** Que pensez-vous de mes photos? **4.** Est-ce que votre appareil est aussi bon que mon appareil? **5.** Où sont vos photos? **6.** Où avez-vous pris vos photos? **7.** Où avez-vous laissé votre appareil? **8.** Où a-t-il acheté son appareil? **9.** Où est celui d'Hélène (*Helen's*)?

III. Donnez en français les réponses indiquées à chacune des questions suivantes:

A. Connaissez-vous les châteaux de la Loire?

1. I know them. I know them all. I don't know them. I don't know them all.
2. I know two of them. I know some of them. I know several of them. I don't know any of them. I don't know a single one.

B. Connaissez-vous les cathédrales gothiques?

1. I know them. I know them all. I don't know them. I don't know them all.
2. I know two of them. I know some of them. I know several of them. I don't know any of them. I don't know a single one.

C. Est-ce qu'on est venu me voir?

1. Yes, someone came. No, no one came. I didn't see anyone.
2. I didn't hear anyone. I didn't hear anything. Several persons came.

D. Qu'est-ce qui est arrivé?

1. Nothing happened. Nothing much. Something interesting.
2. Nothing unusual. Practically nothing. Something else.

E. Que fait Jean ce soir?

1. He has nothing to do. He hasn't much to do. He has practically nothing to do.
2. He has nothing interesting to do. He has something interesting to do.

IV. Répétez les phrases suivantes en ajoutant le pronom démonstratif convenable:

EX.: — Tout le monde l'a regardée.
— **Tout le monde l'a regardée, celle-là.**

1. Il est malin (*clever*). 2. Elle n'est pas bête. 3. Il n'est pas très poli. 4. Il joue bien. 5. Elle ne connaît pas grand-chose à la politique.

(Note that the addition of the demonstrative pronoun simply adds stress to the statement.)

V. Complétez les phrases suivantes en employant le pronom possessif ou démonstratif convenable:

A. 1. La voiture de Mme Frazer est neuve. 2. (*mine*) . . . est vieille. 3. (*John's*) . . . est rouge. 4. (*My father's*) . . . est plus neuve que celle de Jean. 5. (*This one*) . . . n'est pas à moi. 6. (*Those over there*) . . . sont à vendre.

B. 1. Jean a son appareil. 2. Hélène a laissé . . . dans la voiture. (*Her's*) 3. J'ai laissé . . . à l'hôtel. (*mine*) 4. . . . est à la maison. (*Henry's*) 5. . . . que j'ai acheté à Paris prend de bonnes photos. (*The one*) 6. . . . que nous avons vus dans la devanture ont l'air d'être de bonne qualité. (*The ones*)

C. 1. Les emblèmes des rois de France sont assez curieux. 2. . . . est une salamandre. (*François premier's*) 3. . . . que nous avons vus à Blois sont remarquables. (*The ones*) 4. . . . est un porc-épic. (*Louis XII's*) 5. J'aime bien . . . . (*his*) 6. Que pensez-vous de . . . ? (*this one*)

LE CULTIVATEUR

Les Frazer se sont arrêtés dans un village. A la poste, où il est allé pour envoyer une dépêche, Jean parle à un cultivateur de l'endroit. Celui-ci se plaint, selon l'habitude, du temps, de la pluie persistante, du coût de la culture, et des produits qui se vendent mal.

JEAN. —¹Voilà un bien vilain temps pour les récoltes!

LE CULTIVATEUR. —²Ah, monsieur, il vaut mieux ne pas en parler! ³Il y a de quoi désespérer. ⁴L'année dernière, c'était la sécheresse, et cette année, c'est une pluie continuelle.

JEAN. —⁵Je ne crois pas qu'il faille désespérer. ⁶Le temps finira par s'arranger.

LE CULTIVATEUR. —⁷J'espère que vous avez raison. ⁸Je souhaite que la pluie s'arrête et qu'il fasse beau, ⁹mais j'ai peur que mes souhaits ne servent pas à grand-chose . . . ¹⁰Si au moins nos produits se vendaient bien. ¹¹Mais bien que nous soyons obligés de dépenser plus qu'autrefois, ¹²la culture rapporte de moins en moins.

The Frazers have stopped in a village. At the post office, where he went to send a wire, John is talking with a a local farmer. The latter is complaining, as usual, about the weather, the steady rain, the cost of farming, and the low price of produce.

JOHN. —¹This is very bad weather for the crops!

THE FARMER. —²Oh, sir, it's too awful for words. ³It's enough to make you give up (despair). ⁴Last year, it was the drought and this year it's a continual rain.

JOHN. —⁵I don't think one should give up. ⁶The weather will clear up (get better) in time.

THE FARMER. —⁷I hope you are right. ⁸I wish the rain would stop and that the weather would be fine, ⁹but I am afraid my wishes are not going to help much. ¹⁰If only (at least) our products sold well! ¹¹But although we have to spend more than in the past, ¹²farming brings in less and less.

JEAN. —¹³Je croyais que le gouvernement fixait les prix . . .

LE CULTIVATEUR. —¹⁴Oui, mais je crains que nous n'arrivions bientôt plus à joindre les deux bouts. ¹⁵Il faut que nous payions plus cher tout ce que nous achetons, ¹⁶les semences, les engrais, sans compter les machines.

JEAN. —¹⁷Il me semble en effet qu'on voit dans les champs bien plus de machines qu'autrefois.

LE CULTIVATEUR. —¹⁸Maintenant, à moins qu'on aille dans des coins perdus, on ne voit plus de chevaux: ¹⁹rien que des machines. ²⁰Ici, il n'y a pas un seul cultivateur qui n'ait son tracteur. ²¹Il suffit que l'un d'eux en ait un pour que son voisin veuille aussi avoir le sien . . . ²²Voulez-vous que je vous dise ce que j'en pense? ²³Le gouvernement est en train de ruiner le cultivateur!

JEAN. —²⁴Dans mon pays, nous avons un peu les mêmes problèmes.

JOHN. —¹³I thought the government regulated prices.

THE FARMER. —¹⁴Yes, but I'm afraid we will soon not be able to make both ends meet any longer. ¹⁵We have to pay more for everything we buy, ¹⁶seed, fertilizer, not to mention (not counting) farm machinery.

JOHN. —¹⁷It does seem to me, as a matter of fact, (It seems to me, indeed,) that you see far more machines in the fields than in the past.

THE FARMER. —¹⁸Now, unless you go to out-of-the-way places, you won't see any horses any more: ¹⁹nothing but machinery. ²⁰Here, there isn't a single farmer who hasn't his tractor. ²¹If *one* has one it is enough to make his neighbor want to have one too (*his*) . . . ²²Do you want me to tell you what I think (about it)? ²³The government is gradually bankrupting the farmers!

JOHN. —²⁴In my country, we have somewhat the same problems.

I. SUBSTITUTIONS. Répétez les phrases suivantes, en substituant les mots indiqués:

1. Celui-ci se plaint [du temps].

   de la pluie persistante/ de la sécheresse/ du coût des machines/ du prix des produits agricoles

2. Il vaut mieux ne pas [en parler].

   parler de ça/ désespérer/ être découragé/ se plaindre

3. Je souhaite [que la pluie s'arrête].

   qu'il fasse beau/ qu'il fasse moins chaud/ que le temps s'arrange/ que le gouvernement nous aide davantage

4. Il faut que nous payions plus cher [tout ce que nous achetons].

tout ce qu'il nous faut/ ce dont nous avons besoin/ tout ce qui
nous est nécessaire dans nos champs/ tout ce que nous employons

5. Je crains que nous n'arrivions bientôt plus [à joindre les deux bouts].

à acheter des machines/ à acheter des engrais/
à vendre nos produits/ à payer nos impôts

6. Voulez-vous que je vous dise ce que [j'en pense]?

je pense du gouvernement/ je pense du ministre de l'agricul-
ture/ je pense de lui/ je pense des ministres/ je pense d'eux

7. Le gouvernement est en train [de nous ruiner].

de nous aider/ d'aider l'agriculture/ de faire quelque
chose pour l'agriculture/ de s'occuper de nous

II. Répondez en français:

1. Où les Frazer se sont-ils arrêtés? **2.** Pourquoi se sont-ils arrêtés? **3.** A qui
Jean parle-t-il? **4.** De quoi parle-t-il? **5.** Qu'est-ce que le cultivateur lui
répond lorsque Jean lui parle du temps? **6.** Quel temps a-t-il fait l'année
dernière? **7.** Quel temps fait-il cette année? **8.** Que lui dit Jean pour le
consoler? **9.** Est-ce que le cultivateur croit que ses souhaits servent à quelque
chose? **10.** Pense-t-il que la culture rapporte beaucoup? **11.** Par qui les prix
sont-ils fixés? **12.** Est-ce que le cultivateur croit que ces prix sont assez élevés?
13. Que doivent acheter les cultivateurs? **14.** Quel changement Jean
remarque-t-il en ce qui concerne l'agriculture? **15.** Voit-on beaucoup de
chevaux à l'heure actuelle? **16.** Qu'est-ce qui a remplacé les chevaux?
17. Est-ce que la plupart des cultivateurs ont un tracteur? **18.** Qu'est-ce que
l'homme à qui parle Jean pense du gouvernement? **19.** Les problèmes
agricoles existent-ils seulement en France?

III. Demandez à quelqu'un:

1. où sont les Frazer. **2.** à qui Jean parle. **3.** ce que le cultivateur pense
du temps. **4.** s'il pense que le temps va s'arranger. **5.** si la culture coûte
plus qu'autrefois. **6.** si elle rapporte davantage. **7.** si les prix fixés par le
gouvernement sont assez élevés. **8.** ce que les cultivateurs ont besoin d'acheter.
9. s'il y a maintenant beaucoup de chevaux dans la culture. **10.** ce qu'il y
a à leur place. **11.** pourquoi le cultivateur se plaint du gouvernement. **12.** ce
que le cultivateur pense du gouvernement.

LE CULTIVATEUR

IV. Répétez chacune des phrases suivantes en employant **finir par:**

EX.: — Le temps s'arrangera.
     — **Le temps finira par s'arranger.**

1. Il fera beau. **2.** La pluie s'arrêtera. **3.** Le gouvernement ruinera le cultivateur. **4.** Nous abandonnerons la culture. **5.** Je me découragerai. **6.** Nous joindrons les deux bouts.

V. Employez les expressions suivantes dans les phrases indiquées:

1. Il **y a de quoi** (*There's every reason to . . .*)
    (a) se décourager. (b) désespérer. (c) se plaindre. (d) renoncer à la culture.

2. Il **n'y a pas de quoi** (*There's no reason to . . .*)
    (a) se décourager. (b) désespérer. (c) se plaindre. (d) abandonner la culture.

3. Il **a de quoi** (*He has the means to . . .*)
    (a) vivre. (b) acheter une voiture. (c) faire construire une nouvelle maison. (d) acheter des machines.

4. Il **n'a pas de quoi** (*He doesn't have the means to . . .*)
    (a) vivre. (b) acheter une voiture. (c) faire construire une nouvelle maison. (d) acheter des machines.

VI. THÈME.

At the post office of a village where they had stopped because Mrs. Frazer wanted to send a telegram, John spoke to a local farmer. They talked about the weather and the crops, and the farmer complained of both. In France as in the U.S., farmers pay higher and higher prices for what they buy, and they receive less and less for what they sell. Two centuries ago people did not always have enough bread to eat. Even at the beginning of the last century, white bread was still a luxury (**un luxe**). Now France grows (**récolte**) too much wheat, and the French people eat less and less bread. Naturally the farmers are not happy!

Subjonctif: présent et passé composé

69 Formation of the present subjunctive.

A. The endings.

The endings of the present subjunctive of all French verbs (except **être** and **avoir**) are: **-e, -es, -e, -ions, -iez, -ent.**

B. The stem.

The stem of the present subjunctive of regular verbs is the same as as that of the first person plural of the present indicative. Ex.: *Present Indicative:* Nous **donn**ons, nous **finiss**ons, nous **vend**ons; *Present Subjunctive:* je **donn**e, je **finiss**e, je **vend**e.

C. Forms of the present subjunctive of **être** and **avoir** and of regular verbs.

1. être:

je sois, tu sois, il soit, nous soyons, vous soyez, ils soient.

2. avoir:

j'aie, tu aies, il ait, nous ayons, vous ayez, ils aient.

Note that the stem of the present subjunctive of **avoir** is pronounced [ɛ] like the **è** in **près,** thus: [ɛ, ɛ, ɛ, ɛjõ, ɛje, ɛ].

3. donner:

je donne, tu donnes, il donne, nous donnions, vous donniez, ils donnent.

4. finir:

je finisse, tu finisses, il finisse, nous finissions, vous finissiez, ils finissent.

5. vendre:

je vende, tu vendes, il vende, nous vendions, vous vendiez, ils vendent.

70   Use of the present subjunctive.

A. After certain expressions of will, emotion, or necessity.

The subjunctive is used in subordinate clauses introduced by **que** and depending upon certain verbs that express wishing, wanting, desiring; joy, sorrow, happiness, regret, fear; approval or disapproval, etc. Among the verbs of this group which may take the subjunctive, the following are the most frequently used: **vouloir, désirer; aimer mieux, préférer; souhaiter,** *to wish;* **craindre,** *to fear;* **être content, être heureux; regretter; être fâché; avoir peur,** and a number of impersonal expressions such as **il faut que . . ., il vaut mieux que . . ., il suffit que . . .,** etc.

Il faut que **nous payions** plus cher tout ce que nous achetons.
Voulez-vous que **je** vous **dise** ce que j'en pense?
Je souhaite que la pluie **s'arrête** et qu'**il fasse** beau.
J'ai peur que mes souhaits ne **servent** pas à grand-chose.
Il suffit que l'un d'eux en **ait** un **pour que** son voisin **veuille** avoir le sien.

Note that in the above examples the subject of the verb in the subordinate clause is *different* from the subject of the verb in the main clause. You have seen in par. 62 that when the subject of the main verb is the *same* as that of the subordinate verb, the infinitive is used instead of the subjunctive.

Voulez-**vous** que **je** vous **dise** ce que j'en pense? (*Subjunctive*)
Voulez-**vous** me **dire** ce que vous en pensez? (*Infinitive*)

J'ai peur que **vous soyez** en retard. (*Subjunctive*)
J'ai peur d'**être** en retard. (*Infinitive*)

B.   After expressions of possibility.

The subjunctive is normally used in subordinate clauses depending upon expressions that express possibility (but not probability), such as: **Il est possible que, Il se peut que, Il est peu probable, Il n'est pas sûr que.**

Il est possible qu'il **pleuve** demain.
Il se peut qu'il **pleuve** demain.

But note that after expressions that suggest certainty or even probability the indicative is normal.

Il est certain qu'il **pleuvra.**
Il est probable que nous **serons** en retard.

C. After certain conjunctive expressions.

The subjunctive must be used in clauses introduced by certain conjunctive expressions of which the following are the most frequently used: **à moins que,** unless; **avant que,** before; **jusqu'à ce que,** until; **bien que, quoique,** although; **quoi que,** whatever; **pour que,** so that; **de peur que,** for fear that.

Bien que nous **soyons obligés** de dépenser plus qu'autrefois...
Quoi qu'il fassent, les cultivateurs n'arriveront bientôt plus à joindre les deux bouts.
Il suffit que l'un d'eux en **ait** un **pour que** son voisin **veuille** avoir le sien.

Note that after **à moins que** and **avant que** the use of the pleonastic **ne** is optional.

A moins qu'on **aille** dans les coins perdus, ...
A moins qu'on **n'aille** dans les coins perdus, ...

D. After indefinite antecedent or exaggeration.

The subjunctive is used in relative clauses whose antecedent is indefinite or is modified by the word **seul** or by a superlative:

Je ne connais **personne** qui **puisse** vous aider.
C'est **le plus beau** château que **j'aie** jamais vu.
Ici, il n'y a pas **un seul** cultivateur qui **n'ait** son tracteur.

E. After expressions of uncertainty.

The subjunctive is not always used in subordinate clauses that follow verbs expressing a belief, opinion, or expectation such as **croire, penser, espérer, compter:**

(1) After affirmative forms of these verbs the indicative is used:

Je crois qu'il va pleuvoir.
J'espère qu'il viendra.

(2) After negative or interrogative forms, either the indicative or the subjunctive may be used. The subjunctive implies greater uncertainty:

Croyez-vous qu'il pleuvra ce soir? (*Indicative*)
Croyez-vous qu'il pleuve ce soir? (*Subjunctive*)
Je n'espère pas qu'il viendra. (*Indicative*)
Je n'espère pas qu'il vienne. (*Subjunctive*)

71 Subjunctive of irregular verbs.

A. Commonest irregular verbs whose present subjunctive has two stems:

aller: aille, ailles, aille, **all**ions, **all**iez, aillent.
apercevoir: aperçoive, aperçoives, aperçoive, **apercev**ions, **apercev**iez, aperçoivent.
boire: boive, boives, boive, **buv**ions, **buv**iez, boivent.
croire: croie, croies, croie, **croy**ions, **croy**iez, croient.
devoir: doive, doives, doive, **dev**ions, **dev**iez, doivent.
envoyer: envoie, envoies, envoie, **envoy**ions, **envoy**iez, envoient.
mourir: meure, meures, meure, **mour**ions, **mour**iez, meurent.
prendre: prenne, prennes, prenne, **pren**ions, **pren**iez, prennent.
recevoir: reçoive, reçoives, reçoive, **recev**ions, **recev**iez, reçoivent.
tenir: tienne, tiennes, tienne, **ten**ions, **ten**iez, tiennent.
venir: vienne, viennes, vienne, **ven**ions, **ven**iez, viennent.
voir: voie, voies, voie, **voy**ions, **voy**iez, voient.
vouloir: veuille, veuilles, veuille, **voul**ions, **voul**iez, veuillent.

B. Commonest irregular verbs whose present subjunctive has only one stem:

faire: fasse, fasses, fasse, fassions, fassiez, fassent.
pouvoir: puisse, puisses, puisse, puissions, puissiez, puissent.
savoir: sache, saches, sache, sachions, sachiez, sachent.

C. Note that the subjunctive of many irregular verbs follows the pattern of regular verbs and can be derived from the first person plural of the present indicative (see par. 69):

conduire, connaître, construire, courir, cueillir (accueillir), dire, dormir, écrire, lire, mettre, partir, plaindre, plaire, pleuvoir, suivre, vivre.

A. Formation.

The *passé composé* of the subjunctive is composed of the present sub-junctive of the auxiliary verb and the past participle.

> **être: j'aie été, tu aies été, il ait été, nous ayons été, vous ayez été, ils aient été.**
> **avoir: j'aie eu, tu aies eu, etc.**
> **donner: j'aie donné, tu aies donné, etc.**
> **aller: je sois allé, tu sois allé, il soit allé, nous soyons allés, vous soyez allé(s), ils soient allés.**
> **prendre: j'aie pris, tu aies pris, etc.**

B. Use.

Generally speaking, the *passé composé* of the subjunctive is used like the present subjunctive except that it expresses completed action.

> Voilà le plus beau château que **j'aie** jamais **vu.**
> J'ai peur qu'**il se soit trompé** de route.
> Je ne crois pas qu'**il ait plu** cette nuit.
> Bien qu'**ils soient allés** en Touraine, ils n'ont pas vu tous les châteaux.

———

I. EXERCICE D'APPLICATION. Mettez chacune des phrases suivantes au subjonctif, en commençant par **Il faut que . . .:**

1. Je déjeune tout de suite.   **2.** Nous déjeunons à Orléans.   **3.** Je choisis la meilleure route.   **4.** Vous choisissez la meilleure route.   **5.** Henri répond au téléphone.   **6.** Nous répondons aux lettres.   **7.** Je suis à l'heure.   **8.** Vous êtes à l'heure.   **9.** Je serai prêt à partir à sept heures.   **10.** Nous serons prêts à partir à huit heures.   **11.** J'ai de la patience.   **12.** Nous avons de la patience.   **13.** Nous nous levons de bonne heure.   **14.** Vous vous levez de bonne heure.   **15.** Jean va chez les Duplessis.   **16.** Nous allons en ville.   **17.** Jean prend un taxi.   **18.** Il fait signe au chauffeur.   **19.** Nous faisons des emplettes.   **20.** Nous achetons des cadeaux.   **21.** Le chauffeur sait l'adresse des Duplessis.   **22.** Jean envoie une dépêche.   **23.** Il met une lettre à la poste.   **24.** Il dit ce qu'il pense.   **25.** Nous disons toujours ce que nous pensons.

II. SUBSTITUTIONS. Répétez les phrases suivantes, en substituant les mots indiqués:

1. Il vaut mieux [que nous partions tout de suite].

    que vous veniez avec nous/ que nous sachions à quelle heure arrive l'autobus/ que nous allions à Blois/ que nous fassions des courses

2. Il est possible [que nous ayons encore de la pluie].

    que le temps finisse par s'arranger/ qu'il fasse beau demain/ qu'il pleuve encore demain/ que la pluie s'arrête

3. Je regrette que Jean [n'ait pas pu assister au mariage].

    soit allé en Égypte/ ait oublié d'envoyer un cadeau de mariage/ ne soit pas venu me chercher/ se soit levé trop tard

4. (a) Je souhaite [que vous veniez nous voir]. (Subjunctive) (*I wish*)

    que vous restiez prendre le thé/ que vous me disiez votre avis (*opinion*)/ que vous me parliez de votre voyage/ que vous fassiez sa connaissance

    (b) J'espère [que vous viendrez nous voir]. (Indicative) (*I hope and expect*)

    que vous resterez prendre le thé/ que vous me direz votre avis/ que vous me parlerez de votre voyage/ que vous ferez sa connaissance

5. (a) Je ne crois pas [que vous soyez ici à sept heures du matin]. (Subjunctive) (*I doubt*)

    que vous ayez raison/ que vous soyez prêt à sept heures du matin/ que nous puissions partir avant huit heures/ que vous sachiez sa nouvelle adresse

    (b) Je crois [que vous serez ici à sept heures du matin]. (Indicative) (*I really believe*)

    que vous avez raison/ que vous serez prêt à sept heures du matin/ que nous pourrons partir avant huit heures/ que vous savez sa nouvelle adresse

6. (a) Je ne suis pas sûr que Jean [soit à Paris]. (Subjunctive) (*possibility* or *doubt*)

    soit allé visiter le Louvre/ ait fait la connaissance de Charles/ vienne me chercher à l'hôtel/ puisse partir demain

    (b) Il me semble que Jean [est à Paris]. (Indicative) (*probability*)

    est allé visiter le Louvre/ a fait la connaissance de Charles/ viendra me chercher à l'hôtel/ pourra partir demain

III. Combinez deux phrases en une seule, en commençant par l'expression indiquée:

EX.: — (Bien que) Je suis en France depuis deux mois. Je ne suis pas encore allé voir Versailles.

— **Bien que je sois en France depuis deux mois, je ne suis pas encore allé voir Versailles.**

1. (Quoique) Il fait froid. Nous allons faire une promenade. **2.** (Avant que) La nuit tombe. Nous irons visiter le Louvre. **3.** (A moins que) Vous allez au Louvre. Vous ne verrez pas *la Joconde*. **4.** (Bien que) Je sais chanter. Je ne chanterai pas ce soir. **5.** (Quoique) Elle est riche. Elle n'est pas heureuse. **6.** (Bien que) Je fais tout ce que je peux. Je n'arrive pas à joindre les deux bouts.

IV. Répondez affirmativement en employant l'indicatif, puis négativement en employant le subjonctif:

1. Croyez-vous qu'il y ait une place pour Jean dans l'auto des Frazer? **2.** Croyez-vous que Jean sera prêt à partir à sept heures et demie? **3.** Pensez-vous qu'Henri vienne le chercher à sept heures et demie? **4.** Est-elle sûre qu'ils puissent voir tous les châteaux de la Renaissance?

V. Répondez en français, en employant **Il est possible . . .:**

1. Irez-vous en Touraine l'été prochain? **2.** Est-ce que vous faites des emplettes ce soir? **3.** Sortez-vous demain soir? **4.** Saurez-vous parler français couramment à la fin de l'année? **5.** Aurons-nous le temps de visiter toutes les salles du musée? **6.** Serez-vous prêt à partir à sept heures du matin? **7.** Vous couchez-vous de bonne heure ce soir? **8.** Écrirez-vous des lettres dimanche après-midi? **9.** Pouvez-vous venir nous voir dimanche prochain?

VI. Complétez les phrases suivantes en employant le subjonctif du verbe indiqué:

A. Le présent du subjonctif

1. Roger est le seul Français que nous _____. (connaître) **2.** Connaissez-vous quelqu'un qui _____ le grec? (savoir) **3.** Je ne connais personne qui _____ faire mon travail. (pouvoir) **4.** Nous attendrons jusqu'à ce que vous _____. (arriver) **5.** A moins que nous _____ de bonne heure, nous serons en retard. (partir)

B. Le passé composé du subjonctif

1. C'est le plus beau château que nous _____ _____. (visiter) **2.** C'est le livre le plus intéressant que j'_____ _____. (lire) **3.** Nous attendrons jusqu'à ce que vous _____ _____ votre travail. (finir) **4.** Bien que j'_____ _____ la Touraine, j'y retournerai l'été prochain. (voir) **5.** Je suis content que vous _____ _____ me voir. (venir)

SUBJONCTIF: PRÉSENT ET PASSÉ COMPOSÉ

SUR LA ROUTE

Jean et les Frazer voyagent toujours en auto dans la région de la Loire. Il pleut à verse et Henri, qui conduit, ne sait pas trop où ils sont.

John and the Frazers are still traveling by car in the Loire region. It is pouring rain, and Henry, who is driving, is a little hazy as to their whereabouts.

HENRI (*au volant*). —¹Voilà des heures qu'il pleut sans arrêt. ²Il faisait beau quand nous sommes partis; ³il s'est mis à pleuvoir une demi-heure plus tard. ⁴Maintenant on voit à peine à travers le pare-brise, car l'essuie-glace fonctionne mal. ⁵Et écoutez la pluie sur le toit de la voiture.

HENRY (*at the wheel*). —¹It's been raining steadily for hours. ²The weather was fine when we started; ³it began to rain a half hour later. ⁴Now you can scarcely see through the windshield because the windshield wiper isn't working properly. ⁵And listen to the rain on the car roof.

JEAN (*récitant*). —

⁶O bruit doux de la pluie
Par terre et sur les toits!
⁷Pour un cœur qui s'ennuie
O le chant de la pluie!

⁸Dans l'esprit du poète, ⁹il s'agissait d'un autre genre de toit, bien entendu.*

JOHN (*reciting*). —

⁶Oh gentle noise of the rain
On the ground and on the roofs!
⁷For a heart that is desperately sad
Oh the song of the rain!

⁸In the mind of the poet, ⁹it was a question of another sort of roof, of course.

HENRI. —¹⁰Ne dis pas des choses comme ça sans me prévenir! ¹¹J'ai été si surpris que j'ai failli quitter la route.

HENRY. —¹⁰Don't say such things without warning me! ¹¹I was so surprised that I almost ran off the road.

---

* Vers du poète **Paul Verlaine** (1844-1896).

HÉLÈNE. —¹²Cette pluie ne me déplaît pas du tout. ¹³Elle me donne au contraire un sentiment de confort, de bien-être.

HENRI. —¹⁴Je crains que ton bien-être ne soit de courte durée. ¹⁵J'ai l'impression que nous nous sommes trompés de route.

JEAN. —¹⁶J'aperçois là-bas un poteau indicateur. ¹⁷Lisez ce qu'il dit.

HENRI. —¹⁸Je ne peux rien voir à cause de la pluie.

JEAN. —¹⁹Arrête-toi un instant et ouvre la portière.

HENRI (lisant). —²⁰Il dit: G-I-E-N, 65 kilomètres.

HÉLÈNE. —²¹Comment prononce-t-on G-I-E-N?

JEAN. —²²Je crois que GIEN rime avec CHIEN.

HÉLÈNE. —²³Je ne sais jamais comment on prononce les noms propres. ²⁴On écrit REIMS et on dit RINCE, ²⁵LAON et on dit LENT, ²⁶CAEN et on dit QUAND; ²⁷le nom de la rivière LA SAÔNE rime avec BEAUNE. ²⁸Je n'y comprends rien.

HENRI. —²⁹Vraiment, ce n'est pas le moment de discuter l'orthographe. ³⁰Tu ferais mieux de me dire quelle route je dois suivre!

JEAN. —³¹Si je me permets de te donner mon avis, tu n'as guère le choix. ³²Suis celle-ci jusqu'au prochain village. ³³Là, nous verrons bien quelle route il faut prendre.

HELEN. —¹²This rain doesn't bother me at all. ¹³On the contrary it gives me a feeling of comfort, of well-being.

HENRY. —¹⁴I am afraid that your well-being may be short-lived (of short duration). ¹⁵I have the impression that we have taken the wrong road.

JOHN. —¹⁶I see a signpost up ahead. ¹⁷Read what it says.

HENRY. —¹⁸I can't see a thing because of the rain.

JOHN. —¹⁹Stop a moment and open the door.

HENRY (reading). —²⁰It says: G-I-E-N, 65 kilometers.

HELEN. —²¹How do you pronounce G-I-E-N?

JOHN. —²²I think GIEN rhymes with CHIEN.

HELEN. —²³I never know how you pronounce proper names. ²⁴You write REIMS and you say RINCE ²⁵LAON and you say LENT, ²⁶CAEN and you say QUAND; ²⁷the name of the river LA SAÔNE rhymes with BEAUNE. ²⁸I don't get it (understand it at all).

HENRY. —²⁹Really, this is not the time to discuss spelling. ³⁰You would do better to tell me what road to follow.

JOHN. —³¹If I may take the liberty of giving you my opinion, you scarcely have any choice. ³²Follow this one as far as the next village. ³³There we will certainly see what road we must take.

I. SUBSTITUTIONS. Répétez les phrases suivantes, en substituant les mots indiqués:

1. Il s'est mis à pleuvoir [une demi-heure plus tard].

   quand nous nous sommes mis en route/ quand nous sommes partis/ au moment de notre départ/ il y a deux heures

2. Écoutez la pluie [sur le toit de la voiture].

   sur le toit de la maison/ dans la cheminée/ contre les fenêtres/ qui tombe

3. [Ne dites pas des choses comme ça] sans me prévenir.

   Ne partez pas/ Ne vous mettez pas en route/ Ne vous arrêtez pas/ Ne quittez pas la maison

4. J'ai l'impression [que nous nous sommes trompés de route].

   que nous nous sommes trompés de rue/ que nous sommes en retard/ qu'il va pleuvoir/ qu'il va se mettre à pleuvoir

5. J'aperçois là-bas [un poteau indicateur].

   un village/ un poste d'essence (*filling station*)/ le clocher d'une église/ un troupeau de moutons

6. Je ne peux rien voir à cause [de la pluie].

   du brouillard (*the fog*)/ du soleil/ de l'essuie-glace qui fonctionne mal/ des phares (*headlights*) de l'auto qui vient

7. Tu ferais mieux de [me dire quelle route je dois suivre].

   regarder le poteau indicateur/ lire ce qu'il dit/ ne pas te plaindre/ ne pas te plaindre du mauvais temps

8. [Ce n'est pas le moment] de discuter l'orthographe.

   C'est le moment/ C'est le bon moment/ C'est le mauvais moment/ Ce n'est pas le bon moment

9. Suis [celle-ci].

   cette route-ci/ cette rue-ci/ mes conseils/ les conseils de ton père

II. Répétez les phrases suivantes, en remplaçant **commencer à** par **se mettre à**:

1. Il a commencé à pleuvoir. 2. Jean a commencé à réciter un poème. 3. Henri a commencé à se plaindre. 4. Il commence à pleuvoir. 5. Jean commence à réciter un poème. 6. Henri commence à se plaindre. 7. Commencez à travailler. 8. D'habitude je commence à étudier à huit heures.

9. Ce soir je commencerai à étudier plus tôt. 10. Je commencerais à apprendre le russe, si j'avais le temps.

III. Répétez les phrases suivantes, en remplaçant **faire bien** par **faire mieux:**

1. Tu ferais bien de me dire quelle route je dois suivre. 2. Est-ce que nous ne ferions pas bien de partir plus tôt? 3. Vous feriez bien de partir à sept heures et demie au lieu de huit heures. 4. Vous feriez bien de me prévenir quand vous dites ces choses-là. 5. Il aurait bien fait de m'avertir.

IV. Répétez les phrases suivantes en employant le passé composé de **faillir** et l'infinitif:

EX.: — J'ai quitté la route.
— **J'ai failli quitter la route.**

1. L'auto a quitté la route. 2. Nous avons eu un accident. 3. Nous avons pris la mauvaise route. 4. J'ai manqué l'avion. 5. Hélène a laissé son appareil dans le restaurant. 6. Je me suis trompé de route. 7. Ils se sont trompés de route. 8. L'auto est restée en panne (*had a breakdown*).

V. Répondez en français:

1. Où sont Jean et ses amis? 2. Qui conduit l'auto? 3. Quel temps fait-il? 4. Quand s'est-il mis à pleuvoir? 5. Où peut-on entendre la pluie? 6. Quels vers Jean récite-t-il? 7. Qu'est-ce qu'Henri a failli faire quand il a entendu Jean? 8. Est-ce que la pluie déplaît à Hélène? 9. Pourquoi la pluie lui plaît-elle? 10. Que craint Henri? 11. Est-ce qu'il est sur la bonne route? 12. Qu'est-ce qu'il aperçoit là-bas? 13. Pourquoi ne peut-il pas lire l'inscription tout d'abord? 14. Qu'est-ce que Jean lui dit de faire? 15. Que dit l'inscription? 16. Hélène sait-elle toujours comment prononcer les noms propres? 17. Savez-vous où sont les villes que cite Hélène? 18. Que dit Henri à sa sœur qui discute la prononciation des noms propres? 19. Quel conseil Jean donne-t-il à son ami? 20. Pourquoi lui dit-il d'aller jusqu'au prochain village?

VI. Demandez à quelqu'un:

1. s'il fait beau quand Jean et ses amis sont sur la route. 2. s'il pleut depuis longtemps. 3. s'il faisait beau quand ils sont partis. 4. quand il a commencé à pleuvoir. 5. si Henri peut voir à travers le pare-brise. 6. pourquoi il ne

peut pas voir. **7.** si Henri a été surpris. **8.** ce qu'il a failli faire. **9.** ce qu'Hélène pense de la pluie. **10.** quel sentiment la pluie lui donne. **11.** ce que craint Henri. **12.** s'il s'est trompé de route. **13.** ce qu'Henri aperçoit. **14.** s'il peut lire ce qui est écrit sur le poteau indicateur. **15.** où Henri pourra demander quelle route il doit suivre.

VII. Répétez après moi les vers suivants de Paul Verlaine:

> Il pleure dans mon cœur
> Comme il pleut sur la ville;
> Quelle est cette langueur
> Qui pénètre mon cœur?
>
> O doux bruit de la pluie,
> Par terre et sur les toits!
> Pour un cœur qui s'ennuie,
> Oh! le chant de la pluie!
>
> Il pleure sans raison
> Dans ce cœur qui s'écœure!
> Quoi! nulle trahison?
> Ce deuil est sans raison.
>
> C'est bien la pire peine
> De ne savoir pourquoi,
> Sans amour et sans haine,
> Mon cœur a tant de peine.

VIII. THÈME.

The pronunciation of proper names, especially names of small cities, is not always evident to French people **(les Français)**. Whereas **(Tandis que)** common nouns are used everywhere, proper names sometimes have a local pronunciation. And the names of the inhabitants of some of these cities are even stranger **(plus étranges)**. Of course everybody knows that the inhabitants of Paris are called "Parisiens," and those of Marseilles "Marseillais." But sometimes the name of the inhabitant of a city is very different from the name of the city itself **(la ville elle-même)**. You have perhaps heard of the old city of Tours, sur la Loire. But you probably don't know that its inhabitants are called "Tourangeaux," and that those who live at Besançon are called Bisontins. As the French themselves say: "One never knows."

SUR LA ROUTE

Verbes irréguliers

73   A quick look at irregular verbs.

In order to learn irregular verbs, it is absolutely necessary to practice using them. However, it is also instructive to look at them in groups and to see clearly how they differ from regular verbs. You can see almost at a glance that most of the forms of many of them are perfectly regular. The following paragraphs point out the ways in which they are irregular, and the exercises provide practice in using both regular and irregular forms.

The grammar unit should be reviewed occasionally and the exercises should be worked on until you can do them rapidly, correctly, and with confidence.

A. Present indicative.

The present indicative is the only tense of irregular verbs that is practically always irregular.

Instead of having the same stem throughout like regular verbs (see par. 4), irregular verbs usually have two stems, one for the singular and the 3rd plural, and the other for the first and second plural. Ex.: **venir: je viens, tu viens, il vient, nous venons, vous venez, ils viennent; recevoir: je reçois, tu reçois, il reçoit, nous recevons, vous recevez, ils reçoivent.**

Practically all irregular verbs have the present indicative endings **-s, -s, -t, -ons, -ez, -ent.** A few have those of the first conjugation: **-e, -es, -e, -ons, -ez, -ent.**

B. *Imparfait.*

Except for **être**, the *imparfait* of all irregular verbs follows the pattern of regular verbs: the endings are always regular and the stem is always the same as the stem of the first person plural of the present indicative.

C. Future.

Of the 30 irregular verbs mentioned in this lesson, less than a third have an irregular future. For verbs that do have an irregular future (and conditional), it should be noted that the endings are always regular and that the same stem is always used throughout the two tenses.

D. Past participle.

Irregular verbs ending in **-er** always have a past participle in **-é.** Those in **-ir** have a past participle in **-i, -u,** or **-ert.** Those in **-re** have a past participle in **-u, -is, -it,** or **-aint (-eint, -oint).** Those in **-oir** have a past participle in **-u.** Those following the same pattern are grouped together below.

E. Present subjunctive, see par. 71.

NOTE: As the forms of the imperfect subjunctive and the *passé simple* are taken up in Unit 30, they will not be considered here.

74 Indicative of irregular verbs ending in -er.

There are only two verbs in this group: **aller** and **envoyer.** Both are regular except for the present indicative and the future.

A. Aller, *to go.*

— Où **allez-vous,** Monsieur? — **Je vais** à Saint-Cloud.
J'irai au cinéma ce soir.

PRÉSENT: **Je vais, tu vas, il va, nous allons, vous allez, ils vont.**
FUTUR: **J'irai.**

Note that **s'en aller,** *to leave, to go away* has practically the same use and meaning as **partir** except that **s'en aller** is rarely used in compound tenses.

VERBES IRRÉGULIERS

B. Envoyer, *to send.*

On m'**a envoyé** au Vénézuéla.
On m'**envoie** maintenant en Amérique.
Je ne sais pas où on m'**enverra** ensuite.

PRÉSENT: **J'envoie, tu envoies, il envoie, nous envoyons, vous envoyez, ils envoient.**

FUTUR: **J'enverrai.**

Renvoyer, *to send back, to send away* is of course conjugated like **envoyer.**

75 First group of irregular verbs in -ir: **partir, sortir, sentir, servir, dormir,** etc.

These verbs have two stems in the present indicative: **par—part—,
ser—serv—, dor—dorm—,** etc. All the forms of these verbs are regular
except for the present indicative.

A. Partir, *to leave.*

Je pars à midi.
Il faisait beau quand **nous sommes partis.**

PRÉSENT: **Je pars, tu pars, il part, nous partons, vous partez, ils partent.**

B. Sortir, *to go out* (intransitive); *to take out* (transitive).

Il faisait beau quand **nous sommes sortis.**
Je sors le chien tous les soirs.

PRÉSENT: **Je sors, tu sors, il sort, nous sortons, vous sortez, ils sortent.**

C. Sentir, *to smell;* **se sentir,** *to feel.*

Ces roses **sentent** bon.
Je ne **me sens** pas très bien.

PRÉSENT: **Je sens, tu sens, il sent, nous sentons, vous sentez, ils sentent.**

D. Servir, *to serve;* **se servir de,** *to use, to help oneself;* **servir à,** *to be used for;*
servir de, *to serve as, to be used as.*

Marie **sert** le dîner.
Hélène **se sert de** l'appareil de Jean.

Cela ne **sert à** rien. (*That is useless.*)

Le château de Loches **a servi de** prison.

PRÉSENT: **Je sers, tu sers, il sert, nous servons, vous servez, ils servent.**

E. Dormir, *to sleep;* s'endormir, *to fall asleep.*

J'ai **dormi** tout l'après-midi.

Il dort bien la nuit.

Il s'endort de bonne heure.

PRÉSENT: **Je dors, tu dors, il dort, nous dormons, vous dormez, ils dorment.**

NOTE: Compounds of these verbs follow the same pattern of conjugation.

Ex.: **sentir** — **consentir,** *to consent;* **partir** — **repartir,** *to set out again.*

76 Second group of irregular verbs in -ir: venir, tenir.

These verbs have two stems for the present indicative **(viens —
venons)**, an irregular future **(viendrai)** and a past participle in **-u.**

A. Venir, *to come;* venir de (with infinitive) *to have just.*

D'où **venez-vous,** Jean?

Je viens de France.

Est-ce que **vous venez d'**arriver en France?

PRÉSENT: **Je viens, tu viens, il vient, nous venons, vous venez, ils viennent.**
PASSÉ COMPOSÉ: **Je suis venu(e).**
FUTUR: **Je viendrai.**

Revenir, *to come back;* **devenir,** *to become;* **prévenir,** *to warn;* **se souvenir
(de),** *to remember;* **convenir,** *to be suitable, to agree,* are conjugated like
venir.

B. Tenir, *to hold, to keep;* tenir à, *to insist upon, to be eager to.*

Henri **tient à** monter en haut de la tour Eiffel.

PRÉSENT: **Je tiens, tu tiens, il tient, nous tenons, vous tenez, ils tiennent.**
PASSÉ COMPOSÉ: **J'ai tenu.**
FUTUR: **Je tiendrai.**

Retenir, *to retain, to reserve;* **appartenir (à),** *to belong to,* are conjugated
like **tenir.**

VERBES IRRÉGULIERS

77   Third group of irregular verbs in -ir: **ouvrir,** to open; **couvrir,** to cover; **souffrir,** to suffer.

These verbs are regular except for the present indicative and the past participle ending in **-ert.**

Ouvrez la portière de la voiture.
Roger **a ouvert** la lettre.

PRÉSENT: **J'ouvre, tu ouvres, il ouvre, nous ouvrons, vous ouvrez, ils ouvrent.**
PASSÉ COMPOSÉ: **J'ai ouvert.**

78   First group of verbs ending in -re: **connaître, croire, boire, lire.**

Regular except for the present indicative and the past participle.

The past participle of these verbs ends in **-u: connaître — connu, croire — cru, boire — bu, lire — lu.**

A.   Connaître, *to know, to be acquainted with.* (See par. 40.)

Connaissez-vous les Duplessis?
Je ne **connais** pas très bien la France.

PRÉSENT: **Je connais, tu connais, il connaît, nous connaissons, vous connaissez, ils connaissent.**
PASSÉ COMPOSÉ: **J'ai connu.**

B.   Croire, *to believe; to think.*

Je crois que *Gien* rime avec *chien.*
Croyez-vous cette histoire?

PRÉSENT: **Je crois, tu crois, il croit, nous croyons, vous croyez, ils croient.**
PASSÉ COMPOSÉ: **J'ai cru.**

C.   Boire, *to drink.*

Buvez-vous du café? — Oui, **j'en bois** tous les matins.
Il a bu un demi-litre d'eau fraîche.

PRÉSENT: **Je bois, tu bois, il boit, nous buvons, vous buvez, ils boivent.**
PASSÉ COMPOSÉ: **J'ai bu.**

D. **Lire,** *to read.*

Voilà un poteau indicateur. **Lisez** ce qu'il dit.
(Lisant) Il dit: Gien, 65 kilomètres.

PRÉSENT: **Je lis, tu lis, il lit, nous lisons, vous lisez, ils lisent.**
PASSÉ COMPOSÉ: **J'ai lu.**

79 Second group of irregular verbs in -re.

The verbs in this group are regular except for the present indicative
and the past participle.

A. Past participle in -is: mettre — mis, prendre — pris.

1. **Mettre,** to put, to put on; **se mettre à,** to begin.

Je mets mon imperméable quand il pleut.
Il s'est mis à pleuvoir. **J'ai mis** mon imperméable.
Si **je me permets** de te donner mon avis, tu n'as guère le choix.

PRÉSENT: **Je mets, tu mets, il met, nous mettons, vous mettez, ils mettent.**
PASSÉ COMPOSÉ: **J'ai mis.**

Permettre, *to permit;* **promettre,** *to promise;* **remettre,** *to deliver, to put back,* and other compounds of **mettre** are conjugated like **mettre.**

2. **Prendre,** to take.

Quelle route **prenez-vous?** —**Je prends** l'autoroute.
Vous ne **comprenez** pas? — Non, **je** n'y **comprends** rien.
J'ai été si **surpris** que j'ai failli quitter la route.

PRÉSENT: **Je prends, tu prends, il prend, nous prenons, vous prenez, ils prennent.**
PASSÉ COMPOSÉ: **J'ai pris.**

Comprendre, *to understand;* **surprendre,** *to surprise;* **apprendre,** *to learn,* and other compounds of **prendre** are conjugated like **prendre.**

B. Past participle in -it: dire, écrire, conduire.

1. **Dire** to say, to tell.

On écrit *Laon* et **on dit** *lent.*
Ne **dites** pas ces choses-là sans me prévenir.

PRÉSENT: **Je dis, tu dis, il dit, nous disons, vous dites, ils disent.**
PASSÉ COMPOSÉ: **J'ai dit.**

2. Écrire, to write.

On écrit *Caen* et on dit *quand*.
Écrivez votre nom.

PRÉSENT: **J'écris, tu écris, il écrit, nous écrivons, vous écrivez, ils écrivent.**
PASSÉ COMPOSÉ: **J'ai écrit.**

Décrire, *to describe*, is conjugated like **écrire**.

3. Conduire, to drive; to conduct.

Henri **conduit** l'auto.
Il a conduit toute la journée.

PRÉSENT: **Je conduis, tu conduis, il conduit, nous conduisons, vous conduisez, ils conduisent.**
PASSÉ COMPOSÉ: **J'ai conduit.**

Produire, *to produce*, and **construire,** *to build*, are conjugated like **conduire.**

C. Past participle in -i: suivre, suffire.

1. Suivre, to follow; to take (a course).

Suivez cette route jusqu'au prochain village.
Je la **suis** depuis une heure. (*I have been following it for an hour.*)

PRÉSENT: **Je suis, tu suis, il suit, nous suivons, vous suivez, ils suivent.**
PASSÉ COMPOSÉ: **J'ai suivi.**

2. Suffire, to suffice, to be sufficient.

This verb is used mostly as an impersonal verb.

Il suffit d'appuyer sur le bouton. (*All you need do is to . . .*)
Il suffira de partir à sept heures.

PRÉSENT: **Il suffit.**
PASSÉ COMPOSÉ: **Il a suffi.**

80 Verbs ending in -indre.

Plaindre, *to pity;* **se plaindre,** *to complain;* **craindre,** *to fear;* **atteindre,** *to reach, to attain;* **éteindre,** *to extinguish;* **peindre,** *to paint;* **rejoindre,** *to meet, to catch up with.*

The present tense of this group of verbs has two stems. In all cases the plural stem ends en **-gn-:** Je **crains** — nous **craign**ons.

The past participle of these verbs ends in **-int** and is identical with the third person singular of the present tense: **il craint,** il a **craint; il atteint,** il a **atteint; il peint,** il a **peint; il rejoint,** il a **rejoint.**

Craindre, *to fear.*

Je crains que votre bien-être ne soit de courte durée.
Ne **craignez** rien, monsieur.
Henri **se plaint** de la pluie.

Présent: **Je crains, tu crains, il craint, nous craignons, vous craignez, ils craignent.**
Passé composé: **J'ai craint.**

Note that the verbs ending in **-eindre** and **-oindre** have **-e-** or **-o-** in their stem throughout: il **p**eint, elle nous rejoint.

81 Faire, to make, to do.

Il faisait beau quand nous sommes partis.
Mon appareil **fera** l'affaire.
Tu ferais mieux de me dire quelle route il faut prendre.

Présent: **Je fais, tu fais, il fait, nous faisons, vous faites, ils font.**
Passé composé: **J'ai fait.**
Futur: **Je ferai.**

82 Voir, to see; apercevoir, to perceive, to see; recevoir, to receive.

These verbs have a past participle in **-u,** two stems in the present tense, and an irregular future.

Voir

Je vois un village là-bas.
Je verrai ce que je peux faire.

Présent: **Je vois, tu vois, il voit, nous voyons, vous voyez, ils voient.**
Passé composé: **J'ai vu.**
Futur: **Je verrai.**

VERBES IRRÉGULIERS

Apercevoir

J'aperçois là-bas un poteau indicateur.
Je l'ai aperçu de loin.

Présent: **J'aperçois, tu aperçois, il aperçoit, nous apercevons, vous apercevez, ils aperçoivent.**
Passé composé: **J'ai aperçu.**
Futur: **J'apercevrai.**

The conjugation of **recevoir** is like that of **apercevoir.**

I. Mettez chacune des phrases suivantes au pluriel:

1. Je vais à Londres. 2. Je m'en vais demain. 3. J'envoie des cadeaux. 4. Je pars à trois heures. 5. Je sors ce soir. 6. Je me sers de son appareil. 7. Est-ce que tu dors? 8. Est-ce que tu viens avec nous? 9. Qu'est-ce que tu deviens? 10. Est-ce que tu te souviens d'elle? 11. Connais-tu les Duplessis? 12. Crois-tu cette histoire? 13. Bois-tu du café? 14. Il boit du café. 15. Il lit le journal. 16. Il prend l'autobus. 17. Il apprend à conduire. 18. Il dit toujours la vérité. 19. Il écrit des lettres. 20. Il conduit bien. 21. Il ne craint rien. 22. Il ne se plaint pas. 23. Qu'est-ce qu'il fait? 24. Qu'est-ce qu'il aperçoit?

II. Mettez chacune des phrases suivantes au passé composé:

1. Mme Frazer va en France. 2. Elle rejoint Henri. 3. Un jour, en traversant la Place de l'Opéra, elle aperçoit Jean Hughes. 4. Elle le voit de loin. 5. Ils vont ensemble au Café de la Paix. 6. Mme Frazer prend un café-crème. 7. Soudain elle se sent mal. 8. Elle se plaint d'avoir mal au cœur. 9. Elle souffre pendant quelques instants. 10. Elle se remet bientôt. 11. Elle se met à sourire de nouveau. 12. Cette crise est de courte durée. 13. Jean offre de la reconduire à son hôtel. 14. Elle ne veut pas le déranger. 15. Il se permet de la reconduire tout de même. 16. Elle le remercie vivement.

III. Mettez chacune des phrases suivantes au futur:

1. Je m'en vais demain. 2. Il envoie des cadeaux. 3. Il vient nous voir. 4. Il revient la semaine prochaine. 5. Cette auto tient la route. 6. Je me souviens de lui. 7. Il suffit de partir à huit heures. 8. Les pompiers éteignent le feu. (*The firemen are putting out the fire.*) 9. Je vous rejoins tout à l'heure.

10. Je le vois ce soir. 11. Je reçois de ses nouvelles. 12. Il reçoit de mes nouvelles. 13. Qu'est-ce que vous faites? 14. Nous le voyons tous les jours. 15. Ils vont en Touraine. 16. Ils voient les châteaux.

IV. Répondez en français par une phrase complète à chacune des questions suivantes:

1. Où a-t-on envoyé Jean? 2. Est-ce qu'on l'enverra en Afrique cet été? 3. Est-ce que vous sortez tous les soirs? 4. Vous servez-vous de votre appareil tous les jours? 5. Prenez-vous beaucoup de photos? 6. Avez-vous pris des photos l'hiver dernier? 7. Est-ce que Jean vient d'arriver à Paris? 8. D'où vient-il? 9. Les Duplessis viennent-ils dîner avec Jean? 10. Les Frazer viendront-ils le chercher à son hôtel? 11. Comment les Duplessis ont-ils reçu Jean? (à bras ouverts) 12. Est-ce que la terre est couverte de neige aujourd'hui? 13. Connaissez-vous les Frazer? 14. Jean les connaît-il? 15. Buvez-vous beaucoup de café? 16. En avez-vous bu ce matin? 17. Est-ce que vous mettez votre imperméable quand il fait beau? 18. Est-ce qu'il s'est mis à pleuvoir ce matin de bonne heure? 19. Qui conduit l'auto des Frazer? 20. Conduisez-vous souvent? 21. Vos parents conduisent-ils souvent? 22. Craignez-vous la pluie? 23. Vous plaignez-vous quand il pleut? 24. Henri se plaint-il de la pluie? 25. Jean aperçoit-il un poteau indicateur? 26. Est-ce que les Frazer l'aperçoivent aussi? 27. Qui l'a aperçu le premier? 28. Est-ce que vous recevez beaucoup de lettres? 29. Vos parents en reçoivent-ils beaucoup? 30. En avez-vous reçu ce matin? 31. Espérez-vous en recevoir ce soir?

V. THÈME. **Si j'avais une grosse fortune.**

1. I would buy a big house. 2. I would have lots of guests (I would receive a quantity of guests). 3. I would not fear anything. 4. I would lead an extraordinary life. 5. I would paint. 6. I would drive big cars. 7. I would have several houses built. 8. I would not complain of taxes. 9. I would not take the liberty (**se permettre**) of giving advice to everybody. 10. I would sleep late every morning. 11. I would do whatever I wanted to (all that would please me). 12. I would be royally bored.

LES GENDARMES

Jean et les Frazer, en route pour Paris, voient tout à coup deux gendarmes au milieu de la route. Ils ne savent pas ce que veulent ces gendarmes, et la conversation qu'ils ont avec eux ne les renseigne guère.

HENRI. —¹Qu'est-ce que c'est que ça, là-bas, au milieu de la route?

JEAN. —²Tu ne vois pas ce que c'est? ³Regarde leur uniforme. ⁴Ce sont des gendarmes.*

HENRI. —⁵Qu'est-ce qui se passe?

JEAN. —⁶Je n'en sais rien. ⁷Peut-être qu'un crime a été commis.

HENRI. —⁸Que faut-il faire? Faire demi-tour?

JEAN. —⁹Sûrement pas.

HÉLÈNE. —¹⁰Sois sérieux et ralentis. ¹¹Je ne sais pas ce qu'ils veulent, ¹²mais il est certain que ces braves gendarmes ont quelque chose à nous dire. ¹³Voyons de quoi il s'agit.

John and the Frazers, who are on the way to Paris, suddenly see two troopers in the middle of the road. They don't know what the troopers want, and the conversation they have with them is not very informative.

HENRY. —¹What's that, up ahead, in the middle of the road?

JOHN. —²Don't you see what it is? ³Look at their uniforms. ⁴It's troopers.

HENRY. —⁵What's going on?

JOHN. —⁶I have no idea. ⁷Perhaps a crime has been committed.

HENRY. —⁸What must we do? Turn around?

JOHN. —⁹Certainly not.

HELEN. —¹⁰Don't be silly, and slow down. ¹¹I don't know what they want, ¹²but it is certain that those worthy troopers have something to say to us. ¹³Let's see what's up.

---

* Les gendarmes constituent la police nationale. Les membres de la police urbaine s'appellent agents de police ou sergents de ville.

(*Henri s'arrête. Les gendarmes s'approchent.*)

UN DES GENDARMES (*à Henri*). — [14]Veuillez me montrer vos papiers, monsieur.

HENRI. —[15]Lesquels voulez-vous?

LE GENDARME. —[16]Votre passeport, votre permis de conduire et votre police d'assurance. (*Après avoir examiné les papiers:*) [17]Tout est en règle. [18]Vous pouvez continuer.

MME FRAZER. —[19]Pourquoi ne demandes-tu pas à monsieur les renseignements dont tu as besoin?

HENRI. —[20]Tiens, c'est une idée! [21]A quoi est-ce que je pensais? (*Au gendarme:*) [22]Nous voulons aller à Orléans, monsieur. [23]Laquelle des deux routes est la plus courte, [24]celle sur laquelle nous sommes ou celle qui passe par Romorantin? [25]Qu'en pensez-vous?

LE GENDARME. —[26]Il n'y a pas grande différence, monsieur. [27]Si j'étais à votre place, je ne changerais pas de route.

HENRI. —[28]Merci beaucoup, monsieur. (*Ils se remettent en route.*)

HÉLÈNE. —[29]Ce qui me gêne, c'est que nous ne saurons jamais pourquoi ces gendarmes nous ont arrêtés.

HENRI. —[30]Qu'est-ce que ça fait? [31]Ils nous ont remis en liberté, et c'est tout ce qui importe.

(*Henry stops. The troopers come to the car.*)

ONE OF THE TROOPERS (*to Henry*). — [14]Please show me your papers, sir.

HENRY. —[15]Which ones do you want?

THE TROOPER. —[16]Your passport, your driver's license, and your insurance policy. (*After examining the papers:*) [17]Everything is in order. [18]You can go ahead.

MRS. FRAZER. —[19]Why don't you ask the gentleman for the information you need?

HENRY. —[20]Well! That's an idea. [21]What was I thinking about? (*To the trooper:*) [22]We want to go to Orléans. [23]Which of the two roads is the shorter, sir, [24]the one we are on or the one that goes through Romorantin? [25]What do you think (of it)?

THE TROOPER. —[26]There is not much difference, sir. [27]If I were you (If I were in your place), I would not change roads.

HENRY. —[28]Thank you very much, sir. (*They start off again.*)

HELEN. —[29]What bothers me is that we will never know why those troopers stopped us.

HENRY. —[30]What difference does it make? [31]They set us free and that is the only thing that matters.

I. SUBSTITUTIONS. Répétez les phrases suivantes, en substituant les mots indiqués:

1. La conversation qu'ils ont avec eux [ne les renseigne guère].
   ne leur apprend rien/ ne leur apprend pas grand-chose/ ne les éclaire pas/ ne leur dit pas ce qu'ils veulent savoir

2. De quoi [s'agit-il]?
   est-il question/ avez-vous besoin/ parlez-vous/ s'occupe-t-il

3. Voyons [de quoi il s'agit].
   de quoi il est question/ ce qu'ils veu-lent/ ce qu'ils diront/ ce qui se passe

4. Je ne sais pas [ce qui est arrivé].
   ce qui leur est arrivé/ ce qui lui arrivera/ ce qu'il fait à l'heure actuelle/ ce qu'il est devenu (*what has become of him*)/ ce qu'il deviendra

5. Laquelle des deux routes est [la plus courte]?
   la meilleure/ la plus directe/ la mieux entretenue (*kept up*)/ la moins poussiéreuse

6. Si j'étais à votre place je ne changerais pas [de route].
   de chemin/ d'itinéraire/ d'idée/ d'hôtel/ de vêtements

II. SUBSTITUTIONS. **penser de, penser que.** Répétez les phrases suivantes, en substituant les mots indiqués:

1. Que pensez-vous de ce château? Je pense qu'il est [très beau].
   très vieux/ très curieux/ assez intéressant/ fort impressionnant

2. Que pensez-vous de son idée? Je pense qu'elle est [raisonnable].
   originale/ curieuse/ fort intéressante/ extraordinaire

3. Que pensez-vous de ce qu'il a fait? Je pense [qu'il a eu raison].
   qu'il a eu tort/ qu'il se trompe/ qu'il s'est trompé/ qu'il a bien fait (*did the right thing*)

III. Dites en français, en employant l'expression indiquée:

A. penser à

1. What are you thinking about? 2. I am thinking of our trip to Touraine. 3. When I think of it, I think of the rain. 4. Don't you think of the two troopers who stopped us? 5. Naturally, I think of them all the time.

B. à la place (de)

1. If I were you, I wouldn't take the other road. 2. Put yourself in my place. 3. I don't know what I would do if I were in your place. 4. If I were in Henry's place, I would slow down and stop.

IV. Dites à quelqu'un:

1. de ralentir. 2. d'ouvrir la portière. 3. de regarder le poteau indicateur. 4. de faire demi-tour. 5. que vous croyez voir des gendarmes. 6. qu'ils ont l'air de vous attendre. 7. que vous vous doutez de ce qu'ils veulent. 8. qu'ils veulent sans doute regarder vos papiers. 9. que vous avez failli vous tromper de route. 10. que vous finirez bien par arriver à Orléans.

V. Répondez en français:

1. Henri voit-il quelque chose sur la route? 2. Sait-il ce que c'est? 3. Que demande Henri lorsqu'il voit les gendarmes? 4. Comment Jean explique-t-il leur présence? 5. Qu'est-ce qu'Henri propose de faire? 6. Quel conseil Hélène donne-t-elle à son frère? 7. Que font les gendarmes quand l'auto s'arrête? 8. Qu'est-ce qu'un des gendarmes demande à Henri de lui montrer? 9. Quels papiers le gendarme veut-il examiner? 10. Qu'est-ce qu'il dit à Henri après avoir examiné ses papiers? 11. Qu'est-ce que Mme Frazer dit à Henri de demander au gendarme? 12. Henri y avait-il pensé? 13. Où veut-il aller? 14. Combien de routes peut-il prendre pour aller à Orléans? 15. Qu'est-ce qu'il veut savoir au sujet de ces routes? 16. Y a-t-il une grande différence entre les deux? 17. Que ferait le gendarme s'il était à la place d'Henri? 18. Qu'est-ce qui gêne Hélène? 19. Henri pense-t-il que cela importe beaucoup? 20. Qu'est-ce qui importe, à son avis?

VI. Demandez à quelqu'un:

1. ce qu'Henri voit sur la route. 2. s'il sait ce que c'est. 3. ce que c'est qu'un gendarme. 4. si Jean sait ce qui se passe. 5. de quoi il s'agit. 6. ce que les gendarmes demandent à Henri. 7. ce que c'est qu'un passeport. 8. s'il faut un passeport pour voyager en Europe. 9. laquelle des deux routes est la plus courte. 10. ce qu'il ferait s'il était à votre place. 11. ce qui gêne Hélène. 12. ce qui importe.

VII. THÈME.

As he was driving along a narrow road between Bourges and Orléans, Henry saw two men standing on each side of a bridge over a small river. John told him to notice their uniforms. Henry immediately realized that these two gentlemen were gendarmes. "What's going on? What do they want? I haven't done anything . . .," he thought. There was really nothing to be afraid of. Sometimes the police stop passing cars, just to make sure (**s'assurer**) that everything is in order; for instance, to make sure that the car has not been stolen or that the driver has not committed some crime. After looking at Henry's papers, at his passport and driver's license, the gendarmes let him continue (on) his trip.

VIII. Mettez les phrases suivantes au passé, en remplaçant le présent de l'indicatif par le **passé composé** ou l'**imparfait**, selon le cas:

Tout à coup, j'aperçois deux gendarmes qui barrent la route. Qu'est-ce qu'ils nous veulent? Est-ce que par hasard je vais trop vite? Aussitôt, je ralentis et les gendarmes s'approchent de la voiture. L'un d'eux semble tirer un carnet de sa poche. C'est mauvais signe . . .

Mais en réalité ces gendarmes n'ont aucune intention perverse et ils me demandent très aimablement où je vais. Croyant qu'ils me demandent comment je vais, je leur réponds: "Très bien, merci" . . . Ils se mettent à rire, et l'un d'eux me dit que je peux continuer mon voyage.

Ces gendarmes sont de braves gens, qui ne nous veulent aucun mal.

Route en forêt

Pronoms interrogatifs et relatifs

83   Interrogative pronouns that refer to persons.

A. Subject forms: **Qui?** or **Qui est-ce qui?** *Who?*

Qui est allé à Saint-Cloud?   *or*
Qui est-ce qui est allé à Saint-Cloud?

B. Object forms: **Qui?** or **Qui est-ce que?** *Whom?*

1.   Object of a verb.

Qui Jean est-il allé voir?   *or*
Qui est-ce que Jean est allé voir?

2.   Object of a preposition.

A qui Roger a-t-il parlé?
De qui parlez-vous?
Chez qui a-t-il dîné?

Note that **est-ce que** is often used with **qui?** when it is object of a *verb* but that it is less common when **qui?** is the object of a *preposition*.

84   Interrogative pronouns that refer to things, situations, etc. (not to persons).

A. Subject form: **Qu'est-ce qui?** *What?*

Qu'est-ce qui se passe?
Qu'est-ce qui est arrivé?

B. Object forms.

    1. Object of a verb: **Que? Qu'est-ce que?** *What?*

Que faut-il faire? *or*
Qu'est-ce qu'il faut faire?

Qu'avez-vous dit? *or*
Qu'est-ce vous avez dit?

    2. Object of a preposition: **Quoi?** *What?*

De quoi parlez-vous?
A quoi pensez-vous?

Note also that **Quoi?** is used in the word **pourquoi?** and in the expressions **Quoi de nouveau? Quoi de neuf?** *What's new?*

C. Form for asking for a definition.

    The interrogative form for asking for a definition is **Qu'est-ce que c'est que?**

Qu'est-ce que c'est que ça?	What's that?
Qu'est-ce que c'est qu'un permis de conduire?	What's a driver's license?

In formal writing, the form **Qu'est-ce que?** is used.

Qu'est-ce que le surréalisme?

85 The interrogative pronoun **lequel?** (referring to persons or things)

    Lequel? Laquelle? Lesquels? Lesquelles? *Which? Which one? Which ones?* are used to distinguish between persons or things within a group. They may be used as subject or object of a verb or as object of a preposition.

Laquelle des deux routes est la plus courte?
Lequel des peintres impressionnistes préférez-vous?

In combination with the prepositions **à** or **de,** the forms are: **auquel, auxquels, duquel, desquels,** etc.

Duquel de ces châteaux avez-vous pris des photos?

86   Relative pronouns.

As the forms of interrogative and relative pronouns are confusingly similar, it is helpful to distinguish carefully between the way they are used.

A relative pronoun is used to head a subordinate clause that modifies a preceding noun or pronoun.

Jean, **qui** est de passage à Paris, . . .
Les Duplessis, **que** nous connaissons, . . .

87   The relative pronouns **qui** and **que**.

A. The relative pronoun **qui**.

The relative pronoun **qui** (*who, which, that*) is used as the subject of a verb and may refer to persons or things. (Cf. interrogative **qui?** which refers only to persons.)

Jean, **qui** est allé à Saint-Cloud, . . .
La route **qui** passe par Romorantin . . .
Celle **qui** passe par Romorantin . . .

Qui is also used after prepositions, but in this case it refers only to persons.

Les gendarmes **à qui** nous avons parlé . . .
Les amis **chez qui** il a dîné . . .

B. The relative pronoun **que**.

The relative pronoun **que** (*whom, which, that*) is used only as the direct object of a verb and may refer to persons or things. (Cf. interrog. **que?** which refers only to things.)

Le château **que** nous avons visité hier . . .
Les gendarmes **que** nous avons vus hier . . .

In such phrases, **que** MUST be expressed even though in English we are more likely to say: The château we saw . . .

88   The relative pronoun **dont**.

This form, meaning *of whom, of which, about whom, whose,* etc. is equivalent to the preposition **de** and **qui,** or the forms **duquel, desquels,** etc. (See par. 90.) It may refer to persons or things and it is used only after an expressed antecedent.

Pourquoi ne demandes-tu pas les renseignements **dont** tu as besoin?
Le fonctionnaire **dont** nous parlons . . .
Le château **dont** nous avons vu la façade . . .
Celui **dont** nous avons vu l'intérieur . . .

89   Relative pronouns with **ce** as antecedent.

A.   Subject form: **ce qui** *what, that which.*

Ce qui me gêne, c'est que nous ne saurons jamais . . .
Ce qui m'ennuie, . . .
Je ne sais pas **ce qui** s'est passé.

B.   Object form: **ce que** *what, that which.*

Ce que vous dites n'est pas vrai.
Voilà **ce que** j'ai acheté.
Je ne sais pas **ce que** vous voulez dire.
Je n'ai pas trouvé **ce que** je cherchais.

C.   With preposition.

Ce dont j'ai besoin, c'est d'un bon appareil.
C'est **ce dont** il s'agit.
Voilà **ce à quoi** je pensais.

Ce dont and **ce à quoi** are frequent in literary works, but they are little used in spoken French today.

90   The relative pronoun **lequel (laquelle, lesquels, lesquelles).**

These forms, which correspond to **qui** and **que,** are used primarily after prepositions to refer to things:

La route sur **laquelle** nous sommes . . .
Voilà l'appareil avec **lequel** j'ai pris ces photos.

PRONOMS INTERROGATIFS ET RELATIFS

Note that these forms are sometimes used to refer to persons in a sentence where there are two possible antecedents:

Le père de ma femme, **lequel** . . . (*to refer to* père)
Le père de ma femme, **laquelle** . . . (*to refer to* femme)

91 Où (where, when, in which).

Où is of course an adverb; but in addition to its usual meaning (*where?*), it is often used as if it were a relative pronoun and has the meaning *in which* or *when:*

Le jour **où** (*when*) ils sont arrivés à Orléans . . .
La maison **où** (*where or in which*) habitent les Duplessis . . .

(Cf. interrog. **où** which means only *where?*)

D'où venez-vous? *Where are you from?* or *Where have you been?*

92 Use of qui and quoi without an expressed antecedent in indirect questions.

DIRECT QUESTION	INDIRECT QUESTION
Qui est venu?	Savez-vous **qui** est venu?
De qui parle-t-il?	Savez-vous **de qui** il parle?
A quoi pense-t-il?	Savez-vous **à quoi** il pense?

Qui and **quoi** are used similarly after many expressions such as **je ne sais pas, je me demande, j'ignore,** etc.

Je ne sais pas **qui** est venu, **de qui** il parle, **à quoi** il pense.
Je me demande **de quoi** il s'agit, **de qui** il parle, **à quoi** il pense.
J'ignore **de quoi** il s'agit, **de qui** il parle, **à quoi** il pense.

I. SUBSTITUTIONS. Répétez les phrases suivantes, en substituant les mots indiqués:

1. Voilà un château [qui est célèbre].

   qui a été construit au XVIe siècle/ que je ne connaissais pas/ que j'ai visité l'an dernier/ dont nous avons souvent entendu parler/ dont nous allons voir l'intérieur

2. Je verrai [ce qui se passe].

ce qui arrive/ ce que c'est/ de quoi il s'agit/ à quoi vous pensez

3. Dites-moi [ce que vous faites].

ce qu'il a dit/ de qui vous avez parlé/ de quoi vous parlez/ de quoi
vous avez besoin/ à qui vous pensez/ ce que vous pensez de lui

4. Je me demande [qui a téléphoné].

de quoi il s'agissait/ à qui il voulait
parler/ à quoi il pensait/ d'où il vient

II. Demandez à quelqu'un:

1. qui a invité Jean à aller en Touraine. **2.** ce qu'il a répondu. **3.** qui
conduit l'auto de Mme Frazer. **4.** chez qui Jean est allé à son retour à Paris.
5. de quoi Jean et Roger ont parlé, **6.** ce qui se passe sur la route, **7.** qui a
arrêté l'auto des Frazer. **8.** ce que les gendarmes ont demandé. **9.** de quels
renseignements Henri a besoin. **10.** à quoi pensait Henri. **11.** lequel des
châteaux de la Touraine il préfère. **12.** ce qui gêne Henri. **13.** ce que c'est
qu'un passeport. **14.** ce que c'est qu'un permis de conduire. **15.** ce que
c'est qu'un gendarme. **16.** ce qu'il faut faire. **17.** quelle route il faut prendre.
18. ce que veulent les gendarmes.

III. Posez en français la question à laquelle répondrait chacune des phrases suivantes, en employant des pronoms interrogatifs:

1. Henri conduit la voiture. **2.** Il voit des gendarmes. **3.** Ils demandent
les papiers d'Henri. **4.** Henri demande des renseignements. **5.** Il préfère le
château de Chambord. **6.** Il admire l'emblème de Louis XII. **7.** Mme Frazer
préfère celui de Louise de Savoie. **8.** Il y a quelque chose là-bas au milieu de
la route. **9.** Il faut s'arrêter. **10.** Henri parle de la pluie. **11.** La pluie
l'ennuie. **12.** La poésie le gêne.

IV. Posez les questions suivantes par l'expression indirecte, en commençant par **Savez-vous . . . ?**

EX.: — Qu'est-ce qui se passe?
— **Savez-vous ce qui se passe?**

1. Qui est venu me voir? **2.** Qu'est-ce qu'il a dit? **3.** Qui est-ce qui est venu avec
lui? **4.** Qu'est-ce qu'il voulait? **5.** De quoi a-t-il parlé? **6.** De quoi s'agissait-il?
7. Qu'est-ce qui arrivera? **8.** Qu'est-ce qui s'est passé? **9.** Qu'est-ce que c'est qu'une
police d'assurance?

V. Répondez aux questions précédentes, en commençant par **Je ne sais pas . . . .**

VI. Combinez deux phrases en une seule, en employant un pronom relatif:

EX.: — Voilà des photos. Elles me plaisent beaucoup.
— **Voilà des photos qui me plaisent beaucoup.**

A. qui

1. Jean connaît les Duplessis depuis longtemps. Il va les voir à Saint-Cloud. **2.** Henri conduit la voiture. Il voit des gendarmes au milieu de la route. **3.** Henri est le fils de Mᵐᵉ Frazer. Il aime bien conduire. **4.** Mᵐᵉ Frazer a une belle auto. Elle invite Jean à les accompagner en Touraine. **5.** Jean n'a pas grand-chose à faire. Il accepte avec plaisir.

B. que

1. Jean va voir les Duplessis. Il ne les a pas vus depuis longtemps. **2.** Jean montre des photos à Hélène. Il la connaît depuis longtemps. **3.** Voilà de belles photos. Jean les a prises en Touraine. **4.** Il est content de revoir les Frazer. Il les aime beaucoup. **5.** Il visite le château de Blois. Il le connaissait déjà.

C. dont

EX.: — Voilà les photos. Je vous en ai parlé hier.
— **Voilà les photos dont je vous ai parlé hier.**

1. Henri monte en haut de la tour Eiffel. Il en a souvent entendu parler. **2.** Henri demande des renseignements. Il en a besoin. **3.** Ils ont visité plusieurs châteaux. Ils en avaient des photos. **4.** Marie a acheté le pain. Elle en avait besoin. **5.** Henri préfère le château de Chambord. Il en a admiré la façade.

VII. Dites en français:

1. What interests me is the emblem of François premier. **2.** What bothers me is that I am hungry. **3.** What we need is a good dinner. **4.** What we ate at lunch was excellent; but what I want now is some cool water. **5.** Which of those châteaux is the most beautiful? **6.** With which of those cameras did you take these pictures? **7.** Which of these photos do you like best? **8.** What's that? **9.** Don't you know what it is? **10.** I know it is a signpost but I don't know what it says. **11.** Read what it says. **12.** The day (when) **(où)** we left it rained. **13.** The day we took the wrong road, it rained all day long. **14.** John recited a poem of Verlaine in which it was a question of rain on the roof.

Église d'Auvers, Van Gogh

LETTRES

La fin du séjour de Jean en France approche. Le lendemain de son retour à Paris, après son excursion avec les Frazer dans la région de la Loire, il s'occupe de sa correspondance. Voici ce qu'il écrit à Mme* Frazer:*

Hôtel Meurice
Paris, le 24 août

Chère Madame,

[1]Avant de quitter Paris, je tiens à vous remercier encore de votre aimable invitation à vous accompagner en Touraine. [2]J'étais déjà allé dans cette jolie région, mais je ne l'avais pas parcourue en si agréable compagnie. [3]Je regrette un peu, comme vous, que le "Jardin de la France" ait été si copieusement arrosé au cours de notre voyage. [4]Mais la pluie fait pousser les fleurs, et je n'oublierai jamais les fleurs, surtout les belles roses et les énormes dahlias qui semblent pousser partout en Touraine.

[5]D'après ce que m'a dit Henri, vous avez l'intention de rentrer aux États-Unis à la fin du mois prochain. [6]Nous nous reverrons donc sous peu, ce qui sera pour moi un grand plaisir.

[7]D'ici là, chère Madame, je vous prie de faire mes amitiés à Hélène et à Henri, et d'agréer mes hommages respectueux.

Jean

The end of John's stay in France is drawing near. The day after his return to Paris, after his trip with the Frazers to the Loire region, he is taking care of his correspondence. This is what he writes to Mrs. Frazer:

Hotel Meurice
Paris, August 24

Dear Mrs. Frazer:

[1]Before leaving Paris, I *must* thank you again for your kind invitation to go with you to Touraine. [2]I had already been to that lovely part of the country, but I had never traveled through it in such pleasant company. [3]I am a little sorry, as you are, that the "Garden of France" was so copiously sprinkled during our trip. [4]But rain makes flowers grow, and I'll never forget the flowers, especially the fine roses and the huge dahlias, that seem to grow everywhere in Touraine.

[5]According to what Henry told me, you are planning to go back to the United States at the end of next month. [6]So we will meet again soon, and that will be a great pleasure for me.

[7]In the meantime, please say hello to Helen and Henry for me.

Sincerely yours,
John

Il a essayé de donner un coup de fil à l'antiquaire, chez qui il a acheté un service de table destiné à sa sœur. N'ayant pas réussi, il lui envoie la lettre suivante:

Monsieur,

[1]Vous trouverez ci-inclus un mandat-poste de 165 francs en paiement du reliquat dû sur votre facture No. 2.226, datée du 19 courant.

[2]Je crois vous avoir dit, au moment de l'achat, d'envoyer le service de table de façon à ce qu'il arrive à l'adresse indiquée vers le milieu du mois de septembre. [3]Toutefois, je compte passer quelque temps à Philadelphie. [4]Je désire donc que l'envoi arrive à sa destination une quinzaine de jours plus tard. [5]Je vous prie de fixer la date d'expédition qui convient le mieux, en tenant compte des délais imposés par le transport et par les formalités de douane.

Veuillez agréer, Monsieur, mes salutations empressées.

Jean Hughes

Enfin, pendant son absence de Paris, Jean a reçu de Mme Lucien Ferry une invitation à dîner, qu'il est obligé de décliner pour la raison qu'il indique:

Chère Madame,

[1]Rien ne m'aurait donné plus de plaisir que d'accepter votre aimable invitation à dîner mardi prochain. [2]Malheureusement, je ne serai plus à Paris à cette date. [3]J'aurai quitté la France la veille, et je serai sans doute déjà arrivé à Philadelphie.

[4]Je regrette vivement de ne pas pouvoir être des vôtres. [5]J'aurais été heureux de me retrouver chez vous avec des amis communs, [6]au souvenir de qui je vous prie de me rappeler.

Je vous prie, chère Madame, d'agréer mes respectueux hommages.

Jean Hughes

He tried to phone the antique dealer at whose shop he bought a set of dishes for his sister. As he couldn't reach him (on the phone), he sent him the following letter:

Dear Sir:

[1]You will find herewith a money order for 165 francs in payment of the balance due on your bill No. 2,226, dated the 19th of this month.
[2]I think I told you when I bought the set of china to ship it so it would arrive at the address I gave you towards the middle of September. [3]However, I'm expecting to spend some time in Philadelphia. [4]Therefore, I'd like the shipment to reach its destination about two weeks later. [5]Will you please choose the most suitable shipping date, bearing in mind the time required for transportation and getting it through customs?

Sincerely yours,
John Hughes

Lastly, during his absence from Paris, John got a dinner invitation from Mrs. Lucien Ferry which he has to decline for the reason he gives:

Dear Mrs. Ferry:

[1]Nothing would have given me more pleasure than to accept your kind invitation to dinner next Tuesday. [2]Unfortunately I will no longer be in Paris on that date. [3]I will have left France the day before and I will no doubt have arrived in Philadelphia.
[4]I am very sorry indeed that I can't be among your guests. [5]I would have been happy to be at your house again with mutual friends. [6]Will you please remember me to them?

Sincerely yours,
John Hughes

NOTE: In English, it is unusual to go beyond such formulas as "Dear Mr. Blank" and "Sincerely yours" or "Yours very truly"; but in French, the formulas are a little more elaborate.

In a business letter, you begin: *Monsieur* and end: *Veuillez agréer, Monsieur, mes salutations empressées.* (Please accept . . .)

In a letter to a married woman — Mrs. Frazer, for example — you begin: *Chère Madame* and end: *Je vous prie, chère Madame, d'agréer mes hommages respectueux.* Some people avoid using an imperative — even *Veuillez* — in addressing a woman.

In a letter to a high administrative official, you begin: *Monsieur,* or if you know him personally, *Cher Monsieur;* and you end: *Veuillez agréer, Monsieur,* (or *cher Monsieur*) *l'expression de mes meilleurs sentiments.* It is more flattering to say: *Je vous prie, Monsieur, d'agréer . . .*

Young people writing to each other often use a less formal complimentary close such as: *Bien à vous (à toi)* or *Ton vieil ami,* etc.

Some people still include in the complimentary close such phrases as: *Veuillez agréer l'expression de mes sentiments les plus distingués,* or *Veuillez agréer l'expression de ma plus haute considération,* or *Veuillez croire à mes sentiments respectueux et les meilleurs,* etc.; but it is better to use a simple complimentary close than a fancy one.

I. SUBSTITUTIONS. Répétez les phrases suivantes, en substituant les mots indiqués:

1. D'après ce que m'a dit Henri, vous avez l'intention [de rentrer aux États-Unis].

   de passer encore quelques semaines à Paris/
   de faire un voyage en Bretagne/ de visiter
   les châteaux de la Loire/ d'aller dans le Midi

2. Nous nous reverrons donc [sous peu], ce qui sera pour moi un grand plaisir.

   dans trois jours/ avant la fin de l'année/ au
   mois de septembre/ d'aujourd'hui en quinze

3. Je compte partir [d'aujourd'hui en huit].

   la semaine prochaine/ le mois prochain/ demain/ après-demain

4. Je vous enverrai une dépêche [à mon arrivée à New York].

   le lendemain de mon arrivée/ peu après mon
   arrivée/ dès mon arrivée/ en arrivant à New York

5. Je lui ai donné un coup de fil [hier].

la veille de mon départ/ avant-hier/ juste
avant mon départ/ juste avant de partir

6. Il s'occupe [de sa correspondance].

de ses affaires/ des formalités de·douane/ de
son passeport/ de sa police d'assurance

7. Je regrette de ne pas pouvoir [être des vôtres].

vous accompagner/ accepter votre invitation/ aller passer le
week-end chez vous à la campagne/ vous retrouver à cinq heures

8. Je regrette [que le Jardin de la France ait été si copieusement arrosé].

qu'il ait fait si mauvais temps/ qu'il ait fait si chaud/
qu'il ait plu tout le temps/ qu'il ait fait si froid

9. [La fin de son séjour en France] approche.

La fin des vacances/ Le moment de son
départ/ La saison du tourisme/ Noël

II. Employez l'expression indiquée après chacune des phrases suivantes
pour dire à la personne à qui vous écrivez:

EX.: — que vous devez partir bientôt. (dans trois jours)
— **Je dois partir dans trois jours.**

1. que vous voulez la remercier de son aimable invitation. (je tiens à) **2.** que vous
comptez la revoir bientôt. (sous peu) **3.** que vous auriez été heureux d'être de ses
invités. (des vôtres). **4.** que vous la priez de présenter vos amitiés à ses parents. (rappeler au bon souvenir de) **5.** d'agréer vos salutations empressées. (veuillez)

III. Répondez en français:

1. Jean doit-il bientôt quitter la France? **2.** Que fait-il le lendemain de son
retour à Paris? **3.** Pourquoi écrit-il à Mme Frazer? **4.** Avait-il déjà parcouru
la Touraine? **5.** Comment appelle-t-on quelquefois la Touraine? **6.** Quelles
espèces de fleurs a-t-il vues pendant son voyage? **7.** Que dit-il au sujet de la
pluie? **8.** Quand les Frazer ont-ils l'intention de rentrer aux États-Unis?
9. Quand Jean compte-t-il les revoir? **10.** Pourquoi Jean envoie-t-il un mot à
l'antiquaire? **11.** Qu'est-ce qu'il a inclus dans sa lettre? **12.** Quand a-t-il
reçu la facture de l'antiquaire? **13.** Quand lui avait-il dit d'envoyer le service
de table? **14.** Pourquoi veut-il maintenant que l'envoi arrive quinze jours plus
tard? **15.** Qui fixera la date de l'expédition? **16.** De quoi l'antiquaire
devra-t-il tenir compte quand il fixera cette date? **17.** Quelle invitation Jean

a-t-il reçue pendant qu'il était en Touraine? **18.** Pourquoi ne peut-il pas l'accepter? **19.** Où sera-t-il au moment du dîner auquel il est invité? **20.** D'après ce qu'il dit dans sa lettre, connaît-il quelques-uns des autres invités? **21.** Au souvenir de qui demande-t-il à Mme Ferry de le rappeler? **22.** Comment termine-t-il sa lettre?

IV. Demandez à quelqu'un:

1. si Jean va rester encore longtemps en France. **2.** de quoi il s'occupe avant son départ. **3.** ce qu'il tient à faire avant de quitter Paris. **4.** si Jean connaissait déjà la Touraine. **5.** si les fleurs poussent bien en Touraine. **6.** ce qui les fait pousser. **7.** si les Frazer quitteront bientôt la France. **8.** où Jean compte les revoir. **9.** ce que c'est qu'un mandat-poste. **10.** si Jean sera à San Francisco au milieu d'octobre. **11.** s'il aurait été heureux d'accepter l'invitation qu'il a reçue pendant son absence. **12.** pourquoi il lui est impossible de l'accepter. **13.** avec qui il aurait été heureux de se retrouver. **14.** à qui il demande à Mme Ferry de le rappeler.

V. THÈME.

Before leaving for the United States, John wrote several letters.

First of all, he wrote to Mrs. Frazer to thank her for her kind invitation, and to tell her that in spite of the bad weather, he had greatly enjoyed **(apprécié)** the trip to **(dans)** the Loire region.

Then he wrote to the antique dealer from whom **(chez qui)** he had bought a Quimper earthenware table service to tell him to ship it. He added that the dealer knew better than he how long it takes such a shipment to reach its destination, and he asked him to set the most appropriate date.

Finally, he wrote to a lady who had invited him to dinner. He was very sorry not to be able to accept her invitation, but by **(à)** the date set for the dinner, he would be on his way **(en route pour)** to America.

Temps composés/ Voix passive

93 Pluperfect indicative.

A. Formation of the pluperfect.

The pluperfect tense is composed of the past participle of the verb and the *imparfait* of the auxiliary verb.

1. Verbs conjugated with **avoir**:

J'avais acheté, etc.	I had bought, etc.
J'avais fini	I had finished
J'avais vendu	I had sold
J'avais été	I had been
J'avais eu	I had had

2. Verbs conjugated with **être**:

J'étais allé(e)	I had gone
J'étais parti(e)	I had left
J'étais venu(e)	I had come
Je m'étais levé(e)	I had got up
Je m'étais mis(e) à	I had started

B. Use of the pluperfect.

As in English, the pluperfect tense expresses a past action that took place completely before another past action took place.

J'avais fixé la date de mon départ, quand j'ai reçu votre invitation.
J'étais déjà **allé** dans cette jolie région, mais **je ne l'avais jamais parcourue** en si aimable compagnie.

94 Future perfect indicative.

A. Formation of the future perfect.

The future perfect is composed of the past participle of the verb and the future tense of the auxiliary.

1. Verbs conjugated with **avoir**:

J'aurai fini	I shall have finished
J'aurai été	I shall have been
J'aurai eu	I shall have had

2. Verbs conjugated with **être**:

Je serai parti(e)	I shall have left
Il sera parti	He will have gone (away)
Je me serai levé(e)	I shall have got up

B. Use of the future perfect.

As in English, the future perfect tense is used to express an action that will take place in the future before another future action takes place. Note that in French, the second future action is expressed by the future tense whereas in English it is expressed by the present tense.

J'aurai fini mon travail quand vous arriverez. (*I'll have finished* my work when you get here.)

The future perfect is often used to express an action that will have taken place in the future before a specified time.

Je n'aurai pas encore **atteint** San Francisco à cette époque. (*I won't have got* to San Francisco at that time.)
Je serai parti avant son arrivée. (*I'll have left* before he gets here.)

95 The conditional perfect.

A. Formation of the conditional perfect.

The conditional perfect is formed like the future perfect except that the conditional of the auxiliary is used.

1. Verbs conjugated with **avoir**:

J'aurais acheté	I would have bought
J'aurais fini	I would have finished
J'aurais été	I would have been
J'aurais eu	I would have had

2. Verbs conjugated with **être**:

Je serais allé(e)	I would have gone
Je serais parti(e)	I would have left
Je me serais couché(e)	I would have gone to bed

B. Use of the conditional perfect.

This tense is most commonly used in conditional sentences in which the verb in the if-clause is in the pluperfect. It expresses an action that would have taken place, if another action had taken place (compare par. 61). Note, however, that the if-clause is very often implied rather than expressed.

Henri ne **se serait** pas **trompé** de route s'il avait fait attention aux poteaux indicateurs.

J'aurais été heureux de me retrouver chez vous . . .

Rien ne m'**aurait donné** plus de plaisir que d'accepter votre aimable invitation . . .

96 The passive voice.

A. Distinction between the active and the passive voice.

The *active* voice comprises the forms of a verb that express an action made *by the subject* of the verb: **j'accompagne** mon père.

The *passive* voice comprises the forms that express an action that is made *upon the subject:* **Je suis accompagné** par mon père.

B. Formation of the passive voice.

The passive conjugation of a verb consists of the different tenses of the auxiliary **être** and the past participle of the verb.

PRESENT INDICATIVE: **Je suis accompagné(e)**
IMPARFAIT: **J'étais accompagné(e)**
PASSÉ COMPOSÉ: **J'ai été accompagné(e)**
FUTUR: **Je serai accompagné(e)**, etc.

TEMPS COMPOSÉS/ VOIX PASSIVE

Only transitive verbs (those that can take an object) have a passive voice.

C. Examples of the use of the passive voice.

Le château **a été habité** jusqu'à une date récente.
Chenonceaux **a été construit** au milieu de la rivière.
Versailles **a été construit** par Louis XIV.
Henri IV **a été assassiné** en 1610.

NOTE: The passive of verbs + **de.** The passive voice of the following verbs is often followed by **de: être aimé, accompagné, craint, détesté, estimé, honoré, escorté, précédé, respecté, suivi.**

Elle **est aimée de** tout le monde.
Quand il est entré, il **était suivi de** quelques agents de police.

The past participles (adjectives) **couvert** and **entouré** are also followed by **de:**

Les murs étaient **couverts de** belles tapisseries.
Le château de Chenonceaux est **entouré d'**eau.
La terre est **couverte de** neige.

D. Passive verbs in English vs. French.

Reflexive verbs (see par. 42) and active verbs with the indefinite pronoun **on** are often used when the passive voice would be used in English.

Je me suis trompé.	*I was* mistaken.
On m'a donné une pomme.	*I was given* an apple.

Note that **J'ai été trompé** (passive voice) means *I was deceived* (by someone else). You could not use the passive voice of **donner** to say "I was given an apple."

———

I. SUBSTITUTIONS. Répétez les phrases suivantes, en substituant les mots indiqués:

1. Quand votre invitation est arrivée, [j'avais déjà fixé la date de mon départ].
   j'avais déjà quitté Paris/ j'étais déjà parti/ j'avais déjà retenu
   passage sur l'avion/ j'avais déjà accepté d'aller à la campagne

GRAMMAR 28

2. Quand votre dîner aura lieu, [je serai déjà parti].

j'aurai déjà quitté Paris/ j'aurai déjà rejoint ma famille/ je serai déjà retourné en Amérique/ mon père sera arrivé à Paris

3. Le château de Chenonceaux a été [construit par un financier].

confisqué par Henri II/ donné à Diane de Poitiers/ habité par Catherine de Médicis/ acheté par la famille Menier

4. Ce jardin était [entouré de murs].

entouré d'eau/ entouré de forêts/ couvert de fleurs/ couvert de feuilles/ couvert de neige

II. Mettez chacune des phrases suivantes au plus-que-parfait, en ajoutant . . . **quand vous avez téléphoné:**

EX.: — Je suis allé chez le voisin.
— **J'étais allé chez le voisin quand vous avez téléphoné.**

1. Je suis sorti. **2.** Je ne suis pas rentré. **3.** J'ai commencé à travailler. **4.** J'ai retenu passage sur l'avion. **5.** J'ai accepté l'invitation des Frazer. **6.** Je me suis couché. **7.** Nous nous sommes mis à table. **8.** J'ai lu la nouvelle dans le journal. **9.** J'ai mis la lettre à la poste. **10.** J'ai envoyé le télégramme.

III. Mettez chacune des phrases suivantes au futur antérieur (*future perfect*), en ajoutant . . . **quand vous arriverez:**

EX.: — Je finirai mon travail.
— **J'aurai fini mon travail quand vous arriverez.**

1. Je déjeunerai. **2.** Je partirai. **3.** J'écrirai cette lettre. **4.** Je me lèverai. **5.** Je ferai mes bagages. **6.** J'achèterai les billets. **7.** J'aurai le temps de finir ce livre. **8.** J'irai à la banque. **9.** Je m'habillerai.

IV. Mettez chacune des phrases suivantes aux temps composés:

EX.: — S'il pleuvait, je mettrais mon imperméable.
— **S'il avait plu, j'aurais mis mon imperméable.**

1. Si un étranger vous invitait à dîner, accepteriez-vous son invitation? **2.** Si vous aviez le temps, iriez-vous en Touraine? **3.** Si nous pouvions le faire, nous irions voir ce match. **4.** Si Jean était à Paris, il assisterait au mariage de ses amis. **5.** Si Marie savait l'adresse de Jean, elle l'inviterait à dîner.

TEMPS COMPOSÉS/ VOIX PASSIVE

V. Combinez deux phrases en une seule, en employant le plus-que-parfait et le mot **car:**

EX.: — Nous sommes partis de bonne heure. Nous avons décidé d'arriver à Orléans avant midi.

— **Nous sommes partis de bonne heure car nous avions décidé d'arriver à Orléans avant midi.**

1. La route était en mauvais état. Il a plu toute la journée. 2. Je suis rentré chez moi. J'ai oublié mon portefeuille. 3. Je n'ai pas pu vous écrire pendant les vacances. J'ai perdu votre adresse. 4. Je suis allé à l'hôpital. J'ai pris rendez-vous avec le docteur. 5. J'ai passé l'après-midi en ville. J'ai promis de faire des courses pour ma mère. 6. Il était en retard. Il n'a pas pu trouver de taxi.

VI. Répétez les phrases suivantes, en employant la voix passive:

EX.: — On a arrêté Henri.
— **Henri a été arrêté.**

1. On a assassiné Henri IV. 2. On a construit cette cathédrale au douzième siècle. 3. On a peint la maison. 4. On a envoyé Jean au Vénézuéla. 5. On a trouvé beaucoup de pétrole au Vénézuéla. 6. Christophe Colomb a découvert l'Amérique. 7. On a inauguré le canal de Suez en 1869. 8. On a électrifié beaucoup de lignes. 9. Pascal a inventé une machine à calculer. 10. On récolte beaucoup d'olives en Provence.

Henri IV (1553–1610)

Versailles illuminé

DES NOUVELLES DE JEAN

Quatre mois après que Jean eût quitté la France, les Duplessis reçurent de lui la lettre suivante:

Des rives de l'Apure, le 25 novembre

Mes chers amis,

¹Lorsque je quittai la France en septembre dernier, je m'attendais à vous revoir à la fin de mon congé. ²Le sort me fut bien cruel, qui m'envoya sur les rives inhospitalières de l'Apure. ³Mais vous ne savez pas ce que c'est que l'Apure et plût au ciel que moi-même je n'en eusse jamais entendu parler! ⁴L'Apure est une rivière du Vénézuéla, un affluent de l'Orénoque. ⁵Bref, je suis une fois de plus dans la jungle, à un endroit qui n'est guère accessible que par hélicoptère.

⁶Ce n'est pas, quoi que vous puissiez croire, un lieu de déportation pour les indésirables, bien qu'il y en ait quelques-uns — vous vous en rendrez compte tout à l'heure. ⁷Je dirige un camp de prospecteurs dans des régions presque inexplorées du Vénézuéla et de la Colombie. ⁸Tous les matins, mes hommes se rendent par hélicoptère en divers endroits, où ils font exploser des charges de dynamite, de façon à déterminer la configuration du sol. ⁹Ce qui arriva hier à une de nos équipes vous donnera une idée de la vie que nous menons ici.

¹⁰Pourtant, la journée commença comme d'habitude. ¹¹L'hélicoptère vint chercher nos trois hommes le matin et il les déposa dans une clairière au milieu de la jungle. ¹²Là, ils se mirent au travail. ¹³Tout alla bien jusqu'à midi. ¹⁴A ce moment-là des Indiens arrivèrent, et menaçant les intrus des armes les plus diverses, ils s'emparèrent de tout ce que possédaient les prospecteurs, argent, montres, outils, et les dépouillèrent de leurs vêtements. ¹⁵Quand l'hélicoptère revint les chercher le soir, le pilote trouva nos trois hommes qui l'attendaient avec une impatience facile à comprendre. ¹⁶Se douterait-on jamais qu'une telle aventure pût arriver, de nos jours, à d'honnêtes prospecteurs?

Four months after John had left France, the Duplessis received the following letter from him:

From the banks of the Apure,
November 25

Dear Friends:

¹When I left France last September, I expected to see you again at the end of my vacation. ²Fate, which sent me to the inhospitable banks of the Apure, was very cruel. ³But you do not know what the Apure is, and I wish to heaven (might it be pleasing to heaven) that *I* had never heard of it! ⁴The Apure is a river of Venezuela, a tributary of the Orinoco. ⁵In a word, I am once more in the jungle, in a place that is scarcely accessible except by helicopter.

⁶Whatever you might think, it is not a place for deportation of undesirables, although there are a few of them — you shall see in a moment. ⁷I am in charge of a camp of prospectors in some almost unexplored regions of Venezuela and Colombia. ⁸Every morning, my men go by helicopter to various places where they explode charges of dynamite so as to determine the configuration of the ground (lay of the land). ⁹What happened yesterday to one of our crews will give you an idea of the life that we lead here.

¹⁰And yet, the day began as usual. ¹¹The helicopter came to pick up our three men in the morning and it put them down in a clearing in the midst of the jungle. ¹²There, they started to work. ¹³All went well until noon. ¹⁴At that moment some Indians arrived, and threatening the intruders with a variety of weapons, they seized everything the prospectors had: money, watches, tools, and they stripped them of their clothes. ¹⁵When the helicopter came back for them in the evening, the pilot found our three men waiting for him with easily comprehensible impatience. ¹⁶Would one ever suspect that such an adventure could happen these days to honest prospectors?

¹⁷Je ne sais pas combien de temps je resterai ici. ¹⁸Je me dis parfois que vous êtes beaucoup plus sages que moi. ¹⁹Te rappelles-tu, Roger, ce que tu me disais un jour: «Ma vie a été bien tranquille comparée à la tienne»? ²⁰Surtout, ne faites pas du petit Michel un ingénieur, ou tout au moins, qu'il laisse le pétrole tranquille! ²¹Et pourtant . . .

²²J'espère malgré tout vous revoir un de ces jours. ²³En attendant, mes chers amis, puisque ma lettre vous arrivera sans doute vers le Nouvel An, je vous souhaite à tous les trois une joyeuse année et toute sorte de prospérité.

Bien cordialement,
Jean

Marie-Antoinette (1755–1793)

[17]I don't know how long I'll stay here. [18]I sometimes tell myself that you are much wiser than I am. [19]Do you remember, Roger, what you were telling me one day: "My life has been very calm compared to yours"? [20]Above all, don't make an engineer of little Michel, or, at least, let him leave oil alone! [21]And yet . . .

[22]I hope to see you again one of these days in spite of everything. [23]Meanwhile, since my letter will reach you probably around New Year's, I wish all three of you a happy New Year and all sorts of prosperity.

Sincerely yours,
John.

Le Pique-nique, Boucher

I. SUBSTITUTIONS. Répétez les phrases suivantes, en substituant les mots indiqués:

1. Je m'attendais [à vous revoir].
   à vous rejoindre/ à vous retrouver/ à recevoir
   de vos nouvelles/ à retourner en France

2. Vous ne savez pas ce que c'est [que l'Apure].
   qu'un fonctionnaire/ que l'administration/ que la vie
   d'un prospecteur/ que la vie dans des régions inexplorées

3. Bref, je suis une fois de plus [dans la jungle].
   dans un endroit presque inaccessible/ de retour à
   Paris/ de retour en Amérique/ dans l'Amérique du Sud

4. Quoi que vous puissiez [croire], j'ai l'intention de partir le plus tôt possible.
   dire/ me conseiller/ penser/ vous imaginer

5. Qu'il laisse [le pétrole] tranquille.
   la politique/ la médecine/ la physique nucléaire/ la lune

6. J'espère malgré tout [vous revoir un de ces jours].
   ne pas finir mes jours ici/ ne pas rester trop longtemps ici/ m'habituer à la vie que je mène ici/ retourner à Paris un de ces jours

II. Dites en français, en employant les expressions indiquées:

A. s'attendre à (ce que)

1. I was expecting to see you (again) at the end of my leave. 2. Did you expect to receive a letter from Venezuela? 3. No, I was not expecting it. 4. I expected that you would return here at the end of your leave. 5. The Duplessis did not expect to hear (to learn) that John was in the jungle once more.

B. recevoir de ses (leurs) nouvelles

1. They did not expect to hear from him at that time. 2. They had not heard from him for three months. 3. The last time they heard from him, he had just left Paris. 4. I have not heard from them for two weeks.

C. se rendre compte (de, que)

1. You will realize it in a while. 2. Do you realize that prospecting is sometimes a dangerous occupation? 3. Yes, I realize it, after what happened to John's prospectors. 4. Did you realize that there were still unexplored regions in Venezuela? 5. No, I didn't realize it.

D. se douter (de, que)

1. Would one ever suspect that such a thing might happen? 2. The prospectors never suspected that Indians would seize everything they had. 3. The Duplessis did not suspect that John had once more been sent to Venezuela. 4. I suspect what happened. 5. There were Indians near them, but the prospectors did not suspect it.

III. Répondez en français:

1. Depuis combien de temps Jean avait-il quitté la France quand les Duplessis ont reçu de ses nouvelles? 2. De quand sa lettre était-elle datée? 3. Dans quel pays était-il quand il l'a écrite? 4. Qu'est-ce que c'est que l'Apure? 5. En avez-vous jamais entendu parler? 6. De quel fleuve l'Apure est-il un affluent? 7. L'endroit où se trouve Jean est-il facilement accessible? 8. Quel est le meilleur moyen de l'atteindre? 9. Qu'est-ce que Jean fait à cet endroit? 10. Quand l'hélicoptère vint-il chercher les trois hommes? 11. Où les déposa-t-il? 12. Que firent-ils après cela? 13. Qu'est-ce qui se passa à midi? 14. De quoi les Indiens s'emparèrent-ils? 15. Quand l'hélicoptère revint-il chercher les trois hommes? 16. Les prospecteurs étaient-ils heureux de revoir le pilote? 17. Jean sait-il combien de temps il restera au Vénézuela? 18. Qu'est-ce que Roger lui a dit un jour? 19. Quel conseil Jean donne-t-il aux parents du petit Michel? 20. Croit-il vraiment ce qu'il dit? 21. Que souhaite-t-il aux Duplessis en attendant de les revoir? 22. Pourquoi leur adresse-t-il ses souhaits?

IV. Demandez à quelqu'un:

1. de qui les Duplessis reçoivent des nouvelles. 2. la date de la lettre de Jean. 3. l'endroit où est Jean au moment où il écrit sa lettre. 4. ce qu'il pense de l'endroit où il se trouve. 5. quelle est la meilleure façon d'y arriver. 6. si Jean se plaît beaucoup là où il est. 7. de quoi il s'occupe. 8. comment voyagent les équipes de prospecteurs. 9. ce qui s'est passé le matin. 10. ce qui est arrivé à midi. 11. comment les Indiens s'emparèrent de ce que possédaient les prospecteurs. 12. si la vie de Roger est plus tranquille que celle de Jean.

V. THÈME.

Poor John did not expect to be sent back to Venezuela, but he knows that in his profession, one must expect anything. Once more he finds himself in the jungle, with the monkeys, the parrots and the mosquitoes. To amuse himself, he can perhaps go fishing for piranhas. I don't know if you have heard of these little fish. They travel together and are so fierce that they can devour a whole cow in **(en)** half an hour . . . At any rate, John will one of these days be a member of the board of directors **(conseil d'administration)** of a large petroleum company, and he will be seated behind a big desk in one of New York's skyscrapers. In the meantime, he is young and strong, and he is used to **(il a l'habitude de)** living in the jungle. We all wish him luck.

À la recherche du pétrole

Passé simple de l'indicatif/ Imparfait et plus-que-parfait du subjonctif

97   Meaning of the **passé simple**.

The names *passé simple* (simple past) and *passé composé* (compound past) are used to distinguish two past tenses which, generally speaking, have the same meaning: both tenses are used to express an action that took place in the past or a state of being that existed in the past.

Il revint (Il est revenu) à Paris et **il fut** (il a été) content de retrouver ses amis. L'hiver **fut** (a été)* rigoureux et les gens **restèrent** (sont restés) à la maison.

98   Use of the **passé simple**.

The *passé composé* is the normal past tense in spoken French (see par. 5); the *passé simple* is used in literary narrative style and occasionally in formal speech. (Like the *passé composé*, the *passé simple* may be used with the *imparfait*.)

Le bateau venait à peine de quitter la rive lorsque **l'eau commença** (or a commencé) à entrer à l'intérieur.

99   Formation of the **passé simple**.

A. Regular verbs.

The stem of the *passé simple* of verbs of the first conjugation is found by dropping the **-er** ending: **aimer — aim-**; and the endings are **-ai, -as, -a, -âmes, -âtes, -èrent** [e, a, a, am, at, ɛʀ].

---

* On pourrait, bien entendu, employer **était** dans cette phrase.

The stem of the *passé simple* of verbs of the second and third conjugations is found by dropping the **-ir** or **-re** ending; the endings for both conjugations are: **-is, -is, -it, -îmes, -îtes, -irent** [i, i, i, im, it, iʀ].

Examples:

aimer: j'aimai, tu aimas, il aima, nous aimâmes, vous aimâtes, ils aimèrent.
finir: je finis, tu finis, il finit, nous finîmes, vous finîtes, ils finirent.
vendre: je vendis, tu vendis, il vendit, nous vendîmes, vous vendîtes, ils vendirent.

B. Être and avoir.

être: je fus, tu fus, il fut, nous fûmes, vous fûtes, ils furent.
    Pronounced: [fy, fy, fy, fym, fyt, fyʀ]
avoir: j'eus, tu eus, il eut, nous eûmes, vous eûtes, ils eurent.
    Pronounced: [y, y, y, ym, yt, yʀ]

C. Other irregular verbs.

The *passé simple* of irregular verbs cannot be mastered at a glance, but at least one can see quickly which ones are irregular.

As the *passé simple* is used mostly in the third person, only this person will be listed here. All the forms may be found in the Table of irregular verbs, pp. 278–304.

1. The *passé simple* of all verbs ending in **-er** is regular.

2. The *passé simple* of nearly all irregular verbs ending in **-ir** is regular. Notable exceptions:

tenir and **venir**	**courir** and **mourir**
il tint [iltɛ̃], ils tinrent [iltɛ̃ʀ]	il courut, ils coururent
il vint [ilvɛ̃], ils vinrent [ilvɛ̃ʀ]	il mourut, ils moururent

3. The *passé simple* of verbs ending in **-re** often has an irregular stem; but the 3rd person singular ending is always either **-it** or **-ut**.

(*a*)

conduire: il conduisit, ils conduisirent
dire: il dit, ils dirent
écrire: il écrivit, ils écrivirent
faire: il fit, ils firent
mettre: il mit, ils mirent
naître: il naquit, ils naquirent

prendre: il prit, ils prirent
suivre: il suivit, ils suivirent
vaincre: il vainquit, ils vainquirent

(b)

atteindre: il atteignit, ils atteignirent
craindre: il craignit, ils craignirent
peindre: il peignit, ils peignirent
plaindre: il plaignit, ils plaignirent
rejoindre: il rejoignit, ils rejoignirent

Note that the stem of verbs in group (<i>b</i>) is like the stem of the first person plural of the present indicative.

(c)

conclure: il conclut, ils conclurent
connaître: il connut, ils connurent
lire: il lut, ils lurent
vivre: il vécut, ils vécurent

4. The *passé simple* of verbs in **-oir** has an irregular stem and the vowel of the ending is always **u**.

apercevoir: il aperçut, ils aperçurent
boire: il but, ils burent
croire: il crut, ils crurent
devoir: il dut, ils durent
falloir: il fallut (*impersonal*)
pleuvoir: il plut (*impersonal*)
pouvoir: il put, ils purent
recevoir: il reçut, ils reçurent
savoir: il sut, ils surent
valoir: il valut, ils valurent
    Exceptions:
s'asseoir: il s'assit, ils s'assirent
voir: il vit, ils virent

100 Examples of use of the **passé simple** in narrative style.

Lorsque je **quittai** la France, je m'attendais à vous revoir à la fin de mon congé. Le sort me **fut** bien cruel, qui m'**envoya** sur les rives de l'Apure . . .

La journée **commença** comme d'habitude. L'hélicoptère **vint** chercher nos trois hommes et les **déposa** dans une clairière au milieu de la jungle. Là, ils **se mirent** à travailler. Tout **alla** bien jusqu'à midi. A ce moment des Indiens **arrivèrent**, . . . ils **s'emparèrent** de tout ce qu'ils possédaient, argent, montres, outils, et les **dépouillèrent** de leurs vêtements. Quand l'hélicoptère **revint** le soir, le pilote **trouva** nos trois hommes qui l'attendaient avec une impatience facile à comprendre.

Compare:

Bonaparte **mena** en Italie une armée qui **était** victorieuse (*which was already victorious — that is, a victorious army*).

Bonaparte **mena** en Italie une armée qui **fut** victorieuse (*which, after he got there, was victorious*).

101 Imperfect subjunctive.

The imperfect subjunctive forms of all verbs can be inferred from the *passé simple* as follows: drop the last letter of the second person singular and add the endings **-sse, -sses, -^t, -ssions, -ssiez, -ssent**. The third singular of the imperfect subjunctive always has a circumflex accent on the vowel of the ending and ends in a **t**.

A. Regular verbs.

aimer: *passé simple:* tu **aimas**; *imperfect subjunctive:*
aima**sse**, aima**sses**, aim**ât**, aima**ssions**, aima**ssiez**, aima**ssent**.
finir: *passé simple:* tu **finis**; *imperfect subjunctive:*
fini**sse**, fini**sses**, fin**ît**, fini**ssions**, fini**ssiez**, fini**ssent**.
vendre: *passé simple:* tu **vendis**; *imperfect subjunctive:*
vendi**sse**, vendi**sses**, vend**ît**, vendi**ssions**, vendi**ssiez**, vendi**ssent**.

B. Auxiliary verbs.

être: *passé simple:* tu **fus**; *imperfect subjunctive:*
fu**sse**, fu**sses**, f**ût**, fu**ssions**, fu**ssiez**, fu**ssent**.
avoir: *passé simple:* tu **eus**; *imperfect subjunctive:*
eu**sse**, eu**sses**, e**ût**, eu**ssions**, eu**ssiez**, eu**ssent** [ys, ys, y, ysjõ, ysje, ys].

C. Some irregular verbs.

As this tense is used chiefly in the third person, only this person will be given here.

tenir: *passé simple:* il **tint**; *imperfect subjunctive:* il **tînt**, ils **tinssent**.
venir: *passé simple:* il **vint**; *imperfect subjunctive:* il **vînt**, ils **vinssent**.
faire: *passé simple:* il **fit**; *imperfect subjunctive:* il **fît**, ils **fissent**.
craindre: *passé simple:* il **craignit**; *imperfect subjunctive:* il **craignît**, ils **craignissent**.
pouvoir: *passé simple:* il **put**; *imperfect subjunctive:* il **pût**, ils **pussent**.
savoir: *passé simple:* il **sut**; *imperfect subjunctive:* il **sût**, ils **sussent**.

102 Pluperfect subjunctive.

This tense is composed of the past participle of a verb and the imperfect subjunctive of the auxiliary.

Verbs conjugated with **avoir:**

Il eût aimé, Il eût fini, Il eût vendu

Verbs conjugated with **être:**

Il fût allé, Il fût parti, Il fût venu, etc.

103 Uses of tenses in the subjunctive.

A. If the verb of the main clause is in the present or future,

1. an action or a state of being in the present or in the future is expressed by the present subjunctive in the subordinate clause.

Il vaut mieux que **vous veniez** tout de suite.
Il faudra qu'**il vienne** me voir.

2. an action or state in the past is expressed by the *passé composé* of the subjunctive in subordinate clauses.

Je doute qu'**il soit arrivé** à sept heures du matin.
Je ne crois pas qu'**il ait été** très malade.

B. If the verb of the main clause is in a past tense, or the conditional,

1. the verb of the subordinate clause is put in the imperfect subjunctive to express an action that is *present or future in relation to the verb of the main clause.*

Se **douterait**-on jamais qu'une telle aventure **pût** arriver?
Je craignais qu'**il partît** (*would leave*).
J'ai demandé qu'**il répondît** immédiatement.
Je voulais qu'**il vînt** dîner chez nous demain.

2. the verb of the subordinate clause is put in the pluperfect subjunctive to express an action that was *past* in relation to the verb of the main clause.

Plût au ciel que moi-même **je** n'en **eusse** jamais **entendu** parler. (**Plût** is imperfect subjunctive of **plaire:** *Might it please heaven that . . .*)
Je craignais qu'**il fût parti** avant mon arrivée. (. . . *had left* . . .)
Je ne croyais pas qu'**il eût quitté** l'hôpital.

Except for the third person singular, the imperfect and pluperfect subjunctives are now used sparingly even in writing. They are even rarer in conversational French.

———————

I. SUBSTITUTIONS. Répétez les phrases suivantes, en substituant les mots indiqués:

1. L'hélicoptère [vint les chercher].
   les déposa dans une clairière/ s'en alla/ revint
   les chercher le soir/ les trouva dans la jungle

2. La journée [commença] comme d'habitude.
   finit/ se passa/ se termina/ prit fin

3. Les Indiens [arrivèrent].
   les menacèrent/ s'emparèrent de tout ce qu'ils possédaient/
   prirent leur argent/ les dépouillèrent de leurs vêtements

4. Quoi que vous [puissiez croire], . . .
   pensiez/ disiez/ fassiez/ ayez fait

5. Se douterait-on qu'une telle aventure [pût arriver] à d'honnêtes prospecteurs?
   puisse arriver/ ait pu arriver/ arrive/ soit arrivée

6. Bref, je suis [une fois de plus] dans la jungle.
   de nouveau/ de retour/ encore une fois

II. Mettez chacune des phrases suivantes au pluriel:

1. Il arriva. **2.** Il trouva. **3.** Il se reposa. **4.** Il s'en occupa. **5.** Il finit. **6.** Il répondit. **7.** Il réussit. **8.** Il se mit à parler. **9.** Il reçut. **10.** Il s'en aperçut. **11.** Il eut. **12.** Il fut. **13.** Il but de l'eau fraîche. **14.** Il apprit la nouvelle. **15.** Il reconnut. **16.** Il sut. **17.** J'arrivai. **18.** J'allai. **19.** Je trouvai. **20.** Je montai. **21.** J'aperçus. **22.** Je m'aperçus. **23.** Je fus. **24.** Je répondis.

III. Remplacez le passé composé par le passé simple:

1. Jean est arrivé à Paris le 18 août. **2.** Il est descendu à l'hôtel Meurice. **3.** Le lendemain il a décidé d'aller voir les Duplessis. **4.** Il a pris un taxi qu'il a attendu quelque temps. **5.** Roger l'a reçu à bras ouverts. **6.** Il l'a invité à dîner. **7.** Jean a vu pour la première fois le fils des Duplessis. **8.** Il a été très heureux de revoir ses amis. **9.** Un jour qu'il traversait la Place de l'Opéra, Jean a rencontré Mme Frazer et Hélène. **10.** Il a été très étonné de les voir, car il ne savait pas qu'elles étaient à Paris. **11.** Mme Frazer a eu l'amabilité de l'inviter à les accompagner en Touraine. **12.** Le vendredi suivant, ils ont quitté Paris. **13.** Henri est venu chercher Jean à son hôtel à sept heures et demie. **14.** Ils se sont mis en route à huit heures. **15.** Il leur a fallu quatre heures pour aller de Paris à Orléans où ils ont déjeuné. **16.** Le lendemain ils sont allés à Chenonceaux où ils ont visité le château. **17.** Le temps a été désagréable pendant une bonne partie de leur séjour en Touraine. **18.** Malgré cela, Jean a trouvé le voyage fort agréable.

IV. Remplacez **même si** et l'indicatif par **bien que** et le passé composé du subjonctif:

1. Même s'il a plu beaucoup, nos amis ont visité plusieurs beaux châteaux. **2.** Même si Jean avait beaucoup à faire, il a accepté l'invitation de Mme Frazer. **3.** Même si Henri s'est trompé de route, ils sont arrivés sans trop de retard. **4.** Même si Jean a acheté plusieurs cadeaux, il doit en acheter d'autres avant son départ. **5.** Même s'il a déjà vu la plupart des châteaux, il a été content d'aller en Touraine.

V. Répétez les phrases suivantes, en commençant par la phrase indiquée et en employant l'imparfait du subjonctif.

EX.: — Louis XIV voulait . . . Molière est allé à la cour.
— **Louis XIV voulait que Molière allât à la cour.**

A. Louis XIV voulait

1. Molière a joué une nouvelle comédie. **2.** On a construit Versailles. **3.** Le Nôtre a dessiné les jardins. **4.** Molière est venu souvent à Versailles.

B. Le roi ne voulait pas

1. Ses ministres eurent trop d'influence. **2.** On le fit attendre. **3.** On écrivit contre lui. **4.** La noblesse gouverna l'État.

VI. THÈME.

Racine was born at la Ferté-Milon in 1639. He became an orphan early and was reared by his grandmother. He entered **(entrer à)** the school of Port-Royal, where he received an excellent education. He learned Latin and Greek and read most of the Greek and Latin classics. To the great annoyance **(mécontentement)** of his masters, he began to write for the theater.

In Paris, he made the acquaintance of Boileau, La Fontaine, and others. In the course of his career as **(d')** a dramatic author, which lasted about ten **(une dizaine d')** years, he wrote several fine tragedies. In 1677 he gave up **(abandonner)** the theater, got married and, eventually, had five sons and five daughters. For a long time, he lead a family life and he took care of his children's education with great care **(soin).**

At the request **(la prière)** of Mme de Maintenon he composed two religious tragedies, *Esther* and *Athalie,* which were performed at the school of Saint-Cyr. He died in 1699.

Racine was perhaps the greatest French dramatic poet.

Scène de *Phèdre*, de Racine

REFERENCE

MATERIALS

TABLE OF SOUNDS OF THE FRENCH LANGUAGE

As Represented by Symbols of the International Phonetic Alphabet

CONSONANTS

	Bi-labial	Labio-dental	Dental and Alveolar	Palato-alveolar	Palatal	Velar	Uvular
Plosive	p b		t d			k g	
Nasal	m		n		ɲ		
Lateral			l				
Rolled			r*				ʀ
Fricative		f v	s z	ʃ ʒ			
Semi-vowels	w ɥ				j (ɥ)	(w)	

VOWELS

	Front	Central	Back
Close	i y		u
Half-close	e ø	ə	o õ
Half-open	ɛ ɛ̃	œ œ̃	ɔ
Open	a		ɑ ɑ̃

* The symbols [ʀ] and [r] represent two ways of producing "r" in French. The [ʀ] is produced between the back of the tongue and the soft palate, the [r] with the tip of the tongue against the teeth or gums. Only the [ʀ] is used in the phonetic transcriptions in this book, but the alveolar [r] is quite commonly used in the south of France.

HOW
TO IMPROVE
YOUR ACCENT

104 A. Cultivating a new set of speech habits.

Many American students never acquire a good French accent because they try to figure out on the basis of inaccurate or inept rules how the written language "would be" pronounced; and when they *do* try to speak in French, they use their normal American speech habits. The right way to go about it is, (1) to understand that the two languages are fundamentally different both as to patterns of accent and as to the way the sounds of the languages are produced; (2) to listen carefully to one's instructor or to the voices on the tape and imitate as exactly as possible the way they say phrases; and (3) to practice using French phrases *in the French way* until an entirely new set of speech habits has been developed.

In English — and in most other languages, certain syllables are strongly accented and others are given a very weak utterance. In French, on the contrary, words do not have accented syllables, and consequently every pronounced syllable receives an equal amount of emphasis. In saying "Where is the restaurant?" for example, most Americans would say something like: "Where's the rest'runt?" in four syllables, we would put a slight accent on *where* and on the syllable *rest-*, and we would enunciate the vowels of these syllables quite clearly; but we would pronounce the rest of the phrase with so little stress that the vowels *i, e, au,* and *a* of the unstressed syllables would either be dropped or else they would be pronounced *uh* — like the "o" in "committee."

A French person who is not familiar with our system of accented and unaccented syllables, however, would say something like: "Wear eez zee res-tau-rant?" in six clear syllables of equal length and equal stress. You are so used to hearing certain syllables stressed and others unstressed, that you would *think* the Frenchman is merely accenting the wrong syllables. But that is not what he is doing: he is really giving each syllable approximately equal stress as he would in speaking in French. Moreover, he is giving the vowels of each syllable full value and, to make things even worse, he is substituting French sounds for English ones because in French there is no *wh* (as in *where*), no ĭ (as in *is*), and no *th* (as in *the*). Furthermore the French "r" is entirely different from ours, and most of the remaining sounds of French are quite different from their English counterparts.

If you try to speak French the way you speak English, you will sound just as funny as the Frenchman who says "Wear eez zee res-tau-rant?" and you will be much less comprehensible. So it is necessary to overcome your normal speech habits and learn as soon as possible to pronounce French words and phrases as French people do. This takes both intelligence and persistence.

EXERCISES

I. Pronounce the following pairs of words, making it a point to stress the accented syllables in the English words and trying to give equal stress to each syllable in the French words:

> *Eng.* an'-uh-mul, *Fr.* a-ni-mal; *Eng.* min'-uh-rul, *Fr.* mi-né-ral; *Eng.* national (násh-un-ul), *Fr.* na-tio-nal [na-sjɔ-nal].* Note, meanwhile, that in French, syllables tend to begin with a consonant and to end with a vowel (see par. 111).

II. In order to get the pattern of rhythm of French words clearly in mind, say rapidly: tóc-tóc-tóc, a-ni-mal; tóc-tóc-tóc, mi-né-ral; tóc-tóc-tóc, na-tio-nal [na-sjɔ-nal]; tóc-tóc-tóc-tóc-tóc, in-ter-na-tio-nal [ɛ̃-tɛʀ-na-sjɔ-nal].

After practicing a few words and groups of words with equal stress on all syllables, you will be able to pronounce them evenly without establishing the rhythm in advance with the syllable "tóc"; but whenever you find it difficult to catch the rhythm of a phrase, it is helpful to tap the number of pronounced syllables on a table or to revert to the exercise with the syllable "tóc". This, of course, takes time; but you can't expect to overcome the speech habits of a lifetime in five minutes.

---

* The key to pronunciation indicated between square brackets is the International Phonetic Alphabet, which is used for the transcription of all the Conversations (pp. 242-253). This will be studied later; for the time being, the principal objective is to get the habit of giving equal stress to each pronounced syllable of each phrase.

III. Examples from Conversation I. Pronounce the following:

1. (12 syllables, 6 and 6). De passage à Paris, après une longue absence, [də-pa-sa-ʒa-Pa-ʀi, a-pʀɛ-zyn-lõg-ab-sɑ̃s]

2. (Three groups: 1, 5, and 3 syllables):

Treize,	avenue du Palais,	à Saint-Cloud.
[tʀɛz]	[av-ny-dy-pa-lɛ]	[a-sɛ̃-klu]

   Repeat each of the three groups several times and then repeat the entire sentence in nine short, equally stressed syllables.

3. (Three groups: 6, 3, and 5 syllables):

6	C'est près du pont de Saint-Cloud,	[sɛ pʀɛ dy põd sɛ̃-klu]
3	à l'entrée de	[a lɑ̃ tred]
5	l'autoroute de l'Ouest.	[lɔ-to-ʀut də lwɛst]

   Repeat each group several times and then repeat the entire sentence in fourteen short, equally stressed syllables.

4. (3 syllables): Entendu. [ɑ̃ tɑ̃ dy].

5. (5 syllables): Montez, s'il vous plaît. [mõ-te sil vu plɛ]

IV. Listen attentively to the voices on the tapes for the first Conversation, note consciously the rhythm of phrases, and keep trying to imitate the voices until you can utter a string of syllables evenly and effortlessly. Once you develop this skill, it is much easier to acquire correct French pronunciation.

B. French intonation.

French intonation differs from English intonation in at least three ways. The following sentences will roughly illustrate all three differences. (The intonations given below are free from word emphasis.)

Mon père // habite / à Philadelphie.

Mais la sœur / de mon père // est en France.

My father // lives / in Philadelphia.

But my father's / sister // is in France.

First difference. To express continuation, to indicate that a statement is not finished, French sense-groups, such as **Mon père, habite, Mais la sœur, de mon père,** *rise* to the last syllable: . . . **père,** . . . **-bite,** . . . **sœur,** . . . **père:** whereas English sense-groups, such as *My father, lives, But my father's, sister,* tend to *fall after the stressed syllable:* . . . *father, lives,* . . . *father's,* . . . *sister.*

Second difference. To express finality, to indicate that a sentence is ending, French intonation falls continuously, starting with the very *first* syllable of the last sense-group: . . . **Philadelphie,** . . . **est en France;** whereas English intonation falls only *after* the last stressed syllable of the last sense-group: . . . **Philadelphia,** or after the beginning of the last stressed syllable: . . . **France.**

Note 1. The contrast between continuation and finality is well marked in French since continuation is rising and finality falling. In English, both continuation and finality are falling — the difference is only a matter of degree: finality falls lower than continuation.

Third difference. In the rising curves of continuation, French makes a clear distinction between the high rise of *major* continuation, as in **Mon père, de mon père,** and the moderate rise of *minor* continuation, as in **habite, Mais la sœur.** English does not make this distinction, 'or does not stress it to the same extent as French. Between the falling curves of *father* and *lives,* of *father's* and *sister,* no significant difference is made.

Note 2. The continuity of the fall, for finality, and of the rise, for continuation, applies to all the other types of falling or rising intonations in French. For instance, falling questions, such as:

Comment vous appelez-vous?

Où êtes-vous né?

Quel âge avez-vous?

Quelle est votre nationalité?

always begin to fall at the very first syllable.

In English, such questions tend to fall only after the last syllable:

What is your name?

Where were you born?

How old are you?

What is your nationality?

Similarly, rising questions, such as:

Avez-vous des parents?

rise continuously, from the first to the last syllable.
  In English, rising questions, such as:

Have you any relatives?

tend to rise only after the last stressed syllable.

105 Patterns of accent also affect the way you produce the individual
sounds of a language.

As a result of our way of accenting some syllables and slighting
others in English, we tend to pronounce both the consonants and the
vowels that are in accented syllables differently from the way we pronounce them when they are in other positions. Compare the initial and
the final "t" in tem′-per-ate, tal′-ent, tick′-et: the initial "t" is uttered
with a considerable puff of air (called *aspiration*) and the second "t" (in
final position phonetically) is scarcely heard at all. We shall see that in

French, the [t], as well as other pronounced consonants, is completely articulated in practically all positions: **tante, tenter.**

In English we tend to lengthen and diphthongize vowels in accented syllables: day (dā^ɪ), die (di^ɪ), doe (do^ŭ), etc., and to slight those in unaccented syllables. But in French, as there are no accented and unaccented syllables, pronounced vowels have approximately the same pronunciation in different positions. It is extremely unusual for any French vowel other than *e* to have the sound of a so-called mute "e" [ə].

It should be encouraging to note that while our dictionary makers have to resort to dozens of diacritical marks and accent signs in order to indicate the way words are pronounced in English, you will find no table of diacritical marks in a French dictionary: the normal French alphabet suffices for indicating the pronunciation of French words! In this book, we use the International Phonetic Alphabet because the letters of the French alphabet, which are perfectly satisfactory for indicating French pronunciation to a French person, are so closely associated in our minds with the sounds of English that they are misleading for American students.

106 Position of the tongue in speaking French.

As the organs of speech other than the tongue are used in French very much as they are in English, it is not necessary to study their functioning in order to speak French well. But as the tongue is used very differently in the two languages, it is absolutely essential that you learn to use it in new ways if you want to speak French with "a good accent." For example, in English the tip of the tongue is usually turned up when we prepare to pronounce the consonants *t, d, s, z, n, l, r, ch, zh, y,* and some of the vowels; but in French the tip of the tongue is *never turned up*. We shall see that if the tongue is in the right position to produce a given sound, the proper sound is practically sure to be produced.

107 French consonants.

A. Explanation and exercises for the consonants that are pronounced with the tip of the tongue against or near the front teeth: [t, d, s, z, n, l, ʃ, ʒ].

Observe carefully the difference between English and French pronunciation of these sounds, and contrast the pairs of words in English and French. Place the tip of the tongue firmly against the front teeth consciously for each French word and expel as little air as possible. In this way the upper surface of the tongue (not the tip) will be against or near the alveolar ridge (the ridge just behind the upper front teeth) for the French words.

(a) quite different

[t] as in tout.	Contrast Eng. two with Fr. tout.
[d] as in décide.	Contrast Eng. day with Fr. décide.
[n] as in une banane.	Contrast Eng. banana with Fr. une banane.
[l] as in le lit.	Contrast Eng. will with Fr. s'il vous plaît.
[s] as in je sais.	Contrast Eng. say with Fr. Je sais.

(b) only slightly different

[z] as in vous‿avez.	Contrast Eng. zebra with Fr. zèbre.
[ʃ] as in le chauffeur.	Contrast Eng. show with Fr. le chauffeur.
[ʒ] as in jamais.	Contrast Eng. pleasure with Fr. jamais.

Repeat these pairs of words several times, especially the first five, using the tip of the tongue consciously for each English word and moving the tongue forward consciously for each French word. Make the French sounds sound different from the English ones! If you pronounce these consonants as you do in English, your French will never sound like authentic French.

Repeat the following French words and phrases, making it a point to keep the tip of the tongue against the lower front teeth and to use as little breath as possible:

du tabac [dytaba], du thé [dyte], la table, la date, des dates, des dettes, des doutes, il décide, le taxi, l'hôtel, les hôtels, le petit hôtel, entendu, des tomates, le château, s'il vous plaît, du lait, je joue, jamais, janvier, gentil, jeune, joli, juste, la chaise, la chambre, la chance, changer, je change, le chèque, des bananes, Suzanne, la neige.

B. Explanation and exercises for the consonants that are pronounced with the tongue toward the back of the mouth: [k, g, ɲ, ʀ].

[k] and [g] are pronounced approximately as most people pronounce them in English except that, when at the beginning of a word, they are uttered with a greater flow of air in English.

Place the tip of the tongue against the lower front teeth (so that the vowels will be pronounced properly) and expel as little air as possible in pronouncing the French words.

[k] as in le **c**afé	Contrast Eng. **c**offee with Fr. le **c**afé.
[g] as in le **g**az.	Contrast Eng. **g**as with Fr. le **g**az.

Repeat the following:

la carte, la cause, combien, comment, je connais, qui, que, quel, les quais, les courses;
la galerie, le gardien, grave, le guide, le garage, le garçon, la gorge, les gants.

The sound [ɲ] as in "un si**gne**" is the one usually pronounced in English "Swin**gy**our partner." It is pronounced farther back in the mouth than the somewhat similar sound in English "o**ni**on."

Repeat the following words, making it a point to produce the sound [ɲ] in the back of the mouth — if possible:

un signe, le champagne, la Bretagne, l'agneau, le peigne, le règne, nous craignons, Que craignez-vous?

The sound [ʀ] as in "après" has no counterpart in English. To produce the French uvular "r", the back of the tongue is placed close to the soft palate as if to gargle. In order to avoid saying an American "r" unintentionally, the tip of the tongue should be placed more firmly than ever against the lower front teeth and held there. With the tongue in this position: (*a*) Pronounce "ugh" as in English *mug*. (*b*) Repeat and prolong the "gh": ugh-gh-gh-gh. (*c*) With the tongue still in this position, try to repeat this sound without actually pronouncing the [g]. (*d*) Without moving the tongue, make the sound [ʀ] gently. Do not gargle it. Note that when French is spoken with elegance, you scarcely hear the [ʀ] at all. (*e*) Repeat, using as little air as possible. (*f*) Pronounce the following words gently, carefully, and repeatedly:

l'art [laʀ], rare [ʀɑʀ], or [ɔʀ], l'orange [lɔʀɑ̃ʒ], l'aurore [lɔʀɔʀ], horreur [ɔʀœʀ], heureux [øʀø], Paris [paʀi], Marie [maʀi], la mairie [lamɛʀi], Américain [ameʀikɛ̃], après [apʀɛ], très [tʀɛ], frais [fʀɛ], un frère [œ̃ fʀɛʀ], gros [gʀo], gras [gʀa], grec [gʀɛk], gris [gʀi], j'ai appris [ʒe apʀi], avril, péril, rire.

Repeat this exercise daily until you can pronounce the French [ʀ] easily and correctly without thinking about it.

C. Explanation and exercises for the consonants that are pronounced with the lips or lips and teeth without use of the tongue: [p, b, f, v, m].

These sounds are produced as in English except that, when initial, they are uttered with a puff of air in English. Hold a strip of paper before your lips and pronounce English *paper* and French **le papier,** expelling as little air as possible for the French word. The paper should not move for the French word!

[p] as in le **p**apier.	Contrast Eng. **p**aper with Fr. le **p**apier.
[b] as in **b**eaucoup.	Contrast Eng. **b**oat with Fr. **b**eaucoup.
[f] as in la **f**leur.	Contrast Eng. **f**lower with Fr. la **f**leur.
[v] as in **v**ous êtes.	Compare Eng. **v**ow and Fr. **v**ous.
[m] as in **m**ada**m**e.	Compare Eng. **m**ada**m** and Fr. **m**ada**m**e.

The difference between initial **p, b,** and **f** in English and French is striking. The difference between **v** and **m** in the two languages is less noticeable.

Pronounce each of the following words with a strip of paper in front of your lips until you can say them all without causing the paper to move:

1. papa, le papier, un peu, mon père, je ne peux pas partir avec Pierre, la petite poupée en papier;

2. une banane, là-bas, le beurre, beau, bon, la bouche, des bonbons, un beau bouquet, beaucoup de bananes;

3. l'enfant, la famille, la fleur, la feuille, février, des pommes frites, des fraises, mon frère.

108 Vowels.

In pronouncing vowels in accented syllables in English, most of us tend to make them into diphthongs — that is, to insert a short ĭ or ŭ before or after the vowel: *day* (dā^ĭ), *die* (dī^ĭ), *doe* (dō^ŭ), *do* (d^{ŭ}u) or (d^{ĭ}u). But in French, the vowels are pronounced without any diphthongization whatever. Generally speaking, the vowels in French are always short; although some French persons tend to lengthen any vowel that is followed by final [m, n, ʀ, ʒ, j, v, z, vʀ], this practice seems justifiable only if the lengthened syllable is at the end of a phrase. You could slightly lengthen the [ɛ] in **père** in the phrase "Où est votre père?" but not in "Mon père est parti." The older phoneticians used to say the final pronounced syllable of each phrase is accented or at least lengthened; but in reality many French people tend to slight rather than stress the end of a phrase. In any case, it would sound very artificial if the final syllable of all phrases were consciously lengthened.

It is fairly easy to pronounce the French vowels correctly if they are pronounced quickly and without stress, and if the tongue does not move out of position while the vowel is being pronounced.

A glance at the vowels on the Table of Sounds of the French Language (p. 224) shows that most of the vowels are in pairs. It is useful to consult this table frequently until you have a clear picture of the way the vowels are produced.

A. [i] as in "vite" and [y] as in "une minute" are pronounced with the tongue placed forward in the mouth (tip against the lower teeth) with the mouth almost closed. The difference between the two sounds is that the lips are relaxed for the [i] and slightly rounded for the [y]. The tongue position is the same for the two sounds.

Pronounce each of the following pairs of sounds and syllables several times, moving only the lips and holding the tip of the tongue firmly against the lower front teeth:

[i], [y]; [pi], [py]; [bi], [by]; [di], [dy]; [fi], [fy]; [li], [ly]; [vi], [vy]; [ni], [ny]; [ʀi], [ʀy].

Pronounce the following words and syllables:

y, eu; pie, pu; bi-, bu; dit, du; fit, fut; lit, lu; vie, vue; nid, nu; riz, rue.

Repeat this exercise until you can pronounce the symbols and the words just alike.

B. [e] as in "été" and [ø] as in "je peux" are pronounced with the tip of the tongue against the lower front teeth and the mouth opened a trifle wider than for [i] and [y]. The difference between the two sounds is that the lips are relaxed for the [e] and slightly rounded for the [ø]. The tongue position is the same for the two sounds.

Pronounce each of the following pairs of sounds and syllables several times, moving only the lips:

[e], [ø]; [pe], [pø]; [be], [bø]; [fe], [fø]; [ke], [kø]; [ne], [nø]; [se], [sø].

Pronounce the following words and syllables:

ai, œufs; pé-, peu; bé-, bœufs; fé-, feu; quai, queue; né, nœud; cé-, ceux.

IMPROVING YOUR ACCENT

C. [ɛ] as in "il **est,**" [œ] as in "n**eu**f," [ɛ̃] as in "la f**in,**" [œ̃] as in "**un** lit," and [ɔ] as in "la p**o**ste" are all pronounced with the mouth half-open.

The difference between [ɛ] and [œ] is that the lips are slightly rounded and the tongue is slightly farther back for the latter.

Pronounce each of the following pairs of sounds and words several times:

[ɛ], [œ]; celle, seul; serre, sœur; père, peur; mère, meurt.

The difference between [ɛ] and [ɛ̃] is that the latter is pronounced by allowing a part of the air to go into the nasal cavity.

[ɛ], [ɛ̃]; fait, fin; laid, lin; mais, main; paix, pain; c'est, sain.

The difference between [œ] and [œ̃] is that the latter is produced by allowing a part of the air to enter the nasal cavity.

[œ], [œ̃]; un œuf, un bœuf; la peur, le parfum [lə paʀfœ̃].

The difference between [œ] and [ɔ] is that the tongue is still farther back for the latter.

[œ], [ɔ]; heure, or; peur, port; beurre, bord; sœur, sort.

D. [a] as in "**la** t**a**ble", [ɑ] as in "**pa**s encore", and [ɑ̃] as in "**en** France" are pronounced with the mouth well open.

The difference between [a] and [ɑ] is that the tongue is slightly farther back in the mouth for the latter.

[a], [ɑ]; il n'a pas; là-bas, il a passé.

The difference between [ɑ] and [ɑ̃] is that the latter is produced by allowing a part of the air to enter the nasal cavity.

[ɑ], [ɑ̃]; pas, enfant; pas en France; pas encore; là-bas en mer.

E. [o] as in "l'h**ô**tel" and [õ] as in "**bo**n" are pronounced with the mouth half-closed.

[o], [õ]; beau, bon; faux, fond; l'eau, long; mot, mon; nos, non; peau, pont; tôt, ton; sot, son.

F. [u] as in "**vou**s" is pronounced with the mouth practically closed, with the lips rounded and the tongue in the back of the mouth.

[u]; nous, vous, bout, cou, doux, fou, goût, houx, loup, mou.

IMPROVING YOUR ACCENT

Pronounce the following pairs of words, making it a point to move the tongue forward for [y] and back for [u]. The lips remain rounded but the tongue makes the distinction between the sounds. This is a very difficult exercise. It should be repeated many times.

[y], [u]; nu, nous; fut, fou; bu, bout; du, doux; eu [y], houx [u]; lu, loup; mu, mou; pu, poux; rue, roux; su, sou; tu, tout. Pas du tout. Les galeries du Louvre.

G. The mute [ə]. In addition to the open [ɛ] as in "vous êtes" and the close [e] as in "l'été," there is also the mute "e" which, as its name implies, is usually silent (as in **avenue** [avny]). Although it is usually silent, it sometimes has the sound [ə] as in "uné demi-heuré." [yn dəmiœʀ].

Repeat the following phrases, noting that most of the mute "e's" are completely silent:

1. Jé décidé d'aller révoir Marié. 2. Jé monté dans lé taxi. 3. Les Duplessis démeurént avénué dé Longchamp. 4. Si ça né vous fait rien. 5. De rétour.

Repeat the following, noting that some of the mute "e's" are pronounced:

1. Est-cé que nous sommés à Saint-Cloud? 2. Uné demi-heure. 3. Montez, **mon**sieur [məsjø]. 4. Le chauffeur. 5. Venez nous voir. 6. Revénez bientôt.

H. Suggestions for sounding or omitting the mute "e".

There is no easy and dependable rule for sounding or omitting the mute "e's", but the following suggestions may be helpful:

Although mute "e's" were normally pronounced a few hundred years ago, they have now practically disappeared from the spoken language. Generally speaking, (a) mute "e's" are not sounded in phrases which can be easily pronounced without them; (b) if mute "e's" occur initially in two successive syllables as in "Je né parle pas anglais", the first one is pronounced [ə] and the second one is not sounded. Ex.: le chéval, le répas, le pétit déjeuner. But **ce que** is pronounced [skə].

It is customary to sound the [ə] of the article **le** in pronouncing individual words (especially in giving a *dictée*) or at the beginning of a sentence. Ex.: **Le** château est sur la place. But French people tend to omit the mute "e's" even in initial syllables: le̸ château, le̸ chauffeur; re̸marquez; re̸gardez; re̸tournez-vous. This looks difficult, but with a little practice you will be saying [ʒɑ̃nsɛpa] and [lʃofœʀdətɑksi], etc., without feeling self-conscious.

As the rules for writing poetry were developed long ago, when mute "e's" were commonly pronounced, the final "e" preceding a consonant is commonly sounded in reading poetry or in singing. Ex.: **toute ma vie,** which would have three syllables [**tut** ma vi] in conversation, would have five in an operatic aria [**tu** tə ma vi ə].

When in doubt as to the pronunciation of mute "e's" in this book, one can always consult the phonetic transcriptions of the Conversations (pages 242–253).

109 Semi-vowels.

[w], [j], and [ɥ].

A. [w] as in "**voilà**" is pronounced with the lips — approximately as in English.

moi, une poire, la boîte, une fois; oui, Louis, soyez, loyer, voyons.

B. [j] as in **bien** [bjɛ̃] is pronounced with the tip of the tongue against the lower front teeth.

bien, rien, tiens, la fille, gentille, la famille, travailler, vieux [vjø], vieille [vjɛj].

C. [ɥ] as in "**la nuit**" [lanɥi] is produced by saying [y] and [i] in rapid succession. The tip of the tongue should of course be against the lower front teeth and care should be taken to move the lips as little as possible and to avoid making the sound [w].

Repeat the following:

[y] [i], [y] [i], [y] [i], [ɥi], [ɥi], [ɥi].

Repeat this exercise until you can say [ɥi] without a trace of the sound of [w].

IMPROVING YOUR ACCENT

Repeat the following pairs of words and syllables with the same precaution:

nid, nuit; lit, luit; qui, cuit; frit, fruit; si, suis; Brie, bruit; vite, huit; fit, fuit; bi-, buis; j'y, juillet; chien, juin; cite, suite; nage, nuage; tel, actuel; avance, nuance; cède, Suède; cette, cacahuète.

D. [w] as in **oui** is produced with the lips but [ɥ] is produced with the tongue:

oui, huit francs; Louis, lui; enfouit, enfuit.

PHONETIC TRANSCRIPTIONS

Cardinal numbers and Conversations.

CARDINAL NUMBERS

A. In dates, street numbers, telephone numbers, in counting, etc., the cardinal numbers are pronounced as follows:

1. œ̃, yn
(un, une)

2. dø
(deux)

3. tʀwɑ
(trois)

4. katʀ
(quatre)

5. sɛ̃k
(cinq)

6. sis
(six)

7. sɛt
(sept)

8. ɥit
(huit)

9. nœf
(neuf)

10. dis
(dix)

11. õz
(onze)

12. duz
(douze)

13. tʀɛz
(treize)

14. katɔʀz
(quatorze)

15. kɛ̃z
(quinze)

16. sɛz
(seize)

17. dissɛt
(dix-sept)

18. dizɥit
(dix-huit)

19. diznœf
(dix-neuf)

20. vɛ̃
(vingt)

21. vɛ̃teœ̃
(vingt et un)

22. vɛ̃tdø
(vingt-deux)

23. vɛ̃ttʀwɑ
(vingt-trois)

24. vɛ̃katʀ
(vingt-quatre)

25. vɛ̃tsɛ̃k
(vingt-cinq)

26. vɛ̃tsis
(vingt-six)

27. vɛ̃tsɛt
(vingt-sept)

28. vɛ̃tɥit
(vingt-huit)

29. vɛ̃tnœf
(vingt-neuf)

30. tʀɑ̃t
(trente)

31. tʀɑ̃teœ̃
(trente et un)

32. tʀɑ̃tdø, etc.
(trente-deux)

40. kaʀɑ̃t
(quarante)

41. kaʀɑ̃teœ̃
(quarante et un)

42. kaʀɑ̃tdø, etc.
(quarante-deux)

50. sɛ̃kɑ̃t
(cinquante)

51. sɛ̃kɑ̃teœ̃
(cinquante et un)

52. sɛ̃kɑ̃tdø, etc.
(cinquante - deux)

60. swasãt
(soixante)

61. swasãteœ̃
(soixante et un)

62. swasãtdø, etc.
(soixante-deux)

70. swasãtdis
(soixante-dix)

71. swasãteõz
(soixante et onze)

72. swasãtduz, etc.
(soixante-douze)

80. katʀəvẽ
(quatre-vingts)

81. katʀəvẽœ̃, etc.
(quatre-vingt-un)

90. katʀəvẽdis
(quatre-vingt-dix)

91. katʀəvẽõz, etc.
(quatre-vingt-onze)

100. sã
(cent)

101. sã œ̃   **102.** sã dø, etc.
(cent un)   (cent deux)

500. sẽsã
(cinq cents)

501. sẽsã œ̃, etc.
(cinq cent un)

600. sisã
(six cents)

601. sisã œ̃, etc.
(six cent un)

700. sɛtsã
(sept cents)

701. sɛtsã œ̃, etc.
(sept cent un)

800. ɥisã
(huit cents)

801. ɥisã œ̃, etc.
(huit cent un)

900. nœfsã
(neuf cents)

901. nœfsã œ̃
(neuf cent un)

1000. mil   **1001.** mil œ̃, etc.
(mille)   (mille un)

5000. sẽmil
(cinq mille)

1100. õzsã or milsã
(onze cents or mille cent)

6000. simil
(six mille)

1200. duzsã or mildøsã
(douze cents or mille deux cents)

7000. sɛtmil
(sept mille)

1300. tʀɛzsã or miltʀwasã, etc.
(treize cents or mille trois cents)

8000. ɥimil
(huit mille)

2000. dø mil
(deux mille)

9000. nœfmil
(neuf mille)

2100. dømil sã
(deux mille cent)

10.000. dimil
(dix mille)

2200. dømildøsã
(deux mille deux cents)

500.000. sẽsãmil
(cinq cent mille)

2300. dømiltʀwasã, etc.
(deux mille trois cents)

1.000.000. œ̃miljõ
(un million)

B. Cardinal numbers, used purely as adjectives and immediately followed by the nouns they modify, are pronounced as follows:

1. Their final consonants are linked to a word beginning with a vowel.

1. un enfant	œ̃nɑ̃fɑ̃
2. deux enfants	døzɑ̃fɑ̃
3. trois enfants	trwɑzɑ̃fɑ̃
5. cinq enfants	sẽkɑ̃fɑ̃
6. six enfants	sizɑ̃fɑ̃
7. sept enfants	setɑ̃fɑ̃
8. huit enfants	ɥitɑ̃fɑ̃
9. neuf* enfants	nœfɑ̃fɑ̃
10. dix enfants	dizɑ̃fɑ̃

2. The final consonant of 2, 3, 5, 6, 8, 10, is silent before a word beginning with a consonant.

2. deux francs	døfʀɑ̃
3. trois francs	tʀwɑfʀɑ̃
5. cinq francs	sẽfʀɑ̃
6. six francs	sifʀɑ̃
8. huit francs	ɥifʀɑ̃
10. dix francs	difʀɑ̃

3. The pronunciation of the final consonant of 7 and 9 before a word beginning with a consonant is optional.

7. sept francs	setfdɑ̃ *or* sefʀɑ̃
dix-sept francs	dissetfʀɑ̃ *or* dissefdɑ̃
9. neuf francs	nœffʀɑ̃
dix-neuf francs	diznœffʀɑ̃

---

* Note that in **neuf ans** and **neuf heures,** the **f** is pronounced **v.**

CONVERSATIONS

Unit 1

Rətur a paRi.

də pasaʒ a paRi apRɛ zyn lõgapsãs, ʒã yg desid dale Rvwar sɛzami paRizjɛ̃ Rɔʒe e maRi dyplɛsi, mɛ̃tnã maRje e kidmœR dəpɥi kɛlkə tã a sɛ̃klu. il vjɛ̃d fɛRsiɲ aœ̃ ʃofœRdətaksi. lə taksi saRɛt.

(¹oʃofœR.)
ʒã. —²tRɛz, avny dy palɛ a sɛ̃klu. ³sɛ pRɛ dy põd sɛ̃klu, a lãtRed lɔtoRut də lwɛst. lə ʃofœR. —⁴ãtãdy məsjø. mõte silvuplɛ.
ʒã. —⁵vəlõtje. ilja diminyt kə ʒatã œ̃taksi. (ʒã mõt dãltaksi.)
lə ʃofœR. —⁶si sanvufɛRjɛ̃, ʒvɛ pRãdR le ke. ⁷sɛpətɛtRœ̃ pø ply lõ, me(z)õ pɛR mwɛ̃dtã.
ʒã. —⁸kɔmã sa?
lə ʃofœR. ⁹il sõ sãs ynik. —¹⁰lə lõde ke, tut le vwatyR võ dãlmɛm sãs. ¹¹sava boku plyvit.
ʒã. —¹²kõbjɛ̃d tã fotil puRale a sɛ̃klu?
lə ʃofœR. —¹³ilfo ãviRõ vɛ u vɛ̃tsɛ̃ minyt, tutoply(s). ¹⁴lə tã sɛ̃d laRʒã vusave, ¹⁵syRtu puR le ʃofœR də taksi.
ʒã (œ̃pøplytaR). —¹⁶sɔmnudeʒa a sɛ̃klu?
lə ʃofœR. —¹⁷nõməsjø. nusəm tuʒuR apaRi. ¹⁸õnsɛʒamɛ u paRi kɔmãs e u ilfini.

Unit 3

ʃe le dyplɛsi.

Rɔʒe aRsy ʒã a bRa(z)uvɛR, e ʒã a ete tRɛz œRødə Rtruve sõnami kilnavɛpɑ vyd pɥi lõtã. malœRøzmã, maRi ete ã tRɛ̃d fɛRdekuRs o məmãd(ə) laRivedʒã. ãnatãdã sõRtuR, nodøzami paRl dəskilzõfɛ okuR dedø dɛRnjɛRzane.

Rɔʒe. —¹tu a boku vwajaʒe dəpɥitõdepaR ilja døzã, nɛspɑ?
ʒã. —²wi, pɑmal. ³kɔmtylsɛ, ãkitã paRi, ʒə sɥiRtuRne a filadɛlfi. ⁴dəla ʒ(ə) sɥizale a pitsbœrg, u ʒe pɑse kɛlkəmwɑ dã lɛ labɔRatwaR dyn kõpaɲid petRɔl. ⁵pɥiõma ãvwaje o venezɥela.
Rɔʒe. —⁶ty ɛ(z)ale osi o mwajenɔRjã, nɛspɑ?
ʒã. —⁷atã! ʒne pɑzãkɔR finid paRled mɛvwajaʒ . . . ⁸dy venezɥela ʒ(ə)sɥi paRti puR latynizi. ⁹ʒe kite latynizi puR leʒipt, leʒipt puR liRɑk. ¹⁰pɥi ʒe pɑse kɛlkətã a tɛlaviv. ¹¹õmãvwa mɛ̃tnã ozetazyni, pɑseœ̃kõʒed tRwɑ mwɑ kə ʒnepɑ vɔle.

PHONETIC TRANSCRIPTIONS

Rɔʒe. —¹²kõpaʀe alatjen mavi a ete bjẽ tʀɑ̃kil. ¹³dəpɥinɔtʀə maʀjaʒ, maʀi e mwa nu sɔm ʀɛste bjẽ saʒmɑ̃ alamɛzõ, ¹⁴sɔf bjẽnɑ̃tɑ̃dy kɛlkəpti vwajaʒ dagʀemɑ̃.

ʒɑ̃. —¹⁵ʒeʀsy lẽvitasjõ a tõ maʀjaʒ kɑ̃ ʒetɛ dɑ̃ la ʒõgl venezɥeljen. ¹⁶ʒne pɑpyvniʀ asiste alaseremɔni. sɛtɛtʀə lwẽ.

Rɔʒe. —¹⁷ɑ̃ tukɑ, rɛst dine avɛk nu səswaʀ. ¹⁸maʀisʀa ɑ̃ʃɑ̃ted təʀvwaʀ, e nuʀpaʀlʀõ dy bõvjøtɑ̃.

Unit 5

ɶnaksidɑ̃.

maʀi e Rɔʒe õtẽvite ʒɑ̃ adineʃezø. a lafẽ dyʀpɑ, ʒɑ̃ paʀl dɶnaksidɑ̃ kiayljø syʀ lə nil pɑ̃dɑ̃ sõ sejuʀ ɑ̃neʒipt.

ʒɑ̃. —¹maʀi, tõ dine etɛ delisjø. ²ʒənsavɛ pɑdytu, iljadøzɑ̃, kə ty etɛ sibɔnkɥizinjɛʀ.

maʀi. —³ʒapʀesi vivmɑ̃ tõ kõplimɑ̃. ⁴mɛ dinuɶpø skətyafɛ okuʀdəsedødɛʀnjɛʀzane.

ʒɑ̃. —⁵lanedɛʀnjɛʀ asɛtdat, ʒetɛzɑ̃neʒipt. ⁶vusuvnevu dytɛʀiblaksidɑ̃ kiayljø syʀ lə nil?

Rɔʒe. —⁷ʒəmsuvjẽdəkɛlkəʃoz— ⁸ɶ bato ki tʀɑ̃spɔʀtɛ de pasaʒe syʀ lə nil, nɛspɑ?

ʒɑ̃. —⁹ʒetɛ dɑ̃lvwazinaʒ omɔmɑ̃d laksidɑ̃.

Rɔʒe. —¹⁰kɛski ɛtaʀive, oʒyst?

ʒɑ̃. —¹¹vwala. sɛtɛ ɶtʀɛ vjøbato. ¹²dəpɥi swasɑ̃tdizɑ̃, il tʀɑ̃spɔʀtɛ de pasaʒe syʀ lə nil. ¹³iljavɛdlaplas puʀ ynswasɑ̃tɛn də pasaʒe. ¹⁴ləʒuʀ də laksidɑ̃, õnɑ̃na ɑ̃baʀke plydsɑ̃sẽkɑ̃t. ¹⁵lə batovnɛtapɛn dəkite laʀiv, lɔʀskə lo a kəmɑ̃se a ɑ̃tʀe a lẽteʀjœʀ.

maʀi. —¹⁶purkwal kapitɛn nɛtilpɑ ʀtuʀne obɔʀ?

ʒɑ̃. —¹⁷ilaeseje. ¹⁸lə bato etɛ akɛlkəmɛtʀ dybɔʀ kɑ̃ laksidɑ̃ a y ljø. ¹⁹ilete mɛm si pʀedybɔʀ ²⁰kõnalɑ̃se dekɔʀd a deʒɑ̃ syʀlaʀiv dyflœv. ²¹natyʀɛlmɑ̃, plyzil tiʀe syʀlekɔʀd, plylbato sẽklinɛ. ²²ilafini paʀʃaviʀe. ²³ynsɑ̃tɛndəpɛʀsɔn səsõ nwaje. ²⁴la plypaʀ depasaʒen savɛ pɑnaʒe.

maʀi. —²⁵sɛtɑ̃ veʀite yn bjẽ tʀististwaʀ.

Rɔʒe. —²⁶setafʀø, mɛ selavi! . . . ²⁷sinuzaljõ pʀɑ̃dʀləkafe osalõ?

Unit 7

ləpti miʃel

fjɛʀmɑ̃, Rɔʒe e maʀi mõtʀaʒɑ̃ lœʀ fis ləptimiʃel. ʒɑ̃, ki a dotʀə susi, tʀɛt lasɛn avɛk ynẽdylʒɑ̃s leʒɛʀmɑ̃ mɔkøz.

Rɔʒe. —¹ɛskəmiʃel ɛRevɛje, maRi? ²vwala bjẽ dɸʒœR kil dɔR.

maRi. —³ʒkRwa lavwaR ãtãdy Rmɥe dãsõli tutalœR. ⁴vɸtylvwaR, ʒã?

ʒã. —⁵sɛRtɛnmã. ⁶ʒe sisuvã ãtãdy paRledlɥi kəʒtjẽ(z)apsɔlymã a fɛR sakɔnɛsãs.

(dãlaʃãbR dəmiʃel.)

maRi. —⁷ʒ(ə)təpRezãt nɔtR ʒœnfis miʃel.

ʒã. —⁸kɛl ʒãtipti gaRsõ! ⁹R(ə)gaRde se gRãzjɸ blɸ e sə ʒɔli suRiR!

maRi. —¹⁰ilɛ mẽtnãd bɔnymœR, sãdut paRskil a dɔRmi tulapRɛmidi. ¹¹kãtil vjẽd səRevɛje, ilɛkɛlkəfwa dətRɛ mɔvɛzymœR.

ʒã. —¹²ʒepɛnaləkRwaR . . . ¹³kɛlɑʒ atil?

maRi. —¹⁴ilɔRa tRɛzmwɑl pRəmje sɛptãbR e ilpɛz õzkilo.

ʒã. —¹⁵ɛskil sɛmaRʃe?

maRi. —¹⁶vwajõ, ʒã, savɛty maRʃe kãtyavɛœ̃nã?

ʒã. —¹⁷fRãʃmã, ʒənməRapɛlpɑ . . . ¹⁸dajœR, avɛkyntɛlmɛR, u plyto avɛk dətel paRã, Rjẽ nɛtẽpɔsibl.

maRi. —¹⁹o vwala bjẽ nɔtR ʒã, kiadɔRs mɔkedeʒã, ²⁰tutã lœR fəzã dekõplimã.

ʒã. —²¹maRi, tym pRɛt tutsɔRt də mɔvɛz ẽtãsjõ. ²²malgRetu, nusɔm lemejœRzamidymõd, nɛspɑ?

UNIT 9

lə fõksjɔnɛR.

Rɔʒe a de difikylte avɛkyn administRasjõ finãsjɛR. ilRakõta ʒã kɔmã leʃoz səsõ pase.

Rɔʒe. —¹ʒə dwɑ RtuRne sɛtapRɛmidi obyRo dyn administRasjõ finãsjɛR ²mɔkype dyn afɛR dẽpo puR mõnyzin. ³ilsaʒi dyn dɸzjɛmvizit. ⁴la pRəmjɛR fwa, ʒe ete fɔRmalRasy.

ʒã. —⁵kəvɸtydiR? kɛskisɛ pɑse?

Rɔʒe. —⁶kãʒəsɥizãtRe, œ̃nãplwaje ma fɛ kõpRãdR kə ʒəldeRãʒe boku.

ʒã. —⁷sete puRtã sõ metje apRɛtu.

Rɔʒe. —⁸tynsɛpa skəsɛkœ̃fõksjɔnɛR.

ʒã. —⁹sɛ kɛlkœ̃ o sɛRvis dy guvɛRnəmã.

Rɔʒe. —¹⁰pResizemã. tRavaje puR lguvɛRnəmã lɥi dɔn də lɔtoRite. ¹¹ɔR lə guvɛRnəmã lə pɛ dɔRdinɛR ase mal e savinɛ pazɛgzaktəmã pasjɔnãt. ¹²ilɛdõk mekõtã. ¹³ilalẽpResjõ kilne pɑ Rekõpãse dsɛ sɛRvis ¹⁴kɔm il dəvRɛ lɛtR. ¹⁵kɛlkəfwa ilsəvãʒ syR lə pyblik. ¹⁶setãplwaje sɛ vãʒe ã mɔbliʒã a Rəvnir lə vwaR oʒuRdɥi.

ʒã. —¹⁷kɛskiltadi?

Rɔʒe.　—[18]ilmadikə, dapRɛlalɛtRkilmavɛtãvwaje, ʒɔRɛdy vniR ləvwaR lavɛj.　[20]ʒə
lɥi e Repõdy kəʒənavɛ pɑ py, [21]a koz dœ̃ Rãdevudafɛr ẽpɔRtã.　[22]"ẽpɔRtãunõ,
il falɛvniR," matilRepõdy.
　　　[23]il nəma faly kœ̃nẽstã puR mə Rãdrə kõt [24]kilvalɛ mjøn pazẽsiste.　[25]ʒə
sɥi sɔRti ã lɥi dizã kəʒəsRɛzøRødə RəvniR lə vwaR.
ʒã.　—[26]lefõksjɔnɛR sõ paRtu le mɛm, ty sɛ.

UNIT 11

lemwajẽdtRãspɔR.

lemwajẽdtRãspɔR ʃãʒ boku dynepɔkalotR.　otRəfwa le ʒã ale apje, kɛlkəfwa
aʃval uãvwatyR.　mẽtnã ilsdeplasãnoto.　neãmwẽ letRẽ sõtãkɔR tRRɛzãplwaje
ã fRãs.

Rɔʒe.　—[1]õnsədutpɑ [2]kilafalydesjɛkl [3]puR dɔneopaRizjẽ demwajẽdtRãspɔRkɔmɔd.
[4]ʒyskosjɛklədeRnje, pɛRsɔn sɔf paskal, [5]navɛpãse a kReeskõnapɛl [6]letRãspɔR-
ãkɔmœ̃.
ʒã.　—[7]paskal, ləmatɛmatisjẽ, lotœR depãse?
Rɔʒe.　—[8]ã pɛRsɔn.　[9]œ̃ ʒuR ilaylide [10]detabliR de vwatyR pɛjãt puRtRãspɔRte
levwajaʒœR a lẽteRjœRdəlavil.　[11]maløRøzmã, ilnəsəsõpɑ(z)abitɥe tudsɥit a
sõnẽvãsjõ.　[12]boku dãtRø navɛ mɛm pɑdkwa sɔfRiR lənuvomwajẽdtRãspɔR.
[13]aty ãtãdypaRle dməsjø ɔmnɛs?
ʒã.　—[14]nõ, ʒne ʒamɛ ãtãdypaRledlɥi.
Rɔʒe.　—[15]sɛ lɥi ki, paRetil, apRɛzavwaRẽvãte sɛ vwatyRpyblik, [16]lœRadɔnelənõ
dɔmnibys, a kozdəsõnõ: ɔmnɛs, ɔmnibys . . . ty kõpRã?　[17]məsjø ɔmnɛs
apãseasla ozãviRõ də milɥisãtRãt, [18]vɛrlepɔk u lõ sɛ mi a kõstRɥiR leʃmẽdfɛR.
[19]a lœRaktɥɛl, bokudvwajaʒœR sə sɛRv deʃmẽdfɛR [20]e osi dɛzɔtobys, kiõ
syksede ozɔmnibys də məsjø ɔmnɛs.
ʒã.　—[21]ʃenu, letRẽ sɛRv syRtu a tRãspɔRte demaRʃãdiz.
Rɔʒe.　—[22]ʒeãtãdydiR kə letRẽamerikẽ tRãspɔRt də mwẽzãmwẽdvwajaʒœR.
[23]pɑ(z)ãfRãs.　[24]ləʃmẽdfɛR Rɛst lə pRẽsipal mwajẽdtRãspɔR.　[25]leta a depãse
de sɔmenɔRm puR mɔdɛRnizel matɛRjel.　[26]paRtu le liɲ õtete elɛktRifje.
[27]lezɔtoRaj, puR lə tRãspɔR de vwajaʒœR, võtayntRegRãdvitɛs.　[28]sã nu vãte
[29]nuzotRəfRãsɛ avõ Reysi a kRee œ̃ sistɛm [30]ki fɛ ladmiRasjõ de kɔnɛsœR . . .
deʃmẽdfɛR.

Unit 13

ʃe lãtikɛʀ.

ʒã pʀɔfit dəsõseʒuʀapaʀi puʀaʃtedekado destine adepɛʀsɔn kilɥisõʃɛʀ ozetazyni. ɶ̃ʒuʀ, dãzynpətit ʀy vwazin də sẽʒɛʀmẽdepʀe, ilʀəmaʀk aladvãtyʀ dɶ̃nãtikɛʀ ɶ̃sɛʀvis də tabl kilɥiplɛ. ilãtʀ, avɛk lẽtãsjõd laʃte puʀsasɶʀ, silpʀi ãnɛʀezɔnabl.

lãtikɛʀ. —[1]vudezire kɛlkəʃoz, məsjø?

ʒã. —[2]ʒmẽteʀɛs asəsɛʀvis ki ɛ̃taladvãtyʀ də vɔtʀ magazẽ. [3]puʀjevu məlmõtʀe?

lãtikɛʀ. —[4]sɛʀtɛnmã, məsjø. [5]ʒnãnemi kə kɛlkəzeʃãtijõ alavitʀin. [6]lezotʀ pjɛs sõtisi dãsplakaʀ. [7]ʒvɛ vulefɛʀvwaʀ.

ʒã. —[8]kõbjẽ jãnatil ãtu?

lãtikɛʀ. —[9]swasãtkẽz, məsjø. [10]lə sɛʀvis ɛ kõplɛ. [11]ilnimãkpazynsœlpjɛs. [12]avʀɛdiʀ, lɔʀskəʒleaʃte, il mãkeynasjet. [13]mɛ, ʒepym lapʀɔkyʀe ʃezɶ̃nãtikɛʀ dəkõkaʀno.

ʒã. —[14]savevu dupʀɔvjẽ sə sɛʀvis?

lãtikɛʀ. —[15]ʒleaʃtemwamɛm, dãzynvãt ozãʃɛʀ a ʀɛn. [16]il vjẽ dɶ vjø ʃato ã bʀɔtaɲ dõtõ vãdel məbilje apʀɛ desɛ. [17]sedlatʀɛbɛlfajãs dəkẽpɛʀ, məsjø. [18]opʀi ẽdike dəsisãsẽkãt fʀã, set ynɔkazjõ maɲifik.

ʒã. —[19]puvevu vuʃaʀʒed lɛkspedje ãnameʀik? [20]sɛtɶ̃kado puʀmasɶʀ.

lãtikɛʀ. —[21]lesemwa sœlmã sõnadʀɛs. [22]nunuʃaʀʒ(ə)ʀõ də tulʀɛst, ãbalaʒ e fʀe dãvwa.

ʒã. —[23]ɛl ləʀsəvʀa ãbəneta nɛspɑ?

lãtikɛʀ. —[24]nəkʀeɲe ʀjẽ, məsjø. [25]nugaʀãtisõ tunozãvwa.

ʒã. —[26]ãtãdy. [27]ãvwaje lə lɥi vɛʀ ləkẽz septãbʀ. [28]ilnəm ʀɛst ply kavupɛje, nɛspɑ?

Unit 15

yn ʀãkõtʀ.

ɶ̃ʒuʀ kiltʀavɛʀs laplas dəlɔpeʀa, ʒã sətʀuv tutaku fasafas avɛk ɛlen fʀeⁱzɚ esamɛʀ. ilzeʃãʒ də kɔʀdjal pwaɲe dmẽ. nɔte dajɶʀ kə seʀãkõtʀinatãdy apaʀi u ajɶʀ, ãtʀə pɛʀsɔn vənãd peielwaɲe sõ mwẽ ʀaʀ kõ nəl pãsʀɛ, kaʀ le tuʀist fʀekãt le mɛm zãdʀwa.

ʒã. —[1]madam fʀeⁱzɚ! [2]ɛlen! [3]kɛl syʀpʀiz! [4]ʒiɲɔʀe kəvuzetje isi!

madam fʀeⁱzɚ. —[5]mwɑ nõ ply ʒənmədutɛ pɑkəvuzetje a paʀi. [6]ãʀi sʀa sɛʀtɛnmã øʀød vuʀvwaʀ.

ʒã. —[7]ãʀi ɛtosi apaʀi?

PHONETIC TRANSCRIPTIONS

ɛlen. —[8]bjẽsyʀ. [9]mɛ tykɔne mõfʀɛʀ: [10]kã nulɥi avõdik nuziʀjõ fɛʀdezãplɛt setapʀɛmidi, [11]iladeklaʀe kilɛmɛ mjø mõte ã odlatuʀɛfel.

madam fʌe[i]zɤ. —[12]kõbjẽdtã kõtevu ʀɛste apaʀi, ʒã?

ʒã. —[13]ʒə sre ãkɔʀisi yn vẽten dəʒuʀ. [14]ʒɛʀtəny pasaʒ syʀœ̃navjõ kipaʀtiʀa puʀ nju jɔʀk də samdi ãkẽz.

madam fʌe[i]zɤ. —[15]nuziʀõ pɑsel wikɛnd ãtuʀɛn. [16]iljɔʀa ynplaspuʀvu dã nɔtʀ vwatyʀ, sivunave ʀjẽdmjø afɛʀ. [17]mɛ ʒəmʀãkõt kə vunavesãdutpɑ bokudtã avɔtʀ dispozisjõ.

ʒã. —[18]mɛsi. [19]ãsmɔmã, ʒəsɥi libʀ kɔmlɛʀ, eʒəsʀe ãʃãted vuzakõpaɲe. [20]kã avevu lẽtãsjõd paʀtiʀ?

madam fʌe[i]zɤ. —[21]nunumetʀõ(z)ãʀut vɛʀ ɥitœʀ dymatẽ vãdʀədi pʀɔʃẽ. [22]ditnu uvuzet desãdy, e nuvjẽdʀõ vu ʃɛʀʃe.

ʒã. —[23]nəvudeʀãʒepɑ puʀmwa.

ɛlen. —[24]sə nɛ pazœ̃ deʀãʒmã. [25]dɔn sœlmã tõnadʀɛsamamã.

ʒã. —[26]ʒəsɥidesãdyalotel mœʀis. [27]nunuʀtʀuvʀõ vɛʀɥitœʀ. [28]ãnatãdã, dit bjẽ de ʃoz dəmapaʀ a ãʀi, [29]kəʒəʀvɛʀe dajœʀ supø.

Unit 17

a ʃənõso.

ʒã e sezami pɑslaʒuʀne a ʃənõso. il vjɛn də vizite lẽterjœʀ dy ʃato, kõstʀɥi o sezjɛm sjɛkl, e ki ɛtœ̃ de mənymã le plyzelegãd laʀənesãs fʀãsez. ã sɔʀtã, ilzeʃãʒlœʀz ẽpʀɛsjõ.

ɛlen. —[1]ʒadɔʀ səʃato! [2]si ʒavezaʃwsaziʀ ãtʀə tusøk nuzavõvy, ʒə ʃwaziʀe səlɥi si. [3]skim plɛ syʀtu, sɛ kil ɛt ãkɔʀabitabl.

ãʀi. —[4]vudʀɛty iabite?

ɛlen. —[5]sladepã. [6]si ʒavetuskilfo, ʒəsʀɛ tʀezɔʀøzisi. [7]bjẽ nãtãdy, il fodʀɛtavwaʀ dənõbʀø sɛʀvitœʀ: kɥizinje, ʒaʀdinje, ɛtseteʀa, ʀəsəvwaʀ de kãtited ẽvite . . .

ʒã. —[8]kɔm lɛ ʀwadotʀəfwa, paʀegzãpl . . . [9]ãnœ̃mo, ɛlen, tyvudʀe mənecẽʒãʀ dəvi ki, ʒəlkʀẽ, nɛgzistə ply.

ɛlen. —[10]puʀtã, lə ʃato a ete abite ʒyska yn dat ʀɛsãt, nɛspɑ?

ʒã. —[11]mɛwi, paʀ le mənje, ki ãsõ tuʒuʀ pʀəpʀieteʀ. [12]se puʀ sla kəl ʃatod ʃənõso etã mejœ̃ʀ eta kə səlɥid ʃãbəʀ, [13]ki dəpɥi de sjɛkl ʀɛstplyzumwẽvid.

ãʀi. —[14]pɛʀsɔnɛlmã, ʒneʃãʒʀe pɑ ʃãbəʀ puʀ ʃənõso. [15]vy a distãs, lafasad də ʃãbəʀ ɛtinubliabl.

madam fʌe[i]zɤ. —[16]vwajõ, mezãfã, il nə saʒi pɑ deʃãʒe œ̃ʃato puʀœ̃notʀ. [17]nilœ̃ ni lotʀənə vuzapaʀtjẽ.

ɛlen. —[18]kɛlkəʃoz mẽtʀig: [19]puʀkwa atõ kõstʀɥi ynpaʀti dy ʃato o miljø dyn ʀivjɛʀ?

ʒɑ̃. —²⁰ʀjɛ̃d plysĕpl: ²¹katʀin dəmedisis a deside kə si ɛlfəze kõstʀ ᴜ iʀ sɛt galʀi a dɸzetaʒ odsyd la ʀivjɛʀ, ²²ɛl puʀɛ pɑsed lotʀəkote sɑ̃ sɔʀtird ʃezɛl.

ɛlɛn. —²³tjɛ̃, sɛtynide! ²⁴ʒnɔʀɛ ʒamɛ pɑ̃se a sla!

UNIT 19

o ʃatod blwɑ.

kõtinᴜ ɑ̃ lœʀ vizit dəlatuʀɛn, ʒɑ̃ e sɛzami aʀivablwɑ. lə ʃato a ete kõstʀ ᴜ i a difeʀɑ̃tze pɔk e dɑ̃tʀwa stil difeʀɑ̃: lapaʀti la plyzɑ̃sjɛn paʀlwiduz, ynotʀəpaʀti paʀ fʀɑ̃swapʀəmje, e la tʀwazjɛm paʀ gastõ dɔʀleɑ̃, fʀɛʀdə lwitʀɛz. lə gid (dyn-vwamɔnɔtən)

lə gid. —¹nusɔm mɛ̃tnɑ̃, mesjɸ dam, dɑ̃l kabinɛd katʀin də medisis.* ²ʀəmaʀke la dekɔʀasjõ ɑ̃bwaskylte. ³səpanosi kaʃ plyzjœʀzaʀmwaʀ səkʀɛt, u laʀɛn kõsɛʀve de papje, de biʒu, mɛm de pwazõ, ditõ. ⁴iljave plyddɸsɑ̃pano e katʀsœlmɑ̃ dɑ̃tʀɸetemɔbil. ⁵sɸsiʀəsɑ̃blɛ tɛlmɑ̃ asɸla kiletetɛ̃pɔsiblədle distĕge, ⁶mɛmɑ̃lezɛgzaminɑ̃dpʀɛ.

(lə gid e le vizitœʀ kit lə kabinɛdlaʀɛn.)

ɑ̃ʀi. —⁷kɛskɛl fəze depwazõ kɛl kõsɛʀve dɑ̃sõnaʀmwaʀ?

ɛlɛn. —⁸sete pɸtetʀəpuʀ leʒɑ̃ kɛlnɛmɛpa!

madam fɹe ⁱ zɚ. —⁹nə dit pɑ tʀɔdmal də katʀin də medisis. ¹⁰ʒe ɑ̃tɑ̃dydir kɛl vale mjɸk saʀepytasjõ . . .

ɛlɛn. —¹¹la plypaʀ de ʃatok nuzavõ vizite sõ vid. ¹²otʀəfwa, il dəvetɛtʀə mœble. ¹³kə sõ dəvny le mœbl?

ʒɑ̃. —¹⁴mɛmotʀəfwa, le ʃato nave pɑ bokud mœbl, ¹⁵sɔf sɸ ki sɛʀved ʀezidɑ̃s abitᴜel a kɛlkəgʀɑ̃ pɛʀsɔnaʒ. ¹⁶lemœbləkiʀɛste õ dispaʀy pɑ̃dɑ̃ laʀevɔlysjõ.

ɛlɛn. —¹⁷ʒvudʀɛbjɛ̃ pʀɑ̃dʀynfɔtod sɛfnɛtʀ ɔʀned salamɑ̃dʀ.** ¹⁸mɛ ʒe lɛse mõnapaʀɛj dɑ̃ lavwatyʀ. ¹⁹vɸty bjɛ̃m pʀɛtel tjɛ̃?

ʒɑ̃. —²⁰mɛ wi. ²¹ləmjɛ̃n vo sɑ̃dut pɑltjɛ̃. ²²mɛzilfʀa lafɛʀ.

ɛlɛn. —²³ʒənsɛpa mɑ̃ sɛʀviʀ.

ʒɑ̃. —²⁴ʀjɛ̃d ply sɛ̃pl. ²⁵ilsyfid apᴜije syʀ lbutõ.

---

* fam də ɑ̃ridɸ, rwad fʀɑ̃s də kɛ̃z sɑ̃ kaʀɑ̃tsɛt a kɛz sɑ̃ sɛ̃kɑ̃tnœf.

** la salamɑ̃dʀ ete lɑ̃blem də fʀɑ̃swa pʀəmje ʀwadə kɛ̃z sɑ̃ kɛ̃z a kɛ̃z sɑ̃ kaʀɑ̃t sɛt el pɔʀkepiketɛ səlᴜidə lwi duz (katɔʀz sɑ̃ katʀə vɛ̃ dizᴜit a kɛ̃z sɑ̃ kɛz).

Unit 21

lə kyltivatœr.

le fɹeⁱzɚ sə sõtaʀete dɑ̃zœ̃ vilaʒ. a la pɔst uiletale puʀɑ̃vwaje yn depεʃ, ʒɑ̃ paʀl a œ̃ kyltivatœr də lɑ̃dʀwa. səlɥi si səplɛ̃ səlõ labityd dytɑ̃, də la plɥi pεʀsistɑ̃t, dy kudlakyltyʀ, e dε pʀədɥi kis vɑ̃dmal.

ʒɑ̃. —[1]vwala œ̃ bjɛ̃ vilɛ̃ tɑ̃ puʀ le ʀekɔlt.

lə kyltivatœr. —[2]a, məsjø, il vo mjøn pazɑ̃paʀle. [3]il jadkwa dezεspeʀe. [4]lane dεʀnjεʀ, setε la seʃʀεs, e sεt ane sεtynplɥikõtinɥel.

ʒɑ̃. —[5]ʒənkʀwapɑ kil faj dezεspeʀe. [6]lə tɑ̃ finiʀa paʀ saʀɑ̃ʒe.

lə kyltivatœr. —[7]ʒεspεʀkə vuzaveʀezõ. [8]ʒəswεt kə la plɥi saʀεt e kil fas bo, [9]mε ʒe pœʀ kə me swεn sεʀv pazagʀɑ̃ʃoz . . . [10]si o mwɛ̃ no pʀədɥis vɑ̃dε bjɛ̃! [11]mε bjɛ̃ kə nu swajõ əbliʒed depɑ̃se ply kotʀəfwa, [12]lakyltyʀ ʀapɔʀt də mwɛ̃zɑ̃mwɛ̃.

ʒɑ̃. —[13]ʒkʀwaje kəlguvεʀnəmɑ̃ fiksε lepʀi.

lə kyltivatœr. —[14]wi meʒkʀɛ̃ kə nu naʀivjõbjɛ̃toply aʒwɛ̃dʀ le dø bu. [15]il fo kə nu pejõ ply ʃεʀ tuskə nuzaʃtõ, [16]le smɑ̃s, le zɑ̃gʀε, sɑ̃ kõte le maʃin.

ʒɑ̃. —[17]ilmə sɑ̃bl ɑ̃nefε kõvwa dɑ̃ leʃɑ̃ bjɛ̃ plyd maʃin kotʀəfwa.

lə kyltivatœr. —[18]mɛ̃tnɑ̃ amwɛ̃kõnaj dɑ̃ de kwɛ̃ pεʀdy õnvwa plyd ʃəvo: [19]ʀjɛ̃k de maʃin. [20]isi, il nja pɑ(z) œ̃ sœl kyltivatœr ki nε sõ tʀaktœr. [21]il sufi kə lœ̃ dø ɑ̃ netœ̃ puʀkə sõ vwazɛ̃ vœj osi avwaʀ lə sjɛ̃. [22]vulevu kəʒvu diz skə ʒɑ̃ pɑ̃s? [23]lə guvεʀnəmɑ̃ εtɑ̃tʀεd ʀɥinel kyltivatœr.

ʒɑ̃. —[24]dɑ̃ mõ pei, nuzavõ œ̃ pø le mεm pʀɔblεm.

Unit 23

syʀ la ʀut.

ʒɑ̃ e le fɹeⁱzɚ vwajaʒ tuʒuʀ ɑ̃noto dɑ̃ laʀeʒjõd lalwaʀ. il pløtavεʀs e ɑ̃ʀiki kõdɥi nəse pɑtʀə uilsõ.

ɑ̃ʀi. (ovɔlɑ̃). —[1]vwala dezœʀ kil plø sɑ̃zaʀε. [2]il fəze bo kɑ̃ nu sɔm paʀti, [3]il sε mi(z)a plœvwaʀ yn dəmiœʀ ply taʀ. [4]mɛ̃tnɑ̃ õ vwaapεn a tʀavεʀ lə paʀbʀiz kaʀlεsɥiglas fõksjɔnmal. [5]e ekute la plɥi syʀ lə twad la vwatyʀ.

ʒɑ̃ (ʀesitɑ̃).
— [6]o bʀɥi du də la plɥi
paʀ tεʀ e syʀ lε twa!
[7]puʀ œ̃ kœʀ ki sɑ̃nɥi
o lə ʃɑ̃ də la plɥi!
[8]dɑ̃ lεspʀi dy pɔet, [9]il saʒise dœ̃notʀəʒɑ̃ʀ də twa, bjɛ̃nɑ̃tɑ̃dy.

ãʀi.　—[10]nə di pɑ de ʃoz kɔm sa sãm pʀevniʀ!　[11]ʒe ete si syʀpʀi kə ʒe faji kite la ʀut.

ɛlen.　—[12]set plɥi nəm deplɛ pɑ dytu.　[13]ɛl mədɔn o kõtʀeʀ œ̃ sãtimãd kõfəʀ, də bjẽnetʀ.

ãʀi.　—[14]ʒkʀẽ kə tõ bjẽnetʀ nə swad kuʀtə dyre.　[15]ʒe lẽpʀesjõ kə nunu sɔm tʀõped ʀut.

ʒã.　—[16]ʒapeʀswa labɑœ̃pəto-ẽdikatœʀ.　[17]lizeskildi.

ãʀi.　—[18]ʒənpø ʀjẽ vwaʀ a koz də la plɥi.

ʒã.　—[19]aʀettwa œ̃nẽstã e uvʀ la pəʀtjeʀ.

ãʀi (lizã).　—[20]il di: ʒe-i-ə-ɛn swasãt sẽ kiləmetʀ.

ɛlen.　—[21]kəmã pʀənõs tõ ʒe-i-ə-ɛn?

ʒã.　—[22]ʒkʀwakə ʒjẽ ʀimavek ʃjẽ.

ɛlen.　—[23]ʒənsɛ ʒamɛ kəmã õ pʀənõs le nõ pʀəpʀ.　[24]õnekʀi ɛʀ-ə-i-ɛm-ɛs e õ di: ʀẽs, [25]ɛl-a-o-ɛn et õ di lã; [26]se-a-ə-ɛn e õ di kã; [27]lənõd la ʀivjeʀ la son rim avek bon.　[28]ʒnikõpʀã ʀjẽ.

ãʀi.　—[29]vʀemã, snepal məmã də diskyte ləʀtəgʀaf.　[30]ty fʀe mjød mə diʀ kɛl ʀut ʒə dwa sɥivʀ.

ʒã.　—[31]si ʒəm peʀmɛd tə dɔne mõnavi, tyna geʀ ləʃwa.　[32]sɥi selsi ʒysko pʀəʃẽ vilaʒ.　[33]la, nu veʀõ bjẽ kɛl ʀut ilfo pʀãdʀ.

Unit 25

---

le ʒãdaʀm.

ʒã e le fɹei`rɚ, ã ʀut puʀpaʀi, vwa tutaku døʒãdaʀm omiljød la ʀut.　il nəsavpɑ skəvœl seʒãdaʀm, e la kõveʀsasjõ kilzõtavek ø nəle ʀãseɲə geʀ.

ãʀi.　—[1]kɛskə seksa, la bɑ, o miljød la ʀut?

ʒã.　—[2]tyn vwa pɑskəse?　[3]ʀəgaʀd lœʀ ynifəʀm.　[4]sə sõ de ʒãdaʀm.

ãʀi.　—[5]kɛskis pãs?

ʒã.　—[6]ʒnã sɛ ʀjẽ.　[7]pøtetʀ kõ̃ kʀim a ete kəmi.

ãʀi.　—[8]kə fotil feʀ? feʀ dəmituʀ?

ʒã.　—[9]syʀmãpɑ.

ɛlen.　—[10]swa seʀjø e ralãti.　[11]ʒən sepɑs kil vœl, [12]mezilɛ seʀtẽ kəsebʀav ʒãdaʀm õ kɛlkə ʃoz a nu diʀ.　[13]vwajõ də kwa il saʒi.

(ãʀi saʀet.　le ʒãdaʀm sapʀəʃ.)

œ̃ de ʒãdaʀm (a ãʀi).　—[14]vœeje mə mõtʀe vo papje, məsjø.

ãʀi.　—[15]lekel vulevu?

lə ʒãdaʀm.　—[16]vətʀ pɑspəʀ, vətʀə peʀmid kõdɥiʀ e vətʀ pəlis dasyʀãs.　(apʀez-avwaʀ ɛgzamine le papje)　[17]tut ɛtãʀɛgl.　[18]vu puve kõtinɥe.

madam freizɚ.　—[19]puʀkwa nədmãdəty pɑ a məsjø le ʀãseɲmã dõ ty a bəzwẽ?

ãʀi. —²⁰tjẽ, sɛt yn ide! ²¹a kwa ɛskəʒ pãsɛ.

(o ʒãdaʀm) ²²nu vulõzale a ɔʀleã, məsjø. ²³lakɛl de dø ʀut ɛ la ply kuʀt, ²⁴sɛl syʀ
lakɛl nu sɔm u sɛl ki pɑs paʀ ʀəmɔʀãtẽ? ²⁵kã pãse vu?

lə ʒãdaʀm. —²⁶il nja pɑ gʀãd difeʀãs, məsjø. ²⁷si ʒetɛza vɔtʀə plas, ʒən ʃãʒʀɛ
pɑd ʀut.

ãʀi. —²⁸mɛʀsi boku, məsjø, (il sə ʀmɛtã ʀut).

ɛlɛn. —²⁹skim ʒɛn, sɛk nun sɔʀõ ʒamɛ puʀkwa se ʒãdaʀm nuzõtaʀete.

ãʀi. —³⁰kɛskə sa fɛ? ³¹il nuzõʀmi ã libɛʀte, e sɛ tus ki ẽpɔʀt.

Unit 27

lɛtʀ.

la fẽ dy seʒuʀ də ʒã ã fʀãs apʀɔʃ. lə lãdmẽ də sõʀtuʀ a paʀi, apʀɛ sõn-
ɛkskyʀsjõ avɛk le fʁeⁱzʒ· dã la ʀeʒjõd la lwar, il sɔkyp də sakɔʀɛspõdãs. vwasi
skil ekʀi a madam fʁeⁱzʒ·:

> otɛl mœʀis
> paʀi, lə vẽt katʀ u

ʃɛʀ madam:

avãdkite paʀi, ʒə tjẽza vu ʀmɛʀsje ãkəʀ də vɔtʀ emabl ẽvitasjõ a vuzakõpaɲe
ã tuʀɛn. ʒete deʒa ale dã sɛt ʒɔli ʀeʒjõ, meʒən lave ʒamɛ paʀkuʀy ã si agʀeabl
kõpaɲi. ʒə ʀgʀɛt œ̃ pø, kɔm vu, kəl ʒaʀdẽd la fʀãs ɛtete si kɔpjøzmãtaʀoze o kuʀ
də nətʀəvwajaʒ. mɛ la plɥi fɛ puse le flœʀ eʒ(ə)nubliʀe ʒamɛ le flœʀ, syʀtu le
bɛl ʀoz e lezenɔʀm dalja, ki sãbl puse paʀtu ã tuʀɛn.

dapʀɛs kə ma di ãʀi, vuzave lẽtãsjõd ʀãtʀe ozetazyni alafẽdy mwɑ pʀɔʃẽ.
nu nu ʀəveʀõdõk supø, ski sʀa puʀ mwa œ̃ gʀã plɛziʀ.

disi la, ʃɛʀ madam, ʒə vupʀid fɛʀ mezamitje a ɛlɛn e a ãʀi e dagʀee mezɔmaʒ
ʀɛspɛktɥø.

ʒã

il aɛsejed dɔne œ̃ kudfil a lãtikɛʀ ʃeki ila aʃte œ̃ sɛʀvis də tablə dɛstine a sa
sœʀ. nejã pɑ ʀeysi, il lɥi ãvwa la lɛtʀəsɥivãt.

məsjø,
vu tʀuvʀe si ẽkly œ̃ mãda-pɔst də sã swasãtsẽ fʀã ã pɛmã dy ʀəlika dy syʀ
vɔtʀə faktyʀ nymeʀo dømil døsã vɛt sis, date dy diznœf kuʀã.

ʒkʀwa vuzavwaʀ di, o məmãd laʃa, dãvwajel sɛʀvis də tabl də faʃõ askil aʀiv
a ladʀɛs ẽdike vɛʀ lə miljø dy mwãd sɛptãbʀ. tutfwa, ʒkõt pɑse kɛlkətã a filadɛlfi.

ʒdeziʀ dõk kə lãvwa aʀiv a sa dɛstinasjõ yn kɛ̃zɛn dəʒuʀ plytaʀ. ʒvu pʀi də fikse la dat dɛkspedisjõ ki kõvjɛ̃ ləmjø, ã tənã kõt de delɛ ɛ̃poze par lə tʀãspɔʀ e paʀ le fɔʀmalite də dwan.

vœejezagʀee, məsjø, me salytasjõãpʀɛse.

ʒ̃ã yg

ãfɛ̃, pãdã sõnapsãs də paʀi, ʒ̃ã aʀsy də madam lysjɛ̃ feʀi yn ɛ̃vitasjõ a dine, kil ɛtəbliʒed dekline puʀ la ʀɛzõ kil ɛ̃dik:

ʃɛʀ madam:

ʀjɛ̃ nə mɔʀe dɔne plyd plɛziʀ kə daksɛpte vɔtʀɛmabl ɛ̃vitãsjõ adine maʀdi pʀəʃɛ̃. maløʀøzmã, ʒən sʀe plyapaʀi a set dat. ʒɔʀe kite lafʀãs la vej, e ʒəsʀe sãdut deʒa aʀive a filadɛlfi.

ʒə ʀgʀɛt vivmãdən pɑ puvwaʀ ɛtʀə de votʀ. ʒɔʀɛzete øʀø də məʀtʀuve ʃe vu avɛk dezami kəmœ̃, o suvniʀ də ki ʒə vu pʀid mə ʀaple.

ʒə vu pʀi, ʃɛʀ madam, dagʀee me ʀɛspɛktɥø zɔmaʒ.

ʒ̃ã yg

UNIT 29

de nuvɛl də ʒ̃ã.

katʀə mwɑ apʀɛkə ʒ̃ã y kite la fʀãs, le dyplɛsi ʀəsyʀ də lɥi la lɛtʀ sɥivãt.

de ʀiv də lapyʀ, lə vɛ̃tsɛ̃k nɔvãbʀ.

me ʃɛʀzami:

lɔʀskəʒ kite la fʀãs ã sɛptãbʀə dɛʀnje, ʒmatãdɛa vu ʀvwaʀ a la fɛ̃d mõ kõʒe. lə sɔʀ mə fy bjɛ̃ kʀyɛl, ki mãvwaja syʀ le ʀiv inɔspitaljɛʀ də lapyʀ. mɛ vun save paskə sɛ kə lapyʀ, e plytosjel kə mwamɛm ʒnãnys ʒamez ãtãdy paʀle! lapyʀ ɛtyn ʀivjɛʀ dy venezɥela, œ̃naflyã də lɔʀenɔk. bʀɛf, ʒsɥi(z)yn fwad ply dã la ʒõgl, a œ̃nãdʀwa ki nɛ gɛʀ aksɛsiblə kə paʀ elikɔptɛʀ.

snɛpɑ, kwakə vu pɥisje kʀwaʀ, œ̃ ljø də depɔʀtasjõ puʀ lezɛ̃desiʀabl, bjɛ̃ kil jãnɛ kɛlkəzœ̃ — vu vuzã ʀãdʀe kõt tutalœʀ. ʒədiʀiʒ œ̃ kã də pʀɔspɛktœʀ dã de ʀeʒjõ pʀɛskinɛksplɔʀe dy venezɥela ed la kɔlõbi. tu le matɛ̃, mezəm sə ʀãd paʀ elikɔptɛʀ ã divɛʀzãdʀwa, u il fõteksploze de ʃaʀʒ də dinamit, də fasõ a detɛʀmine la kõfigyʀasjõ dy sɔl. ski aʀiva jɛʀ a yn də noz ekip vu dɔnʀa yn ided la vi kə nu mnõ isi.

puʀtɑ̃, la ʒuʀne kɔmɑ̃sa kɔm dabityd. lelikɔpteʀ vɛ̃ ʃeʀʃe no tʀwazɔm lə matɛ̃, e il ledepoza dɑ̃zyn kleʀjeʀ o miljødla ʒõgl. la il səmiʀto tʀavaj. tutala bjɛ̃ ʒyska midi. as mɔmɑ̃ la dezɛ̃djɛ̃ aʀiveʀ, e, mənasɑ̃ lezɛ̃tʀy dezaʀm le ply- diveʀs, il sɑ̃paʀeʀ də tu skə pɔsedɛ le pʀɔspɛktœʀ, aʀʒɑ̃, mõtʀ, uti, e le depujeʀ də lœʀ vɛtmɑ̃. kɑ̃ lelikɔpteʀ ʀəvɛ̃ le ʃeʀʃe lə swaʀ, lə pilɔt tʀuva no tʀwaz ɔm ki latɑ̃dɛavek yn ɛ̃pasjɑ̃s fasila kõpʀɑ̃dʀ. sə dutʀetõ ʒɑmɛ kyn tɛl avɑ̃tyʀ pytaʀived no ʒuʀ a dɔnet pʀɔspɛktœʀ?

ʒən sɛ pa kõbjɛ̃d tɑ̃ ʒə ʀɛstʀe isi. ʒəm di paʀfwa kə vuzet boku ply saʒ kəmwa. təʀapɛlty skə tym dizɛ œ̃ ʒuʀ: «ma vi a ete bjɛ̃ tʀɑ̃kil kõpaʀe a la tjɛn»? syʀtu nə fɛt pɑ dypti miʃel œ̃nɛ̃ʒenjœʀ, u tutomwɛ̃, kil lɛs lə petʀɔl tʀɑ̃kil! e puʀtɑ̃ . . .

ʒɛspɛʀ malgʀe tu vuʀvwaʀ œ̃deseʒuʀ. ɑ̃natɑ̃dɑ̃, me ʃeʀzami, pɥiskə ma letʀ vuzaʀivʀa sɑ̃ dut veʀ lə nuvɛl ɑ̃, ʒvu swɛt a tu le tʀwɑ yn bɔnane e tut sɔʀt də pʀɔspeʀite.

bjɛ̃ kɔʀdjalmɑ̃,

ʒɑ̃

SYLLABICATION

111   Division of words into syllables.

When French words are divided into syllables, each syllable generally begins with a consonant and ends with a vowel.

A. When a single consonant stands between two vowels, the consonant goes with the vowel which follows it: bu-reau, ta-bac, hô-tel, ga-rage, vou-lez.

B. When a double consonant (**tt, dd, pp,** etc.) stands between two vowels:

1. in most cases it represents a single sound and stands in the following syllable: do-**nn**ez [dɔne], a-**ll**ez [ale], exce-**ll**ent [ɛksɛlɑ̃], a-**dd**ition [adisjɔ̃]. In writing, such words are divided: do**n**-**n**ez, a**l**-**l**ez, etc.

2. in some cases it represents two consonants, one of which is pronounced with the previous vowel and one with the following one: a**c**-**c**ident [aksidɑ̃], su**g**-**g**érer [sygʒeʀe].

C. When two or more different consonants stand between vowels:

1. one consonant may go with the vowel which precedes and one with the one which follows: mer-ci, par-lez, res-taurant, ob-ser-vatoire;

2. two consonants may form a consonant cluster* and stand together at the beginning of the following syllable: ta-ble, li-bre, a-près, qua-tre;

3. one consonant may go with the preceding vowel and a consonant cluster* may stand together at the beginning of the next syllable: en-ten-dre, or-ches-tre, mal-gré, em-ploi.

The digraphs **ch, ph, th, gn** (each of which of course represents a single sound) always stand with the vowel which follows.

---

* The following are the consonant clusters which occur commonly: **bl, cl, fl, gl, pl; br, cr, dr, gr, pr, tr, vr.**

It is very important to know how French words are divided into syllables, because certain letters are pronounced one way when they are final in a syllable and in a different way when they are followed in the syllable by a pronounced consonant or by a vowel. For example: in the word **un,** the vowel **u** is followed in the same syllable by the letter **n** and is therefore nasalized, i.e. the word is pronounced [œ̃]; in the word **u-ne,** the vowel **u** is final in the syllable and is not nasalized, i.e. the word is pronounced [yn]. Likewise, **faim** is pronounced [fɛ̃], but **j'ai-me** is pronounced [ʒɛm]. **In-telligent** is pronounced [ɛ̃tɛliʒã], but **i-nutile** is pronounced [inytil].

LINKING

112 Principles of linking.

You have learned to say "les‿hôtels," "les‿Américains," and so on — giving the "s" the sound [z]. When a final consonant which is normally silent is pronounced with the initial vowel of the following word, it is said to be linked. In French, this is called **la liaison,** which means binding together. When linking takes place, two words are bound together: you say [lezotɛl] as if it were one word rather than [le zotɛl] as if it were two. A consonant that is linked should always be pronounced lightly.*

Linking takes place only between words that are closely related syntactically and which naturally fall into rhythmic groups (such as a noun and its modifiers).

EXERCISES

I. With linking.

Repeat the following, making the linking properly (without exaggeration):

A. BETWEEN A NOUN AND ITS MODIFIERS:

1. *Article and noun:*

Les‿enfants. Les‿hôtels. Les‿églises. Les‿heures. Les‿Américains. Les‿étudiants. Les‿Anglais.

2. *Adjective and noun:*

Un bon‿hôtel. Les bons‿hôtels. Les petits‿enfants. Trois‿heures. Six‿heures. Neuf‿heures [nœvœʀ]. Les‿États‿-‿Unis. Les Champs‿-‿Elysées.

3. *Article and adjective:*

Les‿autres restaurants.

---

* Some authorities say that in linking the letter is "carried over" to the next word; but we avoid this term because it suggests to English-speaking students that the letter should be given the importance of an initial consonant.

B. BETWEEN PERSONAL PRONOUN AND VERB:

1. *Normal order:*

Nous‿avons. Vous‿avez. Ils‿ont. Vous‿êtes. Vous‿allez. Ils‿entrent
Ils‿arrivent. Ils‿habitent.

2. *Inverted order:*

Est‿-il? Sont‿-ils? Ont‿-ils?

3. Note that the tendency to bind verb forms together is so strong that if the
third person singular of a verb does not end in a "t", a "t" is inserted between the verb and inverted pronoun anyway: A-t-il? Parle-t-il? Étudie-t-il?

C. BETWEEN THE WORD **pas** AND AN ADVERB OR ADJECTIVE:

Pas‿encore.
Pas‿ici. Pas‿Américain.

D. BETWEEN PREPOSITIONS **dans, en, sans, chez** AND NOUN OR PRONOUN:

dans‿un bon hôtel, sans‿argent, en‿or, chez‿elle.

II. Without linking.

Repeat the following WITHOUT linking and note that linking DOES NOT
take place:

A. Between a noun subject and verb: Jean appelle un taxi. Le train
arrive. Les trains arrivent. Les Anglais aiment les sports.

B. Before words beginning with an aspirate "h": des hors-d'œuvre.

C. The "t" in the number **cent un.**

D. After the word **et:** Roger et elle. Vingt‿et un. (The "t" of **et** is
NEVER pronounced under any circumstances.)

III. Optional linking.

In some cases, linking is optional. When in doubt, you can always
consult the phonetic transcriptions of the Conversations. When linking
is optional, the present trend in France is not to link.

ELISION

113 When elision takes place.

When a vowel is dropped out before a word beginning with a vowel or mute "h," *elision* (**élision**) is said to take place. Elision is possible only in the following words: The **e** in: **je, me, te, se, ce, de, le, ne, que;** the **a** in **la;** and the **i** in the word **si** when it is followed by **il, ils.**

Elision is incorrect before a word beginning with an aspirate "h" or before the word **onze:** le/huit octobre, le/onze mars.

DIACRITICAL SIGNS

114 The different diacritical signs.

The following typographical signs are used either to distinguish between two or more possible pronunciations of a letter, or to distinguish between two words which are pronounced alike and, except for the diacritical marks, are spelled alike. *In no case do these signs indicate that a syllable should be stressed.*

A. The acute accent.

The acute accent (´) (**accent aigu**) is used only on the vowel **e:** l'été, espérer. The **é** is usually pronounced [e], but many French people tend to pronounce it [ɛ].

B. The grave accent.

The grave accent (`) (**accent grave**) is used mostly on **e** followed by a final **s** or **-re:** très, près, après-midi; père, frère, j'espère, ils allèrent. The **è** is always pronounced [ɛ].

This accent is also used on the **a** in the preposition **à,** *to,* to distinguish it from the third person singular of the present indicative of **avoir.**

Likewise it is used on the **a** of the adverb **là,** *there,* to distinguish it from the article **la,** *the,* as well as on the **u** of the adverb **où,** *where,* to distinguish it from the conjunction **ou,** *or.* But **à** is pronounced like **a, là** like **la,** and **où** like **ou.**

C. The circumflex accent.

The circumflex accent (^) **(accent circonflexe)** is found on all the vowels except **y: âme, même, île, hôtel, sûr.** An **â** is usually pronounced [ɑ], **ê** [ɛ], **î** [i], **ô** [o], **û** [y]. It is often said that a circumflex "lengthens" a vowel; but today no French person would lengthen the vowels in l'hôtel, l'île, être, êtes-vous, etc.

D. The cedilla.

The cedilla (ˌ) **(cédille)** under **c (ç)** indicates that the letter is pronounced [s].

E. The diaeresis.

When a diaeresis (¨) **(tréma)** is placed over the second of two vowels, it indicates that the vowel so marked begins a new syllable. **Noël, naïf.** Note, however, that the name **Saint-Saëns** is pronounced [sɛ̃ sɑ̃s].

RELATION BETWEEN SPELLING AND PRONUNCIATION

115 Consonants.

LETTER PRONUNCIATION

b	[b]	in practically all cases: une banane, le bébé.
	[p]	when followed by **t** or **s**: absurde, absent, absolument, obtenir. Silent when final: les soldats de plomb.
c	[k]	when followed by **a, o, u,** or **l, r**: le café, le corps, la curiosité, je crois.
	[s]	when followed by **e, i, y**: c'est, certainement, ici, la bicyclette.
	[k]	usually when final: avec, le sac. Silent in: le tabac, franc, blanc, le porc.
	[g]	in: second, secondaire, anecdote.
ç	[s]	Used only before **a, o, u**: le français, le garçon, j'ai reçu.
cc	[k]	except when followed by **e, i, y**: accorder.
	[ks]	when followed by **e, i, y**: accepter, accident.
ch	[ʃ]	usually: chercher, le chimiste, chez, Charles, architecte.
	[k]	sometimes: un orchestre, le chœur, la psychologie.
d	[d]	in practically all cases: dans, l'addition, madame, le sud. Usually silent when final: le pied, le nid, le hasard, le nord.
	[t]	in: tout de suite, le médecin, quand il . . .
f	[f]	in practically all cases: franc, le café.
	[f]	usually when final: le chef, neuf, le rosbif, un œuf. Silent in: les œufs, les bœufs, la clef.
	[v]	in: neuf heures, neuf ans.
g	[g]	when followed by **a, o, u,** or **l, r**: la gare, grand.
	[ʒ]	when followed by **e, i, y**: gentil, les gens, la girafe, le gymnase.
gg	[gʒ]	when followed by **e, i, y**: suggérer.
gn	[ɲ]	la campagne, la Bretagne, la vigne.
gu	[g]	in: la guerre, le guide.
	[gɥ]	in: aiguille, la linguistique.
	[gy]	in: aigu.
h		Always silent: l'homme, l'hôtel, les hors-d'œuvre.
j	[ʒ]	janvier, je déjeune.

k	[k]	le kilo.
l	[l]	usually pronounced even when final: l'hôtel, le cheval. Silent in: gentil, le fusil, le fils, le pouls.
	[j]	when preceded by **ai** or **ei**: le travail, le soleil, vieil, etc.
ll	[j]	when preceded by **ai, ei, ui**: travailler, vieille.
	[j]	usually when preceded by **i**: la fille, gentille, juillet, la famille.
	[l]	in: ville, village, mille, tranquille, illustrer, etc.
m	[m]	at the beginning of a syllable: aimer, madame, calme. Silent in automne, condamner. When final in a syllable, **m** indicates that the preceding vowel is nasalized but it is not otherwise pronounced: faim [fɛ̃], chambre [ʃɑ̃bʀ], ensemble [ɑ̃sɑ̃bl], important [ɛ̃pɔʀtɑ̃].
mm	[m]	l'homme, comme, comment.
n	[n]	at the beginning of a syllable: nous, une, inutile. When final in a syllable or when followed by a consonant, **n** indicates that the preceding vowel is nasalized but it is not otherwise pronounced: bon [bõ], vingt [vɛ̃], enfant [ɑ̃fɑ̃], intelligent [ɛ̃tɛliʒɑ̃], la France [lafʀɑ̃s]. Silent in **-ent** verb endings.
nn	[n]	bonne, sonner, donnez, l'année.
p	[p]	in practically all cases: le papier, le départ, l'aptitude, le pneu, la psychologie, le psaume. Silent when final: trop, beaucoup, loup, coup. Silent in: le temps, compter, la sculpture, etc.
q, qu	[k]	in practically all cases: qui, que, quel, le coq.
qu	[kw]	in: une aquarelle, un aquarium.
r	[ʀ]	in practically all cases: la rue, très, l'art, vers. Pronounced when final in: le fer, la mer, fier, cher, car, pour, l'hiver, etc. Silent in infinitive ending **-er**, and in: boucher, boulanger, charcutier, épicier, monsieur, léger, premier, volontiers, etc.
s	[s]	at beginning of a word or when preceded or followed by a consonant: absent, sang, aspect, etc.
	[z]	when between vowels: la raison, la maison, les roses.
	[z]	when linked: vous‿avez, sans‿elle, trois‿heures. Usually silent when final: les, tables, lesquels.
	[s]	in: le fils, mars, le sens, tous *(pronoun)*, omnibus, autobus, Reims, Saint-Saëns, etc.
sc	[sk]	when followed by **a, o, u,** or **l, r**: la sculpture, scolaire.
	[s]	when followed by **e, i, y**: la science, le scénario.
ss	[s]	assez, aussi, essayer.

t	[t]	at beginning of a syllable: le temps, l'été, l'amitié.
		Silent when final in verb forms (except in linking) and in most nouns and adjectives: le lit, le restaurant, élégant, différent, cent, vingt, excellent, tout, etc.
	[t]	in: l'est, l'ouest, net, dot, Brest, tact, intact, exact.
th	[t]	le thé, le théâtre, la thèse, le mythe, la cathédrale.
ti	[s]	in: démocratie, initial, patience, etc.
	[sj]	in: **-tion** ration, nation, relation, etc.
v	[v]	in all cases: voulez-vous? avez-vous?
w	[v]	in: le wagon, Waterloo.
	[w]	in: le tramway, le sandwich.
x	[ks]	in: excellent, le luxe, l'index.
	[gz]	in: exact, exemple, examen.
	[s]	in: soixante, and in: dix, six (when final in a phrase).
	[z]	in: dix, six (when linked: dix‿enfants).
		Silent in: dix, six (when followed by a word beginning with a pronounced consonant: dix francs); and in: la paix, la voix, etc.
z	[z]	le zéro, le gaz, zut!
		Silent in **-ez** verb ending, nez and in: chez (except in linking).

116 Vowels.

LETTER	PRONUNCIATION	
a, à	[a]	in most cases: la gare, l'accident, la table, à Paris.
	[ɑ]	in: pas, phrase, vase, etc.
â	[ɑ]	in most cases: âge, âme, pâle, château.
		However, many French people do not distinguish between [ɑ] and [a].
ai	[ɛ]	except when final: j'avais, il avait, il fait, ils avaient.
	[ə]	in: nous faisons, je faisais, tu faisais, etc.
	[e]	when final: j'ai, j'irai.
au	[o]	in most cases: au Canada, haut, il faut, chaud.
	[ɔ]	in: j'aurai, le restaurant, Paul.
ay	[ɛj]	in: essayer, payer, ayez.
	[ei]	in: le pays.
	[aj]	in: La Fayette.
è, ê	[ɛ]	je me lève, le père, la tête, vous êtes.
é	[e]	l'été, espérer, allé.

SPELLING AND PRONUNCIATION

e	[ɛ]	when followed by two consonants or in final syllable when followed by a single pronounced consonant: rester, verte, avec, mettre; and in: il est. Many French people pronounce mes, ces, ses, les, des with an open "e" [ɛ].
	[e]	in final syllable when followed by silent **d, f, r, z**: pied, la clef, le boucher, allez; and in: et, and les, mes, etc.
	[ə]	in: je, me, te, se, ce, le, de, ne, que; and in the first syllable of many words such as: venir, demander, demain, cheval, etc.; but this [ə] is usually omitted in conversation if the phrase is easily pronounced without that vowel.
		Silent in words of more than one syllable when final or when followed by silent **s** or **nt**: ville, robes, parle, parles, parlent.
eau	[o]	le bureau, l'eau, le veau.
ei	[ɛ]	la neige, la peine.
ey	[ɛj]	asseyez-vous.
eu	[œ]	in most cases when followed in the same word by a pronounced consonant: neuf, leur, jeune, Europe.
	[ø]	when final, or when followed by the sound [z] or a silent final consonant: un peu, deux, il veut, les yeux, heureuse.
	[y]	in *passé simple*, imperfect subjunctive, and past participle of avoir: j'eus, etc.; il eût, etc.; il a eu, etc.
i	[i]	ici, inutile, innocent, initial.
o	[ɔ]	except when followed by a silent final consonant or the sound [z] or [sj]: notre, joli, l'école, objet, hors-d'œuvre, les pommes, la note, la dot, la robe, l'oignon.
	[o]	when followed by a silent final consonant or the sound [z] or [sj]: mot, dos, nos, gros, la rose, poser, notion.
ô	[o]	le nôtre, table d'hôte, ôter.
œu	[œ]	when followed in the same word by a pronounced consonant: la sœur, hors-d'œuvre, un œuf, le bœuf.
	[ø]	in the plural forms œufs [ø], bœufs [bø].
oi	[wa]	moi, une poire, la boîte, une fois.
	[wɑ]	trois, le mois, le bois, les pois.
ou, où	[u]	nous, voulez-vous?, toujours, où?, ou.
ou	[w]	when followed by a vowel: Louis, oui, jouer, la douane, souhaiter, ouest.
oy	[waj]	loyer, soyons, voyons.
u	[y]	sur, plus, une, la rue, du café.
ua	[ɥa]	nuage.
ue	[ɥɛ]	actuel, actuellement.

SPELLING AND PRONUNCIATION   *263*

ui	[ɥi]	puis, huit, je suis, la nuit, lui, le bruit, juillet.
uy	[yj]	gruyère.
	[ɥij]	fuyez, ennuyer, appuyer.

117 Nasal vowels.

A. Generally speaking, when vowels are followed in the same syllable by **m, n,** the vowel is nasalized and the **m** or **n** is not pronounced.

LETTER PRONUNCIATION

a	[ɑ̃]	quand, sans, grand, l'anglais, la chambre, allemand.
ae	[ɑ̃]	Caen, Saint-Saëns.
ai	[ɛ̃]	le pain, le bain, la faim, la main.
ao	[ɑ̃]	Laon, le paon.
e	[ɑ̃]	en, ensemble, le temps, le membre, la dent, vendre, emmener [ɑ̃mne], l'ennui, évident.
	[a]	évidemment, solennel, la femme.
	[ɛ̃]	examen, européen, le citoyen.
i	[ɛ̃]	la fin, le vin, vingt, impossible.
ie	[jɛ̃]	bien, rien, le chien, ancien, il tient, vous viendrez, etc.
	[i]	in: ils étudient.
	[jɑ̃]	in: patience, orient, science.
o	[ɔ̃]	on, bon, non, sont, onze, l'oncle, le nom, le nombre, compter.
	[ə]	in: monsieur.
oi	[wɛ̃]	loin, moins, le coin, le point.
u	[œ̃]	un, chacun, lundi, le parfum.
		Many French people do not distinguish between [ɛ̃] and [œ̃].
	[ə]	in a few Latin words: album, postscriptum, maximum.
ui	[ɥɛ̃]	juin.

B. Vowels followed by **mm, nn** are usually not nasalized.

a	[a]	année, constamment, élégamment.
e	[ɛ]	ennemi, prennent, tiennent, viennent.
o	[ɔ]	comme, comment, bonne, sonner, l'homme, nommer, le sommeil, Sorbonne, la monnaie.
i	[i]	innocent, immeuble, immédiat.

VERB FORMS

REGULAR VERBS

118 Formation of regular verbs from key forms.

All the forms of regular verbs can be derived from the following key forms: the present infinitive, the present indicative, the past participle, and the *passé simple*. The following paragraphs explain how the various forms can be derived.

119 Forms that can be derived from the infinitive.

A. Present indicative.

To form the present indicative, you drop the infinitive ending **-er**, **-ir**, or **-re** and add the following endings:

Verbs ending in **-er**: **-e, -es, -e, -ons, -ez, -ent.**
Verbs ending in **-ir**: **-is, -is, -it, -issons, -issez, -issent.**
Verbs ending in **-re**: **-s, -s, —, -ons, -ez, -ent.**

B. Future.

To form the future tense, add to the infinitive* the endings: **-ai, -as, -a, -ons, -ez, -ont.** Examples:

donner	je donne**rai**	*I shall give*
finir	je fini**rai**	*I shall finish*
vendre	je vend**rai**	*I shall sell*

---

* For infinitives of the third conjugation, the **-e** of the **-re** ending is omitted to form the future and the conditional. Ex.: je vendrai, je répondrai; je vendrais, je répondrais, etc.

C. Present conditional.

To form the present conditional, add to the infinitive the endings: **-ais- ais, -ait,- ions, -iez, -aient.** Examples:

donner	je donner**ais**	*I should* or *would give*
finir	je finir**ais**	*I should* or *would finish*
vendre	je vendr**ais**	*I should* or *would sell*

120   Forms that can be derived from the present indicative.

A. Present participle.

To form the present participle, drop the **-ons** of the first person plural of the present indicative and add the ending **-ant.** Examples:

nous donnons	donn**ant**	*giving*
nous finissons	finiss**ant**	*finishing*
nous vendons	vend**ant**	*selling*

B. Imperfect indicative.

To form the imperfect indicative, drop the **-ons** of the first person plural of the present indicative and add the endings: **-ais, -ais, -ait, -ions, -iez, -aient.** Examples:

nous donnons	je donn**ais**	*I was giving*, etc.
nous finissons	je finiss**ais**	*I was finishing*, etc.
nous vendons	je vend**ais**	*I was selling*, etc.

C. Imperative.

To form the imperative, use the following forms of the present indicative without the pronoun subject: the second person singular, the first person plural, and the second person plural. Examples:

tu donnes	**donne(s)***	*give*	nous donnons	**donnons**	*let's give*
tu finis	**finis**	*finish*	nous finissons	**finissons**	*let's finish*
tu vends	**vends**	*sell*	nous vendons	**vendons**	*let's sell*

vous donnez	**donnez**	*give*
vous finissez	**finissez**	*finish*
vous vendez	**vendez**	*sell*

---

* In verbs of the first conjugation, the **s** of the second singular ending is used only when followed by the word **y** or **en.**

D. Present subjunctive.

To form the present subjunctive drop the **-ons** of the first person plural of the present indicative and add the endings: **-e, -es, -e, -ions, -iez, -ent.** Examples:

nous donnons	je donne	*I give**
nous finissons	je finisse	*I finish*
nous vendons	je vende	*I sell*

121 Forms in which the past participle† is used.

A. Compound tenses.

The past participle is used in conjunction with the different tenses of the auxiliary verb **avoir** (in a few cases **être,** see paragraph 10) to form the compound tenses of verbs.

1. *Passé composé.*

To form the *passé composé*, use the present tense of the auxiliary verb with the past participle of the verb. Examples:

j'ai donné	*I gave, I have given*
je suis arrivé	*I arrived, I have arrived*

2. Pluperfect.

To form the pluperfect, use the imperfect tense of the auxiliary verb with the past participle of the verb. Examples:

j'avais donné	*I had given*
j'étais arrivé	*I had arrived*

3. Past anterior.

To form the past anterior (a literary tense which is approximately equivalent to the pluperfect), use the *passé simple* of the auxiliary verb with the past participle of the verb. Examples:

j'eus donné	*I had given*
je fus arrivé	*I had arrived*

---

* The subjunctive forms are translated in several different ways, depending upon the context.
† For the formation of the past participle, see p. 18.

4. Future perfect.

To form the future perfect, use the future tense of the auxiliary verb with the past participle of the verb. Examples:

j'aurai donné   *I shall have given*
je serai arrivé   *I shall have arrived*

5. Conditional perfect.

To form the conditional perfect, use the present conditional of the auxiliary verb with the past participle of the verb. Examples:

j'aurais donné   *I should* or *would have given*
je serais arrivé   *I should* or *would have arrived*

6. Past subjunctive.

To form the *passé composé* of the subjunctive, use the present subjunctive of the auxiliary verb with the past participle of the verb. Examples:

j'aie donné   *I have given*, etc.
je sois arrivé   *I have arrived*, etc.

7. Pluperfect subjunctive.

To form the pluperfect of the subjunctive, use the imperfect subjunctive of the auxiliary verb with the past participle of the verb. Examples:

j'eusse donné   *I had given*, etc.
je fusse arrivé   *I had arrived*, etc.

8. Perfect infinitive.

To form the perfect infinitive, use the present infinitive of the auxiliary verb and the past participle of the verb. Examples:

avoir donné   *to have given*
être arrivé   *to have arrived*

B. Tenses of the passive voice.

The past participle is used in conjunction with the different tenses of the auxiliary verb **être** to form the tenses of the passive voice of transitive verbs (i.e., of verbs normally conjugated with **avoir**).

Examples:

PRESENT INDICATIVE	**je suis** flatté	*I am flattered*
IMPERFECT	**j'étais** flatté	*I was flattered*
FUTURE	**je serai** flatté	*I shall* or *will be flattered*
CONDITIONAL	**je serais** flatté	*I should* or *would be flattered*
PASSÉ COMPOSÉ	**j'ai été** flatté	*I was* or *have been flattered*
PLUPERFECT	**j'avais été** flatté	*I had been flattered*
PAST ANTERIOR	**j'eus été** flatté	*I had been flattered*

Although some of the forms of the passive voice look very complicated, they present no real difficulty either from the point of view of form or meaning. When broken down into their component parts and translated literally into English, they practically always make good sense *and good English*. Examples:

Il avait été tué.	He	had	been	killed.
Vous auriez été étonné.	You	would have	been	surprised.

The English passive voice is by no means always rendered in French by the passive voice. (See use of **faire** with an infinitive, par. 62, C and reflexive verbs, par. 43)

122 Forms that can be derived from the **passé simple**.*

To form the imperfect subjunctive, drop the last letter of the first person singular of the *passé simple*, and add the endings: **-sse, -sses, -^t, -ssions, -ssiez, -ssent.**

PASSÉ SIMPLE		IMPERFECT SUBJUNCTIVE
je donna**i**	*I gave*	je donna**sse**
je fin**is**	*I finished*	je fin**isse**
je vend**is**	*I sold*	je vend**isse**

The vowel preceding the **t** of the third person singular of the imperfect subjunctive always has a circumflex accent. Ex.: donn**â**t, fin**î**t, vend**î**t, e**û**t, f**û**t, etc.

---

*For the formation of the *passé simple*, see paragraph 99, pp. 215–217.

REGULAR VERBS

123 Regular conjugations.

A. Infinitive and tenses formed on it.

INFINITIVE

I **donner**	II **finir**	III **vendre**

FUTURE

je donnerai	je finirai	je vendrai
tu donneras	tu finiras	tu vendras
il donnera	il finira	il vendra
nous donnerons	nous finirons	nous vendrons
vous donnerez	vous finirez	vous vendrez
ils donneront	ils finiront	ils vendront

CONDITIONAL

je donnerais	je finirais	je vendrais
tu donnerais	tu finirais	tu vendrais
il donnerait	il finirait	il vendrait
nous donnerions	nous finirions	nous vendrions
vous donneriez	vous finiriez	vous vendriez
ils donneraient	ils finiraient	ils vendraient

B. Present indicative and tenses that can be formed from it.

PRESENT INDICATIVE

je donne	je finis	je vends
tu donnes	tu finis	tu vends
il donne	il finit	il vend
nous **donnons**	nous **finissons**	nous **vendons**
vous donnez	vous finissez	vous vendez
ils donnent	ils finissent	ils vendent

IMPERATIVE

donne(s)	finis	vends
donnons	finissons	vendons
donnez	finissez	vendez

VERB FORMS

| donnant | finissant | vendant |

je donnais	je finissais	je vendais
tu donnais	tu finissais	tu vendais
il donnait	il finissait	il vendait
nous donnions	nous finissions	nous vendions
vous donniez	vous finissiez	vous vendiez
ils donnaient	ils finissaient	ils vendaient

PRESENT SUBJUNCTIVE

je donne	je finisse	je vende
tu donnes	tu finisses	tu vendes
il donne	il finisse	il vende
nous donnions	nous finissions	nous vendions
vous donniez	vous finissiez	vous vendiez
ils donnent	ils finissent	ils vendent

C. Past participle and tenses in which past participle appears.

1. Verbs conjugated with **avoir.**

PAST PARTICIPLE

| **donné** | **fini** | **vendu** |

PASSÉ COMPOSÉ

| j'ai donné, etc. | j'ai fini, etc. | j'ai vendu, etc. |

PLUPERFECT

| j'avais donné, etc. | j'avais fini, etc. | j'avais vendu, etc. |

PAST ANTERIOR

| j'eus donné, etc. | j'eus fini, etc. | j'eus vendu, etc. |

FUTURE PERFECT

| j'aurai donné, etc. | j'aurai fini, etc. | j'aurai vendu, etc. |

REGULAR VERBS

---------------- CONDITIONAL PERFECT ----------------

| j'aurais donné, etc. | j'aurais fini, etc. | j'aurais vendu, etc. |

---------------- PASSÉ COMPOSÉ SUBJUNCTIVE ----------------

| j'aie donné, etc. | j'aie fini, etc. | j'aie vendu, etc. |

---------------- PLUPERFECT SUBJUNCTIVE ----------------

| j'eusse donné, etc. | j'eusse fini, etc. | j'eusse vendu, etc. |

---------------- PERFECT INFINITIVE ----------------

| avoir donné | avoir fini | avoir vendu |

---------------- PERFECT PARTICIPLE ----------------

| ayant donné | ayant fini | ayant vendu |

2. Verbs conjugated with **être**.

PAST PARTICIPLE	**arrivé** (*from* arriver)
PASSÉ COMPOSÉ	je suis arrivé(e), etc.
PLUPERFECT	j'étais arrivé(e), etc.
PAST ANTERIOR	je fus arrivé(e), etc.
FUTURE PERFECT	je serai arrivé(e), etc.
CONDITIONAL PERFECT	je serais arrivé(e), etc.
PASSÉ COMPOSÉ SUBJUNCTIVE	je sois arrivé(e), etc.
PLUPERFECT SUBJUNCTIVE	je fusse arrivé(e), etc.
PERFECT INFINITIVE	être arrivé(e)(s)
PERFECT PARTICIPLE	étant arrivé(e)(s)

D. *Passé simple* and imperfect subjunctive.

PASSÉ SIMPLE

je donnai	je finis	je vendis
tu donnas	tu finis	tu vendis
il donna	il finit	il vendit
nous donnâmes	nous finîmes	nous vendîmes
vous donnâtes	vous finîtes	vous vendîtes
ils donnèrent	ils finirent	ils vendirent

VERB FORMS

je donnasse	je finisse	je vendisse
tu donnasses	tu finisses	tu vendisses
il donnât	il finît	il vendît
nous donnassions	nous finissions	nous vendissions
vous donnassiez	vous finissiez	vous vendissiez
ils donnassent	ils finissent	ils vendissent

124 Verbs of the first conjugation that are regular except for a slight variation in their stem.

A. Verbs whose stem vowel is a mute "e" (acheter, appeler) have two stems.

1. Whenever in conjugation the mute "e" of the stem vowel is followed by a syllable containing a mute "e", the **e** of the stem vowel is pronounced [ɛ]. This occurs in the following forms: the first, second, and third person singular and the third person plural of the present indicative and the present subjunctive (**-e, -es, -e, -ent**); the second person singular of the imperative (**-e** or **-es**); and the six forms of both the future and conditional (**-erai,** etc., **-erais,** etc.).

2. Whenever the mute "e" of the stem vowel is followed by a syllable containing any vowel other than a mute "e", it is pronounced [ə] as in the infinitive. This phenomenon is reflected in the spelling as follows:

• In **acheter,** *to buy;* **geler,** *to freeze;* **lever,** *to raise;* **mener,** *to lead;* **peser,** *to weigh,* and a few other verbs, the stem vowel is written **è** when followed by a syllable containing a mute "e". Ex.: Present: J'**achète,** tu **achètes,** il **achète,** nous achetons, vous achetez, ils **achètent;** Future: j'**achèterai,** etc.; Conditional: j'**achèterais,** etc.

• In **appeler,** *to call;* **jeter,** *to throw,* and a few other verbs ending in **-eler, -eter,** the final l or t of the stem is doubled when followed by a mute syllable. Ex.: Present: J'**appelle,** tu **appelles,** il **appelle,** nous appelons, vous appelez, ils **appellent;** Future: j'**appellerai,** etc.

B. In **espérer,** *to hope;* **céder,** *to yield;* **préférer,** *to prefer,* and a few other verbs whose stem vowel is **é,** the stem vowel is written **è** and pronounced [ɛ] in the present indicative (and present subjunctive) when followed by a mute syllable. Ex.: Present: J'**espère,** tu **espères,** il **espère,** nous espérons, vous espérez, ils **espèrent.** (In the future and conditional, however, the stem vowel of these verbs is written **é.** Ex.: **J'espérerai.**)

C. Verbs ending in **-cer, -ger, -yer** show a slight variation in the spelling of the stem *but not in its pronunciation.*

   1. In **commencer, avancer,** etc., the final **c** of the stem is written **ç** whenever in conjugation it is followed by an **a** or **o.** Ex.: PRESENT: Je commence, tu commences, il commence, nous **commençons,** vous commencez, ils commencent; PRESENT PARTICIPLE: **commençant;** IMPERFECT: je **commençais,** tu **commençais,** il **commençait,** nous commencions, vous commenciez, ils **commençaient;** PASSÉ SIMPLE: je **commençai,** etc.

   2. In **manger,** *to eat,* and other verbs ending in **-ger,** you write **ge** instead of **g** whenever the following vowel is **a** or **o.** Ex.: PRESENT: je mange, tu manges, il mange, nous **mangeons,** vous mangez, ils mangent; IMPERFECT: je **mangeais,** etc.; PASSÉ SIMPLE: je **mangeai,** etc.

   3. In **ennuyer,** *to bother,* and other verbs ending in **-oyer, -uyer,** you write **i** instead of **y** whenever the following letter is a mute "e". Ex.: il **ennuie,** *but* nous **ennuyons.**

   4. In **payer,** *to pay,* and other verbs ending in **-ayer, -eyer,** you may write **y** throughout the verb or, if you prefer, you may write **i** instead of **y** whenever the following letter is a mute "e". Ex.: Je pa**y**e *or* je pa**i**e, *but* nous pa**y**ons.

AUXILIARY VERBS

125 Conjugation of auxiliary verbs **être** and **avoir**.

SIMPLE TENSES

INFINITIVE

être, *to be*   **avoir,** *to have*

PRESENT INDICATIVE

je suis, *I am*	j'ai, *I have*
tu es	tu as
il est	il a
nous sommes	nous avons
vous êtes	vous avez
ils sont	ils ont

IMPERFECT

j'étais, *I was*	j'avais, *I had*
tu étais	tu avais
il était	il avait
nous étions	nous avions
vous étiez	vous aviez
ils étaient	ils avaient

PASSÉ SIMPLE

je fus, *I was*	j'eus, *I had*
tu fus	tu eus
il fut	il eut
nous fûmes	nous eûmes
vous fûtes	vous eûtes
ils furent	ils eurent

FUTURE

je serai, *I shall* or *will be*	j'aurai, *I shall* or *will have*
tu seras	tu auras
il sera	il aura
nous serons	nous aurons
vous serez	vous aurez
ils seront	ils auront

Conditional

je serais, *I should* or *would be*
tu serais
il serait
nous serions
vous seriez
ils seraient

j'aurais, *I should* or *would have*
tu aurais
il aurait
nous aurions
vous auriez
ils auraient

Present Subjunctive

je sois, *I am*, etc.
tu sois
il soit
nous soyons
vous soyez
ils soient

j'aie, *I have*, etc.
tu aies
il ait
nous ayons
vous ayez
ils aient

Imperfect Subjunctive

je fusse, *I was*, etc.
tu fusses
il fût
nous fussions
vous fussiez
ils fussent

j'eusse, *I had*, etc.
tu eusses
il eût
nous eussions
vous eussiez
ils eussent

Imperative

sois, *be*
soyons
soyez

aie, *have*
ayons
ayez

Present Participle

étant

ayant

COMPOUND TENSES

Past Participle

été

eu

Passé Composé

j'ai été, *I was, I have been*, etc.

j'ai eu, *I had, I have had*, etc.

Pluperfect

j'avais été, *I had been*, etc.   j'avais eu, *I had had*, etc.

Past Anterior

j'eus été, *I had been*, etc.   j'eus eu, *I had had*, etc.

Future Perfect

j'aurai été, *I shall have been*, etc.   j'aurai eu, *I shall have had*, etc.

Conditional Perfect

j'aurais été, *I should* or *would have been*, etc.   j'aurais eu, *I should* or *would have had*, etc.

Passé Composé Subjunctive

j'aie été, *I have been*, etc.   j'aie eu, *I have had*, etc.

Pluperfect Subjunctive

j'eusse été, *I had been*, etc.   j'eusse eu, *I had had*, etc.

Perfect Infinitive

avoir été, *to have been*   avoir eu, *to have had*

Perfect Participle

ayant été, *having been*   ayant eu, *having had*

IRREGULAR VERBS

126 Formation of irregular verbs.

Although the rules for deriving the forms of regular verbs (see paragraphs 118–124) do not apply strictly to all irregular verbs, they do apply to a substantial proportion of their forms (see paragraphs 73–82).

127 Reference list of commonest irregular verbs.

abattre	*see* battre	131*	consentir	*see* dormir	144
s'abstenir	*see* tenir	167	construire	*see* conduire	134
abstraire	*see* traire	168	contenir	*see* tenir	167
accourir	*see* courir	137	contraindre	*see* craindre	138
accueillir	*see* cueillir	141	contredire	*see* dire	143
acquérir		128	contrefaire	*see* faire	147
admettre	*see* mettre	152	convaincre	*see* vaincre	169
aller		129	convenir	*see* venir	171
apercevoir	*see* recevoir	161	coudre		136
apparaître	*see* connaître	135	courir		137
appartenir	*see* tenir	167	couvrir	*see* ouvrir	156
apprendre	*see* prendre	160	craindre		138
assaillir	*see* cueillir	141	croire		139
s'asseoir		130	croître		140
astreindre	*see* craindre	138	cueillir		141
atteindre	*see* craindre	138	se débattre	*see* battre	131
avoir		125	décevoir	*see* recevoir	161
battre		131	découvrir	*see* ouvrir	156
boire		132	décrire	*see* écrire	145
bouillir	*see* dormir	144	se dédire	*see* dire	143
combattre	*see* battre	131	déduire	*see* conduire	134
commettre	*see* mettre	152	défaire	*see* faire	147
comprendre	*see* prendre	160	démentir	*see* dormir	144
compromettre	*see* mettre	152	dépeindre	*see* craindre	138
concevoir	*see* recevoir	161	déplaire	*see* plaire	157
conclure		133	déteindre	*see* craindre	138
conduire		134	détenir	*see* tenir	167
connaître		135	détruire	*see* conduire	134
conquérir	*see* acquérir	128	devenir	*see* venir	171

* Listed by paragraph.

devoir		142
dire		143
discourir	*see* courir	137
disparaître	*see* connaître	135
distraire	*see* traire	168
dormir		144
écrire		145
élire	*see* lire	151
émettre	*see* mettre	152
émouvoir	*see* mouvoir	154
endormir	*see* dormir	144
s'endormir	*see* dormir	144
enfreindre	*see* craindre	138
s'enfuir	*see* fuir	149
entreprendre	*see* prendre	160
entretenir	*see* tenir	167
entrevoir	*see* voir	174
entr'ouvrir	*see* ouvrir	156
envoyer		146
éteindre	*see* craindre	138
être		125
exclure	*see* conclure	133
extraire	*see* traire	168
faire		147
falloir		148
feindre	*see* craindre	138
fuir		149
geindre	*see* craindre	138
haïr		150
inclure	*see* conclure	133
inscrire	*see* écrire	145
interdire	*see* dire	143
intervenir	*see* venir	171
introduire	*see* conduire	134
joindre	*see* craindre	138
lire		151
maintenir	*see* tenir	167
maudire	*see* dire	143
médire	*see* dire	143
mentir	*see* dormir	144
mettre		152
mourir		153
mouvoir		154

naître		155
obtenir	*see* tenir	167
offrir	*see* ouvrir	156
omettre	*see* mettre	152
ouvrir		156
paraître	*see* connaître	135
parcourir	*see* courir	137
partir	*see* dormir	144
parvenir	*see* venir	171
peindre	*see* craindre	138
percevoir	*see* recevoir	161
permettre	*see* mettre	152
plaindre	*see* craindre	138
se plaindre	*see* craindre	138
plaire		157
pleuvoir		158
poursuivre	*see* suivre	166
pourvoir	*see* voir	174
pouvoir		159
prédire	*see* dire	143
prendre		160
prescrire	*see* écrire	145
pressentir	*see* dormir	144
prévenir	*see* venir	171
prévoir	*see* voir	174
produire	*see* conduire	134
promettre	*see* mettre	152
proscrire	*see* écrire	145
provenir	*see* venir	171
recevoir		161
reconduire	*see* conduire	134
reconnaître	*see* connaître	135
recueillir	*see* cueillir	141
réduire	*see* conduire	134
rejoindre	*see* craindre	138
remettre	*see* mettre	152
renvoyer	*see* envoyer	146
repartir	*see* dormir	144
se repentir	*see* dormir	144
reprendre	*see* prendre	160
résoudre		162
ressentir	*see* dormir	144
restreindre	*see* craindre	138

VERB FORMS

128 acquérir, to acquire.

FUTURE
j'acquerrai, etc.; CONDITIONAL j'acquerrais, etc.

PRESENT INDICATIVE
j'acquiers, tu acquiers, il acquiert,
nous acquérons, vous acquérez, ils acquièrent.

IMPERATIVE
acquiers, acquérons, acquérez.

PRESENT PARTICIPLE
acquérant; IMPERFECT j'acquérais, etc.

PRESENT SUBJUNCTIVE
j'acquière, tu acquières, il acquière,
nous acquérions, vous acquériez, ils acquièrent.

PAST PARTICIPLE
acquis; PASSÉ COMPOSÉ j'ai acquis, etc.

PASSÉ SIMPLE
j'acquis, etc.; IMPERFECT SUBJUNCTIVE j'acquisse, etc.

129 aller, to go.

FUTURE
j'irai, etc.; CONDITIONAL j'irais, etc.

PRESENT INDICATIVE
je vais, tu vas, il va,
nous allons, vous allez, ils vont.

IMPERATIVE
va(s), allons, allez.

PRESENT PARTICIPLE
allant; IMPERFECT j'allais, etc.

PRESENT SUBJUNCTIVE
j'aille, tu ailles, il aille,
nous allions, vous alliez, ils aillent.

PAST PARTICIPLE
allé; PASSÉ COMPOSÉ je suis allé, etc.

PASSÉ SIMPLE
j'allai, etc.; IMPERFECT SUBJUNCTIVE j'allasse, etc.

IRREGULAR VERBS

130 s'asseoir, to sit down.

FUTURE
je m'assiérai, etc.; CONDITIONAL je m'assiérais, etc.

PRESENT INDICATIVE
je m'assieds, tu t'assieds, il s'assied,
nous nous asseyons, vous vous asseyez, ils s'asseyent.

IMPERATIVE
assieds-toi, asseyons-nous, asseyez-vous.

PRESENT PARTICIPLE
s'asseyant; IMPERFECT je m'asseyais, etc.

PRESENT SUBJUNCTIVE
je m'asseye, tu t'asseyes, il s'asseye,
nous nous asseyions, vous vous asseyiez, ils s'asseyent.

PAST PARTICIPLE
assis; PASSÉ COMPOSÉ je me suis assis, etc.

PASSÉ SIMPLE
je m'assis, etc.; IMPERFECT SUBJUNCTIVE je m'assisse, etc.

Alternate form of s'asseoir.

FUTURE
je m'assoirai, etc. *or* je m'asseyerai, etc.

CONDITIONAL
je m'assoirais, etc. *or* je m'asseyerais, etc.

PRESENT INDICATIVE
je m'assois, tu t'assois, il s'assoit,
nous nous assoyons, vous vous assoyez, ils s'assoient.

PRESENT PARTICIPLE
s'assoyant; IMPERFECT je m'assoyais, etc.

PRESENT SUBJUNCTIVE
je m'assoie, tu t'assoies, il s'assoie,
nous nous assoyions, vous vous assoyiez, ils s'assoient.

Like **s'asseoir: asseoir,** *to seat,* except that it takes the auxiliary verb **avoir.**

131 battre, to beat.

All forms are regular except:

PRESENT INDICATIVE
je bats, tu bats, il bat,
nous battons, vous battez, ils battent.

Like **battre: abattre,** *to fell, to beat down;* **combattre,** *to fight,* and **se débattre,**
to struggle.

132 boire, to drink.

FUTURE and CONDITIONAL: regular.

PRESENT INDICATIVE
 je bois, tu bois, il boit,
 nous buvons, vous buvez, ils boivent.

IMPERATIVE
 bois, buvons, buvez.

PRESENT PARTICIPLE
 buvant; IMPERFECT je buvais, etc.

PRESENT SUBJUNCTIVE
 je boive, tu boives, il boive,
 nous buvions, vous buviez, ils boivent.

PAST PARTICIPLE
 bu; PASSÉ COMPOSÉ j'ai bu, etc.

PASSÉ SIMPLE
 je bus, etc.; IMPERFECT SUBJUNCTIVE je busse, etc.

133 conclure, to conclude.

FUTURE and CONDITIONAL: regular.

PRESENT INDICATIVE
 je conclus, tu conclus, il conclut,
 nous concluons, vous concluez, ils concluent.

IMPERATIVE
 conclus, concluons, concluez.

PRESENT PARTICIPLE
 concluant; IMPERFECT je concluais, etc.

PRESENT SUBJUNCTIVE
 je conclue, etc.

PAST PARTICIPLE
 conclu; PASSÉ COMPOSÉ j'ai conclu, etc.

PASSÉ SIMPLE
 je conclus, etc.; IMPERFECT SUBJUNCTIVE je conclusse, etc.

Like **conclure: exclure,** *to exclude,* and **inclure,** *to include,* except that the past participle of the latter is **inclus.**

134 conduire, to conduct, to drive.

FUTURE and CONDITIONAL: regular.

PRESENT INDICATIVE
je conduis, tu conduis, il conduit,
nous conduisons, vous conduisez, ils conduisent.

IMPERATIVE
conduis, conduisons, conduisez.

PRESENT PARTICIPLE
conduisant; IMPERFECT je conduisais, etc.

PRESENT SUBJUNCTIVE
je conduise, etc.

PAST PARTICIPLE
conduit; PASSÉ COMPOSÉ j'ai conduit, etc.

PASSÉ SIMPLE
je conduisis, etc.; IMPERFECT SUBJUNCTIVE je conduisisse, etc.

Like **conduire: construire,** *to construct;* **déduire,** *to deduce;* **détruire,** *to destroy;*
introduire, *to introduce;* **produire,** *to produce;* **reconduire,** *to lead back;*
réduire, *to reduce;* **séduire,** *to seduce, to please;* **traduire,** *to translate;* etc.

135 connaître, to know, to be acquainted with.

FUTURE and CONDITIONAL: regular.

PRESENT INDICATIVE
je connais, tu connais, il connaît,
nous connaissons, vous connaissez, ils connaissent.

IMPERATIVE
connais, connaissons, connaissez.

PRESENT PARTICIPLE
connaissant; IMPERFECT je connaissais, etc.

PRESENT SUBJUNCTIVE
je connaisse, etc.

PAST PARTICIPLE
connu; PASSÉ COMPOSÉ j'ai connu, etc.

PASSÉ SIMPLE
je connus, etc.; IMPERFECT SUBJUNCTIVE je connusse, etc.

Like **connaître: apparaître,** *to appear;* **disparaître,** *to disappear;* **paraître,** *to
appear;* **reconnaître,** *to recognize;* etc.

136 coudre, to sew.

FUTURE and CONDITIONAL: regular.

PRESENT INDICATIVE
  je couds, tu couds, il coud,
  nous cousons, vous cousez, ils cousent.

IMPERATIVE
  couds, cousons, cousez.

PRESENT PARTICIPLE
  cousant; IMPERFECT je cousais, etc.

PRESENT SUBJUNCTIVE
  je couse, etc.

PAST PARTICIPLE
  cousu; PASSÉ COMPOSÉ j'ai cousu, etc.

PASSÉ SIMPLE
  je cousis, etc.; IMPERFECT SUBJUNCTIVE je cousisse, etc.

137 courir, to run.

FUTURE
  je courrai, etc.; CONDITIONAL je courrais, etc.

PRESENT INDICATIVE
  je cours, tu cours, il court,
  nous courons, vous courez, ils courent.

IMPERATIVE
  cours, courons, courez.

PRESENT PARTICIPLE
  courant; IMPERFECT je courais, etc.

PRESENT SUBJUNCTIVE
  je coure, etc.

PAST PARTICIPLE
  couru; PASSÉ COMPOSÉ j'ai couru, etc.

PASSÉ SIMPLE
  je courus, etc.; IMPERFECT SUBJUNCTIVE je courusse, etc.

Like **courir: accourir,** *to hasten;* **discourir,** *to discourse;* **parcourir,** *to go over;*
  secourir, *to help;* etc.

138 craindre, to fear.

FUTURE and CONDITIONAL: regular.

PRESENT INDICATIVE
je crains, tu crains, il craint,
nous craignons, vous craignez, ils craignent.

IMPERATIVE
crains, craignons, craignez.

PRESENT PARTICIPLE
craignant; IMPERFECT je craignais, etc.

PRESENT SUBJUNCTIVE
je craigne, etc.

PAST PARTICIPLE
craint; PASSÉ COMPOSÉ j'ai craint, etc.

PASSÉ SIMPLE
je craignis, etc.; IMPERFECT SUBJUNCTIVE je craignisse, etc.

Like **craindre: astreindre,** *to compel;* **atteindre,** *to attain;* **contraindre,** *to compel;* **dépeindre,** *to depict;* **déteindre,** *to fade;* **enfreindre,** *to infringe;* **éteindre,** *to extinguish;* **feindre,** *to feign;* **geindre,** *to groan;* **joindre,** *to join;* **peindre,** *to paint;* **plaindre,** *to pity;* **se plaindre,** *to complain;* **rejoindre,** *to rejoin, to meet;* **restreindre,** *to restrain;* **teindre,** *to dye;* etc.

139 croire, to believe.

FUTURE and CONDITIONAL: regular.

PRESENT INDICATIVE
je crois, tu crois, il croit
nous croyons, vous croyez, ils croient.

IMPERATIVE
crois, croyons, croyez.

PRESENT PARTICIPLE
croyant; IMPERFECT je croyais, etc.

PRESENT SUBJUNCTIVE
je croie, tu croies, il croie,
nous croyions, vous croyiez, ils croient.

PAST PARTICIPLE
cru; PASSÉ COMPOSÉ j'ai cru, etc.

PASSÉ SIMPLE
je crus, etc.; IMPERFECT SUBJUNCTIVE je crusse, etc.

140 croître, to grow.

FUTURE and CONDITIONAL: regular.

PRESENT INDICATIVE
je croîs, tu croîs, il croît,
nous croissons, vous croissez, ils croissent.

IMPERATIVE
croîs, croissons, croissez.

PRESENT PARTICIPLE
croissant; IMPERFECT je croissais, etc.

PRESENT SUBJUNCTIVE
je croisse, etc.

PAST PARTICIPLE
crû; PASSÉ COMPOSÉ j'ai crû, etc.

PASSÉ SIMPLE
je crûs, etc.; IMPERFECT SUBJUNCTIVE je crusse, etc.

141 cueillir, to pick, to gather.

FUTURE
je cueillerai, etc.; CONDITIONAL je cueillerais, etc.

PRESENT INDICATIVE
je cueille, tu cueilles, il cueille,
nous cueillons, vous cueillez, ils cueillent.

IMPERATIVE
cueille(s), cueillons, cueillez.

PRESENT PARTICIPLE
cueillant; IMPERFECT je cueillais, etc.

PRESENT SUBJUNCTIVE
je cueille, etc.

PAST PARTICIPLE
cueilli; PASSÉ COMPOSÉ j'ai cueilli, etc.

PASSÉ SIMPLE
je cueillis, etc.; IMPERFECT SUBJUNCTIVE je cueillisse, etc.

Like **cueillir: accueillir,** to *welcome;* and **recueillir,** to *gather,* to *collect.*
assaillir, to *assail* and **tressaillir,** to *start,* etc. are like **cueillir** except that the
future and conditional are regular.

IRREGULAR VERBS

142 devoir, must, etc.

FUTURE
> je devrai, etc.; CONDITIONAL je devrais, etc.

PRESENT INDICATIVE
> je dois, tu dois, il doit,
> nous devons, vous devez, ils doivent.

IMPERATIVE
> ———

PRESENT PARTICIPLE
> devant; IMPERFECT je devais, etc.

PRESENT SUBJUNCTIVE
> je doive, tu doives, il doive,
> nous devions, vous deviez, ils doivent.

PAST PARTICIPLE
> dû; PASSÉ COMPOSÉ j'ai dû, etc.

PASSÉ SIMPLE
> je dus, etc.; IMPERFECT SUBJUNCTIVE je dusse, etc.

143 dire, to say.

FUTURE and CONDITIONAL: regular.

PRESENT INDICATIVE
> je dis, tu dis, il dit,
> nous disons, vous dites, ils disent.

IMPERATIVE
> dis, disons, dites.

PRESENT PARTICIPLE
> disant; IMPERFECT je disais, etc.

PRESENT SUBJUNCTIVE
> je dise, etc.

PAST PARTICIPLE
> dit; PASSÉ COMPOSÉ j'ai dit, etc.

PASSÉ SIMPLE
> je dis, etc.; IMPERFECT SUBJUNCTIVE je disse, etc.

Like **dire: redire,** *to say again.*

The following verbs are like **dire** except that the 2nd person plural of the present indicative ends in **-disez: contredire,** *to contradict;* **se dédire,** *to retract;* **interdire,** *to prohibit;* **médire,** *to slander;* **prédire,** *to predict.*

Note that **maudire,** *to curse,* is conjugated like **finir** (rather than **dire**) except for the past participle **maudit.**

144 dormir, to sleep.

FUTURE and CONDITIONAL: regular.

PRESENT INDICATIVE
    je dors, tu dors, il dort,
    nous dormons, vous dormez, ils dorment.

IMPERATIVE
    dors, dormons, dormez.

PRESENT PARTICIPLE
    dormant; IMPERFECT je dormais, etc.

PRESENT SUBJUNCTIVE
    je dorme, etc.

PAST PARTICIPLE
    dormi; PASSÉ COMPOSÉ j'ai dormi, etc.

PASSÉ SIMPLE
    je dormis, etc.; IMPERFECT SUBJUNCTIVE je dormisse, etc.

Like **dormir: endormir,** *to put to sleep;* **s'endormir,** *to fall asleep;* etc.

The following verbs are conjugated like **dormir** but the present indicative of each is given in full:

bouillir, *to boil:* bous, bous, bout, bouillons, bouillez, bouillent.

mentir, *to lie,* and **démentir,** *to contradict:* mens, mens, ment, mentons, mentez, mentent.

partir, *to leave,* and **repartir,** *to leave again:* pars, pars, part, partons, partez, partent. (Conjugated with auxiliary **être.**)

se repentir, *to repent:* repens, repens, repent, repentons, repentez, repentent.

sentir, *to feel, to smell;* **consentir,** *to consent;* **pressentir,** *to have a presentiment;* **ressentir,** *to feel:* sens, sens, sent, sentons, sentez, sentent.

servir, *to serve;* **se servir de,** *to use:* sers, sers, sert, servons, servez, servent.

sortir, *to go out:* sors, sors, sort, sortons, sortez, sortent. (Conjugated with auxiliary **être.**)

145 écrire, to write.

FUTURE and CONDITIONAL: regular.

PRESENT INDICATIVE
    j'écris, tu écris, il écrit,
    nous écrivons, vous écrivez, ils écrivent.

IMPERATIVE
    écris, écrivons, écrivez.

PRESENT PARTICIPLE
    écrivant; IMPERFECT j'écrivais, etc.
PRESENT SUBJUNCTIVE
    j'écrive, etc.
PAST PARTICIPLE
    écrit; PASSÉ COMPOSÉ j'ai écrit, etc.
PASSÉ SIMPLE
    j'écrivis, etc.; IMPERFECT SUBJUNCTIVE j'écrivisse, etc.

Like **écrire: décrire,** *to describe;* **inscrire,** *to inscribe;* **prescrire,** *to prescribe;* **proscrire,** *to proscribe;* **souscrire,** *to subscribe;* etc.

146 envoyer, to send.

FUTURE
    j'enverrai, etc.; CONDITIONAL j'enverrais, etc.
PRESENT INDICATIVE
    j'envoie, tu envoies, il envoie,
    nous envoyons, vous envoyez, ils envoient.
IMPERATIVE
    envoie(s), envoyons, envoyez.
PRESENT PARTICIPLE
    envoyant; IMPERFECT j'envoyais, etc.
PRESENT SUBJUNCTIVE
    j'envoie, tu envoies, il envoie,
    nous envoyions, vous envoyiez, ils envoient.
PAST PARTICIPLE
    envoyé; PASSÉ COMPOSÉ j'ai envoyé, etc.
PASSÉ SIMPLE
    j'envoyai, etc.; IMPERFECT SUBJUNCTIVE j'envoyasse, etc.

Like **envoyer: renvoyer,** *to send back, to send away.*

147 faire, to do, to make.

FUTURE
    je ferai, etc.; CONDITIONAL je ferais, etc.
PRESENT INDICATIVE
    je fais, tu fais, il fait,
    nous faisons, vous faites, ils font.
IMPERATIVE
    fais, faisons, faites.

PRESENT PARTICIPLE
faisant; IMPERFECT je faisais, etc.

PRESENT SUBJUNCTIVE
je fasse, etc.

PAST PARTICIPLE
fait; PASSÉ COMPOSÉ j'ai fait, etc.

PASSÉ SIMPLE
je fis, etc.; IMPERFECT SUBJUNCTIVE je fisse, etc.

Like **faire: contrefaire,** *to imitate;* **défaire,** *to undo;* **satisfaire,** *to satisfy;* etc.

148   falloir, must, etc. (impersonal).

FUTURE
il faudra; CONDITIONAL il faudrait.

PRESENT INDICATIVE
il faut.

IMPERATIVE
————

PRESENT PARTICIPLE
——— IMPERFECT il fallait.

PRESENT SUBJUNCTIVE
il faille.

PAST PARTICIPLE
fallu; PASSÉ COMPOSÉ il a fallu.

PASSÉ SIMPLE
il fallut; IMPERFECT SUBJUNCTIVE il fallût.

149   fuir, to flee.

FUTURE and CONDITIONAL: regular.

PRESENT INDICATIVE
je fuis, tu fuis, il fuit,
nous fuyons, vous fuyez, ils fuient.

IMPERATIVE
fuis, fuyons, fuyez.

PRESENT PARTICIPLE
fuyant; IMPERFECT je fuyais, etc.

PRESENT SUBJUNCTIVE
je fuie, tu fuies, il fuie,
nous fuyions, vous fuyiez, ils fuient.

IRREGULAR VERBS

PAST PARTICIPLE
>fui; PASSÉ COMPOSÉ j'ai fui, etc.

PASSÉ SIMPLE
>je fuis, etc.; IMPERFECT SUBJUNCTIVE je fuisse, etc.

Like **fuir: s'enfuir,** *to flee, to escape.*

150 *haïr, to hate.

FUTURE and CONDITIONAL: regular.

PRESENT INDICATIVE
>je hais, tu hais, il hait,
>nous haïssons, vous haïssez, ils haïssent.

IMPERATIVE
>hais, haïssons, haïssez.

PRESENT PARTICIPLE
>haïssant; IMPERFECT je haïssais, etc.

PRESENT SUBJUNCTIVE
>je haïsse, etc.

PAST PARTICIPLE
>haï, PASSÉ COMPOSÉ j'ai haï, etc.

PASSÉ SIMPLE
>je haïs, tu haïs, il haït,
>nous haïmes, vous haïtes, ils haïrent.

IMPERFECT SUBJUNCTIVE
>je haïsse, tu haïsses, il haït, etc.

151 lire, to read.

FUTURE and CONDITIONAL: regular.

PRESENT INDICATIVE
>je lis, tu lis, il lit,
>nous lisons, vous lisez, ils lisent.

IMPERATIVE
>lis, lisons, lisez.

PRESENT PARTICIPLE
>lisant; IMPERFECT je lisais, etc.

---

* The **h** is aspirate in all the forms of **haïr.**

PRESENT SUBJUNCTIVE
je lise, etc.
PAST PARTICIPLE
lu; PASSÉ COMPOSÉ j'ai lu, etc.
PASSÉ SIMPLE
je lus, etc.; IMPERFECT SUBJUNCTIVE je lusse, etc.
Like **lire: élire,** *to elect.*

152 mettre, to put.

FUTURE and CONDITIONAL: regular.
PRESENT INDICATIVE
je mets, tu mets, il met,
nous mettons, vous mettez, ils mettent.
IMPERATIVE
mets, mettons, mettez.
PRESENT PARTICIPLE
mettant; IMPERFECT je mettais, etc.
PRESENT SUBJUNCTIVE
je mette, etc.
PAST PARTICIPLE
mis; PASSÉ COMPOSÉ j'ai mis, etc.
PASSÉ SIMPLE
je mis, etc.; IMPERFECT SUBJUNCTIVE je misse, etc.
Like **mettre: admettre,** *to admit;* **commettre,** *to commit;* **compromettre,** *to compromise;* **émettre,** *to put out, to emit;* **omettre,** *to omit;* **permettre,** *to permit;* **promettre,** *to promise;* **remettre,** *to put back, to hand to;* **soumettre,** *to submit;* **transmettre,** *to transmit;* etc.

153 mourir, to die.

FUTURE
je mourrai, etc.; CONDITIONAL je mourrais, etc.
PRESENT INDICATIVE
je meurs, tu meurs, il meurt,
nous mourons, vous mourez, ils meurent.
IMPERATIVE
meurs, mourons, mourez.
PRESENT PARTICIPLE
mourant; IMPERFECT je mourais, etc.

IRREGULAR VERBS

293

PRESENT SUBJUNCTIVE
je meure, tu meures, il meure,
nous mourions, vous mouriez, ils meurent.

PAST PARTICIPLE
mort; PASSÉ COMPOSÉ je suis mort(e), etc.

PASSÉ SIMPLE
je mourus, etc.; IMPERFECT SUBJUNCTIVE je mourusse, etc.

154   mouvoir, to move.

FUTURE
je mouvrai, etc.; CONDITIONAL je mouvrais, etc.

PRESENT INDICATIVE
je meus, tu meus, il meut,
nous mouvons, vous mouvez, ils meuvent.

IMPERATIVE
meus, mouvons, mouvez.

PRESENT PARTICIPLE
mouvant; IMPERFECT je mouvais, etc.

PRESENT SUBJUNCTIVE
je meuve, tu meuves, il meuve,
nous mouvions, vous mouviez, ils meuvent.

PAST PARTICIPLE
mû; PASSÉ COMPOSÉ j'ai mû, etc.

PASSÉ SIMPLE
je mus, etc.; IMPERFECT SUBJUNCTIVE je musse, etc.

Like **mouvoir: émouvoir,** *to stir;* **s'émouvoir,** *to be stirred;* etc., except that the
past participle is **ému** — without the circumflex accent.

155   naître, to be born.

FUTURE and CONDITIONAL: regular.

PRESENT INDICATIVE
je nais, tu nais, il naît,
nous naissons, vous naissez, ils naissent.

IMPERATIVE
nais, naissons, naissez.

PRESENT PARTICIPLE
naissant; IMPERFECT je naissais, etc.

PRESENT SUBJUNCTIVE
    je naisse, etc.
PAST PARTICIPLE
    né; PASSÉ COMPOSÉ je suis né(e), etc.
PASSÉ SIMPLE
    je naquis, etc.; IMPERFECT SUBJUNCTIVE je naquisse, etc.
Like **naître: renaître,** *to be reborn.*

156 ouvrir, to open.

FUTURE and CONDITIONAL: regular.
PRESENT INDICATIVE
    j'ouvre, tu ouvres, il ouvre,
    nous ouvrons, vous ouvrez, ils ouvrent.
IMPERATIVE
    ouvre(s), ouvrons, ouvrez.
PRESENT PARTICIPLE
    ouvrant; IMPERFECT j'ouvrais, etc.
PRESENT SUBJUNCTIVE
    j'ouvre, etc.
PAST PARTICIPLE
    ouvert; PASSÉ COMPOSÉ j'ai ouvert, etc.
PASSÉ SIMPLE
    j'ouvris, etc.; IMPERFECT SUBJUNCTIVE j'ouvrisse, etc.
Like **ouvrir: couvrir,** *to cover;* **découvrir,** *to discover;* **entr'ouvrir,** *to open slightly;*
    offrir, *to offer, to give;* **souffrir,** *to suffer,* etc.

157 plaire, to please.

FUTURE and CONDITIONAL: regular.
PRESENT INDICATIVE
    je plais, tu plais, il plaît,
    nous plaisons, vous plaisez, ils plaisent.
IMPERATIVE
    plais, plaisons, plaisez.
PRESENT PARTICIPLE
    plaisant; IMPERFECT je plaisais, etc.
PRESENT SUBJUNCTIVE
    je plaise, etc.

PAST PARTICIPLE
plu; PASSÉ COMPOSÉ j'ai plu, etc.

PASSÉ SIMPLE
je plus, etc.; IMPERFECT SUBJUNCTIVE je plusse, etc.

Like **plaire: déplaire,** *to displease.*

Note that **taire,** *to say nothing about,* and **se taire,** *to be silent,* are conjugated like **plaire** except that the 3rd person singular of the present indicative is written without the circumflex accent.

158   pleuvoir, to rain (impersonal).

FUTURE
il pleuvra; CONDITIONAL il pleuvrait.

PRESENT INDICATIVE
il pleut.

PRESENT PARTICIPLE
pleuvant; IMPERFECT il pleuvait.

PRESENT SUBJUNCTIVE
il pleuve.

PAST PARTICIPLE
plu; PASSÉ COMPOSÉ il a plu.

PASSÉ SIMPLE
il plut; IMPERFECT SUBJUNCTIVE il plût.

159   pouvoir, to be able, can, etc.

FUTURE
je pourrai, etc.; CONDITIONAL je pourrais, etc.

PRESENT INDICATIVE
je peux (je puis), tu peux, il peut,
nous pouvons, vous pouvez, ils peuvent.

PRESENT PARTICIPLE
pouvant; IMPERFECT je pouvais, etc.

PRESENT SUBJUNCTIVE
je puisse, tu puisses, il puisse,
nous puissions, vous puissiez, ils puissent.

IMPERATIVE
———

PAST PARTICIPLE
    pu; PASSÉ COMPOSÉ j'ai pu, etc.
PASSÉ SIMPLE
    je pus, etc.; IMPERFECT SUBJUNCTIVE je pusse, etc.

160   prendre, to take.

FUTURE and CONDITIONAL: regular.
PRESENT INDICATIVE
    je prends, tu prends, il prend,
    nous prenons, vous prenez, ils prennent.
IMPERATIVE
    prends, prenons, prenez.
PRESENT PARTICIPLE
    prenant; IMPERFECT je prenais, etc.
PRESENT SUBJUNCTIVE
    je prenne, tu prennes, il prenne,
    nous prenions, vous preniez, ils prennent.
PAST PARTICIPLE
    pris; PASSÉ COMPOSÉ j'ai pris, etc.
PASSÉ SIMPLE
    je pris, etc.; IMPERFECT SUBJUNCTIVE je prisse, etc.
Like **prendre: apprendre,** to learn; **comprendre,** to understand; **entreprendre,**
    to undertake; **reprendre,** to take again, etc.; **surprendre,** to surprise; etc.

161   recevoir, to receive.

FUTURE
    je recevrai, etc.; CONDITIONAL je recevrais, etc.
PRESENT INDICATIVE
    je reçois, tu reçois, il reçoit,
    nous recevons, vous recevez, ils reçoivent.
IMPERATIVE
    reçois, recevons, recevez.
PRESENT PARTICIPLE
    recevant; IMPERFECT je recevais, etc.
PRESENT SUBJUNCTIVE
    je reçoive, tu reçoives, il reçoive,
    nous recevions, vous receviez, ils reçoivent.

IRREGULAR VERBS

PAST PARTICIPLE
 reçu; PASSÉ COMPOSÉ j'ai reçu, etc.

PASSÉ SIMPLE
 je reçus, etc.; IMPERFECT SUBJUNCTIVE je reçusse, etc.

Like **recevoir: apercevoir,** *to catch a glimpse of;* **concevoir,** *to conceive;* **décevoir,** *to deceive;* **percevoir,** *to collect;* etc.

162 résoudre, to resolve, to solve.

FUTURE and CONDITIONAL: regular.

PRESENT INDICATIVE
 je résous, tu résous, il résoud,
 nous résolvons, vous résolvez, ils résolvent.

IMPERATIVE
 résous, résolvons, résolvez.

PRESENT PARTICIPLE
 résolvant; IMPERFECT je résolvais, etc.

PRESENT SUBJUNCTIVE
 je résolve, etc.

PAST PARTICIPLE
 résolu; PASSÉ COMPOSÉ j'ai résolu, etc.

PASSÉ SIMPLE
 je résolus, etc.; IMPERFECT SUBJUNCTIVE je résolusse, etc.

163 rire, to laugh.

FUTURE and CONDITIONAL: regular.

PRESENT INDICATIVE
 je ris, tu ris, il rit,
 nous rions, vous riez, ils rient.

IMPERATIVE
 ris, rions, riez.

PRESENT PARTICIPLE
 riant; IMPERFECT je riais, etc.

PRESENT SUBJUNCTIVE
 je rie, tu ries, il rie,
 nous riions, vous riiez, ils rient.

PAST PARTICIPLE
    ri; PASSÉ COMPOSÉ j'ai ri, etc.
PASSÉ SIMPLE
    je ris, etc.; IMPERFECT SUBJUNCTIVE je risse, etc.
Like **rire: sourire,** *to smile.*

164 savoir, to know.

FUTURE
    je saurai, etc.; CONDITIONAL je saurais, etc.
PRESENT INDICATIVE
    je sais, tu sais, il sait,
    nous savons, vous savez, ils savent.
IMPERATIVE
    sache, sachons, sachez.
PRESENT PARTICIPLE
    sachant; IMPERFECT je savais, etc.
PRESENT SUBJUNCTIVE
    je sache, etc.
PAST PARTICIPLE
    su; PASSÉ COMPOSÉ j'ai su, etc.
PASSÉ SIMPLE
    je sus, etc.; IMPERFECT SUBJUNCTIVE je susse, etc.

165 suffire, to suffice, to be enough.

FUTURE and CONDITIONAL: regular.
PRESENT INDICATIVE
    je suffis, tu suffis, il suffit,
    nous suffisons, vous suffisez, ils suffisent.
IMPERATIVE
    suffis, suffisons, suffisez.
PRESENT PARTICIPLE
    suffisant; IMPERFECT je suffisais, etc.
PRESENT SUBJUNCTIVE
    je suffise, etc.
PAST PARTICIPLE
    suffi; PASSÉ COMPOSÉ j'ai suffi, etc.
PASSÉ SIMPLE
    je suffis, etc.; IMPERFECT SUBJUNCTIVE je suffisse, etc.

166 suivre, to follow.

FUTURE and CONDITIONAL: regular.

PRESENT INDICATIVE
je suis, tu suis, il suit,
nous suivons, vous suivez, ils suivent.

IMPERATIVE
suis, suivons, suivez.

PRESENT PARTICIPLE
suivant; IMPERFECT je suivais, etc.

PRESENT SUBJUNCTIVE
je suive, etc.

PAST PARTICIPLE
suivi; PASSÉ COMPOSÉ j'ai suivi, etc.

PASSÉ SIMPLE
je suivis, etc.; IMPERFECT SUBJUNCTIVE je suivisse, etc.

Like **suivre: poursuivre,** *to pursue.*

167 tenir, to hold.

FUTURE
je tiendrai, etc.; CONDITIONAL je tiendrais, etc.

PRESENT INDICATIVE
je tiens, tu tiens, il tient,
nous tenons, vous tenez, ils tiennent.

IMPERATIVE
tiens, tenons, tenez.

PRESENT PARTICIPLE
tenant; IMPERFECT je tenais, etc.

PRESENT SUBJUNCTIVE
je tienne, tu tiennes, il tienne,
nous tenions, vous teniez, ils tiennent.

PAST PARTICIPLE
tenu; PASSÉ COMPOSÉ j'ai tenu, etc.

PASSÉ SIMPLE
je tins, tu tins, il tint,
nous tînmes, vous tîntes, ils tinrent. IMPERFECT SUBJUNCTIVE je tinsse, etc.

Like **tenir: s'abstenir,** *to abstain;* **appartenir,** *to belong;* **contenir,** *to contain;* **détenir,** *to detain;* **entretenir,** *to keep in good condition;* **maintenir,** *to maintain;* **obtenir,** *to obtain;* **retenir,** *to retain;* **soutenir,** *to sustain.*

168   traire, to milk.

FUTURE and CONDITIONAL: regular.

PRESENT INDICATIVE
    je trais, tu trais, il trait,
    nous trayons, vous trayez, ils traient.

IMPERATIVE
    trais, trayons, trayez.

PRESENT PARTICIPLE
    trayant; IMPERFECT je trayais, etc.

PRESENT SUBJUNCTIVE
    je traie, tu traies, il traie,
    nous trayions, vous trayiez, ils traient.

PAST PARTICIPLE
    trait; PASSÉ COMPOSÉ j'ai trait, etc.

PASSÉ SIMPLE
    ——; IMPERFECT SUBJUNCTIVE ——.

Like **traire: abstraire,** *to abstract;* **distraire,** *to distract;* **extraire,** *to extract;* **soustraire,** *to subtract;* etc.

169   vaincre, to conquer.

FUTURE and CONDITIONAL: regular.

PRESENT INDICATIVE
    je vaincs, tu vaincs, il vainc,
    nous vainquons, vous vainquez, ils vainquent.

IMPERATIVE
    vaincs, vainquons, vainquez.

PRESENT PARTICIPLE
    vainquant; IMPERFECT je vanquis, etc.

PRESENT SUBJUNCTIVE
    je vainque, etc.

PAST PARTICIPLE
    vaincu; PASSÉ COMPOSÉ j'ai vaincu, etc.

PASSÉ SIMPLE
    je vainquis, etc.; IMPERFECT SUBJUNCTIVE je vainquisse, etc.

Like **vaincre: convaincre,** *to convince.*

170 valoir, to be worth.

FUTURE
   je vaudrai, etc.; CONDITIONAL je vaudrais, etc.

PRESENT INDICATIVE
   je vaux, tu vaux, il vaut,
   nous valons, vous valez, ils valent.

IMPERATIVE
   vaux, valons, valez.

PRESENT PARTICIPLE
   valant; IMPERFECT je valais, etc.

PRESENT SUBJUNCTIVE
   je vaille, tu vailles, il vaille,
   nous valions, vous valiez, ils vaillent.

PAST PARTICIPLE
   valu; PASSÉ COMPOSÉ j'ai valu, etc.

PASSÉ SIMPLE
   je valus, etc.; IMPERFECT SUBJUNCTIVE je valusse, etc.

171 venir, to come.

FUTURE
   je viendrai, etc.; CONDITIONAL je viendrais, etc.

PRESENT INDICATIVE
   je viens, tu viens, il vient,
   nous venons, vous venez, ils viennent.

IMPERATIVE
   viens, venons, venez.

PRESENT PARTICIPLE
   venant; IMPERFECT je venais, etc.

PRESENT SUBJUNCTIVE
   je vienne, tu viennes, il vienne,
   nous venions, vous veniez, ils viennent.

PAST PARTICIPLE
   venu; PASSÉ COMPOSÉ je suis venu(e), etc.

PASSÉ SIMPLE
   je vins, tu vins, il vint,
   nous vînmes, vous vîntes, ils vinrent. IMPERFECT SUBJUNCTIVE je vinsse, etc.

Like **venir: convenir,** *to agree, to suit;* **devenir,** *to become;* **intervenir,** *to intervene;* **parvenir,** *to attain;* **prévenir,** *to warn,* etc.; **provenir,** *to come from;* **revenir,** *to come back;* **se souvenir,** *to remember;* etc.

172 vêtir, to clothe.

FUTURE and CONDITIONAL: regular.

PRESENT INDICATIVE
je vêts, tu vêts, il vêt,
nous vêtons, vous vêtez, ils vêtent.

IMPERATIVE
vêts, vêtons, vêtez.

PRESENT PARTICIPLE
vêtant; IMPERFECT je vêtais, etc.

PRESENT SUBJUNCTIVE
je vête, etc.

PAST PARTICIPLE
vêtu; PASSÉ COMPOSÉ j'ai vêtu, etc.

PASSÉ SIMPLE
je vêtis, etc.; IMPERFECT SUBJUNCTIVE je vêtisse, etc.

173 vivre, to live.

FUTURE and CONDITIONAL: regular.

PRESENT INDICATIVE
je vis, tu vis, il vit,
nous vivons, vous vivez, ils vivent.

IMPERATIVE
vis, vivons, vivez.

PRESENT PARTICIPLE
vivant; IMPERFECT je vivais, etc.

PRESENT SUBJUNCTIVE
je vive, etc.

PAST PARTICIPLE
vécu; PASSÉ COMPOSÉ j'ai vécu, etc.

PASSÉ SIMPLE
je vécus, etc.; IMPERFECT SUBJUNCTIVE je vécusse, etc.

174 voir, to see.

FUTURE
je verrai, etc.; CONDITIONAL je verrais, etc.

PRESENT INDICATIVE
je vois, tu vois, il voit,
nous voyons, vous voyez, ils voient.

IRREGULAR VERBS   *303*

IMPERATIVE
    vois, voyons, voyez.

PRESENT PARTICIPLE
    voyant; IMPERFECT je voyais, etc.

PRESENT SUBJUNCTIVE
    je voie, tu voies, il voie,
    nous voyions, vous voyiez, ils voient.

PAST PARTICIPLE
    vu; PASSÉ COMPOSÉ j'ai vu, etc.

PASSÉ SIMPLE
    je vis, etc.; IMPERFECT SUBJUNCTIVE je visse, etc.

Like **voir: entrevoir,** *to catch sight of;* **revoir,** *to see again.*

Note that **prévoir** is like **voir** except that the future and conditional are regular.

Note also that **pourvoir** is like **voir** except that the future and conditional are regular and that the passé simple is **je pourvus,** etc., and the imperfect subjunctive **je pourvusse,** etc.

175   **vouloir,** to want, to will.

FUTURE
    je voudrai, etc.; CONDITIONAL je voudrais, etc.

PRESENT INDICATIVE
    je veux, tu veux, il veut,
    nous voulons, vous voulez, ils veulent.

IMPERATIVE
    veux, voulons, voulez, *or*
    veuille, veuillons, veuillez.

PRESENT PARTICIPLE
    voulant; IMPERFECT je voulais, etc.

PRESENT SUBJUNCTIVE
    je veuille, tu veuilles, il veuille,
    nous voulions, vous vouliez, ils veuillent.

PAST PARTICIPLE
    voulu; PASSÉ COMPOSÉ j'ai voulu, etc.

PASSÉ SIMPLE
    je voulus, etc.; IMPERFECT SUBJUNCTIVE je voulusse, etc.

VOCABULARIES

ABBREVIATIONS

abbr	abbreviation	*interrog*	interrogative
adj	adjective	*intr*	intransitive
adv	adverb	*lang*	language
art	article	*m*	masculine
* (asterisk)	aspirate h	*n*	noun
cond	conditional	*obj*	object
conj	conjunction	*p part*	past participle
conjug	conjugated	*p simple*	passé simple
contr	contraction	*par*	paragraph
dem	demonstrative	*pers*	person, personal
dir object	direct object	*pl*	plural
exclam	exclamatory	*poss*	possessive
f	feminine	*pres*	present
fut	future	*prep*	preposition
imper	imperative	*pron*	pronoun
imperf	imperfect	*rel*	relative
ind	indicative	*sg*	singular
indir obj	indirect object	*subj*	subjunctive
inf	infinitive	*trans*	transitive

FRENCH-ENGLISH

A

à [a] at, in, to, into, for; **à moi** mine

abandonner [abɑ̃dɔne] to give up, to abandon

abondant, abondante [abõdɑ̃, abõdɑ̃t] abundant

abord: d'abord [dabɔR] at first

absence [apsɑ̃s] f absence

absolument [apsɔlymɑ̃] absolutely

accepter [aksɛpte] to accept

accessible [aksɛsibl] accessible

accident [aksidɑ̃] m accident

accompagner [akõpaɲe] to go with

accueillir [akœjiR] to welcome

accuser [akyze] to accuse; **s'accuser** to accuse oneself

achat [aʃa] m purchase

acheter [aʃte] to buy

achever [aʃve] to finish

actif, active [aktif] active

actuel, actuelle [aktɥɛl] present; **à l'heure actuelle** now

actuellement [aktɥɛlmɑ̃] at present

adjectif [adʒɛktif] m adjective; **adjectif possessif** possessive adjective

administration [administRasjõ] f administration; **une administration financière** an office of the Treasury Department

admiration [admiRasjõ] f admiration

admirer [admiRe] to admire

adorer [adɔRe] to love, to adore

adresse [adRɛs] f address

adresser [adRɛse] to send

aéroport [aeRɔpɔR] m airport

affaire [afɛR] f affair; **une affaire d'impôts** a tax question

affecté [afɛkte] affected

affectueux [afɛktɥø] affectionate

affirmativement [afiRmativmɑ̃] affirmatively

affluent [aflyɑ̃] m tributary

affreux [afRø] awful

afin de [afɛ̃də] in order to

Afrique [afRik] f Africa

âge [ɑʒ] m age; **Quel âge a-t-il?** How old is he?

agent [aʒɑ̃] m: **agent de police** policeman

agit: s'agir de [saʒiR də] to be a question of

agité [aʒite] excited

agréable [agReabl] pleasant

agréer [agRee] to accept, to approve

agrément [agRemɑ̃] m pleasure, **voyage d'agrément** pleasure trip

agricole [agRikɔl] agricultural

agriculture [agRikyltyR] f agriculture

aider [ɛde] to help

aile [ɛl] f wing (of bird or of building)

ailleurs [ajœR] elsewhere; **d'ailleurs** besides

aimable [ɛmabl] kind

aimer [ɛme] to love, to like; **aimer mieux** to prefer

iii

air [ɛʀ] *m* air
aise [ɛz]: **bien aise** glad
aisé [ɛze] easy, well-to-do
aisément [ɛzemɑ̃] easily
ajouter [aʒute] to add
aliment [alimɑ̃] *m* food
Allemagne [almaɲ] *f* Germany
allemand [almɑ̃] German
aller [ale] to go; **s'en aller** to go away
alors [alɔʀ] then, in that case
Alpes [alp] *f* Alps
Américain, Américaine [ameʀikɛ̃, ameʀikɛn] (an) American
Amérique [ameʀik] *f* America
ami [ami] *m* friend
amitié [amitje] *f* friendship; **faire mes amitiés à** to say hello to, give my regards to
amour [amuʀ] *m* love
amuser [amyze] to amuse; **s'amuser** to be amused, to have a good time
an [ɑ̃] *m* year (*see par 59*)
ancêtre [ɑ̃sɛtʀ] *m* ancestor
ancien [ɑ̃sjɛ̃] old, former
Angleterre [ɑ̃ɡlətɛʀ] *f* England
année [ane] *f* year (*see par 59*)
anniversaire [anivɛʀsɛʀ] *m* birthday
annonce [anɔ̃s] *f* announcement
Antilles [ɑ̃tij] *f pl* West Indies
antiquaire [ɑ̃tikɛʀ] *m* antique dealer
août [u] *or* [ut] August
apercevoir [apɛʀsəvwaʀ] to see, to perceive
appareil [apaʀɛj] *m* camera
appartement [apaʀtəmɑ̃] *m* apartment
appartenir (à) [apaʀtəniʀ] to belong to
appeler [aple] to call; **s'appeler** to be named
appendicite [apɛ̃disit] *f* appendicitis
apporter [apɔʀte] to bring
apprécier [apʀesje] to appreciate
apprendre [apʀɑ̃dʀ] to learn
approcher [apʀɔʃe] to approach, to draw near; **s'approcher** to approach
approprié [apʀɔpʀije] appropriate
après [apʀɛ] after; **d'après** according to

après-midi [apʀɛmidi] *m* afternoon
Arabie [aʀabi] *f* Arabia; **Arabie saoudite** Saudi Arabia
arbre [aʀbʀ] *m* tree
argent [aʀʒɑ̃] *m* money, silver
argenterie [aʀʒɑ̃tʀi] *f* silverware
arme [aʀm] *f* weapon
armée [aʀme] *f* army
armoire [aʀmwaʀ] *f* cupboard
arranger [aʀɑ̃ʒe] to arrange; **s'arranger** to improve, to clear up
arrêt [aʀɛ] *m* stop, stopping
arrêter [aʀɛte] *trans* to stop, to arrest; **s'arrêter** to stop
arrivée [aʀive] *f* arrival
arriver [aʀive] to arrive, to get to; to happen; to succeed
arroser [aʀoze] to water, to sprinkle
art [aʀ] *m* art; **objet d'art** [ɔbʒɛdaʀ] *m* an article of some artistic value
article [aʀtikl] *m* article
artiste [aʀtist] *m* artist
artistique [aʀtistik] artistic
Asie [asi] *f* Asia
assassiner [asasine] to assassinate
asseoir [aswaʀ] to seat; **s'asseoir** to sit down
assez [ase] enough, pretty much
assidûment [asidymɑ̃] systematically
assiette [asjɛt] *f* plate
assister à [asiste a] to be present at
association [asɔsjasjɔ̃] *f* association; **association sportive** an athletic organization
assurance [asyʀɑ̃s] *f* insurance
assurer: s'assurer [sasyʀe] to make sure; to insure
atteindre [atɛ̃dʀ] to reach
attendre [atɑ̃dʀ] to wait for, to expect; **s'attendre à** to expect
attention [atɑ̃sjɔ̃] *f* attention
attirer [atiʀe] to attract
attraper [atʀape] to catch
aucun, aucune [okœ̃, okyn] (*with* **ne**) not a, no; *pron* none, not a one
au-dessus [odsy] above
augmenter [ɔɡmɑ̃te] to increase, raise

aujourd'hui [oʒuʀdɥi] today
auparavant [opaʀavã] before
auprès de [opʀɛdə] near, with
auquel [okɛl] *see* lequel
aurore [ɔʀɔʀ] *f* dawn
aussi [osi] also, too; aussi . . . que
    as . . . as
aussitôt que [ositokə] as soon as
Australie [ɔstʀali] *f* Australia
auteur [otøʀ] *m* author
auto [ɔto] *or* [oto] *m or f* car
autobus [ɔtobys] *or* [otobys] *m* bus
autorail [ɔtoʀaj] *or* [otoʀaj] *m* fast one-
    car passenger train
autorité [ɔtoʀite] *or* [otoʀite] *f* authority
autoroute [ɔtoʀut] *or* [otoʀut] *f* free-
    way, throughway
autre [otʀ] other
autrefois [otʀəfwa] formerly, long ago
avance: d'avance [davãs] beforehand
avancer [avãse] to go forward
avant de [avãdə] before; avant que
    before
avec [avɛk] with
aventure [avãtyʀ] *f* adventure
avenue [avny] *f* avenue
avertir [avɛʀtiʀ] to warn
avion [avjõ] *m* plane; en avion, par
    avion by plane; avion à réaction
    jet plane
avis [avi] *m* advice, opinion
avocat [avɔka] *m* lawyer
avoir [avwaʀ] to have; pour avoir un
    taxi to get a taxi; avoir à to have
    to; avoir beau to . . . in vain
avril [avʀil] April
Azur [azyʀ] *m* Azure; Côte d'Azur
    the Riviera

B

bagages [bagaʒ] *m pl* baggage
bain: salle de bain [saldəbɛ̃] *f* bath-
    room
bal [bal] *m* ball
Balzac [balzak] 19th century French
    novelist

banane [banan] *f* banana
banque [bɑ̃k] *f* bank
bateau [bato] *m* boat; bateau à voile
    sailboat
bâtir [batiʀ] to build
bavard, bavarde [bavaʀ, bavaʀd]
    chatty, garrulous
beau, belle [bo] [bɛl] beautiful; il
    faisait beau the weather was fine
Beauce [bos] *f* rich agricultural region
    southwest of Paris
beaucoup [boku] much, a great deal
Beaune [bon] city in Burgundy
beauté [bote] *f* beauty
bébé [bebe] *m* baby
belge [bɛlʒ] Belgian
Belgique [bɛlʒik] *f* Belgium
besoin [bəzwɛ̃] *m* need; avoir besoin de
    to need
bétail [betaj] *m* cattle
beurre [bœʀ] *m* butter
bien [bjɛ̃] very; well; bien que al-
    though
bien-être [bjɛ̃nɛtʀ] *m* well-being
bientôt [bjɛ̃to] soon
bière [bjɛʀ] *f* beer
bijou [biʒu] *m* jewel
billet [bijɛ] *m* ticket
blanc, blanche [blɑ̃, blɑ̃ʃ] white
blesser [blɛse] to wound; se blesser to
    be wounded
bleu, bleue [blø] blue
bœuf [bœf] *m* ox
boire [bwaʀ] to drink
bois [bwɑ] *m* wood; en bois sculpté of
    carved wood
bois [bwɑ] *pres ind of* boire
bon, bonne [bõ, bɔn] good; le bon
    vieux temps the good old days;
    sentir bon to smell good
bonjour [bõʒuʀ] good morning, good
    afternoon
bord [bɔʀ] *m* edge, bank, shore
border [bɔʀde] to line
botté [bɔte] wearing boots
bouclé [bukle] buckled, curled
bouledogue [buldɔg] *m* bulldog

bourgeoisie *f* [buʀʒwazi] bourgeoisie
bout [bu]: **joindre les deux bouts** to make both ends meet
bouteille [butɛj] *f* bottle
boutique [butik] *f* shop
bouton [butõ] *m* button, knob
bras [bʀɑ] *m* arm; **à bras ouverts** with open arms
brave [bʀav] good, worthy; brave
bref [bʀɛf] in a word
Brésil [bʀezil] *m* Brazil
Bretagne [bʀətaɲ] *f* Brittany
breton, bretonne [bʀətõ] from Brittany
bridge [bʀidʒ]: **partie de bridge** *f* bridge game; **jouer au bridge** to play bridge
brillant [bʀijɑ̃] bright
brouillard [bʀujaʀ] *m* fog
bruit [bʀɥi] *m* noise
Bruxelles [bʀy(k)sɛl] Brussels
bureau [byʀo] *m* office; desk; **bureau de tabac** tobacco shop
but [by(t)] *m* goal

c

c' *see* ce
ça, cela [sa, sla] that, it
cabinet [kabinɛ] *m* private room, study, office (at home)
cache-nez [kaʃne] *m* scarf (long)
cacher [kaʃe] to hide, conceal
cadeau [kado] *m* present, gift
Caen [kɑ̃] ancient city in Normandy
café [kafe] *m* coffee; **café noir** black coffee; **café au lait** coffee with hot milk; **café-crème** coffee and cream
Caire: Le Caire [lə kɛʀ] *m* Cairo
calculateur [kalkylatœʀ] *m* computer
calculer [kalkyle] to calculate
calme [kalm] *m* calm
camarade [kamaʀad] *m* friend
camion [kamjõ] *m* truck
camp [kɑ̃] *m* camp
campagne [kɑ̃paɲ] *f* country
Canada [kanada] *m* Canada

canadien [kanadjɛ̃] Canadian
canal [kanal] *m* canal
capitaine [kapitɛn] *m* captain
car [kaʀ] because
Carmen [kaʀmɛn] opera by Bizet
carré [kaʀe] square; **un kilomètre carré** one square kilometer
carte [kaʀt] *f* card; menu
carte-postale [kaʀt pɔstal] *f* post card
cas [kɑ] *m* case; **en tout cas** in any case, anyway
casser [kɑse]: **se casser le bras** to break one's arm
cathédrale [katedʀal] *f* cathedral; **cathédrale gothique** Gothic cathedral
catholique [katɔlik] catholic
cause [koz] *f* cause; **à cause de la pluie** because of the rain
ce, c' [sə] it, that, he, she, they
ce, cet, cette; ces [sə, sɛt, sɛt; sɛ] this, that; these, those
céder [sede] to give up, to yield
célèbre [selɛbʀ] famous, celebrated
celui [səlɥi] *m*, **celle** *f*, **ceux** *m pl*, **celles** *f pl*, the one(s); **celui-ci, celle-ci,** this one; **celui-là, celle-là,** that one; **ceux-ci, celles-ci,** these; **ceux-là, celles-là,** those
censé [sɑ̃se] supposed
cent [sɑ̃] one hundred
centaine [sɑ̃tɛn] *f* about a hundred
cependant [səpɑ̃dɑ̃] however
cérémonie [seʀemɔni] *f* ceremony
certain, certaine [sɛʀtɛ̃, sɛʀtɛn] certain; **il est certain** it is certain
certainement [sɛʀtɛnmɑ̃] of course
cesser [sɛse] to stop
ceux [sø] *see* celui
Cézanne [sezan] 19th century French painter
chacun, chacune [ʃakœ̃, ʃakyn] each, each one
chaise [ʃɛz] *f* chair
chambre [ʃɑ̃bʀ] *f* room, bedroom
champ [ʃɑ̃] *m* field
chandail [ʃɑ̃dɑj] *m* sweater

changement [ʃɑ̃ʒmɑ̃] *m* change
changer [ʃɑ̃ʒe] to change
chant [ʃɑ̃] *m* song
chanter [ʃɑ̃te] to sing; **chanter faux** to sing off pitch; **chanter juste** to sing on pitch
charbon [ʃaʁbõ] *m* coal
charge [ʃaʁʒ] *f* charge, load
charger: se charger de [səʃaʁʒe] to take charge of, to take care of
charmant [ʃaʁmɑ̃] charming
chasse [ʃas] *f* hunt
chat [ʃa] *m* cat
château [ʃɑto] *m* château
chauffeur [ʃofœʁ] *m* driver
chavirer [ʃaviʁe] to capsize
chemin [ʃ(ə)mɛ̃] *m* road; **chemin de fer** railroad
cheminée [ʃ(ə)miné] *f* fireplace, chimney
Chenonceaux [ʃənõso] famous Renaissance château
chèque]ʃɛk] *m* check
cher [ʃɛʁ], **chère** dear; **coûter cher** to be expensive
chercher [ʃɛʁʃe] to look for; **aller chercher** to go to get; **chercher à** to try to
cheval [ʃ(ə)val] **chevaux** *m* horse; **à cheval** on horseback
cheveu [ʃ(ə)vø] *m* hair
chez [ʃe] at the home, house, apartment, office, store of
chien [ʃjɛ̃] *m* dog
Chili [ʃili] *m* Chile
Chine [ʃin] *f* China
choisir [ʃwaziʁ] to choose
choix [ʃwa] *m* choice
chose [ʃoz] *f* thing; **quelque chose** something; **autre chose** something else; **pas grand-chose** nothing much; **peu de chose** practically nothing; **dire bien des choses à** to give regards to
chou [ʃu] *m* cabbage
chute [ʃyt] *f* fall; **les chutes du Niagara** Niagara Falls

ci-inclus [siɛ̃kly] herewith
cimetière [simtjɛʁ] *m* cemetery; *Le Cimetière marin* a poem by Paul Valéry
cinéma [sinema] *m* movies; **au cinéma** to, at the movies
cinquante [sɛ̃kɑ̃t] fifty
cire [siʁ] *f* wax
clairière [klɛʁjɛʁ] *f* clearing
clé [kle] *f* key
clocher [kloʃe] *m* steeple
cœur [kœʁ] *m* heart; **savoir par cœur** to know by heart; **avoir mal au cœur** to feel sick; **apprendre par cœur** to learn by heart
coiffe [kwaf] *f* head-dress
coin [kwɛ̃] *m* corner; **coins perdus** out-of-the-way places
collègue [kolɛg[*m* colleague
combien [kõbjɛ̃] how much; **combien de temps** how long
combiner [kõbine] to combine, join
Comédie-Française *f* [komedi fʁɑ̃sɛz] French national theater
commander [komɑ̃de] to order
comme [kom] as; *Comme il vous plaîra As You Like It;* **comme ça** like that; **comme ci comme ça** so-so
commencement [komɑ̃smɑ̃] *m* beginning
commencer [komɑ̃se] to begin
comment [komɑ̃] how; **Comment ça?** How's that?; **Et comment!** And how!
commerçant [komɛʁsɑ̃] *m* merchant; *adj* commercial
commettre [komɛtʁ] to commit
commode [komod] convenient
commun, commune [komœ̃, komyn] common; **transport en commun** common carrier
compagnie [kõpaɲi] *f* company
comparé à [kõpaʁea] compared to
complet, complète [kõplɛ, kõplɛt] complete; full
compliment [kõplimɑ̃] *m* compliment
comprendre [kõpʁɑ̃dʁ] to understand;

Je n'y comprends rien I don't understand it at all; **ça se comprend** that is understandable

compte [kõt] *m* account; **se rendre compte** to realize

compter [kõte] to expect, count on

concerner [kõsɛrne] to concern; **en ce qui concerne l'agriculture** as far as agriculture is concerned

concert [kõsɛr] *m* concert

conclure [kõklyr] to conclude

condition [kõdisjõ] *f* condition; **à quelles conditions** in what circumstances; **à condition de** on condition that

conditionnel [kõdisjɔnɛl] *m* conditional; **conditionnel passé** conditional perfect

conduire [kõdɥir] to drive, to conduct

conférence [kõferãs] *f* lecture

configuration [kõfigyrasjõ] *f* lay (of the land)

confisqué [kõfiske] confiscated

confort [kõfɔr] *m* comfort

confortable [kõfɔrtable] comfortable

congé [kõʒe] *m* leave of absence, vacation

connaissance [kɔnɛsãs] *f* acquaintance; **faire sa connaissance** to meet him, her

connaisseur [kɔnɛsœr] *m* connoisseur

connaître [kɔnɛtr] to know (*see par 40*)

conseil [kõsɛj] *m* advice

conseiller [kõsɛje] to advise

consentir [kõsãtir] to consent

conserver [kõsɛrve] to keep

considérable [kõsiderabl] important

considération [kõsiderasjõ] *f* consideration

considérer [kõsidere] to regard

consoler [kõsɔle] to console, to comfort

constamment [kõstamã] constantly, all the time

constituer [kõstitɥe] to form

construction [kõstryksjõ] *f* building

construire [kõstrɥir] to build

construit [kõstrɥi] *p part of* **construire**

content, contente [kõtã, kõtãt] happy, glad

contexte [kõtɛkst] *m* context

continuel [kõtinɥɛl] continual

continuer [kõtinɥe] to continue, proceed

contraire [kõtrɛr] *m* contrary; **au contraire** on the contrary

convenable [kõvnabl] proper, correct

convenir [kõvnir] to agree, to be suitable

conversation [kõvɛrsasjõ] *f* conversation

copieusement [kɔpjøsmã] copiously

corde [kɔrd] *f* rope

cordial [kɔrdjal] cordial

cordialement [kɔrdjalmã]; **bien cordialement** cordially

correspondance [kɔrɛspõdãs] *f* correspondence

cote [kɔt] *f* quota, share

côte [kot] *f* coast

côté [kote] *m* side; **à côté de** beside; **de l'autre côté** on the other side; **du côté de** in the direction of

coucher: se coucher [skuʃe] to go to bed

couleur [kulœr] *f* color

coup [ku] *m* blow; **tout à coup** suddenly; **coup de fil** a phone call

cour [kur] *f* court, yard

courage [kuraʒ] *m* courage

courageusement [kuraʒøzmã] courageously

courageux, courageuse [kuraʒø, kuraʒøz] courageous

couramment [kuramã] fluently

courant [kurã] current; **le mois courant** this month

courir [kurir] to run

cours [kur] *m* course; **au cours de** in the course of

course [kurs] *f* errand

court, courte [kur, kurt] short

cousin [kuzẽ] *m*, **cousine** [kuzin] *f* cousin

coût [ku] *m* cost

couteau [kuto] *m* knife

coûter [kute] to cost; **coûter cher** to be expensive

couvert [kuvɛʀ] covered, cloudy

couvrir [kuvʀiʀ] to cover

craindre [kʀɛ̃dʀ] to fear

créer [kʀee] to create, establish

crème [kʀɛm] *f* cream

crier [kʀie] to shout, to cry out

crime [kʀim] *m* crime

criminel [kʀiminɛl] *m* criminal

crise [kʀiz] *f* crisis; **crise d'appendicite** appendicitis

croire [kʀwaʀ] to believe, to think

cru [kʀy] *p part of* **croire**

cruel, cruelle [kʀyɛl] cruel

cueillir [kœjiʀ] to pick

cuiller [kɥijɛʀ] *f* spoon

cuire [kɥiʀ] to cook

cuisine [kɥizin] *f* cooking; **faire la cuisine** to cook

cuisinier [kɥizinje] *m*, **cuisinière** [kɥizinjɛʀ] *f* cook

cultivateur [kyltivatœʀ] *m* farmer

culture [kyltyʀ] *f* farming

cure [kyʀ] *f* cure

curieux [kyʀjø] interesting

cygne [siɲ] *m* swan

D

dahlia [dalja] *m* dahlia

Danemark [danmaʀk] *m* Denmark

dangereux [dɑ̃ʒʀø] dangerous

dans [dɑ̃] in, into; **dans quelques années** in *or* within a few years

danser [dɑ̃se] to dance

date [dat] *f* date

datif [datif] *m* dative

davantage [davɑ̃taʒ] more

de [də] of; from; by

décider [deside] to decide

déclaration [deklaʀasjõ] *f* declaration

déclarer [deklaʀe] to declare

décliner [dekline] to decline, to refuse

décoration [dekɔʀasjõ] *f* decoration

découragé [dekuʀaʒe] discouraged

décourager: se décourager [sə dekuʀaʒe] to get discouraged

découverte [dekuvɛʀt] *f* discovery

découvrir [dekuvʀiʀ] to discover

décrire [dekʀiʀ] to describe

défaut [defo] *m* fault

défendre [defɑ̃dʀ] to forbid

défini, définie [defini] definite

Degas [dəga] French Impressionist painter

déjà [deʒa] already

déjeuner [deʒœne] to have lunch

délai [delɛ] *m* delay; the time required

délicieux, délicieuse [delisjø, delisjøz] delicious

demander [dəmɑ̃de] to ask; **se demander** to wonder

demeurer [dəmœʀe] to live, to reside

demi-heure [dəmiœʀ] *f* half an hour

demi-tour [dəmituʀ] *m* half turn; **faire demi-tour** to turn around

démonstratif, démonstrative [demõstratif, demõstrativ] demonstrative

départ [depaʀ] *m* departure

dépêche [depɛʃ] *f* telegram

dépêcher [depeʃe]: **se dépêcher** to hurry

dépendre de [depɑ̃dʀ] to depend upon; **cela dépend** it depends

dépenser [depɑ̃se] to spend

déplacer: se déplacer [sə deplase] to move about, to travel

déplaire à [deplɛʀ] to displease

déportation [depɔʀtasjõ] *f* deportation

déposer [depoze] to put down, to deposit

dépouiller [depuje] to strip

depuis [dəpɥi] since; for (*when used with pres tense*)

dérangement [deʀɑ̃ʒmɑ̃] *m* bother

déranger [deʀɑ̃ʒe] to bother (someone); **se déranger** to bother, to be bothered

dernier, dernière [dɛʀnje, dɛʀnjɛʀ] last

dès que [dɛ kə] as soon as

désagréable [dezagʀeabl] disagreeable

descendre [desãdʀ] to go down; **descendre à un hôtel** to stop at a hotel; **descendre de l'autobus** to get off the bus

désert [dezɛʀ] m desert

désespérer [dezɛspeʀe] to despair, to give up; **de quoi désespérer** enough to make you give up

désirer |deziʀe] to want

dessin [desɛ̃] m drawing, design

destination [dɛstinasjõ] f destination

destiné à [dɛstine a] intended for

détail [detaj] m detail

déterminer [detɛʀmine] to determine

détestable [detɛstabl] hateful

détester [detɛste] to hate, detest

détruit [detʀɥi] destroyed

deuil [dœj] m sorrow

deuxième [døzjɛm] second

devanture [dəvãtyʀ] f shopwindow

devenir [dəvniʀ] to become

devenu [dəvny] p part of **devenir**

deviner [dəvine] to guess

devoir [dəvwaʀ] must, should, ought, to be supposed to; to owe (see par 34 and par 35)

dévoué [devwe] devoted; **Votre bien dévoué** Sincerely yours

Diane de Poitiers [djandəpwatje] favorite of Henri II

différence [difeʀãs] f difference

différent [difeʀã] different

difficile [difisil] difficult

difficulté [difikylte] f difficulty, trouble

dîner [dine] to dine, to have dinner

diplomate [diplɔmat] m diplomat

dire [diʀ] to say, to tell; **cela se dit** that is said

direct, directe [diʀɛkt, diʀɛkt] direct; **l'expression directe** direct discourse; quotation

directement [diʀɛktəmã] directly

diriger [diʀiʒe] to direct

discuter [diskyte] to argue, to discuss

disparaître [dispaʀɛtʀ] to disappear

disposition [dispozisjõ] f disposal; **à votre disposition** at your disposal

disque [disk] m record

distance [distãs] f distance; **à quelle distance de** how far, at what distance; **vu à distance** seen from a distance

distinguer [distɛ̃ge] to distinguish

dites [dit] say (imper of **dire**)

divers, diverse [divɛʀ, divɛʀs] various

dizaine [dizɛn] f about ten

docteur [dɔktœʀ] m doctor

dollar |dɔlaʀ] m dollar

domestique [dɔmɛstik] m or f servant

donc [dõk] then

dont [dõ] whose, of whom, of which; **l'argent dont j'ai besoin** the money I need

dormir [dɔʀmiʀ] to sleep

dort [dɔʀ] pres ind of **dormir**

dos [do] m back

douane [dwan] f customs

doué [dwe] gifted

doute [dut] m doubt; **sans doute** probably

douter [dute] to doubt; **se douter de** to suspect

doux, douce [du, dus] gentle, soft; **bruit doux** gentle noise

douzaine [duzɛn] f dozen

du, de la, des, de, d' some, some of (often not translated in English); from, of, etc.

dû [dy] p part of **devoir**

duquel [dykɛl] see **lequel**

dur [dyʀ] hard

durée [dyʀe] f duration; **de courte durée** of brief duration, short-lived

dynamite [dinamit] f dynamite

E

eau [o] f water

échanger [eʃãʒe] to exchange

échantillon [eʃãtijõ] m sample

échapper [eʃape] to escape

écharpe [eʃaʀp] f scarf

éclairer [eklɛʀe] to enlighten
éclat [ekla] *m* brilliance
écœurer; s'écœurer [ekœʀe] to be sick at heart
école [ekɔl] *f* school
économie [ekɔnɔmi] *f* economy; économie politique economy
écouter [ekute] to listen
écrier: s'écrier [sekʀie] to cry out
écrire [ekʀiʀ] to write; ça s'écrit that is written, spelled
effet [efɛ] *m* effect; en effet indeed, in truth
efforcer: s'efforcer [sefɔʀse] to try hard
effroyable [efʀwajbl] frightful
égal, égale [egal] equal; ça m'est égal it's all the same to me
égaler [egale] to equal
église [egliz] *f* church
Égypte [eʒipt] *f* Egypt
Eiffel: tour Eiffel [tuʀefɛl] *f* tower 300 meters high (1000 ft. approx.) built in Paris in 1889
électrifié [elɛktrifje] electrified
élégant, élégante [elegã, elegãt] elegant
élevé [elve] high
elle [ɛl] she; her; herself
éloigné [elwaɲe] distant
emballage [ãbalaʒ] *m* packing
emballer [ãbale] pack
embarquer [ãbaʀke] to embark; to take on
emblème [ãblɛm] *m* emblem
emparer: s'emparer [sãpaʀe] to seize
empêcher [ãpeʃe] to prevent
emplette [ãplɛt] *f* purchase; faire des emplettes to go shopping
emploi [ãplwa] *m* use
employé [ãplwaje] *m* employee
employer [ãplwaje] to use, employ
empressé [ãpʀɛse]: Veuillez agréer mes salutations empressées Sincerely yours
en [ã] *prep* in, to; *adv* from there; *partitive* of them; il en a assez he

is fed up with it; il veut en finir he wants to be done with it; où en est-il? how far along is he?
enchanté [ãʃãte] delighted
enchère [ãʃɛʀ] *f* auction
encombré [ãkõbʀe] crowded
encore [ãkɔʀ] again; pas encore not yet
endormir [ãdɔʀmiʀ] to put to sleep; s'endormir to fall asleep
endroit [ãdʀwa] *m* place, locality
enfant [ãfã] *m* or *f* child
enfin [ãfɛ̃] finally
enfuir: s'enfuir [sãfɥiʀ] to flee
engrais [ãgʀɛ] *m* fertilizer
engraisser [ãgʀɛse] to put on weight
ennuyer [ãnɥije] to bore; s'ennuyer to be bored, very sad
énorme [enɔʀm] huge
énormément [enɔʀmemã] much, a great deal
enseigner [ãsɛɲe] to teach
ensemble [ãsãbl] together
ensuite [ãsɥit] afterwards, then
entendre [ãtãdʀ] to hear; entendre parler de to hear of; entendre dire que to hear that . . .
entendu [ãtãdy] agreed, all right; bien entendu of course
enthousiaste [ãtuzjast] enthusiastic
entier, entière [ãtje, ãtjɛʀ] entire, whole
entourer [ãtuʀe] to surround
entre [ãtʀ] between; entre eux among them; combien d'entre eux? how many of them?
entrée [ãtʀe] *f* entrance
entrer [ãtʀe] to go in
entretenu [ãtʀətəny] kept up
envie [ãvi] *f* desire
environ [ãviʀõ] about, approximately
envoi [ãvwa] *m* shipment
envoyer [ãvwaje] to send
épicerie [episʀi] *f* grocery store
époque [epɔk] *f* period
épouvantable [epuvãtabl] dreadful
équipe [ekip] *f* team, crew
erreur [ɛʀœʀ] *f* error

escalier [ɛskalje] m staircase
escorter [ɛskɔʀte] to escort
espèce [ɛspɛs] f kind
espérer [ɛspeʀe] to hope
esprit [ɛspʀi] m mind
essayer [esɛje] to try
essence [esãs] f gas; poste d'essence m filling station
essuie-glace [esɥiglas] m windshield-wiper
estampe [ɛstãp] f print
estimé [ɛstime] esteemed
estimer [ɛstime] to esteem
établir [etabliʀ] to establish, set up
établissement [etablismã] m establishment
étage [etaʒ] m story; à deux étages two stories high
état [eta] m state, condition
États-Unis [etazyni] m pl United States
éteindre [etɛ̃dʀ] to extinguish, put out
étendre [etãdʀ] to stretch; s'étendre to extend
étonnant, étonnante [etɔnã, etɔnãt] astonishing
étranger [etʀãʒe] m stranger
être [ɛtʀ] to be; être censé to be supposed to
étroit [etʀwa] narrow
étudiant [etydjã] m, étudiante [etydjãt] f student
étudier [etydje] to study
Europe [œʀɔp] f Europe
Européen, Européenne [œʀɔpeɛ̃, œʀɔpeɛn] European
eux [ø] they, them
évidemment [evidamã] evidently
exact, exacte [ɛgzakt] exactly true, correct
exactement [ɛgzaktəmã] exactly, precisely
examiner [ɛgzamine] to examine
excellent [ɛksɛlã] excellent
excursion [ɛkskyʀsjõ] f trip
excuse [ɛkskyz] f excuse
excuser [ɛkskyze] to excuse; s'excuser to apologize

exemple [ɛgzãpl] m example; par exemple for example
exercice [ɛgzɛʀsis] m exercise
exister [egziste] to exist
expédier [ɛkspedje] to ship
expédition [ɛkspedisjõ] f shipment
expérience [ɛkspeʀjãs] f experiment
explication [ɛksplikasjõ] f explanation
exploser [ɛksploze] to explode
expression [ɛkspʀɛsjõ] f expression
exquis [ɛkski] exquisite
extraordinaire [ɛkstʀ(a)ɔʀdinɛʀ] extraordinary

F

façade [fasad] f front, façade
face [fas] f face; face à face face to face
fâché [fɑʃe] angry, sorry, annoyed
facile [fasil] easy
facilement [fasilmã] easily
façon [fasõ] f way; une façon de parler a way of speaking; de façon à ce que so that
facture [faktyʀ] f bill
faïence [fajãs] f earthenware, pottery
faillir [fajiʀ] to fail; faillir and infinitive to . . . almost . . .
faim [fɛ̃] f hunger; mourir de faim to starve to death
faire [fɛʀ] to make, to do; faire signe to signal; il fait beau the weather is fine; si ça ne vous fait rien if it's all right with you; cela se fait that is done; faire voir to show; faire bien de to be right in; faire des vers to write poetry; qu'est-ce que ça fait? what difference does that make? cela ne fait rien it does not make any difference
falloir [falwaʀ] to be necessary; must; to require, to take (see par 36)
famille [famij] f family
fatiguer: se fatiguer [sə fatige] to get tired
faudra [fodʀa] future of falloir
fauteuil [fotœj] m arm-chair

favorable [favɔʀabl] favorable
fée [fe] *f* fairy
femme [fam] *f* woman, wife; **femme de chambre** *f* parlor-maid
fenêtre [fnɛtʀ] *f* window
fer [fɛʀ] *m* iron; **chemin de fer** *m* railroad; **fer forgé** wrought iron
fermer [fɛʀme] to close
fête [fɛt] *f* festivity, party
feu [fø] *m* fire
feuille [fœj] *f* leaf
février [fevʀie] February
fiancé, fiancée [fjãse] fiancé, fiancée
ficher: se ficher [fiʃe] to laugh at
fier, fière [fjɛʀ] proud
fièrement [fjɛʀmã] proudly
fil [fil] *m* wire; **coup de fil** telephone call
fille [fij] *f* girl, daughter; **jeune fille** girl
film [film] *m* film
fils [fis] *m* son
fin [fɛ̃] *f* end
finance [finãs] *f* finance
financier [finãsje] *m* financier; **financier, financière** [finãsjɛʀ] *adj* of or pertaining to finance
finir [finiʀ] to finish, to end; **il a fini par** he finally . . .; **le temps finira par s'arranger** the weather will eventually clear up
fixer [fikse] to fix, to stabilize; **fixer les prix** to fix prices
fleur [flœʀ] *f* flower
fleuve [flœv] *m* river
fois [fwa] *f* time; **une seule fois** a single time
fonctionnaire [fõksjɔnɛʀ] *m* government employee
fonctionner [fõksjɔne] to work
football [futbal] *m* football
forcer [fɔʀse] to force
forêt [fɔʀɛ] *f* forest
formalité [fɔʀmalite] *f* formality
forme [fɔʀm] *f* form
formule [fɔʀmyl] *f* formula
fort, forte [fɔʀ, fɔʀt] *adj* strong; **fort** *adv* very

fortifié [fɔʀtifje] fortified
fortune [fɔʀtyn] *f* fortune; **une grosse fortune** a considerable amount of money
fourchette [fuʀʃɛt] *f* fork
frais, fraîche [fʀɛ, fʀɛʃ] cool
frais [fʀɛ] *m* cost, expense; **frais d'envoi** cost of shipping
franc [fʀã] *m* franc, monetary unit of France
français [fʀãse] *m* French (language); **français, française** *adj* French; **Français, Française** a French person
franchement [fʀãʃmã] frankly
fréquenté [fʀekãte] frequented
fréquenter [fʀekãte] to keep company with
frère [fʀɛʀ] *m* brother
froid [fʀwa] cold
fruits [fʀɥi] *m pl* fruit
fumer [fyme] to smoke

G

gagner [gaɲe] to earn
galerie [galʀi] *f* gallery
gant [gã] *m* glove
garantir [gaʀãtiʀ] to guarantee
garçon [gaʀsõ] *m* boy
garder [gaʀde] to keep; **se garder de** to avoid
gare [gaʀ] *f* railroad station
gazeux [gazø] effervescent, bubbly
geler [ʒəle] to freeze
gendarme [ʒãdaʀm] *m* member of the national police
gêner [ʒɛne] to bother
Genève [ʒənɛv] Geneva
genou [ʒnu] *m* knee
genre [ʒãʀ] *m* kind, sort
gens [ʒã] *f pl* people; **des gens riches** rich people
gentil, gentille [ʒãti, ʒãtij] nice
gentiment [ʒãtimã] politely, kindly
Gien [ʒjɛ̃] small town in Loire valley
glissant [glisã] slippery

gothique [gɔtik] Gothic

gouvernement [guvɛʀnəmɑ̃] m government

gramme [gʀam] m gram

grand, grande [gʀɑ̃, gʀɑ̃d] tall, large

grand-chose [gʀɑ̃ʃoz]: pas grand-chose nothing much

grandi [gʀɑ̃di] grown

gras, grasse [gʀa] fat

gratte-ciel [gʀɑtsjɛl] m skyscraper

gratuit [gʀatɥi] free

gris [gʀi] grey

gros, grosse [gʀo, gʀos] large, big

grossir [gʀosiʀ] to enlarge, to swell

guère [gɛʀ] scarcely (used with ne)

guerre [gɛʀ] f war

guide [gid] m guide

H

habile [abil] skilful

habiller [abije] trans to dress (someone); s'habiller to dress (oneself)

habitable [abitabl] livable, inhabitable

habitant [abitɑ̃] m inhabitant

habiter [abite] to live, reside

habitude [abityd] f habit; d'habitude usually

habituer: s'habituer [sabitɥe] to get used to

*haine [ɛn] f hatred

*hardi, hardie [aʀdi] bold

*hardiment [aʀdimɑ̃] boldly

*hasard [azaʀ] m chance

*haut [o] high; en haut de to the top of; parler haut to speak in a loud voice; parler bas to speak in a low voice; La tour Eiffel a 300 mètres de haut The Eiffel Tower is 300 meters high

*hauteur [otœʀ] f height

*Havre: Le Havre [lə avʀ] m Havre

*hélas [elɑs] alas

hélicoptère [elikɔptɛʀ] m helicopter

hésiter [ezite] to hesitate

heure [œʀ] f hour; à l'heure on time;

de bonne heure early; à l'heure actuelle now

heureux, heureuse [øʀø, øʀøz] happy

hier [jɛʀ] yesterday

histoire [istwaʀ] f story, history

hiver [ivɛʀ] m winter

*Hollande [ɔlɑ̃d] f Holland

Homère [ɔmɛʀ] Homer

hommage [ɔmaʒ] m homage; Agréez mes hommages respectueux Sincerely yours

homme [ɔm] m man

honnête [ɔnɛt] honest, respectable

honorer [ɔnɔʀe] to honor

hôpital [ɔpital] m hospital

horreur [ɔʀoœʀ] f horror

horrible [ɔʀibl] horrible

humeur [ymœʀ] f humor; de bonne humeur in a good mood

I

ici [isi] here; now

idée [ide] f idea

ignorer [iɲɔʀe] to be unaware, not to know

il [il] he, it

île [il] f island; l'Ile d'Orléans island in the Saint Lawrence River

Iliade [iljad] f Iliad, Greek epic poem

imaginer: s'imaginer [simaʒine] to imagine

imparfait [ɛ̃paʀfɛ] m imperfect tense

impatience [ɛ̃pasjɑ̃s] f impatience

impératif [ɛ̃peʀatif] m imperative

imperméable [ɛ̃pɛʀmeabl] m raincoat

importance [ɛ̃pɔʀtɑ̃s] f importance

important [ɛ̃pɔʀtɑ̃] important

importer [ɛ̃pɔʀte] to be important; tout ce qui importe all that's important

imposé [ɛ̃poze] imposed, necessitated by

impossible [ɛ̃pɔsibl] impossible

impôt [ɛ̃po] m tax

impression [ɛ̃pʀɛsjɔ̃] f impression

impressionnant [ɛ̃pʀɛsjɔnɑ̃] impressive

impressionniste [ɛ̃pʀɛsjɔnist] *m* impressionist

inaccessible [inaksɛsibl] inaccessible

inattendu, inattendue [inatɑ̃dy] unexpected

inaugurer [inogyʀe] to open officially

incliner: s'incliner [sɛ̃kline] to list, to lean

inclus [ɛ̃kly] included; ci-inclus herewith

indésirable [ɛ̃deziʀabl] undesirable

indicatif [ɛ̃dikatif] *m* indicative

Indien [ɛ̃djɛ̃] *m* Indian

indiquer [ɛ̃dike] to indicate

indirect, indirecte [ɛ̃diʀɛkt] indirect; expression indirecte indirect discourse

indulgence [ɛ̃dylʒɑ̃s] *f* indulgence

industriel, industrielle [ɛ̃dystʀiɛl] industrial

inexploré [inɛksploʀe] unexplored

infinitif [ɛ̃finitif] *m* infinitive

ingénieur [ɛ̃ʒenjœʀ] *m* engineer; ingénieur-chimiste chemical engineer

ingrat [ɛ̃gʀa] ungrateful

inhospitalier, inhospitalière [inɔspitalje, inɔspitaljeʀ] inhospitable

inoubliable [inubliabl] unforgettable

inscription [ɛ̃skʀipsjɔ̃] *f* inscription, what is written

instant [ɛ̃stɑ̃] *m* moment

intelligent, intelligente [ɛ̃teliʒɑ̃, ɛ̃teliʒɑ̃t] intelligent

intention [ɛ̃tɑ̃sjɔ̃] *f* intention, meaning

intéressant, intéressante [ɛ̃teʀɛsɑ̃, ɛ̃teʀɛsɑ̃t] interesting, worthwhile

intéresser [ɛ̃teʀɛse] to interest; s'intéresser to be interested

intérêt [ɛ̃teʀɛ] *m* interest

intérieur [ɛ̃teʀjœʀ] *m* interior

interrogatif, interrogative [ɛ̃teʀɔgatif, ɛ̃teʀɔgativ] interrogative

intriguer [ɛ̃tʀige] to intrigue

intrus [ɛ̃tʀy] *m* intruder

inventer [ɛ̃vɑ̃te] to invent

invention [ɛ̃vɑ̃sjɔ̃] *f* invention

inverse [ɛ̃vɛʀs]: en sens inverse in the opposite direction

inversion [ɛ̃vɛʀsjɔ̃] *f* inversion, inverted order

invitation [ɛ̃vitasjɔ̃] *f* invitation

invité [ɛ̃vite] *m* guest

inviter [ɛ̃vite] to invite

Iraq [iʀak] Iraq

iris [iʀis] *m* iris

Israël [isʀaɛl] Israel

issue [isy] *f* issue

itinéraire [itineʀɛʀ] *m* itinerary

J

jamais [ʒamɛ] ever, never; ne . . . jamais never

janvier [ʒɑ̃vje] January

Japon [ʒapɔ̃] *m* Japan

jardin [ʒaʀdɛ̃] *m* garden

jardinier [ʒaʀdinje] *m* gardener

jeu [ʒø] *m* game; jeu de mots play on words

jeune [ʒœn] young; jeune fille girl

La Joconde [ʒɔkɔ̃d] *f Mona Lisa*

joindre [ʒwɛ̃dʀ] to join; joindre les deux bouts to make both ends meet

joli, jolie [ʒɔli] pretty

joliment [ʒɔlimɑ̃] very, quite

jouer [ʒwe] to play, to gamble; jouer au tennis to play tennis

joueur [ʒwœʀ] *m* player

jour [ʒuʀ] *m* day; de nos jours these days, in our time

journal [ʒuʀnal] *m* paper

journée [ʒuʀne] *f* day (duration)

juger [ʒyʒe] judge; juger bon (de) to see fit (to)

juif, juive [ʒɥif] Jew

juillet [ʒɥijɛ] July

juin [ʒɥɛ̃] June

jungle [ʒɔ̃gl] *f* jungle

jupe [ʒyp] *f* skirt

jus [ʒy] *m* juice

jusqu'à [ʒyska] until; as far as, to; jusqu'à ce que until

juste [ʒyst] just; **au juste** precisely, exactly

K

kilo [kilo] *m* kilogram, 1000 grams (2.2 pounds approximately)

kiosque [kjɔsk] *m* newspaper stand

L

là [la] there

la *see* **le**

laboratoire, labo [labɔʀatwaʀ] [labo] *m* laboratory

laine [lɛn] *f* wool

laisser [lɛse] to leave; to let

lait [lɛ] *m* milk

lancer [lɑ̃se] to throw

Laon [lɑ̃] city northeast of Paris

laquelle [lakɛl] *see* **lequel**

lard [laʀ] *m* bacon

large [laʀʒ] wide; **la rue a 20 mètres de large** the street is 20 meters wide

largeur [laʀʒœʀ] *f* width

laver [lave] to wash

le, la, les *art* the; *pron* him, her, it; them

légèrement [leʒɛʀmɑ̃] slightly

lendemain: (le) lendemain [lɑ̃dmɛ̃] *m* the next day, the day after

lequel, laquelle, lesquels, lesquelles [lǝkɛl, lakɛl, lekɛl, lekɛl] *rel pron* which; *interrog pron* which?

leur, leurs [lœʀ, lœʀ] their

lever [lǝve] to raise; **se lever** to get up; **le rideau se lève** the curtain goes up

liberté [libɛʀte] *f* liberty

libre [libʀ] free

lieu [ljø] *m* place; **avoir lieu** to take place; **au lieu de** instead of

ligne [liɲ] *f* line

limonade [limɔnad] *f* lemonade

lire [liʀ] to read

lit [li] *m* bed

litre [litʀ] *m* liter (9/10 of a quart, approximately)

livre [livʀ] *f* pound

livre [livʀ] *m* book

loin (de) [lwɛ̃ dǝ] far from

Loire [lwaʀ] *f* Loire river

Londres [lõdʀ] London

long, longue [lõ, lõg] long; **La Seine a 800 km de long** The Seine is 800 kilometers long; **le long des quais** along the quais

longtemps [lõtɑ̃] a long time, long

longueur [lõgœʀ] *f* length

lorsque [lɔʀskǝ] when

lot [lo] *m* lot

Louise de Savoie [lwizdǝsavwa] mother of François Ier

lourd [luʀ] heavy

Louvre [luvʀ] *m* former royal palace that now houses museums

lui [lɥi] he, himself; to him, to her; him

lundi [lœ̃di] *m* Monday

lune [lyn] *f* moon

luxe [lyks] *m* luxury

lycée [lise] *m* secondary school

Lyon [ljõ] Lyons

M

machine [maʃin] *f* machine

magasin [magazɛ̃] *m* store

magnifique [maɲifik] wonderful, magnificent

maigrir [mɛgʀiʀ] to lose weight

main [mɛ̃] *f* hand

maintenant [mɛ̃tnɑ̃] now

mais [mɛ] but; **mais oui** of course; **mais si** yes I do (*after negative*)

maison [mɛzõ] *f* house; **à la maison** at home; **maison de campagne** country house

maître [mɛtʀ] *m* master, teacher

mal [mal] *m* evil, pain; **avoir mal au cœur** to feel sick; *adv* badly; **pas mal** not bad; **pas mal de** quite a bit; **se faire mal** to hurt oneself, **de mal en pis** from bad to worse

malade [malad] sick

malgré [malgʀe] in spite of

malheur [malœʀ] *m* misfortune, unhappiness; **par malheur** unfortunately

malheureusement [maløʀøzmɑ̃] unfortunately

malheureux, malheureuse [maløʀø, maløʀøz] unhappy

malin [malɛ̃] clever; shrewd

maman [mamɑ̃] *f* mother

mandat-poste [mɑ̃dapɔst] *m* money order

manger [mɑ̃ʒe] to eat

manière [manjɛʀ] *f* manner; **de manière à** so as to

manquer (de) [mɑ̃ke] to fail, to miss; to be missing: **une assiette manque** one plate is missing; **j'ai manqué de tomber** I almost fell

manteau [mɑ̃to] *m* cloak, coat

marchandise [maʀʃɑ̃diz] *f* goods, freight

marche: se mettre en marche [səmɛtɑ̃maʀʃ] to start

marché [maʀʃe]: *m* **marché aux Puces** Flea Market

marcher [maʀʃe] to walk

mardi [maʀdi] Tuesday; **le mardi** on Tuesdays

mariage [maʀjaʒ] *m* marriage

marier [maʀje]: **se marier** to get married

mars [maʀs] March

Marseille [maʀsɛj] Marseilles

match [matʃ] *m* game (*sports*)

matériel [mateʀjɛl] *m* equipment

mathématicien [matematisjɛ̃] mathematician

matin [matɛ̃] *m* morning

matinée [matine] *f* forenoon

mauvais, mauvaise [mɔvɛ, mɔvɛz] bad, wrong; **sentir mauvais** to smell bad

me [mə] me, to or for me, myself

mécontent [mekɔ̃tɑ̃] discontent

mécontentement [mekɔ̃tɑ̃tmɑ̃] *m* annoyance

médecin [mɛtsɛ̃] *m* doctor

médecine [mɛtsin] *f* medicine

médicament [medikamɑ̃] *m* medicine

meilleur, meilleure [mɛjœʀ] better; **le meilleur** the best

membre [mɑ̃bʀə] *m* member

même [mɛm] *adj* same; *adv* even

menacer [mənase] to threaten

ménagère [menaʒɛʀ] *f* housewife

mener [məne] to lead

mer [mɛʀ] *f* sea

merveille [mɛʀvɛj] *f* a marvel; **à merveille** marvelously

métier [metje] *m* business, profession

mètre [mɛtʀ] *m* meter (39.36 inches)

métro [metʀo] *m* Paris subway

mettre [mɛtʀ] to put; **se mettre à** to begin; **se mettre en route** to start; **se mettre en marche** to start

meuble [mœbl] *m* a piece of furniture; **meubles** furniture, furnishings

meubler [mœble] to furnish

Mexique [mɛksik] *m* Mexico

midi noon; **le Midi** the South of France

mien, mienne [mjɛ̃, mjɛn] mine

mieux [mjø] *adv* better; **on ne peut mieux** extremely well; **de mieux en mieux** better and better

milieu [miljø] *m* middle

minéral [mineʀal] mineral; **l'eau minérale** mineral water

ministre [ministʀ] *m* cabinet member

minuit [minɥi] *m* midnight

minute [minyt] *f* minute

mis [mi] *p part of* **mettre**

mobile [mɔbil] mobile

mobilier [mɔbilje] *m* furnishings

mode [mɔd] *f* style; **à la mode de** in the style of

moderniser [mɔdɛʀnize] to modernize

moi [mwa] I, me

moindre [mwɛ̃dʀ] *adv* less; **le moindre** the least

moins [mwɛ̃] *adj* less; **le moins** the least; **à moins que** unless; **de moins en moins** less and less; **au moins** at least

mois [mwɑ] *m* month

moissonneuse-batteuse [mwasɔnøz-ba-tøz] *f* combine (harvester-thresher)

moment [mɔmɑ̃] *m* moment; **au moment de** at the time of; **au moment où** when; **un petit moment** a short time

mon, ma, mes [mɔ̃, ma, mɛ] my

monde [mɔ̃d] *m* world; **du monde** in the world (*after a superlative*)

monotone [mɔnɔtɔn] monotonous

monsieur [məsjø] *m* gentleman; sir, Mr.; **messieurs dames** ladies and gentlemen (informal)

montagne [mɔ̃taɲ] *f* mountain

monter [mɔ̃te] to go up; to get in (a car); to get on (a train, bus, ship, plane)

montre [mɔ̃tʀ] *f* watch

Montréal [mɔ̃real] Montreal

montrer |mɔ̃tʀe] to show

monument [mɔnymɑ̃] *m* monument

moquer: se moquer de [sə mɔke də] to kid, make fun of

moqueur, moqueuse [mɔkœʀ] ironical

mort, morte [mɔʀ, mɔʀt] *p part of* **mourir**

mot [mo] *m* word; **un mot** short letter

motocyclette [mɔtɔsiklɛt] *f* motorcycle

mourir [muʀiʀ] to die

mouton [mutɔ̃] *m* sheep

moyen [mwajɛ̃] *m* means

Moyen-Orient [mwajɛn-ɔʀjɑ̃] *m* Middle East

mur [myʀ] *m* wall

murmurer [myʀmyʀe] to murmur

musée [myze] *m* museum

musicien [myzisjɛ̃] *m* musician

musique [myzik] *f* music

N

nager [naʒe] to swim

nageur [naʒœʀ] *m* swimmer

naître [nɛtʀ] to be born

national, nationale [nasjɔnal] national

naturel [natyʀɛl] natural

naturellement [natyʀɛlmɑ̃] of course, obviously

ne: **ne . . . pas** not; **ne . . . plus** no longer; **ne . . . guère** scarcely; **ne . . . jamais** never; **ne . . . que** only; **ne . . . rien** nothing; **ne . . . personne** nobody; **ne . . . ni . . . ni** neither . . . nor

né [ne] *p part of* **naître**

néanmoins [neɑ̃mwɛ̃] nevertheless

nécessaire [neseseʀ] necessary

négatif, négative [negatif, negativ] negative

négativement [negativmɑ̃] in the negative

neige [nɛʒ] *f* snow

neiger [nɛʒe] to snow

netteté [nɛtte] *f* clarity

nettoyer [nɛtwaje] to clean up

neuf [nœf] nine

nez [ne] *m* nose

nid [ni] *m* nest

Noël [nɔɛl] Christmas

nœud [nø] *m* knot

nom [nɔ̃] *m* name; noun

nombre [nɔ̃bʀ] *m* number

nombreux, nombreuse [nɔ̃bʀø, nɔ̃bʀøz] numerous

non [nɔ̃] no

notre, nos [nɔtʀ, no] *adj* our; **le nôtre** [notʀ] *poss pron* ours

Notre-Dame de Paris [nɔtʀədam də paʀi] cathedral built in 12th and 13th centuries on the Île de la Cité

nous [nu] we; us, ourselves; to or for us

nouveau, nouvel, nouvelle [nuvo, nuvɛl, nuvɛl] new; **de nouveau** again

La Nouvelle-Orléans [lanuvɛlɔʀleɑ̃] *f* New Orleans

nouvelles [nuvɛl] *f pl* news

noyer: se noyer [sə nwaje] to be drowned

nu [ny] naked

nuage [nɥaʒ] *m* cloud

nuageux [nɥaʒø] cloudy
nucléaire [nykleɛʀ] nuclear
nuit [nɥi] f night
numéro [nymeʀo] m number

O

obéir [ɔbeiʀ] to obey
objet [ɔbʒe] m object; purpose
obliger [ɔbliʒe] to oblige
obscurité [ɔbskyʀite] f obscurity
occasion [ɔkazjõ] f occasion; bargain
occuper [ɔkype] to occupy; s'occuper
    de to take care of
octobre [ɔktɔbʀ] October
œil [œj] m eye
œuf [œf] m egg
œuvre [œvʀ] f work
offrir [ɔfʀiʀ] to give, to offer; s'offrir
    to afford, to buy
olive [ɔliv] f olive
ombrelle [õbʀɛl] f parasol
omnibus [ɔmnibys] m bus
on, l'on [õ, lõ] one, you, we, they,
    someone, people
onze [õz] eleven
opérer [ɔpeʀe] to operate (on)
opinion [ɔpinjõ] f opinion
or [ɔʀ] m gold
ordinaire [ɔʀdinɛʀ] ordinary; d'or-
    dinaire ordinarily
ordinateur [ɔʀdinatœʀ] m computer
ordre [ɔʀdʀ] m order; donner l'ordre
    to give orders
Orléans [ɔʀleã] city on the Loire river
orné [ɔʀne] ornamented, decorated
orner [ɔʀne] to adorn, decorate
orthographe [ɔʀtɔgʀaf] f spelling
oser [oze] to dare
où [u] where, when, in which
oublier (de) [ublie də] to forget
ouest [wɛst] m west
outil [uti] m tool
ouvert, ouverte [uvɛʀ, uvɛʀt] open; à
    bras ouverts with open arms
ouvrir [uvʀiʀ] to open

P

paiement [pɛmã] m payment
pain [pɛ̃] m bread; loaf; loaf of bread
paire [pɛʀ] f pair
palais [pale] m palace
panne [pan] f breakdown
panneau [pano] m panel
papiers [papje] m papers
par [paʀ] by; par une phrase com-
    plète with a complete sentence
paradis [paʀadi] m paradise
paraître [paʀɛtʀ] to appear; paraît-il
    it seems
parapluie [paʀaplɥi] m umbrella
parc [paʀk] m park
parce que [paʀskə] because
parcourir [paʀkuʀiʀ] to go through
pardon [paʀdõ] m pardon
pare-brise [paʀbʀiz] m windshield
parent [paʀã] m parent, relative
parfois [paʀfwa] sometimes
parisien, parisienne [paʀizjɛ̃, paʀizjɛn]
    Parisian
parler [paʀle] to speak, talk; parler
    bas to speak in a low voice; parler
    haut to speak in a loud voice
parmi [paʀmi] among
parole [paʀɔl] f word
part [paʀ] f part; de ma part as for me;
    à part le pétrole aside from the
    oil
participe [paʀtisip] m participle; par-
    ticipe passé past participle; par-
    ticipe présent present participle
particulier [paʀtikylje] m a (private)
    person, an individual
particulièrement [paʀtikyljɛʀmã] in
    particular; specially
partie [paʀti] f part; faire partie de to
    be a part of, belong to; faire une
    partie de bridge to play bridge
partir [paʀtiʀ] to leave, set out
partitif [paʀtitif] m partitive
partout [paʀtu] everywhere
parvenir à [paʀvəniʀ a] to succeed in
pas: ne . . . pas not

passage [pasaӡ] *m* passage; **de passage à** passing through, temporarily in

passager [pasaӡe] *m* passenger

passé [pɑse] *m* past; **passé composé** compound past tense

passeport [paspɔʀ] *m* passport

passer [pɑse] to pass, to hand; to spend (time); **se passer** to happen; **passer par** to go through

passionnant [pasjɔnɑ̃] very interesting

patiemment [pasjamɑ̃] patiently

patience [pasjɑ̃s] *f* patience

patient, patiente [pasjɑ̃, pasjɑ̃t] patient

pauvre [povʀ] poor; unfortunate

pavé [pave] paved

pavillon [pavijɔ̃] *m* lodge; **pavillon de chasse** hunting lodge

payant [pɛjɑ̃] for pay

payer [pɛje] to pay

pays [pɛi] *m* country

paysage [pɛizaӡ] *m* landscape

peau [po] *f* skin

peindre [pɛ̃dʀ] to paint

peine [pɛn] *f* trouble, misery, sorrow; **à peine** scarcely; **j'ai peine à** I find it hard to; **ce n'est pas la peine** it isn't worth the trouble

peintre [pɛ̃tʀə] *m* painter

peinture [pɛ̃tyʀ] *f* painting

pendant [pɑ̃dɑ̃] during; **pendant . . . que** while

pensée [pɑ̃se] *f* thought

penser [pɑ̃se] to think; **je pense à Marie** I am thinking of Marie; **penser de** to hold an opinion about; **que pensez-vous d'elle?** what do you think of her?; **penser** *with infinitive* to expect to

pension [pɑ̃sjɔ̃] *f* room and board; boardinghouse

perdre [pɛʀdʀ] to lose, to waste

perdu [pɛʀdy] far away

permettre [pɛʀmɛtʀ] to permit, make possible; **se permettre de** to take the liberty of

permis [pɛʀmi] *m* permit; **permis de conduire** driver's license

péril [peʀil] *m* danger

Pérou [peʀu] *m* Peru

persistant [pɛʀsistɑ̃] persistent

personnage [pɛʀsɔnaӡ] *m* personage

personne [pɛʀsɔn] *f* person

personnellement [pɛʀsɔnɛlmɑ̃] personally

perte [pɛʀt] *f* loss

peser [pəze] to weigh

petit, petite [pəti, pətit] little, small

pétrole [petʀɔl] *m* oil

peu [pø] *m* little; **Dites-nous un peu** Just tell us; **peu à peu** little by little; **c'est peu de chose** it is practically nothing; **à peu près** about; **sous peu** soon; **tant soit peu** slightly

peur [pœʀ] *f* fear; **avoir peur** to be afraid; **de peur de** for fear of

peut-être [pøtɛtʀ] perhaps, maybe

phare [faʀ] *m* headlight

pharmacie [faʀmasi] *f* drug store

photo [fɔto] *f* photograph

photographique [fɔtɔgʀafik]: **appareil photographique** *m* camera

physique [fizik] *f* physics

pianiste [pjanist] *m* or *f* pianist

piano [pjano] *m* piano

pièce [pjɛs] *f* piece; play

pied [pje] *m* foot; **aller à pied** to walk

pilote [pilɔt] *m* pilot

pipe [pip] *f* pipe

pire [piʀ] worse (*adj*); **le pire** the worst

pis [pi] worse (*adv*); **de mal en pis** worse and worse, from bad to worse

placard [plakaʀ] *m* cupboard

place [plas] *f* place; seat; room; passage; **à votre place** if I were in your place; **de la place** room; **à la place des chevaux** instead of horses; **Place de l'Opéra** large square in front of the Paris Opera

plaindre [plɛ̃dʀ] to pity; **se plaindre** to complain

plaire (à) [plɛʀ a] to please; **s'il vous plaît** please (if it is pleasing to you)

plaisir [plɛziʀ] *m* pleasure
plan [plɑ̃] *m* plan; map
planter [plɑ̃te] to plant
plat [pla] *m* dish
plateau [plato] *m* tray
pleurer [plœʀe] to cry, to weep
pleuvoir [plœvwaʀ] to rain; **il pleut
à verse** it is pouring
pli [pli] *m* fold
plu [ply] *p part of* **pleuvoir**
plu [ply] *p part of* **plaire**
pluie [plɥi] *f* rain
plupart: (la) plupart [plypaʀ] *f* most
of; **la plupart des gens** most
people
plus [ply] more; **plus . . . que** more
than; **plus . . . plus** the more . . .
the more; **plus . . . moins** the
more . . . the less; **tout au plus** at
most
plusieurs [plyzjœʀ] several
plût [ply] *imperf subj of* **plaire; plût au
ciel** would to heaven
plutôt [plyto] rather
pluvieux [plyvjø] rainy
pneu [pnø] *m* tire
poème [pɔɛm] *m* poem
poésie [pɔezi] *f* poetry
poète [pɔɛt] *m* poet
poignée [pwaɲe] *f* handful; **poignée de
main** handshake
point [pwɛ̃] *m* point; **au point de vue**
from the point of view
poire [pwaʀ] *f* pear
poison [pwazõ] *m* poison
poisson [pwasõ] *m* fish
police [pɔlis] *f* police; **agent de police**
policeman; **police d'assurance** insurance policy
policier [pɔlisje]; **roman policier** *m*
detective story
politique [pɔlitik] political
pomme [pɔm] *f* apple
pompier [põpje] *m* fireman
pont [põ] *m* bridge
population [pɔpylasjõ] *f* population
porc [pɔʀ] *m* pork

porc-épic [pɔʀkepik] *m* porcupine
port [pɔʀ] *m* postage, shipping charges;
port
porte [pɔʀt] *f* door
portefeuille [pɔʀtəfœj] *m* wallet
porter [pɔʀte] to wear; to carry
portière [pɔʀtjɛʀ] *f* door (of car or
train)
portrait [pɔʀtʀɛ] *m* portrait
poser [poze] to put; to ask (a question)
posséder [posede] to possess
possessif, possessive [posɛsif, posɛsiv]
possessive
poste [pɔst] *f* post office; **poste d'essence** *m* filling station
pot [po] *m* pot
poteau indicateur [potoɛ̃dikatœʀ] *m*
signpost
pour [puʀ] to, in order to; for; **pour
que** so that
pourquoi [puʀkwa] why
poursuivre [puʀsɥivʀ] to pursue, to
trail; **se poursuivre** to be carried
on
pourtant [puʀtɑ̃] however
pousser [puse] to grow
pouvoir [puvwaʀ] to be able, can;
cela se peut that is possible;
pouvoir *m* power
précéder [pʀesede] to precede
précis [pʀesi] precise; **à huit heures
précises** at exactly eight o'clock
précisément [pʀesizemɑ̃] exactly
préférer [pʀefeʀe] to prefer, to like
better
premier, première [pʀəmje, pʀəmjɛʀ]
first
prendre [pʀɑ̃dʀ] to take; **prendre le
thé** to have tea; **prendre fin** to end
préoccupation [pʀeɔkypasjõ] *f* pre-
occupation
préposition [pʀepozisjõ] *f* preposition
près (de) [pʀɛ də] near; **de très près**
very closely; **à peu près** about
présence [pʀezɑ̃s] *f* presence
présent [pʀezɑ̃] *m* present; present
tense

présenter [pʀezɑ̃te]′ to introduce; **se présenter** to introduce oneself

presque [pʀɛsk] almost

presser [pʀɛse] to press

prêt, prête [pʀɛ, pʀɛt] ready

prêter [pʀɛte] to lend; to attribute

prévenir [pʀevniʀ] to warn

prier (de) [pʀie də] to beg, request

prière [pʀiɛʀ] f prayer, request

pris [pʀi] p part of **prendre**

prise [pʀiz] f the capture, fall; **la prise de Troie** the fall of Troy

prison [pʀizõ] f prison

prix [pʀi] m price; prize

probable [pʀɔbabl] probable

probablement [pʀɔbabləmɑ̃] probably

problème [pʀɔblɛm] m problem

prochain, prochaine [pʀɔʃɛ̃, pʀɔʃɛn] next

proche [pʀɔʃ] adj near

procurer: se procurer [səpʀɔkyʀe] to get, procure

production [pʀɔdyksjõ] f production

produire [pʀɔdɥiʀ] to produce

produit [pʀɔdɥi] m product

professeur [pʀɔfɛsœʀ] m teacher, professor

profiter (de) [pʀɔfite də] to take advantage of

progrès [pʀɔgʀɛ] m progress

projet [pʀɔʒɛ] m project, plan

promenade [pʀɔmnad] f walk; **faire une promenade** to take a walk

promener: se promener [pʀɔmne] to take a walk

promettre (de) [pʀɔmɛtʀə də] to promise

pronom [pʀɔnõ] m pronoun

pronominal: verbes pronominaux [vɛʀb pʀɔnɔmino] reflexive verbs

prononcer [pʀɔnõse] to pronounce

prononciation [pʀɔnõsjasjõ] f pronunciation

propos [pʀɔpo] **à propos de** in connection with

proposer [pʀɔpoze] to propose, to suggest

propre [pʀɔpʀ] proper, clean; **les noms propres** proper names

propriétaire [pʀɔpʀietɛʀ] m owner

propriété [pʀɔpʀiete] f property, estate

prospecteur [pʀɔspɛktœʀ] m prospector

prospection [pʀɔspɛksjõ] f prospecting

prospérité [pʀɔspeʀite] f prosperity

protestant [pʀɔtɛstɑ̃] Protestant

provenir (de) [pʀɔvniʀ də] to come from

prudemment [pʀydamɑ̃] prudently, carefully

prudent, prudente [pʀydɑ̃, pʀydɑ̃t] prudent, careful

pu [py] p part of **pouvoir**

public [pyblik] m the public

puis [pɥi] then, afterwards

puits [pɥi] m well

pull-over [pylovɛʀ] m pullover

Q

quai [ke] m wharf

qualité [kalite] f quality

quantité [kɑ̃tite] f quantity; **des quantités** lots

quarante [kaʀɑ̃t] forty

quart [kaʀ] m quarter

quartier [kaʀtje] m quarter, part of a city

que [kə] rel pron whom, which; interrog pron what?; conjunction that

Québec [kebɛk] city in Canada

quel, quelle, quels, quelles [kɛl] what?

quelque(s) [kɛlkə] some; **quelque temps** a little time

quelquefois [kɛlkəfwa] sometimes

quelqu'un, quelques-uns [kɛlkœ̃, kɛlkəzœ̃] someone, some

question [kɛstjõ] f question

queue [kø] f tail; **faire la queue** to stand in line

qui [ki] rel pron who, which; interrog pron who? whom?

Quimper [kɛ̃pɛʀ] city in Brittany; well-known make of pottery

quinzaine [kɛ̃zɛn] *f* about fifteen; **une quinzaine** two weeks

quinze [kɛ̃z] fifteen

quitter [kite] to leave

quoi [kwa] what; **de quoi** the means, the wherewithal; **il n'y a pas de quoi** don't mention it; you are welcome

quoi que [kwakə] whatever

quoique [kwakə] although

R

raconter [rakɔ̃te] to tell, relate

raison [rɛzɔ̃] *f* reason

raisonnable [rɛzɔnabl] reasonable

ralentir [ralɑ̃tir] to slow down

rappeler [raple] to call back; **se rappeler** to recall, remember; **rappelez-moi au bon souvenir de** remember me to

rapport [rapɔr] *m* term paper; report

rapporter [rapɔrte] to bring in

rare [rar] rare

rarement [rarmɑ̃] seldom

rat [ra] *m* rat

ravi [ravi] delighted

ravissant [ravisɑ̃] entrancing

récent [resɑ̃] recent

recevoir [rəsəvwar] to receive; to have guests

réciter [resite] to recite

réclame [reklam] *f* advertising

réclamer [reklame] to ask for

récolte [rekɔlt] *f* crop, harvest

récolter [rekɔlte] to harvest, to produce

récompenser [rekɔ̃pɑ̃se] to reward

reconduire [rəkɔ̃dɥir] to take (a person) back (home)

reconnaître [rəkɔnɛtr] to recognize

reculer [rəkyle] to back off, to go backwards, to withdraw

redescendre [rədesɑ̃dr] to go back down

réfléchir [refleʃir] to think, to reflect

réfrigérateur [refriʒeratœr] *m* refrigerator

refuser (de) [rəfyzedə] to refuse to

regagner [rəgaɲe] to go back to

regarder [rəgarde] to look at

région [reʒjɔ̃] *f* region

règle [rɛgl] *f* rule; **en règle** in order

regretter (de) [rəgrɛte] to be sorry, to regret

Reims [rɛ̃s] Rheims, city northeast of Paris

reine [rɛn] *f* queen

rejoindre [rəʒwɛ̃dr] to meet, join, catch up with

relatif [rəlatif] relative

relation [rəlasjɔ̃] *f* relation

reliquat [rəlika] *m* balance, remainder

remarquer [rəmarke] to notice

remercier (de) [rəmɛrsje də] to thank (for)

remettre [rəmɛtr] to deliver; to put back; **remettre en liberté** to set free; **se remettre** to recover, to start again; **se remettre en route** to start on one's way again

remonter [rəmɔ̃te] to go back up

remplacer [rɑ̃plase] to replace; **en remplaçant** replacing

remuer [rəmɥe] to stir

Rennes [rɛn] city in Brittany

Renaissance [rənɛsɑ̃s] *f* Renaissance (French Renaissance was late 15th century and 16th century)

rencontre [rɑ̃kɔ̃tr] *f* chance meeting

rencontrer [rɑ̃kɔ̃tre] to meet

rendez-vous [rɑ̃devu] *m* engagement

rendre [rɑ̃dr] to give back; **se rendre compte** to realize; **se rendre à** to go to

Renoir [rənwar] French Impressionist painter (1841-1919)

renoncer (à) [rənɔ̃se a] to give up

renseignement(s) [rɑ̃sɛɲmɑ̃] *m* information

renseigner [rɑ̃sɛɲe] to inform

renvoyer [rɑ̃vwaje] to send back

réparer [repare] to repair

reparler [rəparle] to talk over

repartir [rəpartir] to set out again

repas [Rəpɑ] *m* meal
répéter [Repete] to repeat
répondre (à) [RepõdRa] to answer
réponse [Repõs] *f* answer; **en réponse** in answer
repos [Rəpo] *m* rest
reposer: se reposer [səRpoze] to rest
représentation [RəpRezɑ̃tasjõ] *f* show, performance
réputation [Repytasjõ] *f* reputation
résidence [Rezidɑ̃s] *f* residence; **résidence habituelle** usual dwelling
résolu [Rezɔly] *p part of* résoudre
résoudre [RezudR] to solve
respecter [Respɛkte] to respect
respectueux, respectueuse [Respɛktɥø, Respɛktɥøz] respectful
responsabilité [Respõsabilite] *f* responsibility
ressembler (à) [Rəsɑ̃ble] to resemble, to look like
ressortir [RəsɔRtiR] to go out again
reste [Rɛst] *m* remainder, rest
rester [Rɛste] to stay; to remain; to be left
résultat [Rezylta] *m* result
retard [RətaR] *m* lateness; **en retard** late
retenir [RətniR] to engage, reserve
retomber [Rətõbe] to fall again
retour [RətuR] *m* return; **de retour** back
retourner [RətuRne] to go back
retrouver [RətRuve] to meet, meet again; **se retrouver** to meet
réussir à [ReysiRa] to succeed in
réveil [Revɛj] *m* alarm clock
réveillé [Reveje] awake
réveiller [Reveje] to waken (someone); **se réveiller** to wake up, waken
revenir [RəvniR] to come back
revoir [RəvwaR] to see again; **au revoir** good-bye, I'll be seeing you
Révolution [Revɔlysjõ] *f* the French Revolution (began in 1789)
revue [Rəvy] *f* review
rhume [Rym] *m* a cold

riche [Riʃ] rich
rideau [Rido] *m* curtain
rien [Rjɛ̃] nothing; **ne . . . rien** nothing; **rien du tout** nothing at all
rigoureux, rigoureuse [RiguRø, RiguRøz] severe
rimer [Rime] to rhyme
rire [RiR] to laugh
risquer (de) [Riske də] to risk
rive [Riv] *f* bank (of river)
rivière [RivjɛR] *f* river
riz [Ri] *m* rice
robe [Rɔb] *f* dress
roi [Rwa] *m* king
roman [Rɔmɑ̃] *m* novel
Romorantin [Rɔmɔrɑ̃tɛ̃] town southeast of Blois
rosbif [Rɔsbif) *m* roast beef
route [Rut] *f* road; **se mettre en route** to start out; **tenir la route** to stay on the road
rue [Ry] *f* street
ruiner [Rɥine] to ruin (financially), to bankrupt
Russie [Rysi] *f* Russia

S

sage [saʒ] well-behaved, orderly, wise
sagement [saʒmɑ̃] sensibly, quietly
sain [sɛ̃]: **sain et sauf** safe and sound
Saint-Cloud [sɛ̃klu] suburb on west side of Paris
Saint-Germain-des-Prés [sɛ̃ʒɛRmɛ̃ dePRe] popular part of the Left Bank in Paris
saison [sɛzõ] *f* season
salamandre [salamɑ̃dR] *f* salamander
salle [sal] *f* lecture room, exhibition room; **salle de bain** bathroom
salon [salõ] *m* living room
salutation [salytasjõ] *f* greeting; **Veuillez agréer mes salutations empressées** Sincerely yours
samedi [samdi] Saturday; **le samedi** on Saturdays

santé [sɑ̃te] *f* health

la Saône [lason] river flowing into the Rhône at Lyons

sauf [sɔf] except, excepting; **sain et sauf** safe and sound

sauter [sote] to jump

savamment [savamɑ̃] learnedly

savant, savante [savɑ̃, savɑ̃t] learned

savoir [savwaʀ] to know, know how (*see par 40*); **faire savoir** to inform; **je n'en sais rien** I have no idea

scène [sɛn] *f* scene

sculpture [skyltyʀ] *f* sculpture

se [sə] himself, herself, oneself, itself, themselves; to or for himself, etc.

seau [so] *m* pail

sécheresse [seʃʀɛs] *f* drought

second, seconde [səgõ, səgõd] second

secret, secrète [səkʀɛ, səkʀɛt] secret

secrétaire [səkʀetɛʀ] *m* secretary

Seine [sɛn] *f* Seine river

séjour [seʒuʀ] *m* stay, sojourn

selon [səlõ] according to

semaine [səmɛn] *f* week

sembler [sɑ̃ble] to seem

semence [səmɑ̃s] *f* seed

sénateur [senatœʀ] *m* senator

sens [sɑ̃s] *m* direction; sense; **sens unique** one-way (street)

sentiment [sɑ̃timɑ̃] *m* feeling

sentir [sɑ̃tiʀ] to smell; **sentir bon** to smell good; **se sentir** to feel

septembre [sɛptɑ̃bʀ] September

sergent de ville [sɛʀʒɑ̃dvil] *m* city policeman

sérieusement [seʀjøzmɑ̃] seriously

sérieux, sérieuse [seʀjø, seʀjøz] serious; **soyez sérieux** don't be silly

service [sɛʀvis] *m* service; **service de table** a set of dishes

servir [sɛʀviʀ] to serve; **servir de** to be used as; **servir à** to serve as; **ça ne sert à rien** that's useless; **se servir de** to use; **en vous servant de** using

serviteur [sɛʀvitœʀ] *m* servant

ses [sɛ] *see* **son**

seul, seule [sœl] alone; **une seule fois** a single time

seulement [sœlmɑ̃] only; just

si [si] if; *with imperf* what if; **si grand** so tall; **mais si** oh yes (*denying a negative*)

siècle [sjɛkl] *m* century; **au vingtième siècle** in the 20th century

sien, sienne [sjɛ̃, sjɛn] *poss pron* his, her, its

sieste [sjɛst] *f* siesta, afternoon nap

signe [siɲ]: **faire signe** to signal

signifier [siɲifje] to mean

simple [sɛ̃pl] simple

situation [situasjõ] *f* situation

sixième [sizjɛm] sixth

ski [ski] *m* ski

société [sɔsjete] *f* corporation; society

sœur [sœʀ] *f* sister

soi [swa] oneself

soif [swaf] *f* thirst; **avoir soif** to be thirsty

soir [swaʀ] *m* evening

soirée [swaʀe] *f* evening (duration)

soixantaine [swasɑ̃tɛn] *f* about sixty

soixante-dix [swasɑ̃tdis] seventy

soleil [sɔlɛj] *m* sun

sombre [sõbʀə] dark

somme [sɔm] *f* sum

son, sa, ses [sõ, sa, sɛ] his, her, its, one's

sonner [sɔne] to ring

sonnette [sɔnɛt] *f* bell

sort [sɔʀ] *m* fate

sorte [sɔʀt] *f* kind; **toute sorte de** all sorts of

sortie [sɔʀti] *f* exit; **à la sortie** as (he) left

sortir [sɔʀtiʀ] to go out; *trans* to take out

sot [so] silly; stupid

souci [susi] *m* care

soucoupe [sukup] *f* saucer

Soudan [sudɑ̃] *m* country in Africa

souffrir [sufʀiʀ] to suffer

souhait [swɛ] *m* wish

souhaiter [swɛte] to wish

souligné [suliɲe] underlined
sourire [suRiR] *m* smile
sourire [suRiR] to smile
sous [su] under; **sous peu** soon
souvenir [suvniR] *m* memory: **rappelez-moi au souvenir de** remember me to
souvenir: se souvenir de [sə suvniR də] to remember
souvent [suvã] often
soyez [swaje] *imperative of* **être**
sport [spɔR] *m* sport
sportif, sportive [spɔRtif, spɔRtiv] pertaining to sports, athletic
stade [stad] *m* stadium
Stendhal [stɛ̃dal] 19th century French novelist
style [stil] *m* style
succéder à [syksɛdea] to follow, to succeed
sucre [sykR] *m* sugar
Suède [syɛd] *f* Sweden
suffire [syfiR] to suffice, to be sufficient; **il suffit de** it is enough to
suggérer [sugʒeRe] to suggest
Suisse [syis] *f* Switzerland
suite: tout de suite [tudsyit] immediately
suivant, suivante [syivã, syivãt] following
suivre [syivR] to follow
sujet [syʒɛ] *m* subject; **au sujet de** about
superlatif, superlative [sypɛRlatif-iv] superlative
sur [syR] on, over
sûr [syR] sure; **bien sûr** certainly
sûrement [syRmã] surely
surpeuplé [syRpøple] overcrowded
surprendre [syRpRãdR] to surprise
surpris [syRpRi] *p part of* **surprendre**
surprise [syRpRiz] *f* surprise
surréalisme [syRRealism] *m* surrealism
surtout [syRtu] especially
survoler [syRvɔle] to fly over
sympathique [sɛ̃patik] congenial, likeable

T

table [tabl] *f* table; **à table** at the table
tableau [tablo] *m* picture
tâcher (de) [taʃe] to try to
taille [taj] *f* size
taire: se taire [sətɛR] to remain silent
tant [tã] so much; **tant que** as long as
tapisserie [tapisRi] *f* tapestry
tard [taR] late; **un peu plus tard** a little later
tas [tɑ] *m* pile; **un tas de choses** lots of things
tasse [tas] *f* cup
taxi [taksi] *m* taxi
te [tə] you, yourself, to you, for you
tel, telle [tɛl] such
Tel-Aviv [tɛlaviv] Tel Aviv
télégramme [telegRam] *m* telegram
téléphoner [telefɔne] to telephone
télévision [televizjɔ̃] *f* TV
tellement [tɛlmã] so much
température [tãpeRatyR] *f* temperature
temps [tã] *m* time; weather
tenir [təniR] to hold; **en tenant compte** bearing in mind, taking into account; **tenir à** to insist upon
terminer: se terminer [sətɛRmine) to end
terre [tɛR] *f* earth; **par terre** on the ground
terrestre [tɛRɛstRə] earthly
terrible [tɛRiblə] terrible
thé [te] *m* tea
théâtre [teatR] *m* theater
tiens! [tjɛ̃] (*imperative of* **tenir**) well!
tiers [tjɛR] *m* third
timbale [tɛ̃bal] *f* cup (of metal)
timbre [tɛ̃bR] *m* stamp
tirer [tiRe] to pull; **se tirer d'affaire** to get along
tiroir [tiRwaR] *m* drawer
toi [twa] you, yourself
toit [twa] *m* roof
tomber [tɔ̃be] to fall, to fall down
ton, ta, tes [tɔ̃, ta, tɛ] your

tort [tɔʀ] *m* wrong; **il a tort** he is wrong

tôt [to] soon

toujours [tuʒuʀ] always, still

tour [tuʀ] *f* tower

Touraine [tuʀɛn] *f* region around Tours

tourisme [tuʀism] *m* tourism

touriste [tuʀist] *m* tourist

tout, toute, tous, toutes [tu, tut, tu, tut] *adj and pron* all; **tout le temps** all the time; **toute l'année** all year; **tous les jours** every day; **tous** [tus] *pron* all; **tout** *adv;* **tout au plus** at most; **tout en faisant des compliments** while paying compliments; **tout à l'heure** a while ago, in a little while *(depending on the tense of the verb)*; **tout à coup** suddenly

toutefois [tutfwa] however

tracteur [tʀaktœʀ] *m* tractor

trahison [tʀaizɔ̃] *f* betrayal, foul play

train [tʀɛ̃] *m* train; **en train de** in the act of

traiter [tʀɛte] to treat

tranquille [tʀɑ̃kil] calm

transport [tʀɑ̃spɔʀ] *m* transportation

transporter [tʀɑ̃spɔʀte] to transport, carry

travail [tʀavaj], **travaux** *m* work

travailler [tʀavaje] to work

travers: à travers [atʀavɛʀ] through

traverser [tʀavɛʀse] to cross

trentaine [tʀɑ̃tɛn] *f* about thirty

trente [tʀɑ̃t] thirty

très [tʀɛ] very

triste [tʀist] sad

troisième [tʀwazjɛm] third

tromper [tʀɔ̃pe] to deceive; **se tromper** to be mistaken; **se tromper de route** to miss the road

trop [tʀɔ] *or* [tʀo] too; **trop de mal** too much evil, too many bad things

troupeau [tʀupo] *m* flock

trouver [tʀuve] to find; **comment trouve-t-il le dîner?** how does he like the dinner?; **il le trouve ex-** cellent he thinks it is excellent; **se trouver** to be

T.S.F. [te ɛs ɛf] **(télégraphie sans fil)** *f* radio

tuer [tɥe] to kill; **se tuer** to kill oneself

Tuileries, les [tɥilʀi] Parisian park

Tunisie [tynizi] *f* Tunisia

U

un, une [œ̃, yn] a; one; **l'un, l'une, les uns, les unes** the one(s); **l'un et l'autre** both; **ni l'un ni l'autre** neither

uniforme [ynifɔʀm] *m* uniform

unique [ynik]: **sens unique** one-way (street)

urbain [yʀbɛ̃] urban

urgent [yʀʒɑ̃] urgent

usine [yzin] *f* factory, manufacturing company

utile [ytil] useful

V

vacances [vakɑ̃s] *f pl* vacation

vaincre [vɛ̃kʀ] to conquer, to vanquish

vais [vɛ] *pres tense of* **aller**

valoir [valwaʀ] to be worth; **il vaut mieux** it is better; **il vaut autant** it is just as well; **il vaudrait mieux** it would be better

vanter [vɑ̃te]: **se vanter** to boast

vase [vaz] *m* vase

vaste [vast] large

vaut [vo] *pres ind of* **valoir**

végétation [veʒetasjɔ̃] *f* vegetation

veille [vɛj] *f* the day before

venant [vənɑ̃] *pres part of* **venir**

vendeur [vɑ̃dœʀ] *m* seller

vendre [vɑ̃dʀ] to sell; **se vendre bien** to sell well; **on a vendu après décès** they sold after the death of the owner

Vénézuéla [venezɥela] *m* Venezuela

vénézuélien, vénézuélienne [venezɥeljɛ̃, venezɥeljɛn] of Venezuela

venger [vɑ̃ʒe]: **se venger** to get revenge

venir [vəniʀ] to come; **venir de** *with inf* to have just . . . ; **venir chercher** to come and get

vente [vɑ̃t] *f* sale; **vente aux enchères** auction

verbe [vɛʀb] *m* verb

vérité [veʀite] *f* truth; **en vérité** in truth, truly

verre [vɛʀ] *m* glass

vers [vɛʀ] *m* verse; **faire des vers** to write poetry

vers [vɛʀ] *prep* towards, about

Versailles [vɛʀsaj] city west of Paris

vert [vɛʀ] green

vertu [vɛʀty] *f* virtue

vêtement [vɛtmɑ̃] *m* clothing

veuillez [vœje] (*imperative of* **vouloir**) please

viande [vjɑ̃d] *f* meat

vice [vis] *m* vice

victorieux, victorieuse [viktɔʀjø, viktɔʀjøz] victorious

vide [vid] empty

vie [vi] *f* life, living

vieux, vieille [vjø, vjɛj] old

vif, vive [vif, viv] alive, lively

vigoureux [viguʀø] sturdy

vilain, vilaine [vilɛ̃, vilɛn] ugly, bad, nasty, disagreeable

village [vilaʒ] *m* village

ville [vil] *f* city

vin [vɛ̃] *m* wine

vingtaine [vɛ̃tɛn] *f* about twenty

violemment [vjɔlamɑ̃] violently

violent, violente [vjɔlɑ̃, vjɔlɑ̃t] violent

visiter [vizite] to visit, go through

visiteur [vizitœʀ] *m* tourist

vite [vit] fast, quickly

vitesse [vitɛs] *f* speed

vitrine [vitʀin] *f* shopwindow; showcase

vivement [vivmɑ̃] keenly, deeply

vivre [vivʀ] to live

vœu [vø] *m* wish

voilà [vwala] there is, there are; **voilà . . . que** *with pres tense* for

voile [vwal] *f* sail

voir [vwaʀ] to see

voisin, voisine [vwazɛ̃, vwazin] *noun* neighbor; *adj* near, neighboring

voisinage [vwazinaʒ] *m* neighborhood

voiture [vwatyʀ] *f* car; carriage; vehicle

voix [vwa] *f* voice

volant [vɔlɑ̃] *m* steering wheel

voler [vɔle] to steal; **que je n'ai pas volé** that I have earned (that I have not stolen)

volontiers [vɔlõtje] willingly, gladly

volumineux [vɔlyminø] bulky

vont [võ] *present tense of* **aller**

votre, vos [vɔtʀ, vo] your

vôtre: le vôtre [ləvotʀ] *poss pron* yours

vouloir [vulwaʀ] to want, desire; **je veux bien** I am willing; **voulez-vous?** do you want to?; **je veux dire** I mean (*see par 38*)

vous [vu] you, yourself, to or for you

voyage [vwajaʒ] *m* trip; **en voyage** on a trip; **voyage d'agrément** pleasure trip

voyager [vwajaʒe] to travel

voyageur [vwajaʒœʀ] *m* traveler

voyons! [vwajõ] come now! let's see! (*imperative of* **voir**)

vrai, vraie [vʀɛ] true; **à vrai dire** to tell the truth

vraiment [vʀɛmɑ̃] really, truly

vu [vy] *p part of* **voir**

vue [vy] *f* view

W

week-end [wikɛnd] *m* weekend

Y

y [i] there; to it, to them; **il y a** there is, there are; **il y a dix ans que** *with present tense* for ten years

yeux [jø] (*pl of* **œil**) *m* eyes

Z

zéro [zeʀo] *m* zero; **zéro heure** 12 midnight

zone [zon] *f* zone

ENGLISH-FRENCH

A

a un *m*, une *f*

able: to be able to pouvoir

about *prep* vers; *adv* à peu près, environ; sur, au sujet de; **how about going . . . ?** si nous allions . . . ?

above sur, au-dessus de; **above all** surtout

absence absence *f*

absolutely absolument

abundant abondant *m*, abondante *f*

accept: to accept accepter

accessible accessible

accident accident *m*

according to d'après, selon

account: on my account pour moi, à cause de moi

accuse: to accuse accuser; **to accuse oneself** s'accuser

acquaintance connaissance *f; to make the acquaintance of* faire la connaissance de

acquainted: to be acquainted with connaître

across en face de, de l'autre côté de; **to walk across** traverser

address adresse *f*

administration administration *f*

admire: to admire admirer

advantage: to take advantage of profiter de

adventure aventure *f*

advice conseil *m; to give advice to* donner des conseils à

advise: to advise to conseiller de

affirm: to affirm affirmer

affirmative affirmatif *m*, affirmative *f*

affirmatively affirmativement

afford s'offrir

afraid: to be afraid of avoir peur de

Africa Afrique *f*

African Africain *m*, Africaine *f*

after après; **after spending two weeks** . . . après avoir passé quinze jours

afternoon après-midi *m; in the afternoon* l'après-midi

afterwards après, ensuite

again de nouveau, encore; **to do again** refaire; **to see again** revoir

against contre

age âge *m*

ago il y a; **a long time ago** il y a longtemps

agree: to agree to consentir à; **to agree with** être de l'avis de

agricultural agricole

ahead devant, là-bas; **up ahead** là-bas; **to go ahead** continuer

air air *m*

alas hélas

Algeria Algérie *f*

alive vivant

all tout, toute, tous, toutes; **all of them**

tous, toutes; **not at all** pas du tout; **in all** en tout

allow: to allow to laisser, permettre de

all right bon, bien, pas mal; **if it is all right with you** si ça ne vous fait rien

almost presque; **I almost ran off the road** j'ai failli quitter la route

alone seul *m*, seule *f;* **to leave alone** laisser tranquille

along le long de; **to take along** emporter; **to come along** accompagner

Alps les Alpes

already déjà

also aussi

although bien que, quoique

always toujours

A.M. du matin

America Amérique *f*

American américain *m*, américaine *f;* **Americans** les Américains

among parmi; **to be among your guests** être des vôtres

amount somme *f*

amuse: to amuse oneself s'amuser

amusing amusant *m*, amusante *f*

and et

angry: to be angry être fâché

animal animal *m*

announce: to announce annoncer

announcement annonce *f*

annoy: to annoy ennuyer

annoyance mécontentement *m*, ennui *m*

another un autre, une autre; **another time** une autre fois

answer réponse *f*

answer: to answer répondre à

antique dealer antiquaire *m*

anxious: to be anxious to tenir à

any du, de la, de l', des, de; en; **not any** ne . . . pas de; **not any more, not any longer** ne . . . plus

anyone quelqu'un; **not anyone** ne . . . personne

anything tout; **not anything** rien

anyway d'ailleurs

apart: to tell apart distinguer

apartment appartement *m*

apologize: to apologize s'excuser (de)

appendicitis appendicite *f*, crise d'appendicite *f*

apple pomme *f*

appointment rendez-vous *m*

appreciate: to appreciate apprécier

approach: to approach approcher, s'approcher de

appropriate *adj* qui convient

April avril *m*

Arabia Arabie *f*

architect architecte *m*

are: there are il y a; **aren't they?** n'est-ce pas?

arm bras *m;* **with open arms** à bras ouverts

around (*place*) autour de; (*time*) vers; environ

arrive: to arrive arriver

art art *m*

artist artiste *m*

artistic artistique

as comme, pendant que; **as . . . as** aussi . . . que; **so as to** pour que, de façon à

aside à part

ask: to ask demander; **to ask someone for information** demander des renseignements à quelqu'un

asleep endormi *m*, endormie *f;* **to be asleep** dormir; **to fall asleep** s'endormir

assassination assassinat *m*

assiduously assidûment

astonish: to astonish étonner

astonishing étonnant *m*, étonnante *f*

at à, chez; **at the** au, à la, à l'; **at the Duplessis'** chez les Duplessis; **at about six o'clock** vers six heures

attain: to attain atteindre

attend: to attend assister à, aller à

attention attention *f;* **to pay attention to** faire attention à, tenir compte de

attract: to attract attirer

attribute: to attribute attribuer

auction vente aux enchères *f;* **at auction** aux enchères
August août *m*
author auteur *m*
authority autorité *f*
automobile voiture *f,* auto *f*
avenue avenue *f*
avoid: to avoid éviter, se garder de
await: to await attendre
awake réveillé
awake: to awake se réveiller
away: to go away s'en aller, partir; **to send away** renvoyer
awful: it's too awful for words il vaut mieux ne pas en parler

B

baby bébé *m*
bachelor vieux garçon *m*
back: to be back être de retour; **to go back** retourner, rentrer; **to step back** reculer
bad mauvais *m,* mauvaise *f;* vilain *m* vilaine *f*
badly mal
baggage bagages *m pl*
balance reliquat *m*
banana banane *f*
bank banque *f; (river)* rive *f*
bankrupt: to bankrupt ruiner
bargain occasion *f*
be: to be être; *(place)* se trouver; **there is, there are** il y a; **to be out** être sorti; **to be cold** avoir froid; **to be right** avoir raison; **the office is in Paris** le bureau se trouve à Paris; **I am to** je dois; **I was to** je devais; **it is better** il vaut mieux; **it is just as well** il vaut autant
bear: to bear in mind tenir compte de
beautiful beau, bel *m;* belle *f;* beaux *m pl;* belles *f pl*
beauty beauté *f*
because parce que; **because of** à cause de

become: to become devenir; **what became of him?** qu'est-ce qu'il est devenu?
bed lit *m; to go to bed* se coucher, se mettre au lit
been été *p part of* être
beer bière *f*
before *(time)* avant, avant de, avant que, auparavant; *(place)* devant; **the year before** l'année précédente; **before finishing** avant de finir
beg: to beg to prier de
begin: to begin to commencer à, se mettre à; **it began to rain** il s'est mis à pleuvoir; **to begin to laugh** se mettre à rire
beginning commencement *m,* début *m*
behind derrière
Belgium Belgique *f*
believe: to believe croire, penser
belong: to belong to appartenir à, être à
besides d'ailleurs, en outre, et puis
best *adj* le meilleur, la meilleure, les meilleurs, les meilleures; *adv* le mieux; **at best** tout au plus
better *adj* meilleur, meilleure, meilleurs, meilleures; *adv* mieux; **it's better** il vaut mieux; **nothing better** rien de mieux; **to do better** faire mieux (de)
between entre
big grand, grande; gros, grosse
bill facture *f*
billfold portefeuille *m*
bit: a bit un peu; **quite a bit** pas mal
board: on board à bord; **to go on board** monter à bord, s'embarquer; **room and board** pension *f*
boast: to boast se vanter
boat bateau *m*
bold hardi *m,* hardie *f*
boldly hardiment
book livre *m*
bore: to bore ennuyer; **to be bored** s'ennuyer

born né; **to be born** naître; **he was born in Paris** il est né à Paris

both les deux, l'un et l'autre

bother dérangement *m*

bother: to bother gêner, ennuyer, déranger; **It's no bother** ce n'est pas un dérangement

bottle bouteille *f*

boy garçon, jeune homme; *pl* jeunes gens

bread pain *m;* **a loaf of bread** un pain

break: to break casser, briser

brick brique *f*

bridge pont *m;* bridge *m*

brilliance éclat *m*

bring: to bring apporter; **to bring in (income)** rapporter; **to bring back** rapporter

Brittany Bretagne *f*

broad vaste, large

brother frère *m*

Brussels Bruxelles

build: to build construire; **to have . . . built** faire construire

building construction *f*

bulldog bouledogue *m*

burn: to burn brûler

burning *adj* brûlant *m*, brûlante *f*

bus autobus *m*

business affaire *f*, métier *m;* **business engagement** rendez-vous d'affaires *m*

busy: to be busy être en train de, s'occuper de, être occupé à

but mais, cependant; **nothing but** rien que

butcher boucher *m*

butter beurre *m*

button bouton *m*

buy: to buy acheter

by par, de, en; **by leaving early** en partant de bonne heure

C

cab taxi *m*

Cabinet member ministre *m*

Cairo Le Caire

call: to call appeler; **to call back** rappeler; **to be called** s'appeler

calm tranquille

camera appareil (photographique) *m*

camp camp *m*

can (pouvoir) **I can** je peux; **you can** vous pouvez, on peut

Canada Canada *m*

canal canal *m*

cane canne *f*

capital capitale *f*

captain capitaine *m*

car voiture *f*, auto *f;* **by car** en auto

card carte *f;* **to play cards** jouer aux cartes

care soin *m*, souci *m;* **to take care of** s'occuper de

career carrière *f*

careful: to be careful not to se garder de

carriage voiture *f*, carrosse *m*

carry: to carry porter, transporter; **to carry away** emporter

carved sculpté

case cas *m;* **in any case** en tout cas

cashier's window caisse *f*

castle château *m*

cat chat *m*

catch: to catch attraper; **to catch up with** rejoindre

cathedral cathédrale *f*

cease: to cease to cesser de

cemetery cimetière *m*

century siècle *m;* **in the 16th century** au seizième siècle

ceremony cérémonie *f*

certain certain *m*, certaine *f*

certainly certainement

chair chaise *f*

chance hasard *m;* **by a lucky chance** par un hasard heureux; **chance meeting** rencontre *f*

change: to change changer de

charge: to take charge of s'occuper de, se charger de; **to be in charge of** s'occuper de

charming charmant *m*, charmante *f*
château château *m*
chatty bavard *m*, bavarde *f*
cheap bon marché, à bon marché
child enfant *m or f*
chimney cheminée *f*
China Chine *f*
china vaisselle *f*, faïence *f;* **a set of**
    china un service de table
choice choix *m*
choose: to choose choisir
church église *f*
cigarette cigarette *f*
circular circulaire
city ville *f*
civil: civil servant fonctionnaire *m*
clarity netteté *f*
class classe *f*
classicism classicisme *m*
classics classiques *m pl*
clean propre
clear: to clear up (*weather*) s'arranger
clearing clairière *f*
close: to close fermer
closely de près
clothes vêtements *m*
Coca-Cola Coca-Cola *m*
coffee café *m;* **to have coffee** prendre
    le café
cold froid *m*, froide *f*, frais *m*, fraîche *f;*
    it is cold il fait froid; **I am cold** j'ai
    froid
college collège *m*
color couleur *f;* **what color?** de quelle
    couleur?
come: to come venir; **to come to** (*be*
    present at) assister à; (*to get near*)
    s'approcher de; **to come out** sortir,
    paraître; **to come back** revenir; **to**
    come in entrer; **to come with**
    accompagner; **to come from** pro-
    venir de; **to come for** venir cher-
    cher; **to come along** accompagner;
    to have (someone) come faire
    venir (quelqu'un)
comedy comédie *f*
comfort confort *m*

commit: to commit commettre
common commun *m*, commune *f*
company compagnie *f*, usine *f*
comparison: in comparison with com-
    paré à
complain: to complain se plaindre
complete complet *m*, complète *f*
completely complètement
compliment compliment *m;* **to pay a**
    compliment faire un compliment
compose: to compose composer
comprehensible facile à comprendre;
    that is comprehensible cela se
    comprend
conceal: to conceal cacher
concert concert *m*
conclude: to conclude conclure
condition condition *f*, état *m;* **in good**
    condition en bon état; **on condi-**
    tion that à condition que
conduct: to conduct conduire
configuration configuration *f*
conquer: to conquer vaincre
consent: to consent to consentir à
console: to console consoler
construction construction *f*
continual continuel
continue: to continue continuer à, se
    poursuivre
contrary contraire; **on the contrary** au
    contraire
control: to be under (someone's) con-
    trol dépendre de (quelqu'un)
convenient commode
conversation conversation *f*
convincing convaincant *m*, convain-
    cante *f*
cook cuisinier *m*, cuisinière *f*
cook: to cook faire la cuisine
cool frais *m*, fraîche *f*
copiously copieusement
correspondence correspondance *f*
cost coût *m*, frais *m pl*
cost: to cost coûter
could (pouvoir): **I could** je pouvais, j'ai
    pu, je pourrais; **I could have**
    j'aurais pu

council conseil *m;* **executive council** conseil d'administration *m*

count: to count on compter sur; **not counting** sans compter

country pays *m,* campagne *f;* **out in the country** à la campagne; **a part of the country** une région

courageous courageux *m,* courageuse *f*

courageously courageusement, avec courage

course cours *m;* **a French course** un cours de français; **of course** bien entendu, naturellement, bien sûr; **in the course of** au cours de

court cour *f*

cousin cousin *m,* cousine *f*

cover: to cover with couvrir de

cow vache *f*

crazy: to be crazy about adorer

cream crème *f;* **coffee with cream** café-crème *m*

crew équipe *f*

crime crime *m*

criminal criminel *m,* criminelle *f*

crisis crise *f*

criticize: to criticize critiquer, dire du mal de

crop récolte *f*

cross: to cross traverser

cruel cruel *m,* cruelle *f*

cry: to cry pleurer, crier; **to cry out** s'écrier

culture culture *f*

cup tasse *f;* **a silver cup (for a child)** une timbale d'argent

cupboard armoire *f,* placard *m*

curtain rideau *m*

customs douane *f;* **to get through customs** accomplir les formalités de douane

cute joli *m,* jolie *f;* gentil *m,* gentille *f*

D

dahlia dahlia *m*

danger danger *m*

dangerous dangereux *m,* dangereuse *f*

dare: to dare oser

date date *f;* **on this date** à cette date

date: to date dater

daughter fille *f*

day jour *m,* journée *f;* **per day, a day** par jour; **all day** toute la journée; **every day** tous les jours; **that day** ce jour-là; **the day before** la veille; **the next day, the day after** le lendemain; **day after tomorrow** après-demain; **today** aujourd'hui; **someday** un jour; **to our day** jusqu'à nos jours; **these days** de nos jours; **the good old days** le bon vieux temps

dead mort *m,* morte *f*

deal: a good deal of beaucoup (de)

deal: to deal in faire le commerce de, vendre

dealer marchand *m,* marchande *f;* **antique dealer** antiquaire *m*

dear cher *m,* chère *f*

death mort *f,* décès *m*

deceive: to deceive tromper

December décembre *m*

decide: to decide to décider de, vouloir

decline: to decline décliner, refuser de

decoration décoration *f*

delay délai *m,* retard *m*

delicious délicieux *m,* délicieuse *f*

delighted enchanté

deliver: to deliver remettre

Denmark Danemark *m*

departure départ *m*

depend: to depend on dépendre de

deportation déportation *f*

describe: to describe décrire

desert désert *m*

design dessin *m*

design: to design dessiner; **to have designed** faire dessiner

desk bureau *m*

despair: to despair désespérer

dessert dessert *m*

destination destination *f*

destined destiné

determine: to determine déterminer
detest: to detest détester
development développement *m*
devour: to devour dévorer
die: to die mourir
difference différence *f;* **it makes no difference** ça ne fait rien
different différent *m*, différente *f*
difficult difficile
dine: to dine dîner
dinner dîner *m;* **to have dinner** dîner
diplomat diplomate *m*
direction sens *m*, direction *f*
disappear: to disappear disparaître
discontent mécontent
discover: to discover découvrir
discovery découverte *f*
discuss: to discuss discuter
dish plat *m*
display étalage *m;* **on display** à l'étalage
displease: to displease déplaire à
disposal disposition *f;* **at your disposal** à votre disposition
distance distance *f;* **from a distance** à distance
distant éloigné
distinguish distinguer
do: to do faire; **to do again** refaire; **all you have to do** vous n'avez qu'à, il suffit de; **to do well to** faire bien de; **my camera will do** mon appareil fera l'affaire
doctor médecin *m*, docteur *m*
dog chien *m*
door porte *f*, portière *f*
dot: at eight o'clock on the dot à huit heures précises
double double; **double gallery** galerie à deux étages *f*
doubt doute *m;* **no doubt** sans doute
doubt: to doubt douter de
down: to go down descendre; **to put down** déposer; **downtown** en ville
dramatic dramatique
dress robe *f*
dress: to dress s'habiller; **to be dressed** être habillé; **to get dressed** s'habiller
drill: to drill (for oil) faire des forages
drilling forage *m*
drink: to drink boire; **to drink coffee** prendre le café
drive: to drive conduire
driver chauffeur *m;* **driver's license** permis de conduire *m*
drought sécheresse *f*
drown: to drown se noyer
drugstore pharmacie *f*
duke duc *m*
duration durée *f*
during pendant, au cours de
duty devoir *m*, fonction *f*
dynamite dynamite *f*

E

each *adj* chaque; *pron* chacun, chacune; **each one** chacun
eager: to be eager to tenir à
early de bonne heure, tôt
earn: to earn gagner
earth terre *f*, sol *m*
earthenware faïence *f;* **Quimper earthenware** faïence de Quimper
easily facilement
easy facile, simple; **nothing easier** rien de plus facile
eat: to eat manger
economic économique
edge bord *m*
education éducation *f*
effect effet *m*
egg œuf *m*
Egypt Égypte *f*
Egyptian égyptien *m*, égyptienne *f*
eight huit
eighteen dix-huit
eighth huitième
eighty quatre-vingts
either: either . . . or soit . . . soit; **not . . . either** ne . . . non plus; **nor I (either)** ni moi non plus
electrify: to electrify électrifier

elegant élégant *m*, élégante *f*
eleven onze
eleventh onzième
else: something else quelque chose d'autre, autre chose; **nothing else** rien d'autre
elsewhere ailleurs
emblem emblème *m*
employee employé *m;* **government employee** fonctionnaire *m*
empty vide, inhabité
end fin *f*, bout *m;* **to make both ends meet** joindre les deux bouts
end: to end finir, achever
engineer ingénieur *m;* **chemical engineer** ingénieur-chimiste *m*
England Angleterre *f*
English anglais *m*, anglaise *f*
enjoy: to enjoy aimer, apprécier
enormous énorme
enough assez; **it is enough that** il suffit que; **it is enough to** il y a de quoi
enter: to enter entrer; **to enter a room** entrer dans une chambre; **to enter school** entrer à l'école
enthusiastic enthousiaste
entire entier *m*, entière *f*
entirely tout à fait, entièrement
entrance entrée *f*
errand course *f*, emplette *f;* **to do errands** faire des courses
escape: to escape échapper à
escort: to escort escorter
especially surtout
establish: to establish établir
esteem: to esteem estimer
Europe Europe *f*
European européen *m*, européenne *f*
even même
evening soir *m*, soirée *f;* **in the evening** le soir; **every evening** tous les soirs
event événement *m*
eventually dans la suite
ever jamais

every chaque; **every morning** chaque matin, tous les matins
everybody tout le monde, chacun
everyone chacun, tout le monde, on
everything tout
everywhere partout
evident évident *m*, évidente *f*
exact exact *m*, exacte *f*
exactly exactement, justement; **exactly true** exact
examine: to examine examiner
example exemple *m;* **for example** par exemple
excellent excellent *m*, excellente *f*
except, excepting sauf, excepté
exchange: to exchange échanger
exist: to exist exister
expect: to expect compter sur, s'attendre à, attendre, penser; **I am expecting a letter** j'attends une lettre
expensive cher *m*, chère *f;* **to be expensive** coûter cher
explain expliquer
explode: to explode exploser, faire exploser
exploration exploration *f*
explosion explosion *f*
extend: to extend s'étendre
extinguish: to extinguish éteindre
extraordinary extraordinaire
eye œil *m*, yeux *pl*

F

façade façade *f*
face face *f;* **face to face** face à face
factory usine *f*, compagnie *f*
fail: to fail to manquer de
fall chute *f*, prise *f;* **Niagara Falls** les chutes du Niagara
fall: to fall tomber; **to fall down** tomber; **to fall asleep** s'endormir
familiar familier *m*, familière *f*
family famille *f;* **family life** vie de famille *f*

famous célèbre; fameux *m*, fameuse *f*

far loin; **far from** loin de; **as far as** jusqu'à; **as far as you can see** à perte de vue; **how far?** à quelle distance?; **how far along is your work?** où en sont vos travaux?

farm ferme *f*; *adj* agricole; **farm products** produits agricoles

farmer cultivateur *m*

farming culture *f*, agriculture *f*

fashionable à la mode, mondain

fast vite; **how fast?** à quelle vitesse?

fate sort *m*

father père *m*

fault faute *f*

favorable favorable

fear crainte *f*, peur *f*; **for fear that** de crainte que, de peur que

fear: to fear craindre, avoir peur de

February février *m*

feed: to feed nourrir; **to be fed** se nourrir; **he is fed up with it** il en a assez

feel: to feel sentir, se sentir, croire; **to feel urged to** tenir à; **to feel sick** se sentir mal, avoir mal au cœur

feeling sentiment *m*

fertilizer engrais *m*

festivity fête *f*

few *adj* quelques; **a few yards away** à quelques mètres; *adv* peu, peu de; *pron* quelques-uns, quelques-unes; **a few of them** quelques-uns d'entre eux, quelques-unes d'entre elles; **fewer and fewer** de moins en moins

field champ *m*

fierce féroce

fifteen quinze; **about fifteen** une quinzaine

fifteenth quinzième

fifth cinquième

fifty cinquante; **about fifty** une cinquantaine

fill: to fill remplir de, être plein de; **filled with** plein de, pleine de

film film *m*

finally enfin, finalement, finir par *and infinitive;* **it finally turned over** il a fini par chavirer

finance finance *f*

financier financier *m*

find: to find trouver

fine beau, belle, beaux, belles; joli, jolie; **the weather is fine** il fait beau; **fine!** entendu!

finish: to finish finir (de), achever de

first premier *m*, première *f;* **Francis the First** François premier; **May 1st** le premier mai; *adv* d'abord; **first of all** tout d'abord

fish poisson *m*

fishing pêche *f;* **to go fishing** aller à la pêche, aller pêcher

fit: to see fit juger bon de

five cinq

fix: to fix fixer

flaw défaut *m*

flee: to flee s'enfuir

flower fleur *f*

fluently couramment

fly: to fly voler, aller par avion; **to fly over** survoler

follow: to follow suivre, prendre (une route)

following suivant *m*, suivante *f;* **the following day** le lendemain

fond: to be fond of aimer

food aliment *m*

foot pied *m*

for pour, depuis, pendant; **I have been waiting for ten minutes** il y a dix minutes que j'attends; **it has been raining for two hours** voilà deux heures qu'il pleut, il pleut depuis deux heures

forbid: to forbid to défendre de

force: to force to obliger à, forcer à

forget: to forget to oublier de

former: the former celui-là, celle-là, ceux-là, celles-là

formerly autrefois

forty quarante; **about forty** une quarantaine

forward: to go forward avancer
four quatre
fourteen quatorze
fourth quatrième
franc franc *m*
France France *f*
Francis François
frankly franchement
free libre; **to set free** mettre en liberté
freeway autoroute *f*
freeze: to freeze geler
French français *m*, française *f;* **the French people** les Français
Friday vendredi *m*
friend ami *m*, amie *f;* **a friend of mine** un de mes amis, une de mes amies
from de, depuis, d'après; **from the** du, de la, de l', des
front: in front of devant
fruit fruit *m;* **I like fruit** j'aime les fruits
full plein *m*, pleine *f*
fun: to make fun of se moquer de
furnished meublé *m*, meublée *f*
furnishings mobilier *m sg*
furniture meubles *m pl*
future futur *m*, avenir *m*

G

gallery galerie *f*
game jeu *m*, match *m;* **a rugby game** un match de rugby
garden jardin *m*
gardener jardinier *m*
gas essence *f*
gay gai *m*, gaie *f*
generally d'ordinaire, d'habitude, généralement
Geneva Genève
gentle doux *m*, douce *f*
gentleman monsieur *m;* **gentlemen** messieurs
German allemand, allemande
Germany Allemagne *f*
get: to get prendre, obtenir, recevoir, se procurer; **to get in, to get into** entrer, monter dans; **to get out**
sortir, descendre; **to get off** descendre; **to get there** arriver; **to get up** se lever; **to go to get** aller chercher; **to come to get** venir chercher; **to get used to** s'habituer à; **I don't get it at all** je n'y comprends rien
girl jeune fille *f*
give: to give donner; **to give up** abandonner, renoncer à; **to give up hope** désespérer
glad content *m*, contente *f;* heureux *m*, heureuse *f;* **glad to** volontiers
gladly volontiers
glass verre *m*
glove gant *m*
go: to go aller, marcher, se rendre; **to go back** retourner; **to go in** entrer; **to go out** sortir; **to go away** partir, s'en aller; **to go up** monter; **to go down** descendre; **to go with** accompagner; **to go and see** aller voir; **to go and get** aller chercher; **to go through** traverser, visiter; **to go ahead** continuer; **what's going on?** qu'est-ce qui se passe?; **don't go out of your way** ne vous dérangez pas; **it couldn't be going better** ça marche on ne peut pas mieux
goal but *m*
good *adj* bon, bonne, bons, bonnes
good-bye au revoir
goods marchandises *f pl*
Gothic gothique
govern: to govern gouverner
government gouvernement *m*
gradually graduellement, peu à peu
granddaughter petite-fille *f*
grandmother grand-mère *f*
greatly beaucoup, grandement
Greek grec *m*, grecque *f*
green vert *m*, verte *f*
ground terre *f*, sol *m;* **on the ground** par terre
grow: to grow *intr* pousser; *trans* faire pousser, récolter

grown-up grande personne *f*
guarantee: to guarantee garantir
guest invité *m;* to be among your guests être des vôtres
guide guide *m*

H

habit habitude *f*
habitual habituel *m,* habituelle *f*
hair cheveu, cheveux *m*
half *adj* demi *m,* demie *f; noun* moitié *f;* half an hour une demi-heure; an hour and a half une heure et demie
hand main *f*
hand: to hand over passer, donner
happen: to happen arriver, se passer; to happen to arriver à, devenir; what happened to him? qu'est-ce qui lui est arrivé?
happy heureux *m,* heureuse *f;* content, contente
hard fort; it was raining so hard il pleuvait tant, il pleuvait si fort
hardly à peine, ne . . . guère; hardly worthy peu digne
hat chapeau *m;* high hat chapeau haut de forme
haul: to haul transporter
have: to have avoir; to have to falloir, avoir à, devoir; to have something done faire faire quelque chose; to have coffee prendre le café
he il, lui, c'
head tête *f*
health santé *f*
hear: to hear entendre; to hear of entendre parler de; to hear that entendre dire que; to hear from someone recevoir des nouvelles de quelqu'un
heart cœur *m;* to know by heart savoir par cœur
heaven ciel *m*
helicopter hélicoptère *m*

hello bonjour; say hello to dites bien des choses de ma part à, dites bien le bonjour à
help: to help aider à; to help oneself se servir
her *poss adj* son, sa, ses; *pers pron* la, l'; lui, elle
here ici; here is, here are voici; here and there çà et là
herewith ci-inclus
hers le sien, la sienne, les siens, les siennes
herself elle-même
hesitate: to hesitate to hésiter à
high haut *m,* haute *f;* de haut; élevé, élevée; 300 meters high 300 mètres de haut; a high price un prix élevé
him le, lui; to him lui, à lui
himself lui-même
his *poss adj* son, sa, ses; *poss pron* le sien, la sienne, les siens, les siennes
hold: to hold tenir
Holland Hollande *f*
home: at home à la maison, chez (moi); to go back home rentrer (à la maison)
Homer Homère
honest honnête
honor honneur *m*
honor: to honor honorer
hope: to hope espérer
horse cheval *m,* chevaux *pl*
hospital hôpital *m,* hôpitaux *pl*
hot chaud *m,* chaude *f*
hotel hôtel *m*
hour heure *f;* half an hour une demi-heure
house maison *f;* at your house chez vous
how comment; how much, how many combien; how long? combien de temps?; to know how savoir *and infinitive;* how is that? comment cela?
however pourtant, cependant
huge énorme, vaste

humor humeur *f*; **in a good humor** de bonne humeur

hundred cent; **about a hundred** une centaine

hungry: to be hungry avoir faim

hunting *f*; **to go hunting** aller à la chasse; **hunting lodge** pavillon de chasse *m*, château de chasse *m*

hurry: to hurry se dépêcher; **to be in a hurry** être pressé

I

I je, moi

idea idée *f*

if si, s'; **if only** si au moins

Iliad (**the**) l'*Iliade*

imagine: to imagine imaginer, s'imaginer

immediately immédiatement, tout de suite

impatience impatience *f*

imply: to imply impliquer

important important *m*, importante *f*

impossible impossible

impression impression *f*

in dans, en, à, de; **in Paris** à Paris; **in France** en France; **in Canada** au Canada; **in the U.S.** aux États-Unis; **in the 16th century** au seizième siècle; **in November** en novembre, au mois de novembre; **in the spring** au printemps; **in summer** en été; **in the fall** en automne; **in winter** en hiver; **in an hour** dans une heure, en une heure; **in the morning** le matin; **at seven in the morning** à sept heures du matin

inaugurate: to inaugurate inaugurer

income revenu *m*

inconvenience: to inconvenience déranger

indeed en effet, vraiment

Indian Indien *m*, Indienne *f*

indicate: to indicate indiquer

indirect indirect *m*, indirecte *f*

industrial industriel *m*, industrielle *f*

influence influence *f*

information renseignements *m pl*

inhabitant habitant *m*

inhospitable inhospitalier *m*, inhospitalière *f*

insist: to insist upon tenir à

installation installation *f*

instance: for instance par exemple

instead: instead of au lieu de

insurance assurance *f*

intelligent intelligent *m*, intelligente *f*

interest intérêt *m*

interest: to interest intéresser; **to be interested in** s'intéresser à

interesting intéressant *m*, intéressante *f*

interior intérieur *m*

intrigue: to intrigue intriguer

introduce: to introduce introduire, présenter

intruder intrus *m*

invent: to invent inventer

invention invention *f*

invitation invitation *f*

invite: to invite to inviter à

Iraq Iraq

iron fer *m*

is est; **it is** c'est; **it is cold** il fait froid; **it is better** il vaut mieux; **it is just as well** il vaut autant

island île *f*

Israel Israël

it il, elle, ce, cela; **it is** c'est, il est, elle est; *dir obj* le, l', la; *indir obj* y; **of it** en; **it makes no difference** cela ne fait rien

its son, sa, ses

J

January janvier *m*

Japan Japon *m*

jewel bijou *m*

juice jus *m*

July juillet *m*

June juin *m*

jungle jungle *f*

just exactement, tout simplement, seulement, ne . . . que; **to have just** venir de *and infinitive;* **it is just as well** il vaut autant

K

keenly vivement
keep: to keep garder, conserver, tenir
key clé *f*
kid: to kid se moquer de
kill: to kill tuer; **to kill oneself** se tuer
kilogram kilogramme *m,* kilo *m;* **five francs a kilogram** cinq francs le kilo
kilometer kilomètre *m*
kind genre *m,* espèce *f*
kind *adj* aimable
kindness amabilité *f*
king roi *m*
know: to know savoir, connaître; **to know how** savoir *and infinitive;* **not to know** ignorer; **to let someone know** faire savoir à quelqu'un; **I didn't know** j'ignorais
knowingly savamment
known connu *m,* connue *f;* **well-known** bien connu, bien connue

L

laboratory laboratoire *m*
lack: to lack manquer de
lady dame *f,* femme *f*
land terre *f*
landscape paysage *m*
large grand *m,* grande *f;* gros *m,* grosse *f;* vaste
last *adj* dernier *m,* dernière *f;* **at last** enfin; **last night** hier soir; **last Sunday** dimanche dernier; **last year** l'année dernière, l'an dernier
last: to last durer
late tard, en retard; **it is late** il est tard; **I am late** je suis en retard; **not later than** dès
Latin *noun* latin *m; adj* latin *m,* latine *f*

latter: the latter celui-ci, celle-ci, ceux-ci, celles-ci
law loi *f*
lawyer avocat *m*
laying établissement *m,* construction *f*
lead: to lead mener, conduire; **to lead a life** mener une vie
leaf feuille *f*
learn: to learn apprendre (à), savoir, entendre dire
least *adj* moindre; **at least** au moins
leave congé *m*
leave: to leave quitter, s'en aller, partir, laisser; **I left** je suis parti; **I left Paris** j'ai quitté Paris; **I left my watch at home** j'ai laissé ma montre à la maison; **all I have left is** il ne me reste plus que; **to leave alone** laisser tranquille
lecture conférence *f*
left: to be left rester; **I have one left** il m'en reste un
lend: to lend prêter
less moins de, moins que; **less and less** de moins en moins
let: to let laisser, permettre de
letter lettre *f*
liberty liberté *f;* **to take the liberty of** se permettre de
license permis *m;* **driver's license** permis de conduire *m*
lie: to lie down se coucher
life vie *f*
like comme; **Isn't that just like John** Voilà bien notre Jean
like: to like aimer, plaire, trouver, vouloir; **did you like it?** est-ce que cela vous a plu? **would you like to?** voudriez-vous?
line ligne *f*
list: to list (*boat*) pencher, s'incliner
listen: to listen to écouter
liter litre *m;* **half a liter** un demi-litre; **five francs a liter** cinq francs le litre
little *adj* petit, petite; *adv* peu; **a little** un peu; **little by little** peu à peu

livable habitable

live: to live vivre; **to live in** demeurer, habiter; **lived in** habité; **enough to live on** de quoi vivre

load charge *f*

loaf: a loaf of bread un pain

local local, du lieu, du pays

Loire la Loire *f*

London Londres

long *adj* long *m*, longue *f*; de long; *adv* longtemps; (*time*) **how long?** combien de temps? depuis combien de temps?; (*distance*) **how long is the road?** quelle est la longueur de la route?; **the road is 700 kms long** la route a 700 kms de long; **will it take you long?** vous faudra-t-il longtemps?; **no longer, any longer** ne . . . plus; **as long as** (*time*) tant que, (*since*) puisque

look: to look regarder, sembler, avoir l'air; **to look at** regarder; **to look for** chercher; **to look like** ressembler à; **to look over (a place)** visiter

lose: to lose perdre

lost perdu *m*, perdue *f*

lot: a lot of, lots of beaucoup de, quantité de; **lots of money** une grosse fortune

loud fort *m*, forte *f*; haut *m*, haute *f*; **to speak in a loud voice** parler haut

love: to love aimer, adorer; **his loved ones** les personnes qui lui sont chères

lovely joli *m*, jolie *f*; charmant *m*, charmante *f*

low bas *m*, basse *f*; **to speak in a low voice** parler bas

lucky heureux *m*, heureuse *f*; **to be lucky** avoir de la chance

lunch déjeuner *m*

lunch: to lunch déjeuner

luxury luxe *m*

M

machine machine *f*

machinery machines *pl*

madam madame *f*

magnificent magnifique

mail: to mail mettre (une lettre) à la poste

main principal *m*, principale *f*, principaux *m pl*, principales *f pl*

majesty majesté *f*

make: to make faire, (*followed by adj*) rendre; **it makes no difference** ça ne fait rien

man homme *m;* **old man** mon vieux

many beaucoup de; **so many** tant de; **too many** trop de; **how many?** combien?

March mars *m*

marriage mariage *m*

married marié; **to get married** se marier

marry: to marry se marier

master maître *m*

matter: to matter importer; **what's the matter?** qu'est-ce qu'il y a?; **what's the matter with him?** qu'est-ce qu'il a?

May mai *m*

may (pouvoir); **may I?** est-ce que je peux? pourrais-je?

maybe peut-être

me me, moi

mean: to mean vouloir dire

meaning intention *f*, sens *m*, signification *f*

means moyen *m*

meantime: in the meantime en attendant, d'ici là

meanwhile en attendant

meat viande *f*

Mediterranean Méditerranée *f*

meet: to meet rencontrer, retrouver, rejoindre, faire la connaissance de; **to meet again** se retrouver

meeting rencontre *f*, réunion *f*

member membre *m*

memory mémoire *f;* **if I remember correctly** si j'ai bonne mémoire

merchant marchand *m*, marchande *f*

meter mètre *m*

Mexico Mexique *m*

middle milieu *m;* **in the middle of** au milieu de

Middle East Moyen-Orient *m*

midnight minuit *m*

midst: **in the midst of** au milieu de

might (pouvoir): **I might** je pourrais; **whatever you might think** quoi que vous puissiez croire

milk lait *m*

million million *m*

mind esprit *m;* **to bear in mind** tenir compte de

mine le mien, la mienne, les miens, les miennes; **it is mine** c'est à moi; **a friend of mine** un de mes amis

mineral minéral *m*, minérale *f*

minister ministre *m*

ministry ministère *m*

minute minute *f*

miss: **to miss** manquer, se tromper de; **one plate was missing** une assiette manquait; **I am missing one plate** il me manque une assiette; **I missed the road** je me suis trompé de route

Mississippi Mississippi *m*

mistaken: **to be mistaken** se tromper

modern moderne

modernize moderniser

moment moment *m;* **a moment, for a moment** un moment, un instant; **in a moment** tout à l'heure; **at that moment** à ce moment-là

Mona Lisa la Joconde

Monday lundi *m*

money argent *m;* **money order** mandat-poste *m*, mandat *m*

monkey singe *m*

month mois *m;* **in the month of** au mois de; **the 19th of this month** le 19 courant

monument monument *m*

mood humeur *f*

more plus, de plus, davantage; **not . . . any more** ne . . . plus; **more than** (*quantity*) plus de, (*comparison*) plus que; **the more . . . the more** plus . . . plus; **once more** une fois de plus

morning matin *m*, matinée *f;* **in the morning** le matin; **every morning** tous les matins; **seven o'clock in the morning** sept heures du matin

mosquito moustique *m*

most la plupart; **most of them** la plupart d'entre eux; **at the most** tout au plus

mother mère *f*

mountain montagne *f*

movable mobile

move; **to move** remuer

movie film *m*, cinéma *m*

moving *adj* mouvant *m*, mouvante *f*

Mr. Monsieur

Mrs. Madame

much beaucoup; **very much** beaucoup; **too much** trop; **so much** tant; **not much** (*indefinite*) pas grand-chose

murder: **to murder** assassiner

murder assassinat *m*

museum musée *m*

music musique *f*

must (devoir, falloir): **he must be** il doit être; **there must be** il doit y avoir

mutual commun *m*, commune *f*

my mon, ma, mes

myself moi-même

N

name nom *m;* **to be named** s'appeler; **proper name** nom propre

narrow étroit *m*, étroite *f*

national national *m*, nationale *f*

nationality nationalité *f*

naturally naturellement, bien entendu

near *prep* près de, à côté de; *adj* proche

necessary nécessaire; **it is necessary** il faut

need besoin *m*

need: to need avoir besoin de

negative négatif *m*, négative *f*

negatively négativement

neighbor voisin *m*, voisine *f*

neighborhood voisinage *m*

neither ni l'un ni l'autre; **neither . . . nor** ne . . . ni . . . ni

never jamais, ne . . . jamais

new nouveau *m*, nouvel *m*, nouvelle *f*, nouveaux *m pl*, nouvelles *f pl* neuf *m*, neuve *f;* **New Year's Day** le Nouvel An, le Jour de l'An

New Orleans La Nouvelle-Orléans

news nouvelles *f pl;* **a piece of news** une nouvelle

newspaper journal *m*, journaux *pl*

next prochain *m*, prochaine *f;* **the next day** le lendemain; **next time** la prochaine fois; *adv* ensuite, alors; **next to you** près de vous

nice gentil *m*, gentille *f;* aimable; **it's nice of him** c'est gentil de sa part

nicely gentiment

night nuit *f;* **at night** le soir, la nuit; **tonight** ce soir; **last night** hier soir; **that night** ce soir-là

Nile Nil *m*

nine neuf

nineteen dix-neuf

nineteenth dix-neuvième

ninety quatre-vingt-dix

ninth neuvième

no non, ne . . . pas de; aucun, aucune; **I have no idea** je n'en sais rien

nobility noblesse *f*

nobody personne, ne . . . personne

noise bruit *m*

none aucun, aucune; ne . . . aucun

noon midi *m*

no one personne, ne . . . personne

nor ni; **neither . . . nor** ne . . . ni . . . ni

North Nord *m;* **North Africa** l'Afrique du Nord

not ne . . . pas; **not at all** pas du tout; **not much** pas beaucoup, pas grand-chose

nothing rien; **nothing at all** rien du tout; **nothing much** pas grand-chose; **nothing but** rien que; **practically nothing** peu de chose; **nothing easier** rien de plus simple

notice: to notice remarquer

noun nom *m*

novel roman *m*

November novembre *m*

now maintenant, actuellement

nowhere nulle part

number nombre *m*, numéro *m;* **numbers of servants** de nombreux domestiques

O

oats avoine *f*

obey: to obey obéir à

object objet *m*

obviously naturellement

occupation occupation *f*

o'clock heure *f;* **at four o'clock** à quatre heures

October octobre *m*

of de; **of the** du, de la, de l', des; **of it, of them** en

offer: to offer offrir

office bureau *m*, cabinet *m*

official fonctionnaire *m*

often souvent

oil pétrole *m;* **oil company** compagnie de pétrole *f*

OK entendu; **everything is OK** tout est en règle

old vieux *m*, vieil *m*, vieille *f*, vieux *m pl*, vieilles *f pl;* ancien *m*, ancienne *f;* âgé *m*, âgée *f;* **how old is he?** quel âge a-t-il?

on sur, en, dans; **on time** à l'heure; **on Saturday** samedi; **on arriving** en arrivant; **on the street** dans la rue

once une fois, une seule fois, autrefois; **once more** une fois de plus; **once a year** une fois par an

one un, une; l'un, l'une; on; **this one** celui-ci; **that one** celui-là; **the one**

celui; **the one . . . the other** l'un
. . . l'autre

only *adj* seul; *adv* seulement, ne . . . que;
if only si au moins

open ouvert *m*, ouverte *f*

open: to open ouvrir

operate: to operate opérer

operation opération *f;* **in operation** en
opération

opinion avis *m*

opposite opposé; **opposite direction**
l'autre sens *m*

orange orange *f*

order ordre *m;* **money order** mandat-
poste *m;* **in order to** afin de; **by
order of** sur l'ordre de; **everything is in order** tout est en règle

order: to order commander

Orinoco Orénoque

ornamented with orné de

orphan orphelin *m*, orpheline *f*

other autre; **some . . . others** les uns . . .
d'autres; **the other one** l'autre

ought (devoir): **you ought to go** vous
devriez aller; **you ought to have
gone** vous auriez dû aller

our notre, nos

ours le nôtre *m*, la nôtre *f*, les nôtres *pl*

ourselves nous-mêmes

out: to go out sortir; **to be out** être
sorti

outside dehors; **at the outside** tout au
plus

over sur, au-dessus de; **over 1000
square kilometers** plus de 1.000
kilomètres carrés; **over there** là-
bas

owe: to owe devoir

own: to own posséder, être propriétaire
de

owner propriétaire *m or f*

P

pack: to pack emballer, faire ses
bagages

packing emballage *m*

page page *f;* **on page 89** à la page 89

paint: to paint peindre

painting peinture *f*, tableau *m*

pair paire *f*

palace palais *m*, château *m*

panel panneau *m*

paper papier *m*, journal *m*

parasol ombrelle *f*

pardon pardon *m*

parent parent *m*, parente *f*

Paris Paris *m*

Parisian Parisien *m*, Parisienne *f*

park parc *m*

parrot perroquet *m*

part partie *f;* **to be a part of** faire
partie de

pass: to pass passer; **to pass through**
être de passage, traverser; **passing
cars** les autos qui passent

passage passage *m*, (*on a plane*) place *f*

passenger passager *m*, passagère *f*

passport passeport *m*

past passé *m;* **in the past** autrefois

patience patience *f*

patiently patiemment, avec patience

pay: to pay payer, rapporter; **to pay
for** payer; **to pay more** payer plus
cher; **to pay a compliment** faire
un compliment

payment paiement *m*

pea pois *m;* **green peas** petits pois

pear poire *f*

pen stylo *m*

people gens *f pl;* monde *m;* on; **the
French people** les Français

per: per month par mois

perform: to perform jouer

performance représentation *f*

perfume parfum *m*

perhaps peut-être

period époque *f*

permit: to permit to permettre de

person personne *f*

personage personnage *m*

personal personnel *m*, personnelle *f*

personally personnellement

petroleum pétrole *m*

Philadelphia Philadelphie

piano piano *m;* **to play the piano** jouer du piano

pick: to pick cueillir, ramasser; **to pick up (someone)** venir chercher (quelqu'un)

picture photographie *f,* photo *f,* tableau *m*

piece pièce *f,* morceau *m*

pilot pilote *m*

pink rose

piranha piranha (*kind of fish*)

pity: to pity plaindre

place endroit *m,* lieu *m;* **to take place** avoir lieu; **in your place** à votre place; **out-of-the-way places** des coins perdus

plan plan *m,* projet *m*

plan: to plan avoir l'intention de

plane avion *m*

plate assiette *f*

play: to play jouer; **to play the violin** jouer du violon; **to play tennis** jouer au tennis

player joueur *m,* joueuse *f;* **a card player** un joueur de cartes

pleasant agréable

please: to please plaire à; **please** s'il vous plaît, je vous en prie

pleasure plaisir *m;* **a pleasure trip** un voyage d'agrément

plenty beaucoup de

P.M. de l'après-midi, du soir

poet poète *m*

poetry poésie *f;* **to write poetry** faire des vers

point: on the point of faillir *and infinitive*

poison poison *m*

police police *f;* **troopers, state police** gendarmes *m pl*

policy police *f;* **insurance policy** police d'assurance

poor pauvre

poorly mal

population population *f*

porcupine porc-épic *m*

possible possible; **that is possible** cela se peut; **it's possible that** il se peut que; **to make possible** permettre de

post card carte-postale *f*

post office bureau de poste *m,* poste *f*

pound livre *f;* **three francs a pound** trois francs la livre

practically presque, à peu près; **practically all you have to do is** il suffit presque de

praise: to praise célébrer, louer; **so lavishly praised** si célébré

precede: to precede précéder

precisely exactement, au juste

prefer: to prefer préférer, aimer mieux

present cadeau *m,* cadeaux *pl*

present: at present à l'heure actuelle, à présent

press: to press presser, appuyer sur

prettily joliment

pretty *adj* joli *m,* jolie *f; adv* assez

prevent: to prevent empêcher de

price prix *m*

prince prince *m*

print estampe *f*

prison prison *f*

private *adj* particulier *m,* particulière *f;* **private families** des particuliers

probable probable

probably sans doute

problem problème *m,* affaire *f*

produce: to produce produire

product produit *m*

profession profession *f*

professor professeur *m*

profit: to profit profiter de

progress progrès *m*

progress: to progress progresser, avancer, faire des progrès

promise: to promise to promettre de

pronoun pronom *m*

pronounce: to pronounce prononcer

pronunciation prononciation *f*

proper propre; **the proper time to** le moment de; **it is proper** il convient de; **proper noun** nom propre *m*

propose: **to propose to** proposer de
prospecting prospection *f*
prospector prospecteur *m*
prosperity prospérité *f*
proud fier *m*, fière *f*
proudly fièrement
provide: to provide donner, fournir
prudent prudent *m*, prudente *f*
prudently prudemment
pull: to pull tirer
purchase achat *m*, emplette *f*
purchase: to purchase acheter, se
    procurer
purpose: to serve the purpose faire
    l'affaire
put: to put mettre; **to put on** mettre;
    to put back remettre; **to put down**
    déposer

Q

quadruped quadrupède *m*
quality qualité *f*
quantity quantité *f*
quarter quart *m;* **a quarter of an hour**
    un quart d'heure; **a quarter past**
    et quart; **a quarter to** moins le
    quart
queen reine *f*
question question *f;* **it is a question of**
    il s'agit de
quickly vite
quiet tranquille
quietly tranquillement, sagement
quite tout à fait, assez
quote: to quote citer

R

radio radio *f*, T.S.F. *f*
rage rage *f*
railroad chemin de fer *m*
rain pluie *f*
rain: to rain pleuvoir; **it is raining** il
    pleut; **it was raining** il pleuvait
raincoat imperméable *m*
raise: to raise élever

rare rare
rate: at any rate en tout cas
rather plutôt, assez, un peu
reach: to reach atteindre: **to reach its**
    destination arriver à destination
read: to read lire
ready prêt *m*, prête *f*
realize: to realize se rendre compte de
really vraiment
rear: to rear élever (un enfant)
reason raison *f;* **there is good reason to**
    il y a de quoi
reasonable raisonnable
receive: to receive recevoir
recently récemment; **until recently**
    jusqu'à une date récente
recite: to recite réciter
recognize: to recognize reconnaître
recover: to recover se remettre
red rouge
refrigerator réfrigérateur *m*
refuse: to refuse to refuser de
regards: give my regards to dites bien
    des choses de ma part à
region région *f*
regret: to regret to regretter de
regulate: to regulate fixer
reign règne *m*
relation relation *f*
relative parent *m*, parente *f*
religious religieux *m*, religieuse *f*
remain: to remain rester
remarkable remarquable
remember: to remember se rappeler,
    se souvenir de; **if I remember cor-**
    rectly si j'ai bonne mémoire
Renaissance Renaissance *f*
repeat: to repeat répéter
replace: to replace remplacer
reply: to reply répondre
represent: to represent représenter
reputation réputation *f*
request demande *f*, prière *f*
request: to request prier de
require: to require exiger, imposer
research recherche *f*
resemble: to resemble ressembler à

reserve: to reserve retenir; **to reserve passage** retenir une place
residence résidence *f*
respect: to respect respecter
responsibility responsabilité *f*
rest reste *m*
rest repos *m*
rest: to rest se reposer
retain: to retain retenir
return retour *m*
return: to return retourner; **to return home** rentrer
revolution révolution *f*
reward: to reward récompenser
rhyme: to rhyme rimer
rich riche; **to be rich** avoir une grosse fortune
richly richement
ride: to ride aller en auto, aller à bicyclette
right *adj* bon, bonne; **the right road** la bonne route; **at the right time** au bon moment; *adv* **right now** en ce moment; *adv* **right away** tout de suite
right: to be right to avoir raison de, faire bien de
ring: to ring sonner
risk: to risk risquer de
rival rival *m*, rivale *f*
river fleuve *m*, rivière *f*
road route *f;* **the wrong road** la mauvaise route
roast beef rosbif *m*
roll petit pain *m*
roof toit *m*
room chambre *f*, salle *f*, place *f;* **living room** salon *m;* **there is room** il y a de la place
rope corde *f*
rose *noun* rose *f*, *adj* rose
royal royal *m*, royale *f*
royally royalement
rugby rugby *m*
run: to run courir; marcher: **my car was not running well** mon auto ne marchait pas bien; **to run off the road** quitter la route
Russia Russie *f*
Russian russe

S

sad triste; **to be sad** s'ennuyer
Sahara le Sahara
salad salade
salamander salamandre *f*
same même; **the same** le même, la même, les mêmes; **the same one** le même, la même; **it's all the same to me** ça m'est égal
sample échantillon *m*
sand sable *m*
satisfied satisfait *m*, satisfaite *f*
Saturday samedi *m*
Saudi Arabia l'Arabie saoudite
say: to say dire; **they say** on dit, dit-on; **that is to say** c'est-à-dire
scarcely à peine, ne . . . guère
scholar savant *m*
school école *f*
sculpture sculpture *f*
sea mer *f*
season saison *f*
seat place *f*
second second *m*, seconde *f;* deuxième
secret secret *m*, secrète *f*
see: to see voir, apercevoir; **to see again** revoir; **to go and see** aller voir; **to see fit to** juger bon de
seed semence *f*
seem: to seem sembler, paraître, avoir l'air de
Seine Seine *f*
seize: to seize s'emparer de
seldom rarement
sell: to sell vendre, se vendre; **if only our products sold well** si au moins nos produits se vendaient bien
send: to send envoyer, expédier; **to send back, to send away** renvoyer; **to send off** expédier
sentence phrase *f*

September septembre *m;* **last September** en septembre dernier
serious sérieux *m,* sérieuse
servant: public servant fonctionnaire *m*
serve: to serve servir; **to serve the purpose** faire l'affaire
set: set of dishes service de table *m*
set: to set mettre, poser, fixer, établir; **to set out** partir
seven sept
seventeen dix-sept
seventh septième
seventy soixante-dix
several plusieurs
severe rigoureux *m,* rigoureuse *f*
she elle, c'
shelter: to shelter oneself from s'abriter de
ship: to ship expédier, envoyer
shipment envoi *m*
shipping envoi *m,* expédition *f*
shop magasin *m;* **tobacco shop** bureau de tabac *m;* **shopwindow** devanture *f*
shop: to shop, to go shopping faire des courses, faire des emplettes
shore rive *f,* bord *m*
short court *m,* courte *f;* **short-lived** de courte durée
shortly sous peu; **shortly after** peu après
should (devoir): **you should** vous devriez; **you should have** vous auriez dû
show: to show montrer, faire voir
shrub arbuste *m*
sick malade
side côté *m*
siesta sieste *f*
signal: to signal faire signe à
signpost poteau indicateur *m*
silly: don't be silly soyez sérieux
silver argent *m*
simple simple
since (*time*) depuis, (*result*) puisque
sing: to sing chanter; **to sing in tune** chanter juste; **to sing out of tune** chanter faux
single seul, seule
Sir Monsieur
sister sœur *f*
sit: to sit s'asseoir, être assis; **to sit down at the table** se mettre à table
site emplacement *m,* lieu *m*
situation situation *f*
six six
sixteen seize
sixteenth seizième
sixth sixième
sixty soixante
skillful habile
skyscraper gratte-ciel *m*
sleep: to sleep dormir
slightest le moindre, la moindre, les moindres
slippery glissant *m,* glissante *f*
slow: to slow down ralentir
small petit *m,* petite *f*
smell: to smell sentir; **to smell good** sentir bon; **to smell bad** sentir mauvais
smile sourire *m*
smile: to smile sourire
smoke: to smoke fumer
snow neige *f*
snow: to snow neiger
so aussi, si, ainsi, donc; **so that** pour que; **so as to** pour, de façon à; **so so** comme ci comme ça; **and so on** et cetera
solve: to solve résoudre
some du, de la, de l', des; *adj* quelque *sg,* quelques *pl; pron* en; quelquesuns, quelques-unes; les uns, les unes; **some of them** quelques-uns (d'entre eux); **some . . . others** les uns . . . d'autres
someone quelqu'un
something quelque chose; **something else** autre chose; **something interesting** quelque chose d'intéressant
sometimes quelquefois, parfois

somewhat un peu

son fils *m*

song chanson *f*, chant *m*

soon tôt, bientôt, sous peu; **as soon as** dès que, aussitôt que

sorry: to be sorry to regretter de, être fâché de

sort sorte *f*, espèce *f*

south sud *m; adv* **south** au sud; **southwest** au sud-ouest

space place *f*

speak: to speak parler; **to speak in a loud voice** parler haut; **to speak in a low voice** parler bas

spelling orthographe *f*

spend: to spend (*time*) passer, (*money*) dépenser

spite: in spite of malgré

splendid splendide

sport sport *m*

spot endroit *m*

spring printemps *m;* **in the spring** au printemps

sprinkle: to sprinkle arroser

square place *f*

square *adj* carré *m*, carrée *f;* **a square kilometer** un kilomètre carré

stadium stade *m*

stagecoach diligence *f*

staircase escalier *m*

stamp timbre *m*

stand kiosque *m;* **a newspaper stand** un kiosque à journaux

standing debout

start: to start commencer; (*on one's way*) partir, se mettre en route

State État *m*

stay séjour *m*

stay: to stay rester, s'arrêter; **to stay for dinner** rester dîner; **he is staying at the Hotel Meurice** il est descendu à l'hôtel Meurice

steadily sans arrêt

steal: to steal voler

still toujours, encore

stir: to stir remuer

stock: rolling stock matériel *m*

stolen volé

stone pierre *f*

stop: to stop arrêter, s'arrêter

story (*narrative*) histoire *f*, **story** (*floor*) étage *m*

straight droit *m*, droite *f;* **straight ahead** tout droit

strange étrange

straw: this is the last straw c'est la fin de tout

street rue *f;* **one way street** sens unique *m*

strip: to strip dépouiller de

strong fort *m*, forte *f*

student étudiant *m*, étudiante *f*

study: to study étudier

suburb faubourg *m*

succeed: to succeed in réussir à, arriver à

such un tel, une telle, de tels, de telles; **such a mother** une telle mère; **such pleasant company** une si agréable compagnie

Sudan Soudan *m*

sudden soudain *m*, soudaine *f*

suddenly tout à coup

suffer: to suffer souffrir

suffice: to suffice for suffire à

sufficient: it is sufficient to il suffit de

sugar sucre *m*

suggest: to suggest proposer de

suit: to suit convenir à

suitable convenable, qui convient, bon à *and infinitive;* **the most suitable date** la date qui convient le mieux

summer été *m;* **in summer** en été

sun soleil *m*

Sunday dimanche *m*

suppose: to suppose supposer; **to be supposed to** devoir, être censé

sure sûr *m*, sûre *f;* **to make sure** s'assurer

surprise surprise *f*

surprise: to surprise surprendre

surprised surpris *m*, surprise *f*, étonné

surround: to surround entourer; **surrounded by water** entouré d'eau

suspect: to suspect se douter de
swan cygne *m*
sweater chandail *m*
Sweden Suède *f*
sweet doux *m*, douce *f*
swim: to swim nager
Switzerland Suisse *f*
systematically assidûment

T

table table *f;* **to sit down at the table** se mettre à table
take: **to take** prendre, emporter, mener, conduire; falloir: **how long does it take?** combien de temps faut-il?, **it would take two hours** il faudrait deux heures; **to take up** monter; **to take out** sortir; **to take place** avoir lieu; **to take on (passengers)** embarquer; **to take advantage of** profiter de; **to take care of** s'occuper de
taking prise *f*
talk conversation *f*
talk: **to talk** parler; **to talk about** parler de
tall grand *m*, grande *f;* de haute taille
tapestry tapisserie *f*
tax impôt *m*
taxi taxi *m;* **taxi driver** chauffeur de taxi *m*
teach: **to teach** enseigner à
teacher maître *m*
team équipe *f*
telegram dépêche *f*
telephone téléphone *m*
telephone: **to telephone** téléphoner, donner un coup de fil
tell: **to tell** dire, parler de, raconter; **to tell about** parler de; **to tell oneself** se dire; **to tell apart** distinguer
temperature température *f*
ten dix
tennis tennis *m;* **to play tennis** jouer au tennis

tenth dixième
terrible terrible
than que, (*with numbers*) de
thank: **to thank** remercier; **to thank for** remercier de; **thank you** merci
that (those) *dem adj* ce *m*, cet *m*, cette *f*, ces *pl;* ce . . . -là, cette . . . -là, ces . . . -là; **that** *dem pron* celui *m*, celle *f*, ceux *m pl*, celles *f pl;* cela; **that** *rel pron* qui, que; lequel, laquelle, lesquels, lesquelles; **all that** tout ce qui, tout ce que; **that** *conj* que; **that's a sad story** c'est une triste histoire; **that depends** cela dépend; **that which** ce qui, ce que, ce dont
the le, la, l', les
theater théâtre *m*
their *poss adj* leur *sg*, leurs *pl*
theirs *poss pron* le leur, la leur, les leurs
them les, leur; eux, elles; **of them** en, d'entre eux
themselves eux-mêmes, elles-mêmes
then (*time*) alors, puis, ensuite; (*result*) alors, ainsi, donc
theology théologie *f*
there là, y; **there is, there are** il y a; **here and there** çà et là
these *dem adj* ces, ces . . . -ci; *dem pron* ceux-ci *m*, celles-ci *f*
they ils, elles, on, ce
thing chose *f*
think: **to think** penser, croire, trouver; **to think about** penser à; **what do you think of it?** qu'en pensez-vous?; **I thought it was excellent** je l'ai trouvé excellent
third troisième; **one third** un tiers
thirsty: **to be thirsty** avoir soif
thirteen treize
thirteenth treizième
thirty trente; **seven-thirty** sept heures et demie
this *dem adj* ce *m*, cet *m*, cette *f;* ce . . . -ci, cet . . . -ci, cette . . . -ci; **this** *dem pron* celui *m*, celle *f;* celui-ci, celle-ci; **this one** celui-ci, celle-ci

those *dem adj* ces, ces . . . -là; *dem pron* ceux, ceux-là *m*, celles, celles-là *f*

thousand *adj* mille, *noun* millier *m*

threaten: to threaten menacer

through à travers; **to go through** traverser, visiter, parcourir

throw: to throw lancer, jeter

Thursday jeudi *m*

ticket billet *m*

tie cravate *f*

till jusqu'à

time temps *m*, heure *f*, moment *m*, fois *f*, délai *m*, époque *f*; **a long time** longtemps; **at the time of** au moment de; **at the time when** au moment où; **at this time** en ce moment; **in time** éventuellement; **of the time** du temps, de l'époque; **to have time to** avoir le temps de; **this is not the time to** ce n'est pas le moment de; **to have a good time** s'amuser bien; **to ask for the time (of day)** demander l'heure

tire pneu *m*

tired fatigué *m*

to à, en, pour, chez, vers; **to Arabia** en Arabie; **to Venezuela** au Vénézuéla; **to Paris** à Paris; **it's ten to four** il est quatre heures moins dix

tobacco tabac *m*

today aujourd'hui

together ensemble

tomorrow demain

tonight ce soir

too trop, aussi; **too much, too many** trop de

tool outil *m*

top haut *m*; **to the top of** en haut de

towards vers

tower tour *f*; **the Eiffel Tower** la tour Eiffel

town ville *f*; **downtown** en ville

tractor tracteur *m*

tragedy tragédie *f*

trail: to trail poursuivre

train train *m*

transport: to transport transporter

transportation transport *m*

travel: to travel voyager; **to travel through** parcourir

traveler voyageur *m*

Treasury Department administration financière *f*

tree arbre *m*

tributary affluent *m*

trip voyage *m*; **on a trip** en voyage; **to take a trip** voyager; **to have a good trip** faire bon voyage

trooper gendarme *m*

trouble peine *f*; **to have trouble in** avoir de la peine à; **it is not worth the trouble** ce n'est pas la peine

Troy Troie

true vrai *m*, vraie *f*; **exactly true** exact

truth vérité *f*; **to tell the truth** à vrai dire

try: to try to essayer de, tâcher de, chercher à; **to try hard** s'efforcer de; **to try in vain** avoir beau *and infinitive*

Tuesday mardi *m*

Tunisia Tunisie *f*

turn: to turn tourner; **to turn over** se retourner, (*boat*) chavirer; **to turn around** faire demi-tour, se retourner

twelfth douzième

twelve douze, une douzaine; **twelve o'clock** (*noon*) midi, (*midnight*) minuit

twentieth vingtième

twenty vingt

twice deux fois

two deux

U

under sous, dessous

understand: to understand comprendre

undesirable indésirable *m*

unexpected inattendu *m*, inattendue *f*

unexpectedly d'une façon inattendue

unexplored inexploré

unforgettable inoubliable

unfortunately malheureusement, par malheur

unhappy malheureux *m*, malheureuse *f*

United States États-Unis *m pl;* **in the U.S.** aux États-Unis

university université *f*

unless à moins que

unlikely peu probable

unpleasant désagréable

until jusqu'à, jusqu'à ce que; **until when?** jusqu'à quel moment?

unusual rare

up: to go up monter; **up the Eiffel Tower** en haut de la tour Eiffel

upon sur, à

use: to use employer, se servir de; **to be used (everywhere)** être employé (partout); **to be used as** servir de; **to be used to** avoir l'habitude de; **to get used to** s'habituer à; **I used to go** j'allais

usual ordinaire; habituel; **as usual** comme d'habitude

usually d'ordinaire, d'habitude

V

vacation vacances *f pl,* congé *m;* **on vacation** en vacances

vain: in vain avoir beau *and infinitive*

various divers, *m,* diverse *f*

vegetation végétation *f*

vehicle voiture *f*

Venezuela Vénézuéla *m*

vengeance: to take vengeance se venger

verse vers *m,* poésie *f*

very très, fort, bien

victorious victorieux *m,* victorieuse *f*

view vue *f;* **from the point of view of** au point de vue de

village village *m*

violent violent *m,* violente *f*

violently violemment

visit visite *f*

visit: to visit visiter; aller voir

visitor visiteur *m*

W

wait: to wait for attendre; **to wait in line** faire la queue

waiter garçon *m*

wake up: to wake up se réveiller

waken s'éveiller, se réveiller

walk promenade *f;* **to take a walk** faire une promenade

walk: to walk marcher, aller à pied; **to walk into** entrer dans; **to walk across** traverser

wall mur *m*

want: to want vouloir, désirer

warm chaud *m,* chaude *f;* **it is warm** il fait chaud

warn: to warn avertir, prévenir

was: I was j'étais; **I was to** je devais

wash: to wash laver; **to wash one's hands** se laver les mains

waste: to waste perdre

watch montre *f*

water eau *f*

way chemin *m,* route *f;* moyen *m,* façon *f;* **on the way to** en route pour; **all the way to** jusqu'à; **by the way** d'ailleurs; **don't go out of your way** ne vous dérangez pas; **out-of-the-way places** des coins perdus; **a way of talking** une façon de parler; **the best way to get there** la meilleure façon d'y aller; **on his way to** en route pour

wealth fortune *f,* richesse *f*

weapon arme *f*

wear: to wear porter

weather temps *m;* **how is the weather?** quel temps fait-il?; **the weather is fine (beautiful)** il fait beau

wedding mariage *m*

Wednesday mercredi *m*

week semaine *f;* **a week from today** d'aujourd'hui en huit; **two weeks from today** d'aujourd'hui en quinze; **all week long** toute la semaine; **weekend** week-end *m*

weigh: to weigh peser

welcome: to welcome accueillir, recevoir

well *adv* bien; **it's just as well** il vaut autant; **to do well to** faire bien de

well-being bien-être *m*

west ouest *m;* à l'ouest

what? *interrog adj* quel? quelle? quels? quelles?; **what** *interrog pron* que? qu'est-ce que? qu'est-ce qui? quoi?; **what is?** qu'est-ce que c'est que?; what *rel pron* ce qui, ce que, quoi; **what is . . .** ce que c'est que; **what!** *exclam* quoi!; **let's see what's up** voyons de quoi il s'agit

whatever quoi que; **whatever he does** quoi qu'il fasse

wheat blé *m*

wheel roue *f;* **steering wheel** volant *m*

when quand, lorsque, où, au moment où, au moment de

whenever quand, chaque fois que

where où

whereas tandis que

which? *interrog adj* quel? quelle? quels? quelles?; *interrog pron* lequel? laquelle? lesquels? lesquelles?; **which one?** lequel? laquelle?; **which ones?** lesquels? lesquelles?; **which** *rel pron* qui, que; lequel, laquelle, lesquels, lesquelles; **of which** dont; **in which** où, dans lequel, etc.; **that which** ce qui, ce que, ce dont

while tandis que, pendant que, en, tout en; **a while ago, in a while** tout à l'heure; **while waiting for her** en attendant son retour

white blanc, *m* blanche *f*

who? *interrog pron* qui? qui est-ce qui?; **who** *rel pron* qui; lequel, laquelle, lesquels, lesquelles

whole entier *m,* entière *f;* **a whole cow** une vache tout entière; **whole days** des journées entières

whom? *interrog pron* qui?; **whom** *rel pron* que, qui; **of whom, about whom** dont

whose? *interrog pron* à qui?; **at whose house?** chez qui?; **whose** *rel pron* dont, de qui

why pourquoi

wide large, de large; **how wide is . . . ?;** quelle est la largeur de . . . ?; **ten yards wide** dix mètres de large

widow veuve *f*

wife femme *f*

willing: to be willing vouloir bien

window fenêtre *f;* **shopwindow** devanture *f*

windshield pare-brise *m;* **windshield wiper** essuie-glace *m*

wine vin *m*

wing aile *f;* **a two-story wing** une galerie à deux étages

winter hiver *m*

wise sage

wish souhait *m*

wish: to wish désirer, souhaiter; **I wish to heaven that** plût au ciel que; **to wish good luck to** souhaiter bonne chance à

with avec, auprès de

within dans; **within a few years** dans quelques années

without sans; **without leaving the house** sans sortir de chez elle

woman femme *f*

wonder: to wonder se demander

wood bois *m;* **carved wood** bois sculpté

word mot *m;* (*spoken*) parole *f;* **in a word** en un mot

work travail *m,* travaux *pl*

work: to work travailler

world monde *m*

worry souci *m*

worry: to worry s'inquiéter; **don't worry** soyez tranquille

worse *adj* pire; *adv* pis; **from bad to worse** de mal en pis

worst *adj* le pire, la pire, les pires

worth: **to be worth** valoir

worthy brave; bon, bonne; digne; **those worthy policemen** ces braves gendarmes

write: to write écrire

wrong *adj* mauvais *m*, mauvaise *f*

wrong: to be wrong to avoir tort de

Y

yard mètre *m* (*approximately*)

year an *m*, année *f*; **every year** tous les ans, chaque année; **every three years** tous les trois ans

yellow jaune

yes oui, si; **yes I do** mais si

yesterday hier

yet encore, déjà, cependant; **not yet** pas encore; **and yet . . .** et cependant . . .

yield production *f*, récolte *f*

you vous, on; tu, te, toi; **if I were you** si j'étais à votre place

young jeune

your votre, ton

yours le vôtre, la vôtre, les vôtres; le tien, la tienne, les tiens, les tiennes; **is it yours?** est-ce à vous?

yourself vous-même, vous-mêmes

Z

zero zéro *m*

Index

lx

future: formation § 119 (B); of regular verbs § 123 (A); of **être** and **avoir** § 125; in conditional sentences § 50 (B, 2); after **quand, lorsque,** etc. § 50 (B, 3); in set expressions § 50 (B, 4); instead of the imperative § 50 (B, 5)

future perfect: formation and use § 94, 121 (A, 4), 123 (C, 1)

geographical names, § 14
grand, § 29 (A)
gros, § 29 (B)

haïr, § 150

il est, ils sont: distinguished from **c'est, ce sont,** footnote p. 59

imperative: formation § 51 (A); 120 (C); of regular verbs § 51 (A), 123 (B); of **être** and **avoir** § 51 (B), 125; of irreg. verbs § 51 (C); of reflexive verbs § 51 (D); forms before **en** § 51 (A); use of personal pronouns with affirmative imperative § 49 (A); use of personal pronouns with negative imperative § 49 (B)

imperfect indicative: formation § 120 (B); of regular verbs § 123 (B); of **être** and **avoir** § 125; of **devoir** § 34 (A); distinguished from the *passé composé* § 15, 18; commonest uses § 16; special uses § 17

imperfect subjunctive: formation and use § 101, 103 (B, 1), 122; of regular verbs § 123 (D); of **être** and **avoir** § 101 (B); of a few irreg. verbs § 101 (C)

impersonal verbs: see **falloir, pleuvoir** and special uses of **faire, valoir, suffire**

indefinite: see "adjectives", "articles", "pronouns"

indirect discourse: use of the imperfect § 17 (E); use of the conditional § 61 (B)

infinitive: verbs followed by **de** and infinitive § 62 (A); verbs followed by **à** and infinitive § 62 (B); verbs followed by infinitive without a preposition § 62 (C); use of prepositions other than **de** and **à** with infinitive § 63; used instead of the subj. § 70 (A); after **savoir** § 40 (A, 1); tenses formed from the infinitive § 119, 123 (A)

infinitive, perfect: of regular verbs § 63 (B), 123 (C, 1); of **être** and **avoir** § 125; used after **après** § 63 (B); formation § 121 (A, 8)

interrogative forms: of the pres. ind. § 4 (C); of the *passé composé* § 7

interrogative pronouns: see "pronouns, interrogative"

interrogative word order: questions by inversion and with **est-ce que** § 4 (C); in the *passé composé* § 7

irregular verbs: patterns of irregular verbs § 73, 126; list of commonest irregular verbs § 127; ending in **-er** § 74; ending in **-ir** § 75-77; ending in **-re** § 78-79; ending in **-indre** § 80; use of **devoir, falloir, pouvoir, vouloir, savoir** § 34-40

jeter, § 124 (A, 2)
jeune, § 29 (C)
jusqu'à ce que, with subj. § 70 (C)

l', le, la, les: see "article, definite" and "pronouns, personal, (unstressed forms)"

lequel: interrogative pronoun § 85; relative pronoun § 90

lever, § 124 (A, 2)
liaison, § 112
linking, § 112
lire, § 78 (D), 151; pres. subj. § 71 (C); *passé simple* § 99 (C, 3)
lorsque, with future § 50 (B, 3)
lui, leur, § 47 (B, 3); word order of pronouns § 47 (C); with imperative § 49
l'un, l'autre, § 68 (F)

Maps

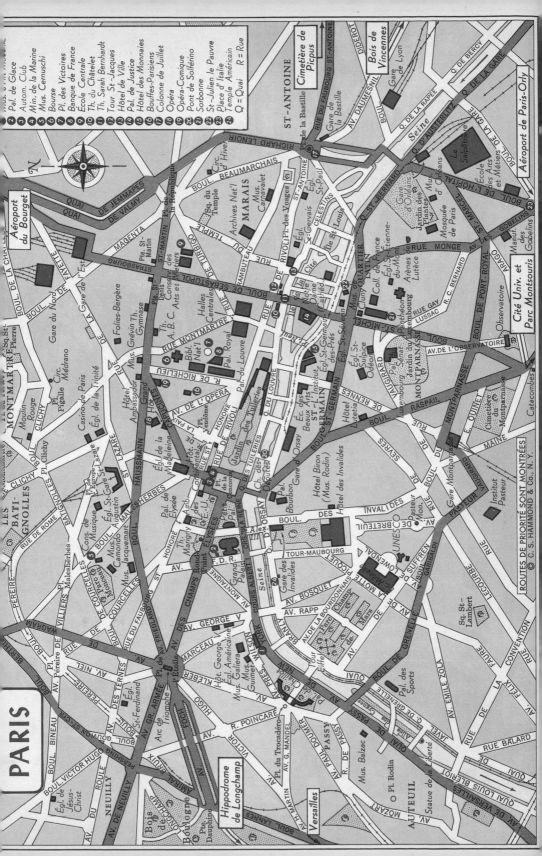

PARIS

① Mus. d'Art Moderne
② Pal. de Glace
③ Autom. Club
④ Min. de la Marine
⑤ Mus. Cernuschi
⑥ Bourse
⑦ Pl. des Victoires
⑧ Banque de France
⑨ École Centrale
⑩ Th. du Châtelet
⑪ Th. Sarah Bernhardt
⑫ Tour St-Jacques
⑬ Hôtel de Ville
⑭ Pal. de Justice
⑮ Hôtel des Monnaies
⑯ Bouffes-Parisiens
⑰ Colonne de Juillet
⑱ Opéra
⑲ Opéra-Comique
⑳ Pont de Solférino
㉑ Sorbonne
㉒ St-Julien le Pauvre
㉓ Place d'Italie
㉔ Temple Américain
Q = Quai   R = Rue

ROUTES DE PRIORITÉ SONT MONTRÉES
© C. S. HAMMOND & Co., N.Y.

Aéroport du Bourget

Aéroport de Paris-Orly

Cité Univ. et Parc Montsouris

St-Antoine

Cimetière de Picpus

Bois de Vincennes

Hippodrome de Longchamp

Versailles

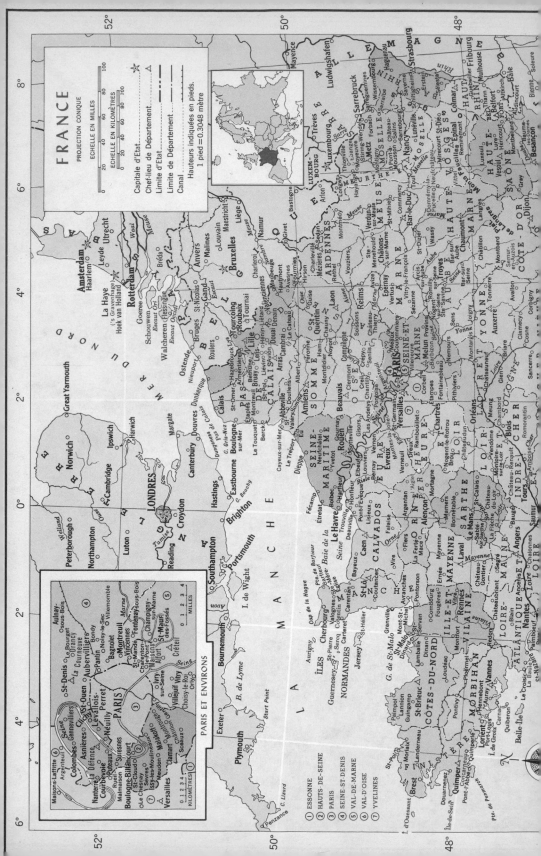

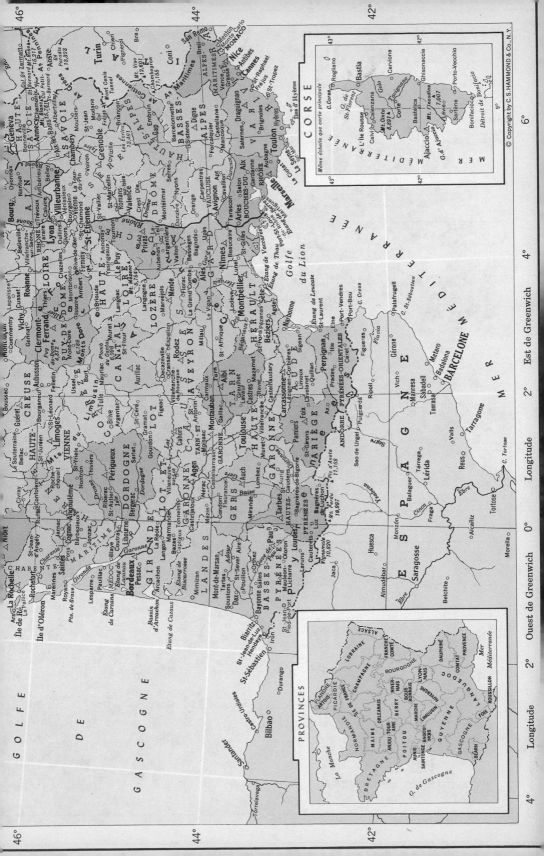

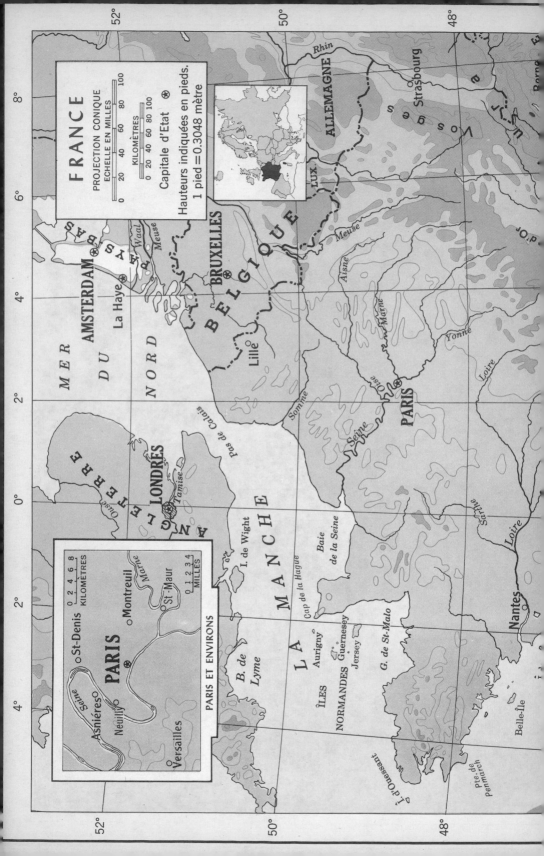

FRANCE

PROJECTION CONIQUE

ECHELLE EN MILES

0   20   40   60   80   100

KILOMÈTRES

0   20   40   60   80   100

⊛ Capitale d'Etat

Hauteurs indiquées en pieds.
1 pied = 0.3048 mètre

ALLEMAGNE

Rhin

Strasbourg

Vosges

LUX.

JO.P.

Meuse

Aisne

Marne

Yonne

Oise

Loire

PARIS ⊛

Seine

Somme

BELGIQUE

BRUXELLES ⊛

Lille ○

Meuse

Waal

PAYS-BAS

AMSTERDAM ⊛

La Haye ○

M E R

D U

N O R D

Pas de Calais

ANGLETERRE

Ouse

Tamise

LONDRES ⊛

I. de Wight

B. de
Lyme

L A   M A N C H E

Cap de la Hague

Baie
de la Seine

ÎLES
NORMANDES

Aurigny ○

Guernesey ○
Jersey ○

G. de St-Malo

Pte. de
Penmarch

I. d'Ouessant

Belle-Île

Nantes

Loire

Sarthe

PARIS ET ENVIRONS

St-Denis ○

Asnières ○

Seine

PARIS ⊛

Neuilly ○

Montreuil ○

Marne

St-Maur ○

Versailles ○

0   2   4   6   8
KILOMÈTRES

0 1 2 3 4
MILES

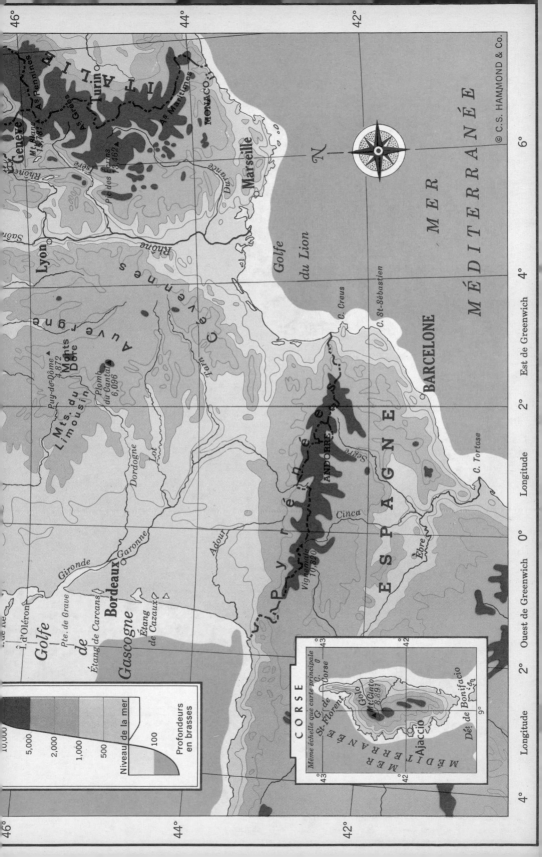

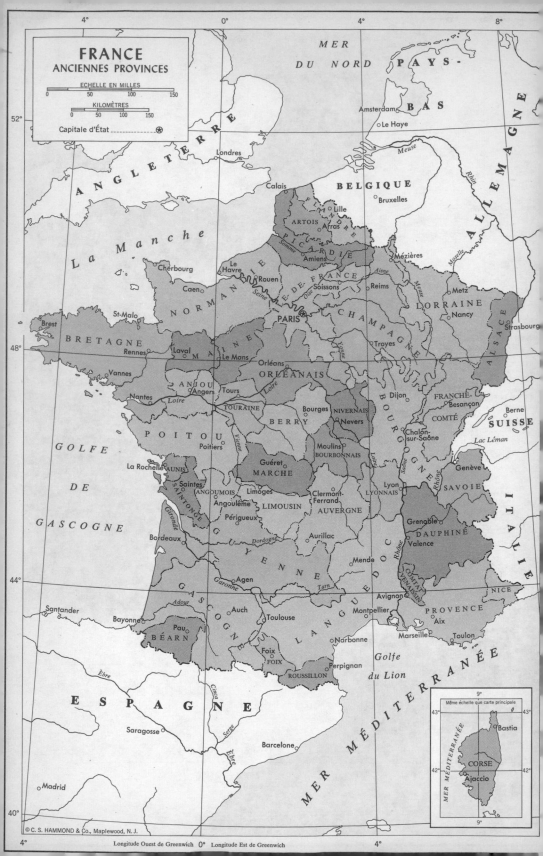

FRANCE
ANCIENNES PROVINCES

ECHELLE EN MILLES

0   50   100   150

KILOMÈTRES

0   50   100   150

Capitale d'État .... ⊛

MER DU NORD PAYS-

Amsterdam
Le Haye

BAS

ANGLETERRE

Londres

La Manche

BELGIQUE

Calais
Bruxelles
Lille
FLANDRE
ARTOIS
Arras
Mézières
PICARDIE
Amiens
Somme
Aisne

ALLEMAGNE

Metz
Moselle
LORRAINE
Nancy
Rhin
Strasbourg
ALSACE

Cherbourg
Le Havre
Rouen
Caen
Seine
NORMANDIE
ÎLE-DE-FRANCE
Soissons
Oise
Reims

St-Malo
Brest
BRETAGNE
Rennes
Vannes
Laval
MAINE
Le Mans

PARIS

CHAMPAGNE
Troyes
Marne

Orléans
ORLÉANAIS
Dijon
FRANCHE-
COMTÉ
Besançon
Berne
SUISSE

ANJOU
Angers   Tours
TOURAINE
Nantes
Loire
Loire
BERRY
Bourges
NIVERNAIS
Nevers
BOURGOGNE
Chalon-
sur-Saône
Lac Léman

POITOU
Poitiers
Vienne
Moulins
BOURBONNAIS
Saône
Lyon
LYONNAIS
Genève
SAVOIE

GOLFE
DE
GASCOGNE

La Rochelle
AUNIS
Saintes
SAINTONGE
ANGOUMOIS
Angoulême
Gironde
Bordeaux
GUYENNE
Dordogne

Guéret
MARCHE
Limoges
LIMOUSIN
Périgueux

Clermont-
Ferrand
AUVERGNE
Aurillac

Grenoble
DAUPHINÉ
Valence
Rhône

ITALIE

Mende

Agen
Garonne
Tarn
GASCOGNE
LANGUEDOC
Rhône
COMTAT
VENAISSIN
Avignon
NICE

Santander
Bayonne
Pau
BÉARN
Auch
Toulouse
Montpellier
Aix
PROVENCE
Marseille
Toulon

Ebre

Foix
FOIX
Narbonne
ROUSSILLON
Perpignan
Golfe
du Lion

MER MÉDITERRANÉE

ESPAGNE

Ebre
Cinca
Serre

Saragosse
Madrid
Barcelone

Même échelle que carte principale

43°   43°

MER MÉDITERRANÉE
Bastia
CORSE
42°   42°
Ajaccio

9°   9°

40°

52°

48°

44°

4°   0°   4°   8°

4°   Longitude Ouest de Greenwich   0°   Longitude Est de Greenwich   4°